Ōoku

● THE INNER CHAMBERS

by **Fumi Yoshinaga**

D0896227

VOL. **17**

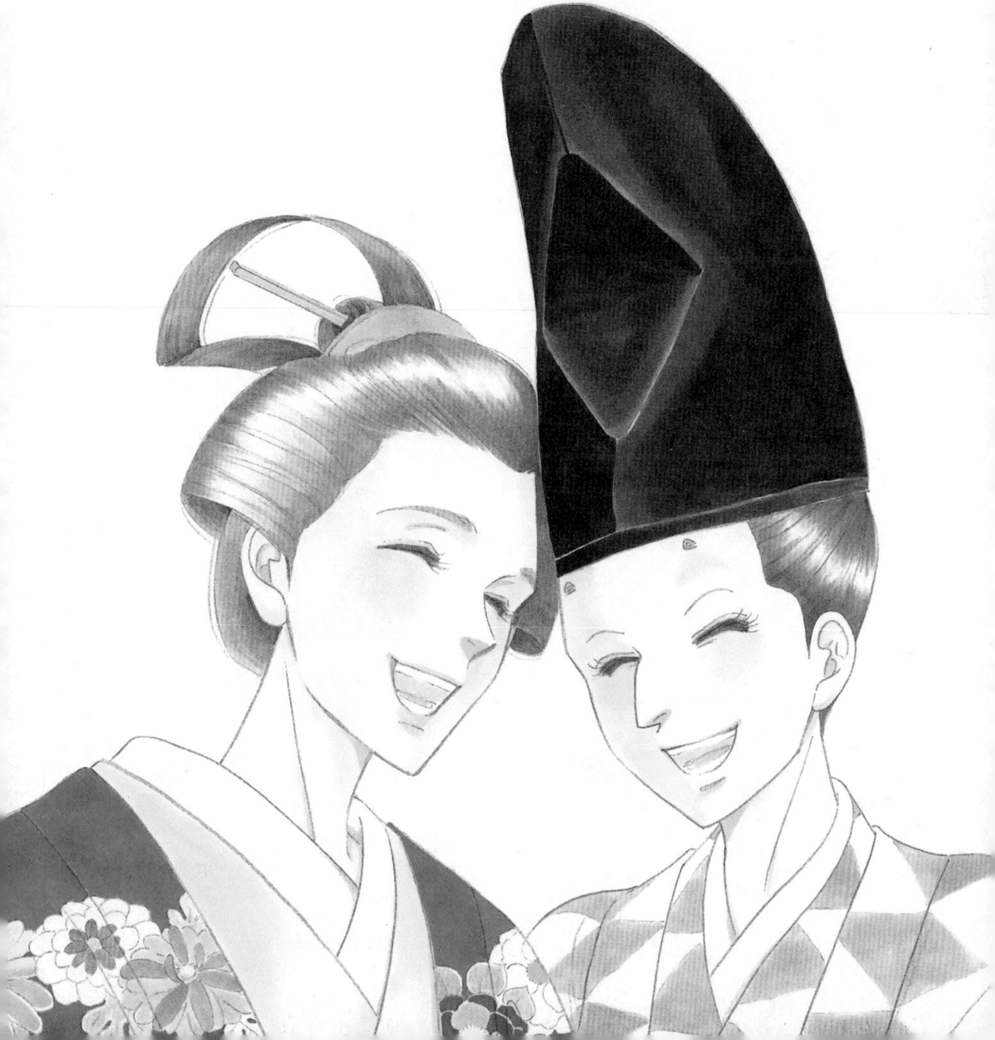

THE INNER CHAMBERS

CAST *of* CHARACTERS

From the birth of the "inverse Inner Chambers" to its zenith, to eradicating the Redface Pox, and now to the end of Tokugawa rule...?

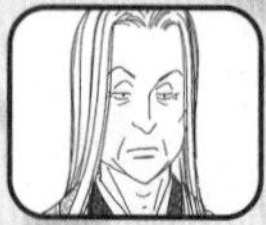

SENIOR CHAMBERLAIN

LADY KASUGA

↓

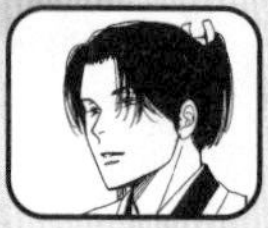

MADE-NOKOJI ARIKOTO (SIR O-MAN)

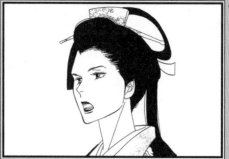

TOKUGAWA IEMITSU (III)

Impersonated her father, Iemitsu, at Lady Kasuga's urging after he died of the Redface Pox. Later became the first female shogun.

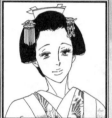

TOKUGAWA TSUNAYOSHI (V)

SENIOR CHAMBERLAIN

EMONNOSUKE

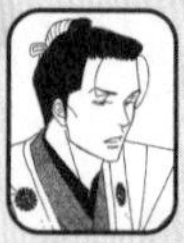

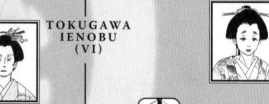

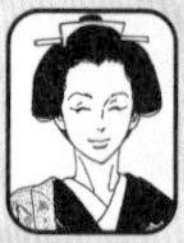

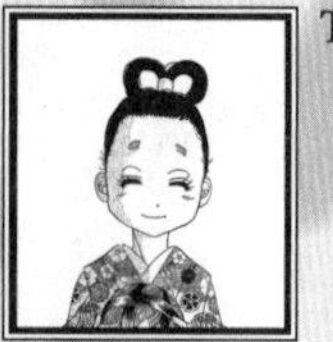

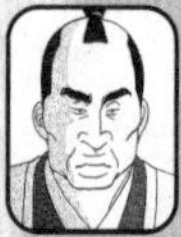

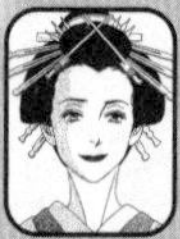

PRIVY COUNCILLOR

YANAGISAWA YOSHIYASU

TOKUGAWA TSUNASHIGE

TOKUGAWA IENOBU (VI)

TOKUGAWA IETSUGU (VII)

TOKUGAWA IETSUNA (IV)

SENIOR CHAMBERLAIN

EJIMA

PRIVY COUNCILLOR

MANABE AKIFUSA

PRIVY COUNCILLOR

KANO HISAMICHI

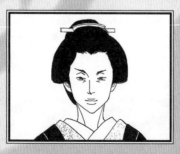

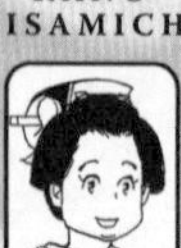

TOKUGAWA YOSHIMUNE (VIII)

Third daughter of Mitsusada, the second head of the Kii branch of the Tokugawa family. Acceded to domain lord and then, upon the death of Ietsugu, to shogun. Imposed and lived by a strict policy of austerity, dismissing large numbers of Inner Chambers courtiers and pursuing policies designed to increase income to the treasury.

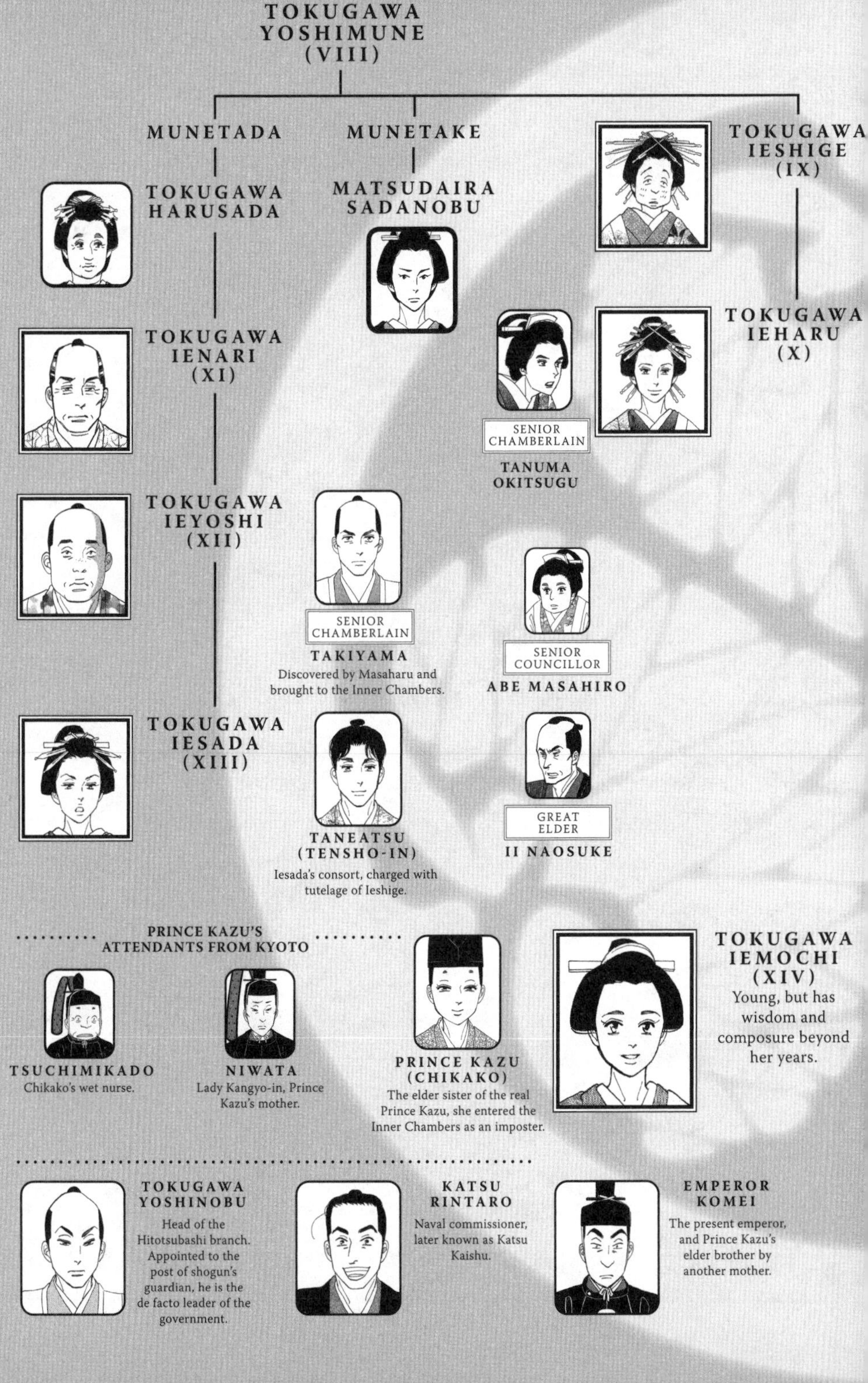
TOKUGAWA YOSHIMUNE (VIII)
MUNETADA
MUNETAKE
TOKUGAWA IESHIGE (IX)
TOKUGAWA HARUSADA
MATSUDAIRA SADANOBU
TOKUGAWA IEHARU (X)
TOKUGAWA IENARI (XI)
SENIOR CHAMBERLAIN
TANUMA OKITSUGU
TOKUGAWA IEYOSHI (XII)
SENIOR CHAMBERLAIN
TAKIYAMA
Discovered by Masaharu and brought to the Inner Chambers.
SENIOR COUNCILLOR
ABE MASAHIRO
TOKUGAWA IESADA (XIII)
TANEATSU (TENSHO-IN)
Iesada's consort, charged with tutelage of Ieshige.
GREAT ELDER
II NAOSUKE
PRINCE KAZU'S ATTENDANTS FROM KYOTO
TSUCHIMIKADO
Chikako's wet nurse.
NIWATA
Lady Kangyo-in, Prince Kazu's mother.
PRINCE KAZU (CHIKAKO)
The elder sister of the real Prince Kazu, she entered the Inner Chambers as an imposter.
TOKUGAWA IEMOCHI (XIV)
Young, but has wisdom and composure beyond her years.
TOKUGAWA YOSHINOBU
Head of the Hitotsubashi branch. Appointed to the post of shogun's guardian, he is the de facto leader of the government.
KATSU RINTARO
Naval commissioner, later known as Katsu Kaishu.
EMPEROR KOMEI
The present emperor, and Prince Kazu's elder brother by another mother.

TABLE *of* CONTENTS

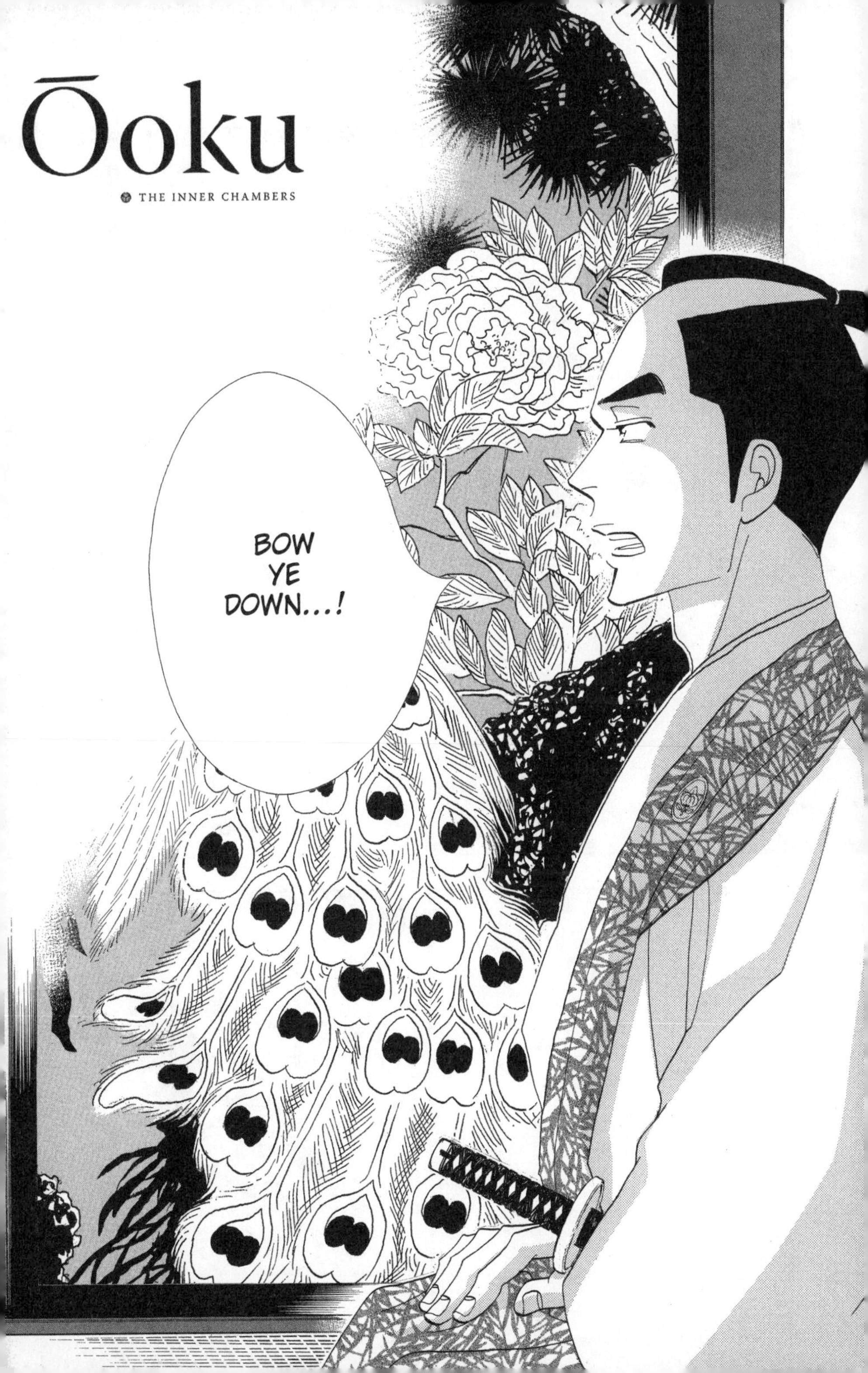
Ōoku
THE INNER CHAMBERS
BOW YE DOWN...!

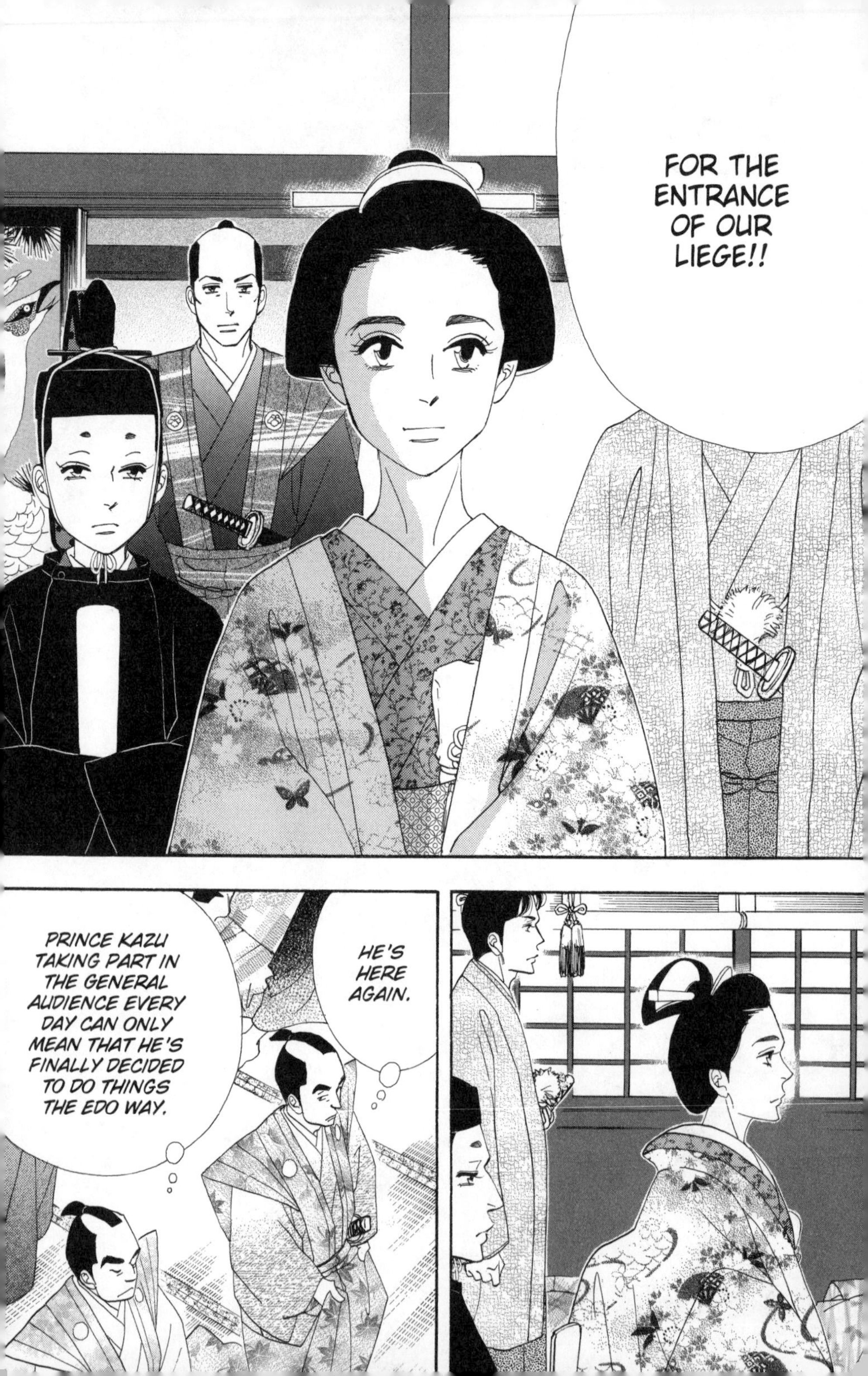
FOR THE ENTRANCE OF OUR LIEGE!!
HE'S HERE AGAIN.
PRINCE KAZU TAKING PART IN THE GENERAL AUDIENCE EVERY DAY CAN ONLY MEAN THAT HE'S FINALLY DECIDED TO DO THINGS THE EDO WAY.

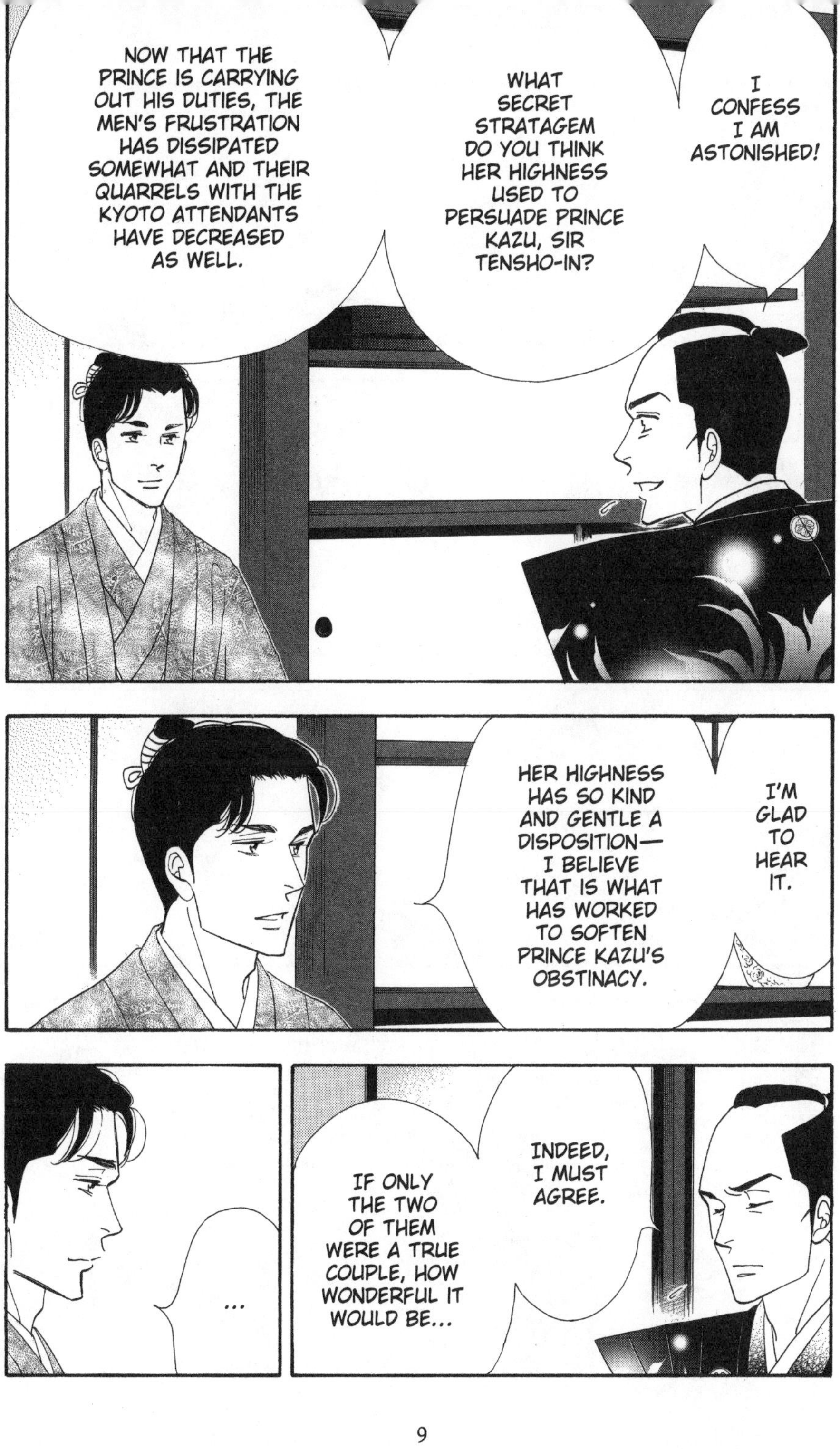
I CONFESS I AM ASTONISHED!
WHAT SECRET STRATAGEM DO YOU THINK HER HIGHNESS USED TO PERSUADE PRINCE KAZU, SIR TENSHO-IN?
NOW THAT THE PRINCE IS CARRYING OUT HIS DUTIES, THE MEN'S FRUSTRATION HAS DISSIPATED SOMEWHAT AND THEIR QUARRELS WITH THE KYOTO ATTENDANTS HAVE DECREASED AS WELL.
I'M GLAD TO HEAR IT.
HER HIGHNESS HAS SO KIND AND GENTLE A DISPOSITION— I BELIEVE THAT IS WHAT HAS WORKED TO SOFTEN PRINCE KAZU'S OBSTINACY.
INDEED, I MUST AGREE.
IF ONLY THE TWO OF THEM WERE A TRUE COUPLE, HOW WONDERFUL IT WOULD BE...
...

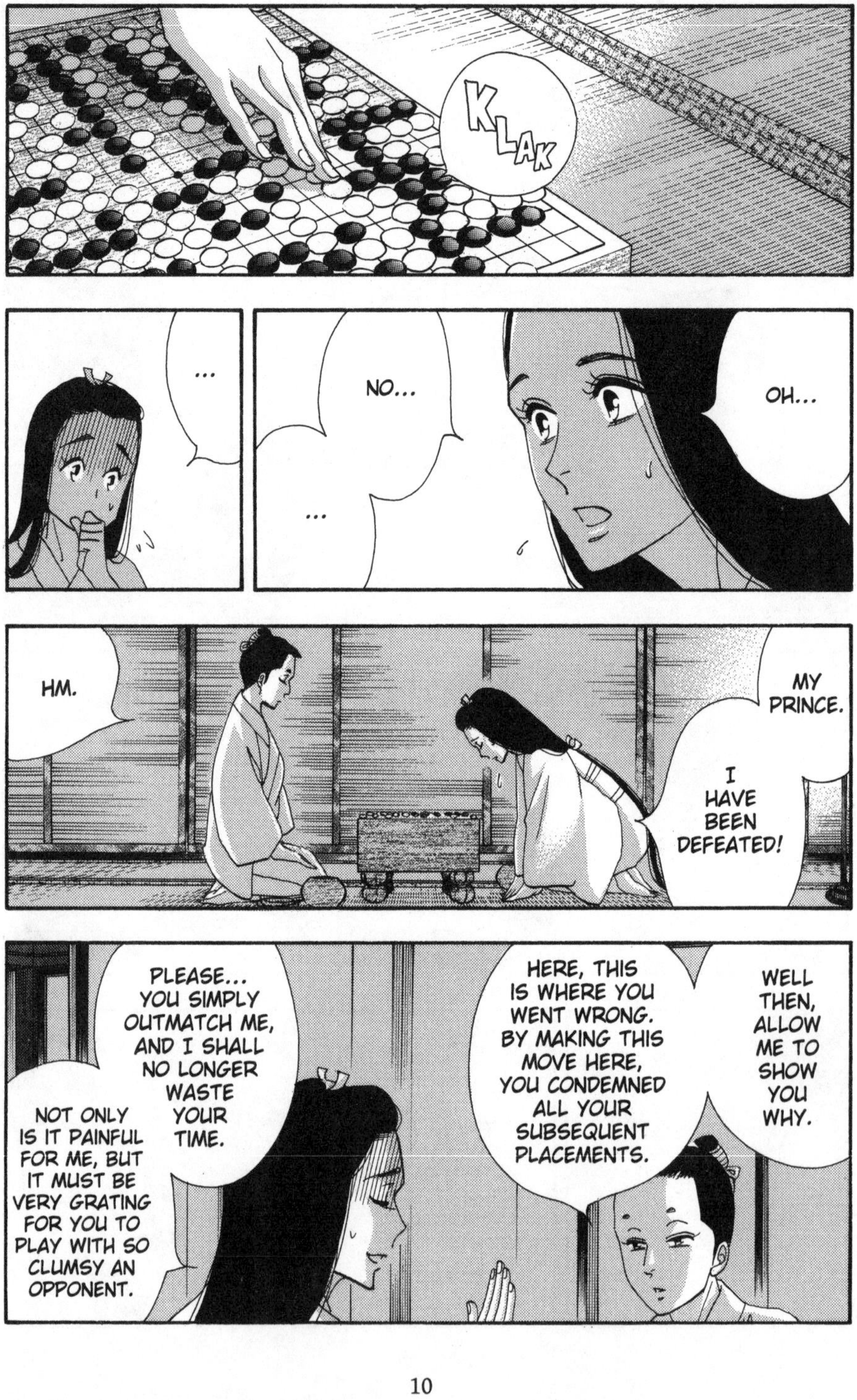
KLAK
OH...
NO...
...
...
MY PRINCE.
I HAVE BEEN DEFEATED!
HM.
WELL THEN, ALLOW ME TO SHOW YOU WHY.
HERE, THIS IS WHERE YOU WENT WRONG. BY MAKING THIS MOVE HERE, YOU CONDEMNED ALL YOUR SUBSEQUENT PLACEMENTS.
PLEASE... YOU SIMPLY OUTMATCH ME, AND I SHALL NO LONGER WASTE YOUR TIME.
NOT ONLY IS IT PAINFUL FOR ME, BUT IT MUST BE VERY GRATING FOR YOU TO PLAY WITH SO CLUMSY AN OPPONENT.

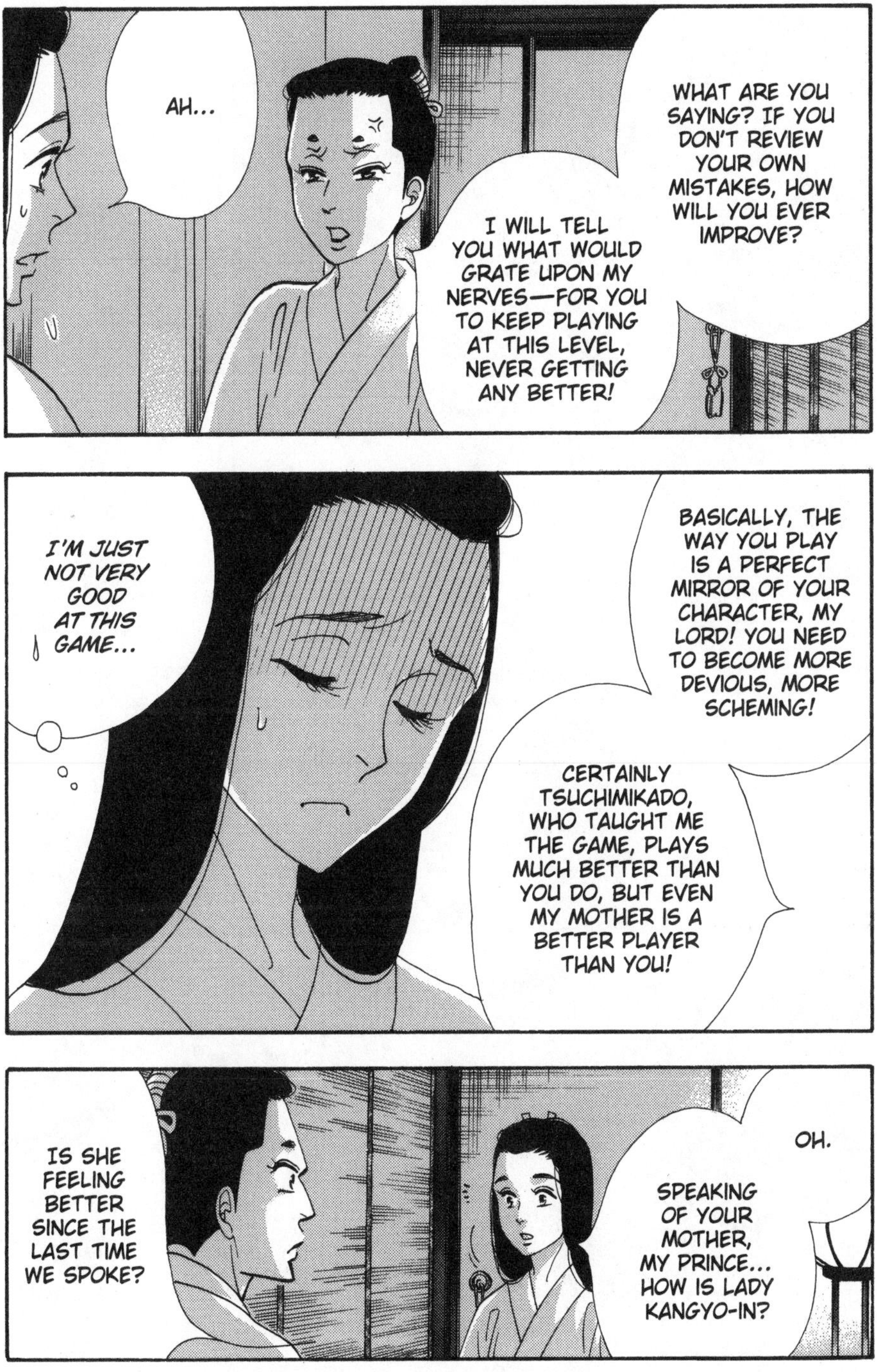
WHAT ARE YOU SAYING? IF YOU DON'T REVIEW YOUR OWN MISTAKES, HOW WILL YOU EVER IMPROVE?
I WILL TELL YOU WHAT WOULD GRATE UPON MY NERVES—FOR YOU TO KEEP PLAYING AT THIS LEVEL, NEVER GETTING ANY BETTER!
AH...
BASICALLY, THE WAY YOU PLAY IS A PERFECT MIRROR OF YOUR CHARACTER, MY LORD! YOU NEED TO BECOME MORE DEVIOUS, MORE SCHEMING!
CERTAINLY TSUCHIMIKADO, WHO TAUGHT ME THE GAME, PLAYS MUCH BETTER THAN YOU DO, BUT EVEN MY MOTHER IS A BETTER PLAYER THAN YOU!
I'M JUST NOT VERY GOOD AT THIS GAME...
OH.
SPEAKING OF YOUR MOTHER, MY PRINCE... HOW IS LADY KANGYO-IN?
IS SHE FEELING BETTER SINCE THE LAST TIME WE SPOKE?

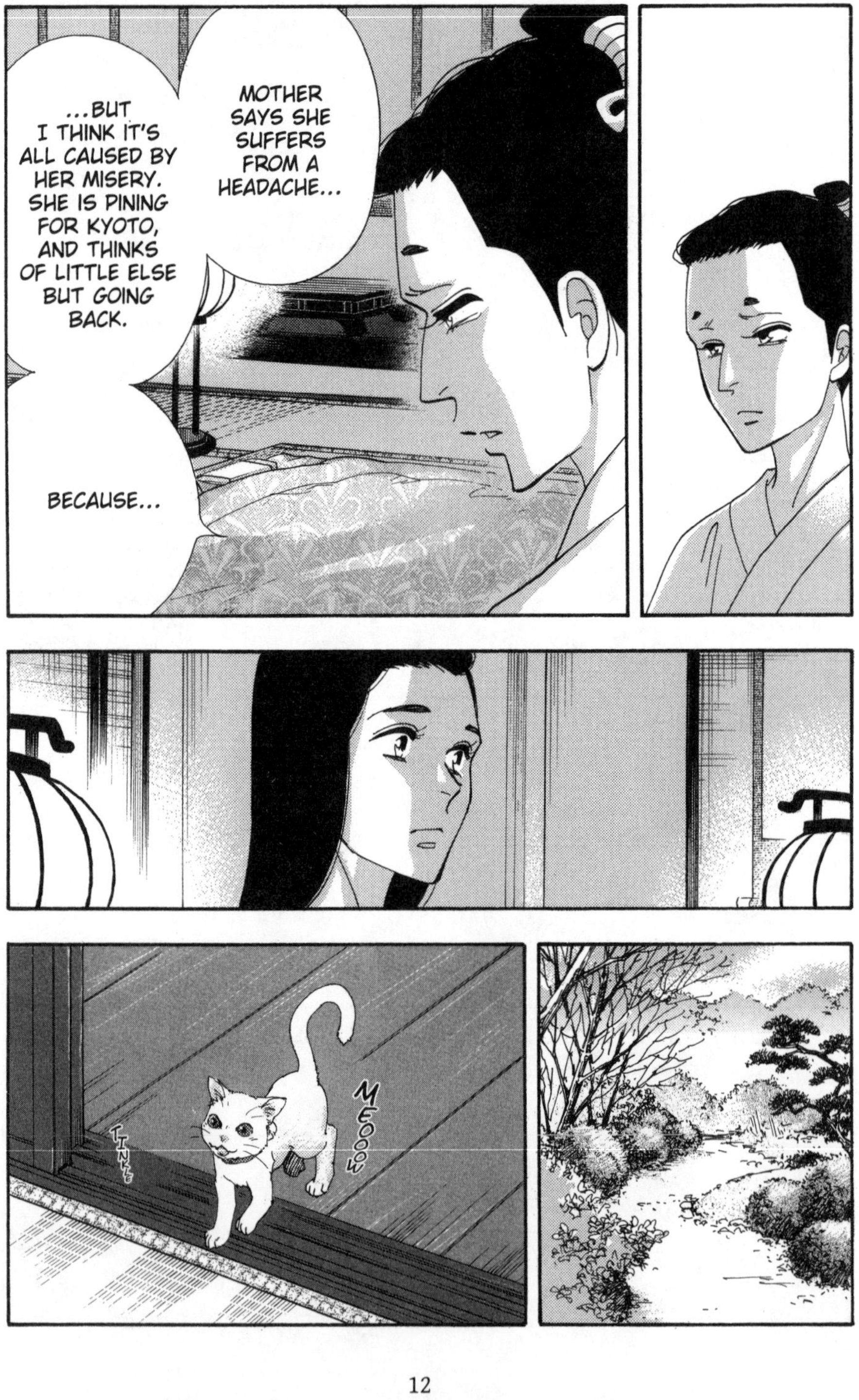
MOTHER SAYS SHE SUFFERS FROM A HEADACHE...
...BUT I THINK IT'S ALL CAUSED BY HER MISERY. SHE IS PINING FOR KYOTO, AND THINKS OF LITTLE ELSE BUT GOING BACK.
BECAUSE...
MEOOOW
TINKLE

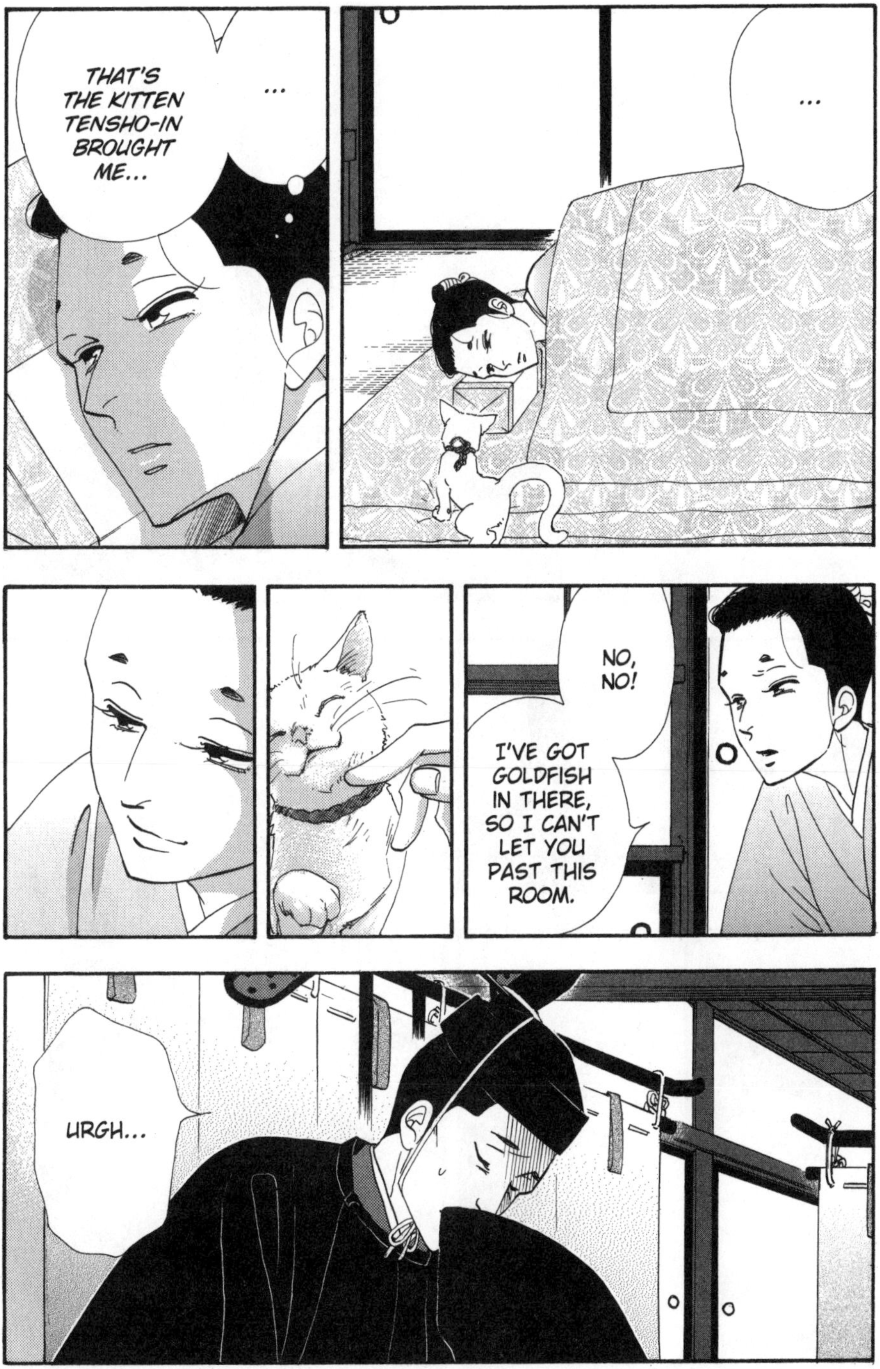
...
...
THAT'S THE KITTEN TENSHO-IN BROUGHT ME...
NO, NO!
I'VE GOT GOLDFISH IN THERE, SO I CAN'T LET YOU PAST THIS ROOM.
URGH...

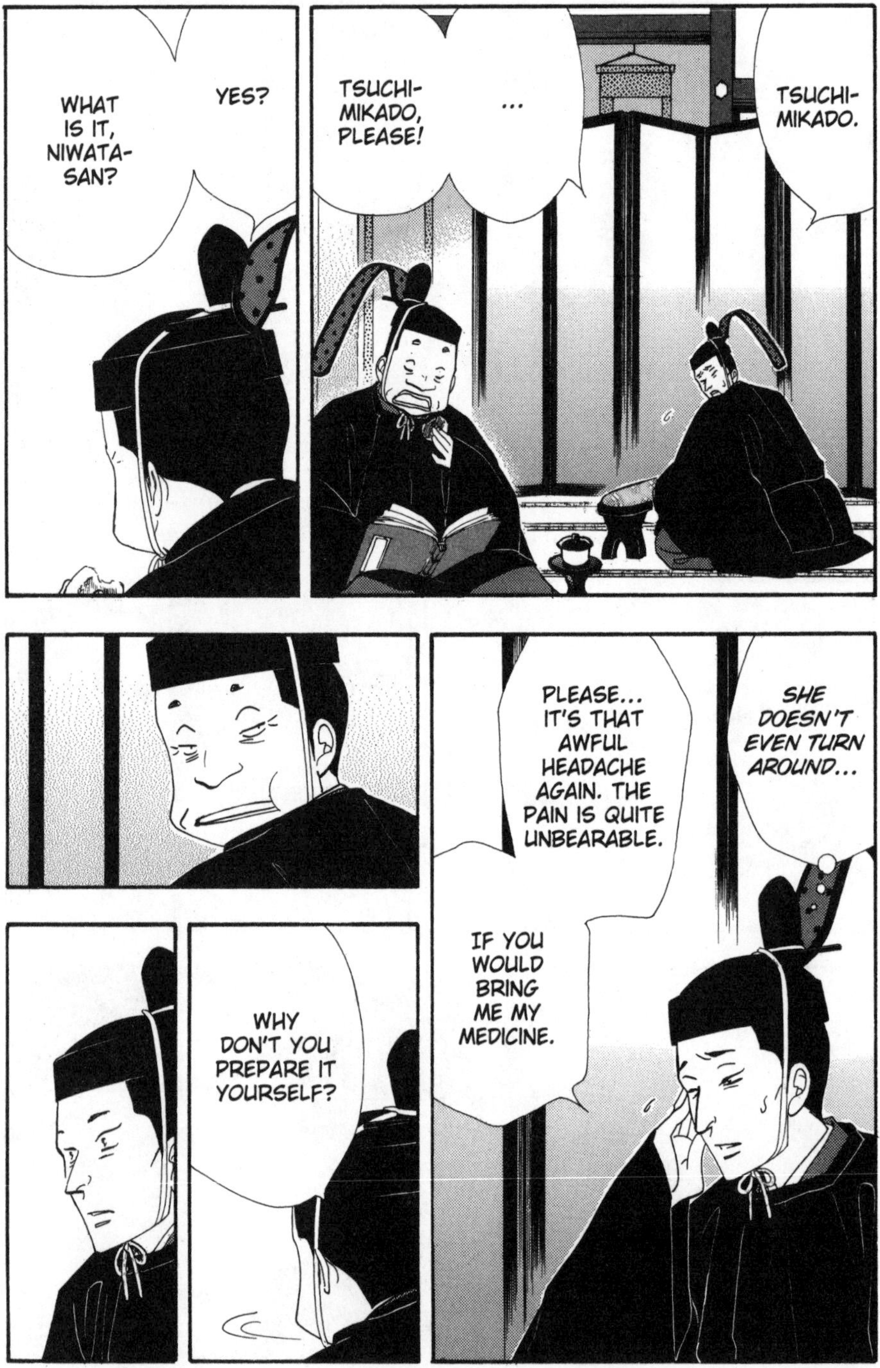
TSUCHI-MIKADO.
...
TSUCHI-MIKADO, PLEASE!
YES?
WHAT IS IT, NIWATA-SAN?
SHE DOESN'T EVEN TURN AROUND...
PLEASE... IT'S THAT AWFUL HEADACHE AGAIN. THE PAIN IS QUITE UNBEARABLE.
IF YOU WOULD BRING ME MY MEDICINE.
WHY DON'T YOU PREPARE IT YOURSELF?

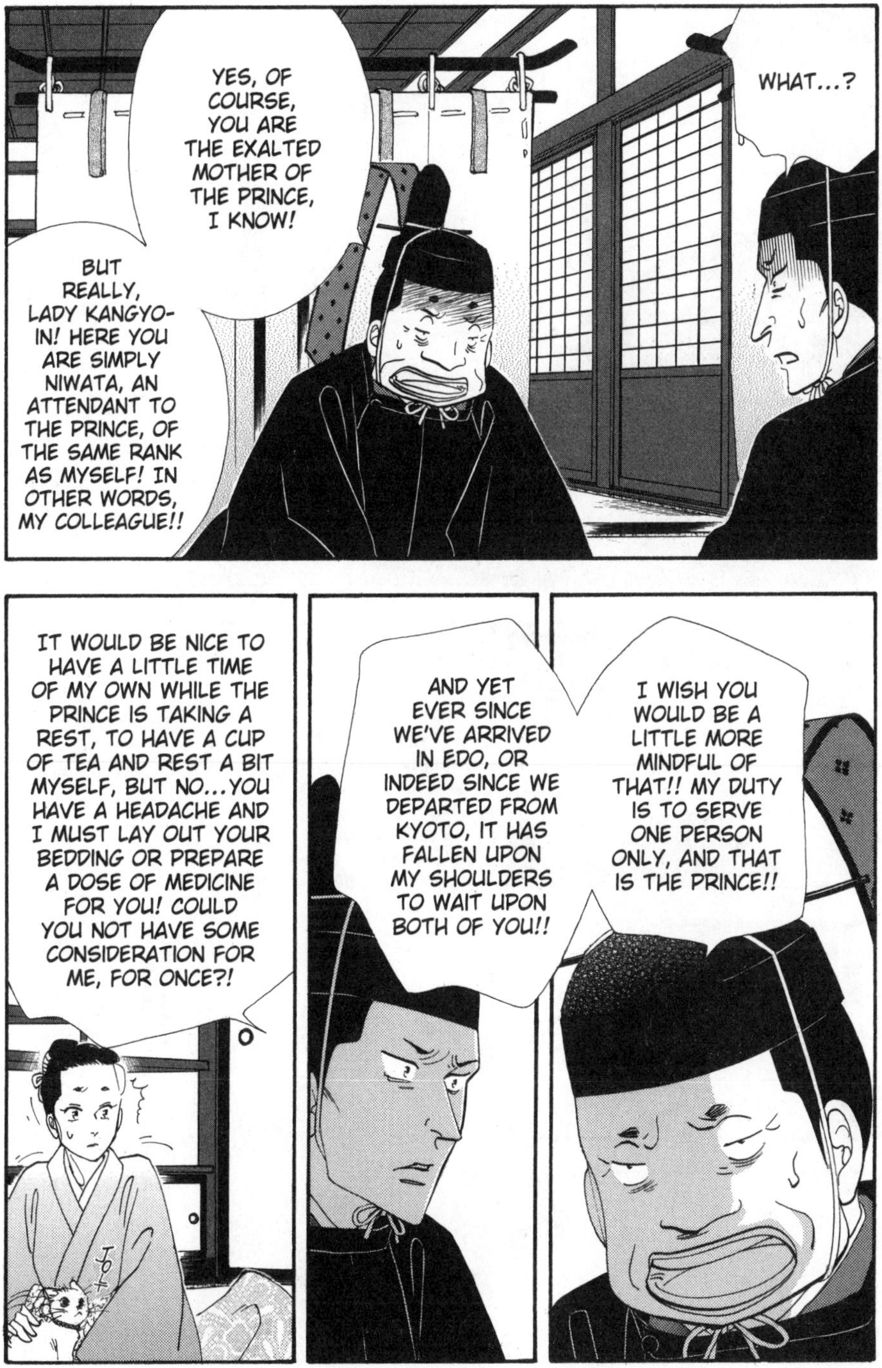
WHAT...?
YES, OF COURSE, YOU ARE THE EXALTED MOTHER OF THE PRINCE, I KNOW!
BUT REALLY, LADY KANGYO-IN! HERE YOU ARE SIMPLY NIWATA, AN ATTENDANT TO THE PRINCE, OF THE SAME RANK AS MYSELF! IN OTHER WORDS, MY COLLEAGUE!!
I WISH YOU WOULD BE A LITTLE MORE MINDFUL OF THAT!! MY DUTY IS TO SERVE ONE PERSON ONLY, AND THAT IS THE PRINCE!!
AND YET EVER SINCE WE'VE ARRIVED IN EDO, OR INDEED SINCE WE DEPARTED FROM KYOTO, IT HAS FALLEN UPON MY SHOULDERS TO WAIT UPON BOTH OF YOU!!
IT WOULD BE NICE TO HAVE A LITTLE TIME OF MY OWN WHILE THE PRINCE IS TAKING A REST, TO HAVE A CUP OF TEA AND REST A BIT MYSELF, BUT NO...YOU HAVE A HEADACHE AND I MUST LAY OUT YOUR BEDDING OR PREPARE A DOSE OF MEDICINE FOR YOU! COULD YOU NOT HAVE SOME CONSIDERATION FOR ME, FOR ONCE?!

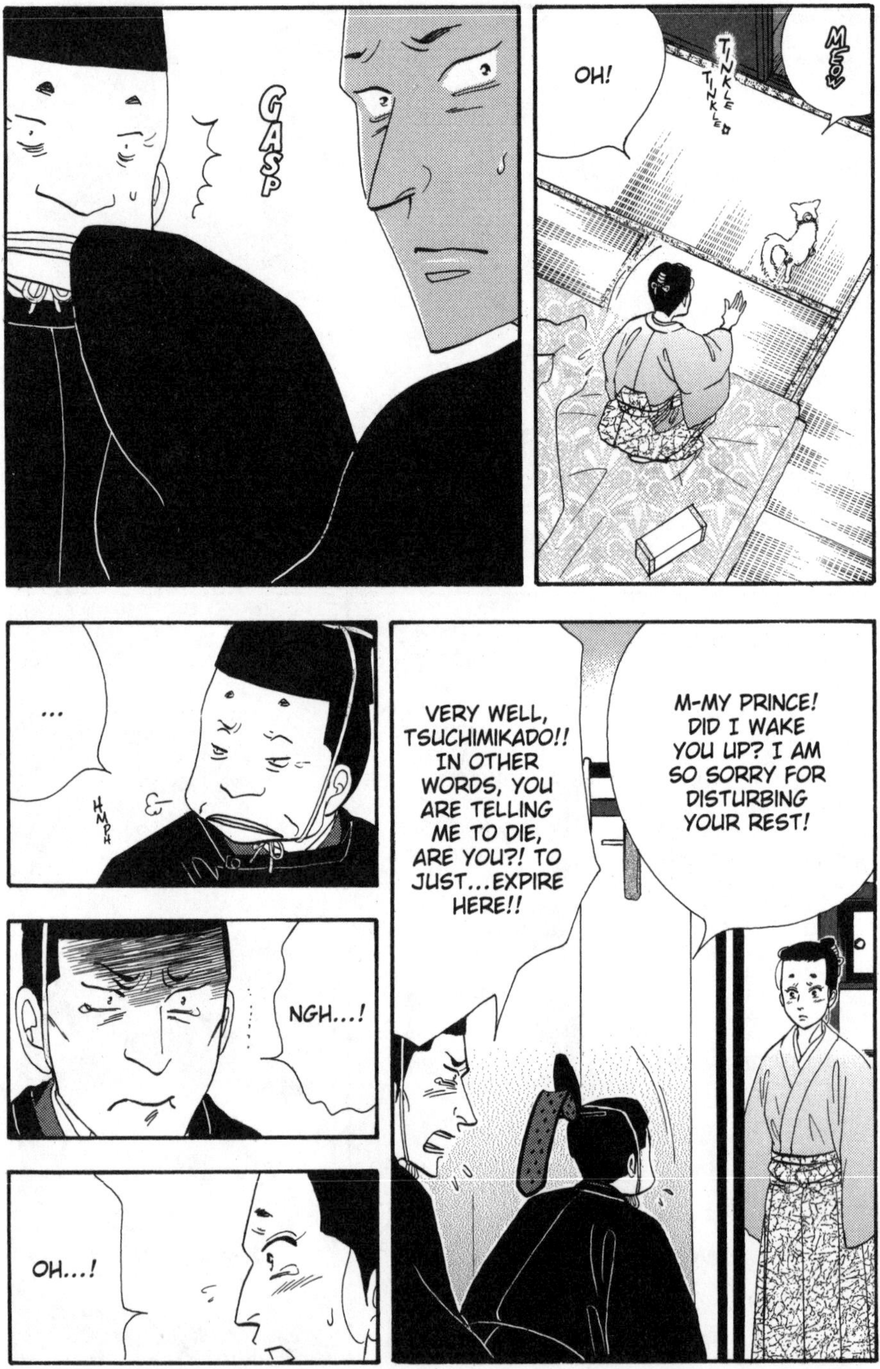
MEOW
TINKLE TINKLE
OH!
GASP
M-MY PRINCE! DID I WAKE YOU UP? I AM SO SORRY FOR DISTURBING YOUR REST!
VERY WELL, TSUCHIMIKADO!! IN OTHER WORDS, YOU ARE TELLING ME TO DIE, ARE YOU?! TO JUST...EXPIRE HERE!!
...
HMPH
NGH...!
OH...!

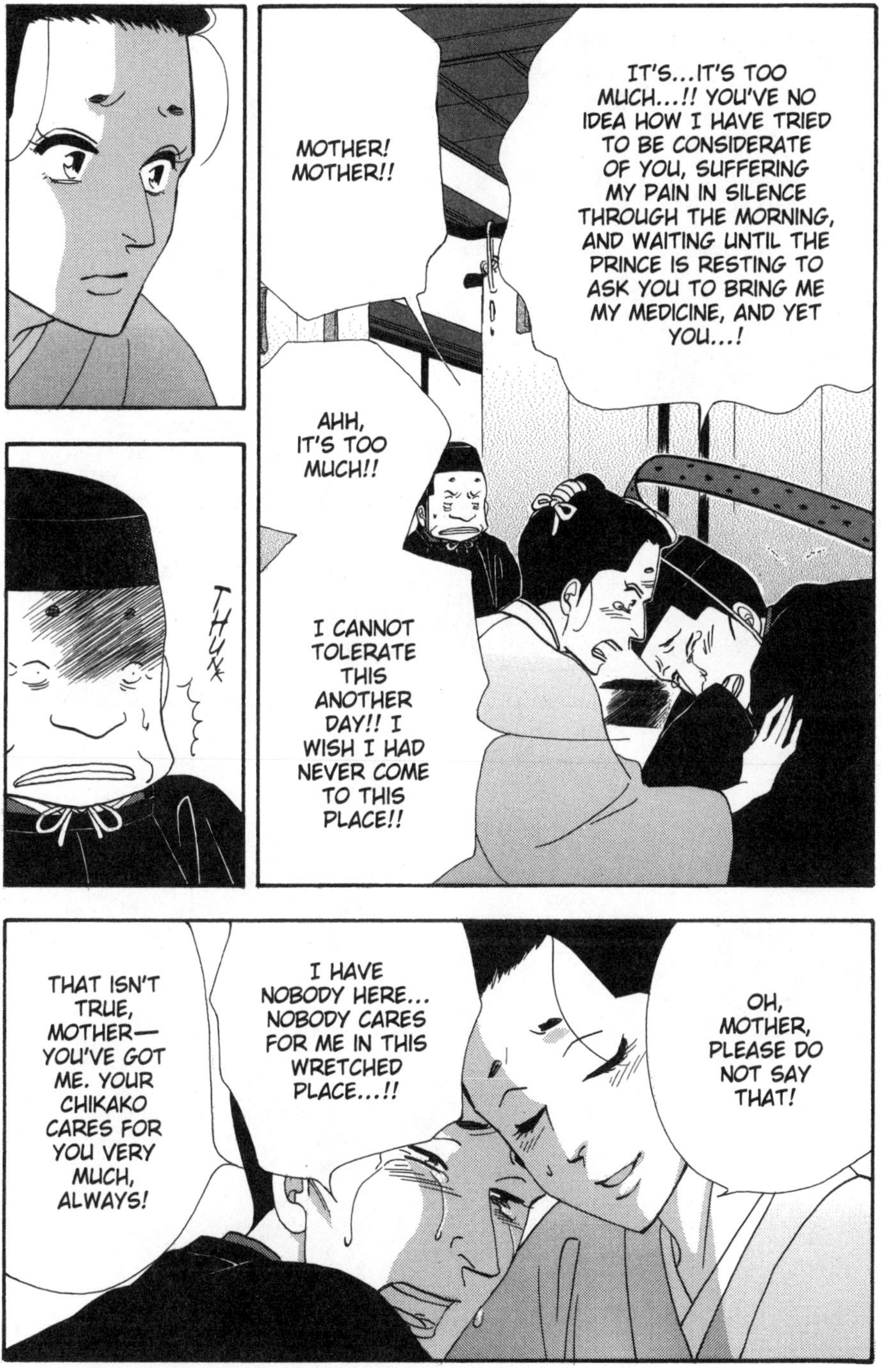
IT'S...IT'S TOO MUCH...!! YOU'VE NO IDEA HOW I HAVE TRIED TO BE CONSIDERATE OF YOU, SUFFERING MY PAIN IN SILENCE THROUGH THE MORNING, AND WAITING UNTIL THE PRINCE IS RESTING TO ASK YOU TO BRING ME MY MEDICINE, AND YET YOU...!
MOTHER! MOTHER!!
AHH, IT'S TOO MUCH!!
I CANNOT TOLERATE THIS ANOTHER DAY!! I WISH I HAD NEVER COME TO THIS PLACE!!
OH, MOTHER, PLEASE DO NOT SAY THAT!
I HAVE NOBODY HERE... NOBODY CARES FOR ME IN THIS WRETCHED PLACE...!!
THAT ISN'T TRUE, MOTHER— YOU'VE GOT ME. YOUR CHIKAKO CARES FOR YOU VERY MUCH, ALWAYS!

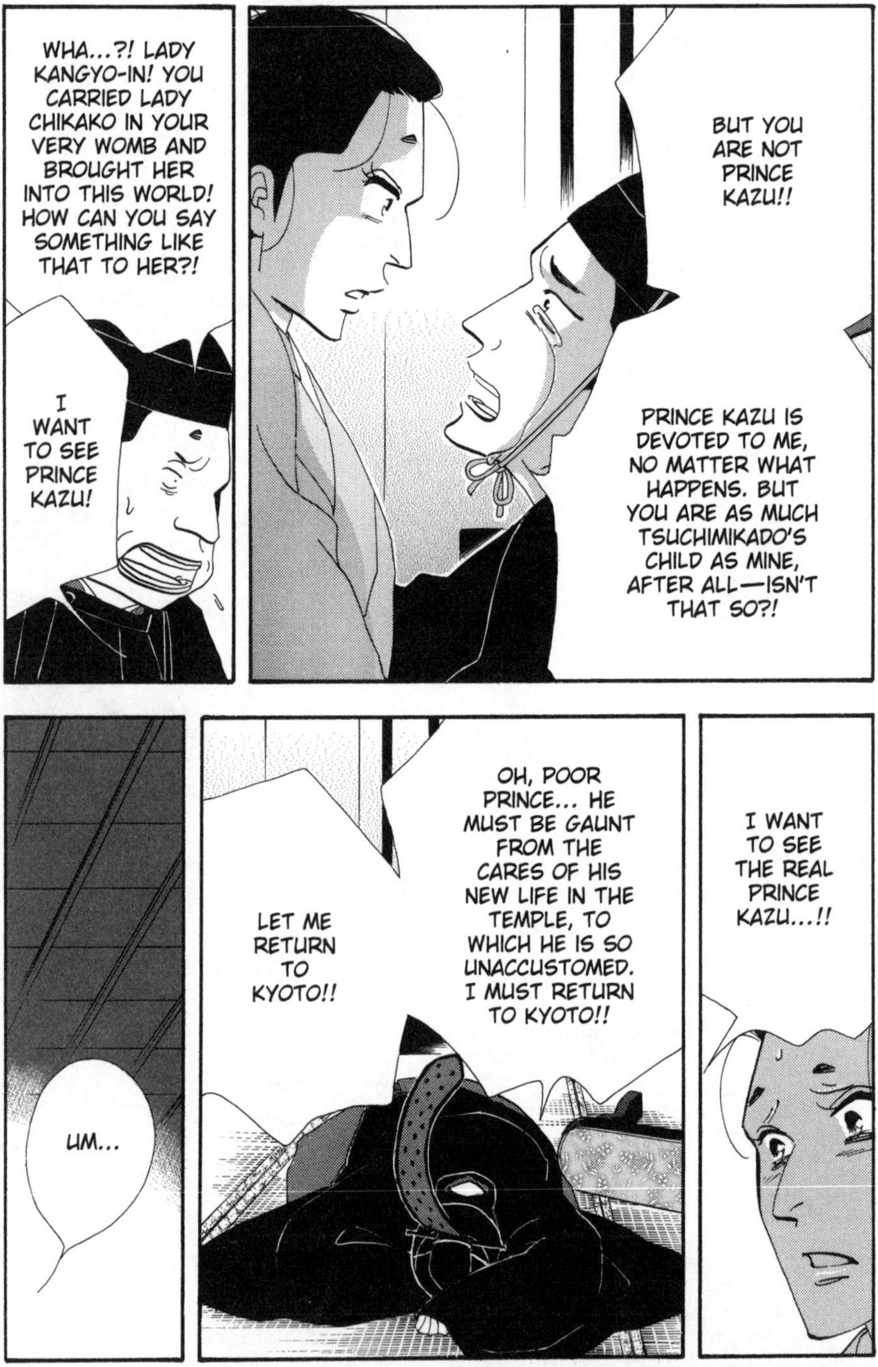
BUT YOU ARE NOT PRINCE KAZU!!
PRINCE KAZU IS DEVOTED TO ME, NO MATTER WHAT HAPPENS. BUT YOU ARE AS MUCH TSUCHIMIKADO'S CHILD AS MINE, AFTER ALL—ISN'T THAT SO?!
WHA...?! LADY KANGYO-IN! YOU CARRIED LADY CHIKAKO IN YOUR VERY WOMB AND BROUGHT HER INTO THIS WORLD! HOW CAN YOU SAY SOMETHING LIKE THAT TO HER?!
I WANT TO SEE PRINCE KAZU!
I WANT TO SEE THE REAL PRINCE KAZU...!!
OH, POOR PRINCE... HE MUST BE GAUNT FROM THE CARES OF HIS NEW LIFE IN THE TEMPLE, TO WHICH HE IS SO UNACCUSTOMED. I MUST RETURN TO KYOTO!!
LET ME RETURN TO KYOTO!!
UM...

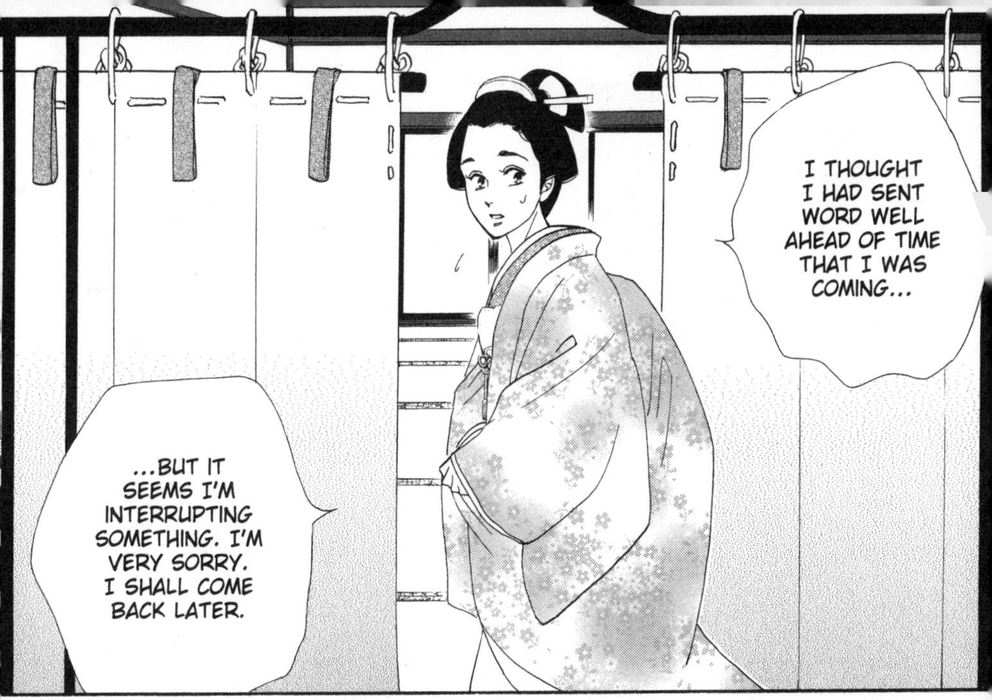
I THOUGHT I HAD SENT WORD WELL AHEAD OF TIME THAT I WAS COMING...
...BUT IT SEEMS I'M INTERRUPTING SOMETHING. I'M VERY SORRY. I SHALL COME BACK LATER.
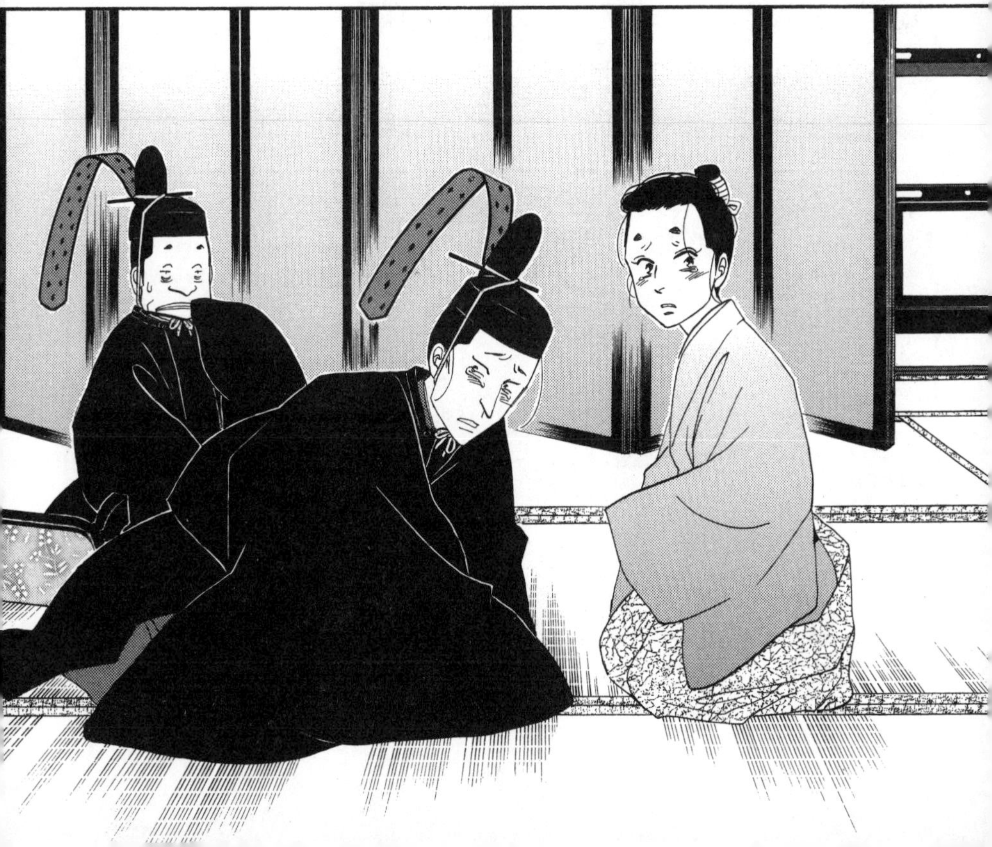

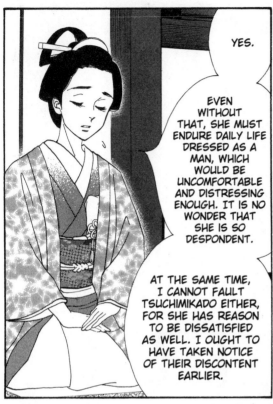

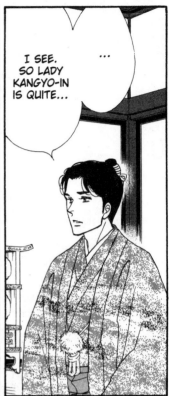

...
I SEE. SO LADY KANGYO-IN IS QUITE...
YES.
EVEN WITHOUT THAT, SHE MUST ENDURE DAILY LIFE DRESSED AS A MAN, WHICH WOULD BE UNCOMFORTABLE AND DISTRESSING ENOUGH. IT IS NO WONDER THAT SHE IS SO DESPONDENT.
AT THE SAME TIME, I CANNOT FAULT TSUCHIMIKADO EITHER, FOR SHE HAS REASON TO BE DISSATISFIED AS WELL. I OUGHT TO HAVE TAKEN NOTICE OF THEIR DISCONTENT EARLIER.
BUT WHAT DO YOU INTEND TO DO, YOUR HIGHNESS?
IF THE PROBLEM IS THE NEED FOR MORE FEMALE ATTENDANTS... CAN MORE WOMEN BE BROUGHT INTO THE INNER CHAMBERS?
I HAVE SOMEONE IN MIND WHO WOULD BE IDEAL.
TAKIYAMA.
M'LORD.

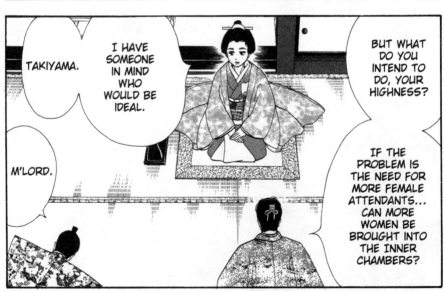

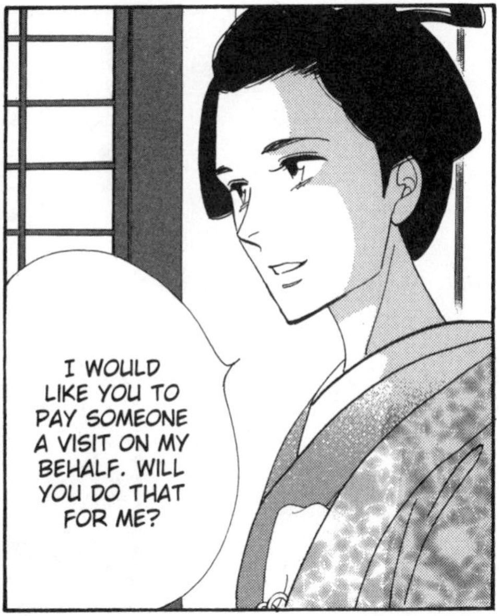
I WOULD LIKE YOU TO PAY SOMEONE A VISIT ON MY BEHALF. WILL YOU DO THAT FOR ME?
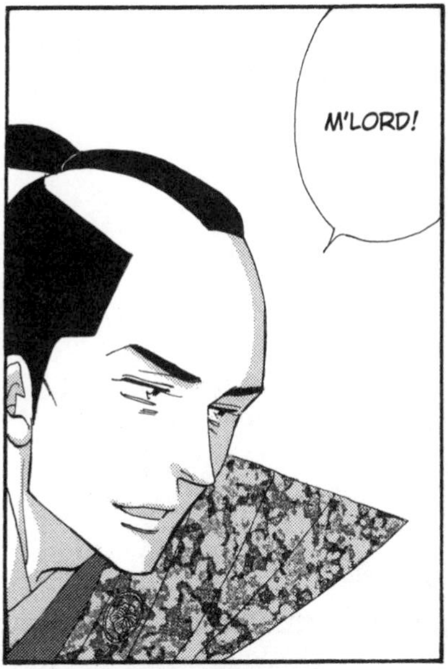
M'LORD!
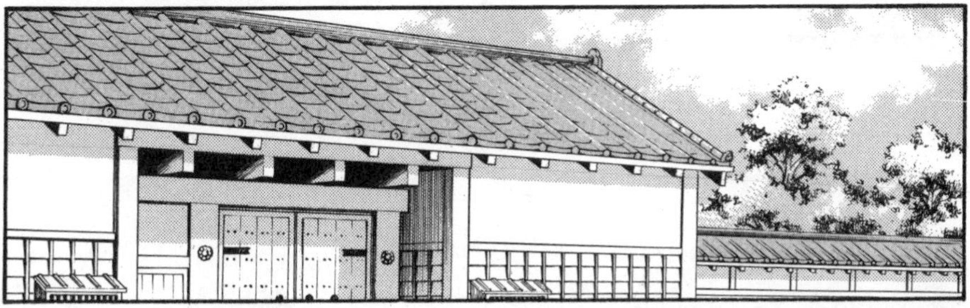
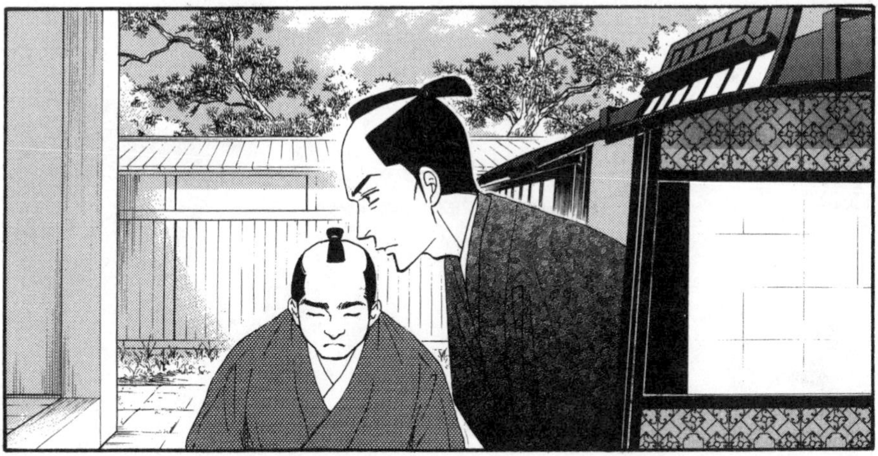

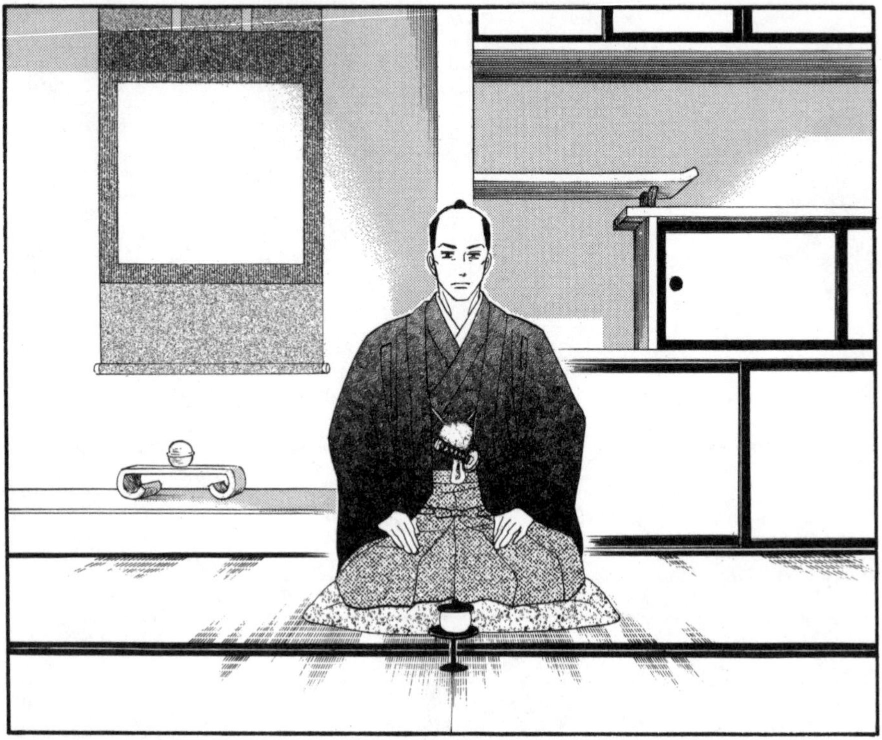

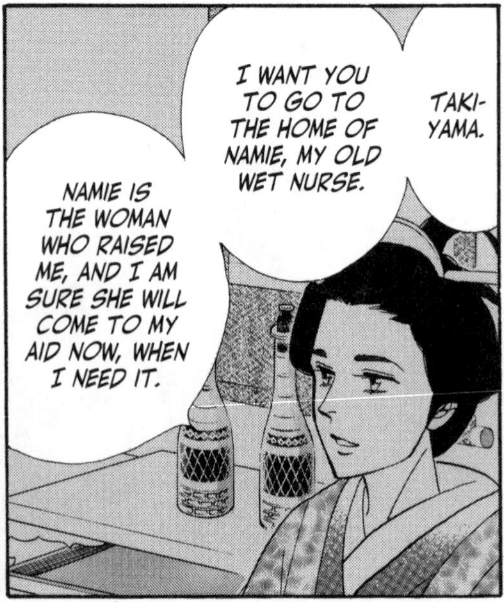
TAKI-YAMA.
I WANT YOU TO GO TO THE HOME OF NAMIE, MY OLD WET NURSE.
NAMIE IS THE WOMAN WHO RAISED ME, AND I AM SURE SHE WILL COME TO MY AID NOW, WHEN I NEED IT.

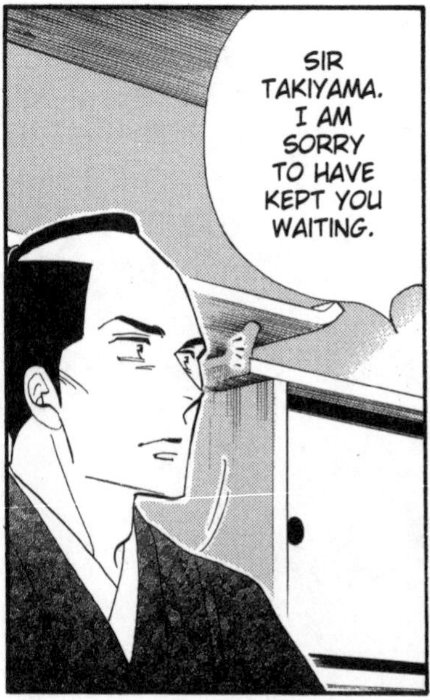
SIR TAKIYAMA. I AM SORRY TO HAVE KEPT YOU WAITING.

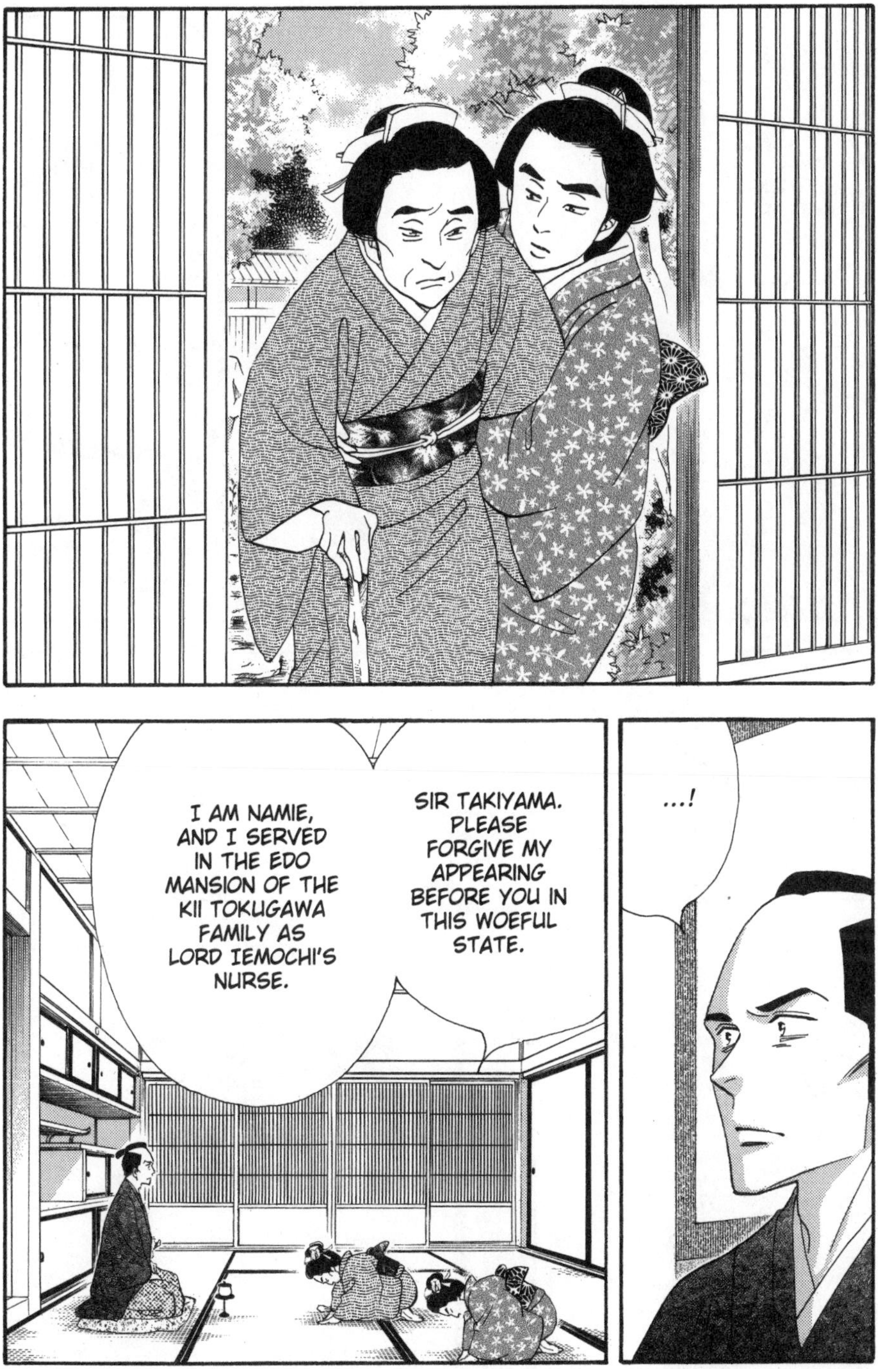
...!
SIR TAKIYAMA. PLEASE FORGIVE MY APPEARING BEFORE YOU IN THIS WOEFUL STATE.
I AM NAMIE, AND I SERVED IN THE EDO MANSION OF THE KII TOKUGAWA FAMILY AS LORD IEMOCHI'S NURSE.

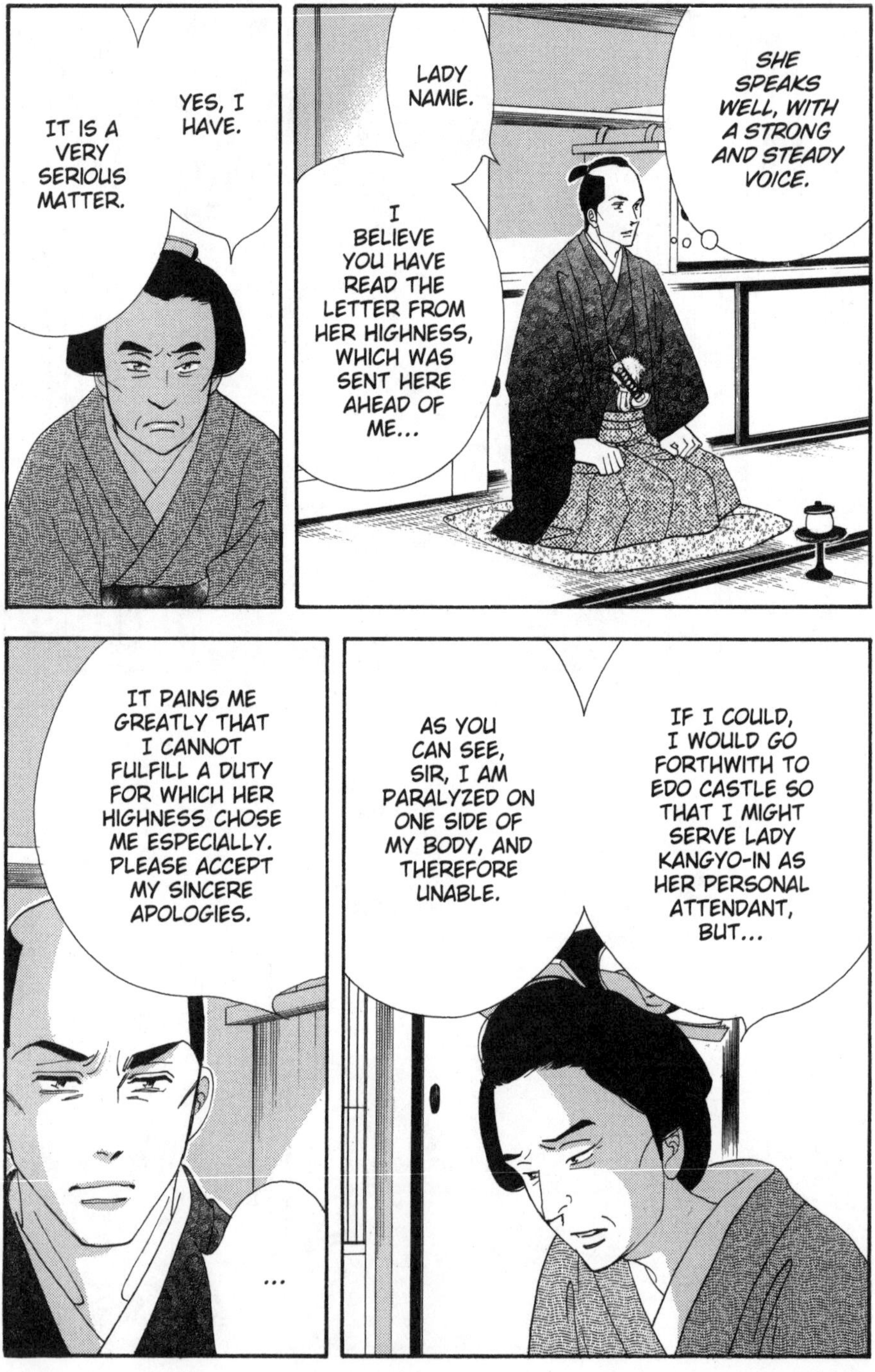
SHE SPEAKS WELL, WITH A STRONG AND STEADY VOICE.
LADY NAMIE.
I BELIEVE YOU HAVE READ THE LETTER FROM HER HIGHNESS, WHICH WAS SENT HERE AHEAD OF ME...
YES, I HAVE.
IT IS A VERY SERIOUS MATTER.
IF I COULD, I WOULD GO FORTHWITH TO EDO CASTLE SO THAT I MIGHT SERVE LADY KANGYO-IN AS HER PERSONAL ATTENDANT, BUT...
AS YOU CAN SEE, SIR, I AM PARALYZED ON ONE SIDE OF MY BODY, AND THEREFORE UNABLE.
IT PAINS ME GREATLY THAT I CANNOT FULFILL A DUTY FOR WHICH HER HIGHNESS CHOSE ME ESPECIALLY. PLEASE ACCEPT MY SINCERE APOLOGIES.
...

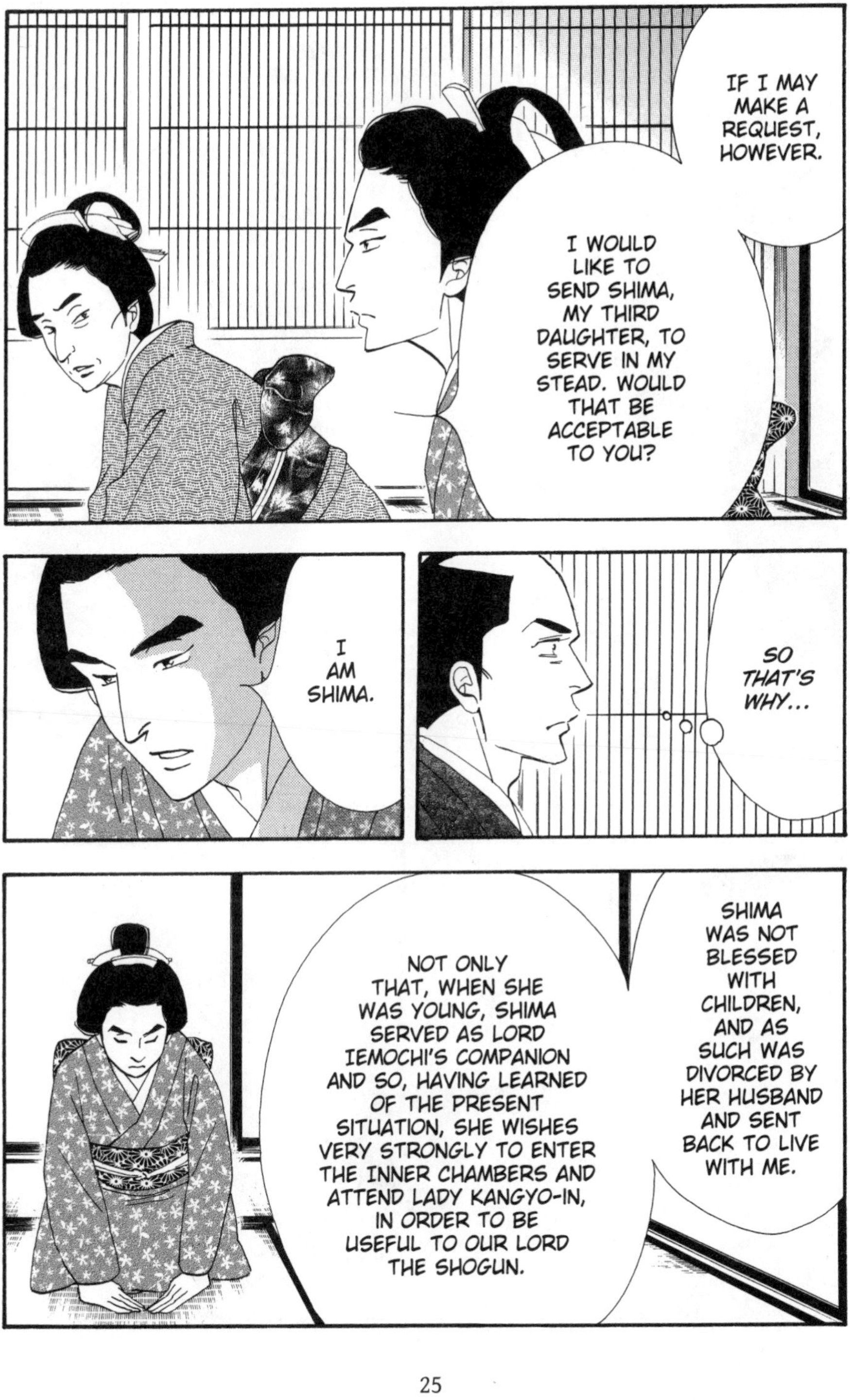
IF I MAY MAKE A REQUEST, HOWEVER.
I WOULD LIKE TO SEND SHIMA, MY THIRD DAUGHTER, TO SERVE IN MY STEAD. WOULD THAT BE ACCEPTABLE TO YOU?
SO THAT'S WHY...
I AM SHIMA.
SHIMA WAS NOT BLESSED WITH CHILDREN, AND AS SUCH WAS DIVORCED BY HER HUSBAND AND SENT BACK TO LIVE WITH ME.
NOT ONLY THAT, WHEN SHE WAS YOUNG, SHIMA SERVED AS LORD IEMOCHI'S COMPANION AND SO, HAVING LEARNED OF THE PRESENT SITUATION, SHE WISHES VERY STRONGLY TO ENTER THE INNER CHAMBERS AND ATTEND LADY KANGYO-IN, IN ORDER TO BE USEFUL TO OUR LORD THE SHOGUN.

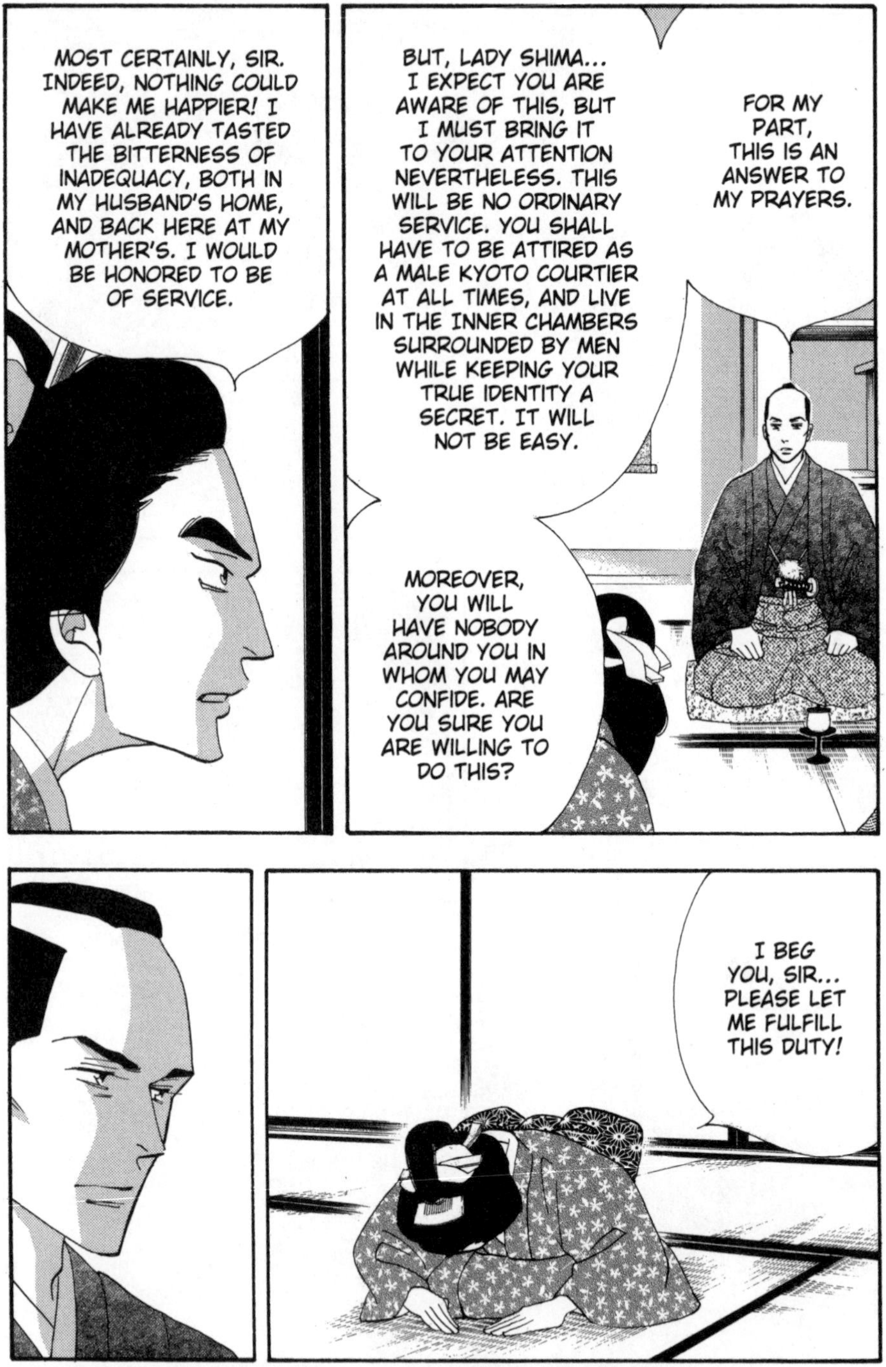
FOR MY PART, THIS IS AN ANSWER TO MY PRAYERS.
BUT, LADY SHIMA... I EXPECT YOU ARE AWARE OF THIS, BUT I MUST BRING IT TO YOUR ATTENTION NEVERTHELESS. THIS WILL BE NO ORDINARY SERVICE. YOU SHALL HAVE TO BE ATTIRED AS A MALE KYOTO COURTIER AT ALL TIMES, AND LIVE IN THE INNER CHAMBERS SURROUNDED BY MEN WHILE KEEPING YOUR TRUE IDENTITY A SECRET. IT WILL NOT BE EASY.
MOREOVER, YOU WILL HAVE NOBODY AROUND YOU IN WHOM YOU MAY CONFIDE. ARE YOU SURE YOU ARE WILLING TO DO THIS?
MOST CERTAINLY, SIR. INDEED, NOTHING COULD MAKE ME HAPPIER! I HAVE ALREADY TASTED THE BITTERNESS OF INADEQUACY, BOTH IN MY HUSBAND'S HOME, AND BACK HERE AT MY MOTHER'S. I WOULD BE HONORED TO BE OF SERVICE.
I BEG YOU, SIR... PLEASE LET ME FULFILL THIS DUTY!

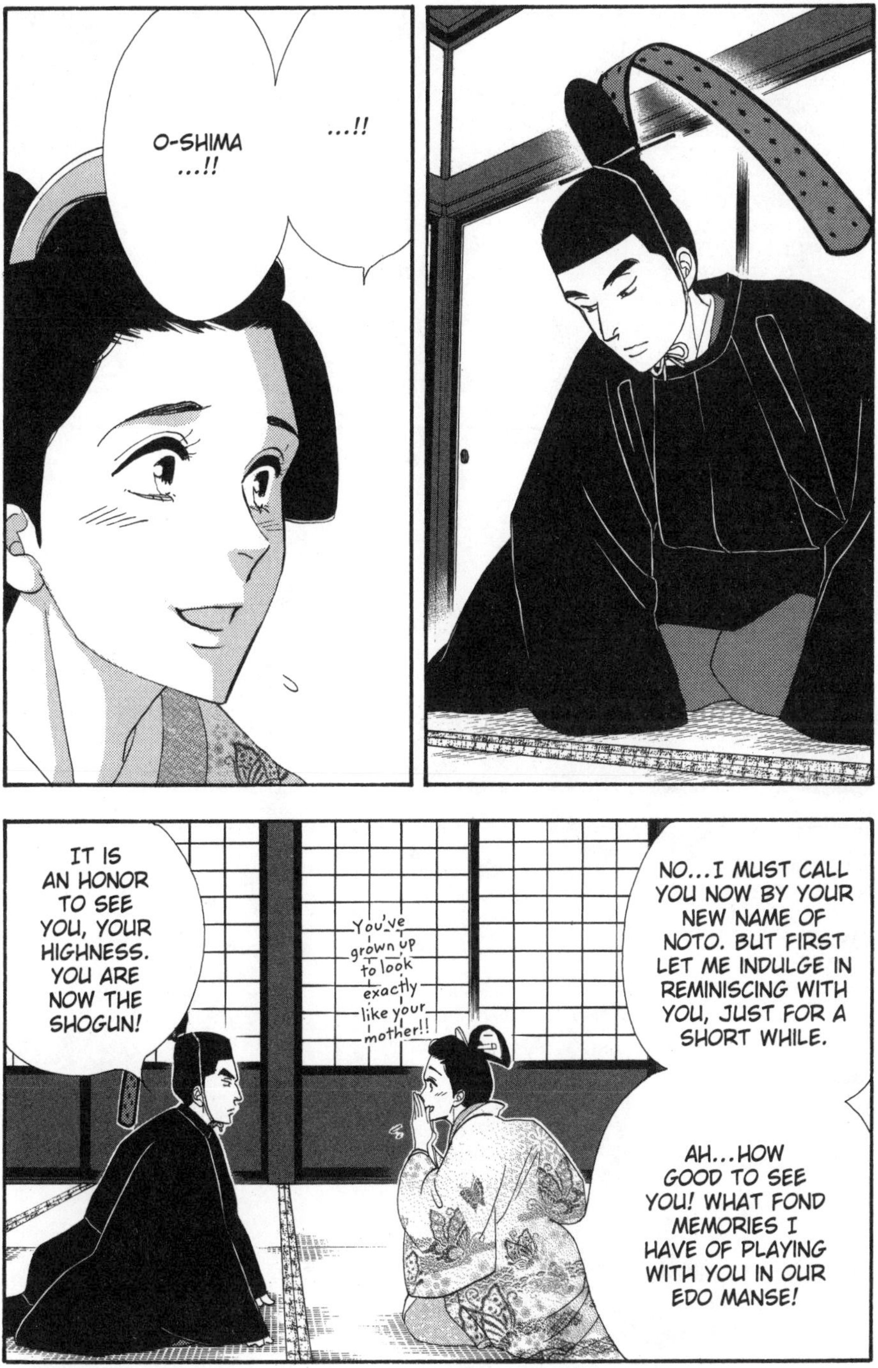
...!!
O-SHIMA ...!!
NO...I MUST CALL YOU NOW BY YOUR NEW NAME OF NOTO. BUT FIRST LET ME INDULGE IN REMINISCING WITH YOU, JUST FOR A SHORT WHILE.
AH...HOW GOOD TO SEE YOU! WHAT FOND MEMORIES I HAVE OF PLAYING WITH YOU IN OUR EDO MANSE!
You've grown up to look exactly like your mother!!
IT IS AN HONOR TO SEE YOU, YOUR HIGHNESS. YOU ARE NOW THE SHOGUN!

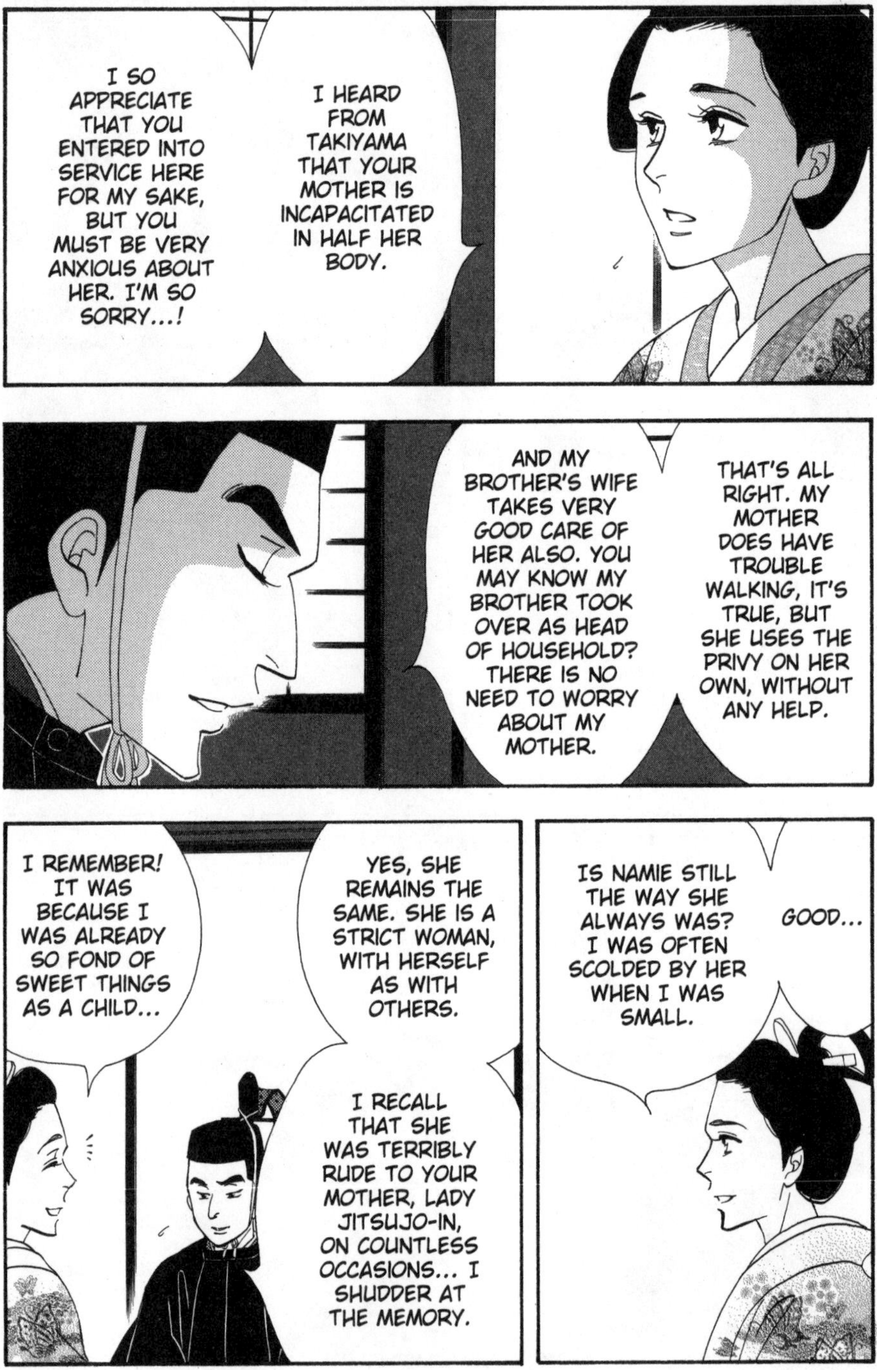
I HEARD FROM TAKIYAMA THAT YOUR MOTHER IS INCAPACITATED IN HALF HER BODY.
I SO APPRECIATE THAT YOU ENTERED INTO SERVICE HERE FOR MY SAKE, BUT YOU MUST BE VERY ANXIOUS ABOUT HER. I'M SO SORRY...!
THAT'S ALL RIGHT. MY MOTHER DOES HAVE TROUBLE WALKING, IT'S TRUE, BUT SHE USES THE PRIVY ON HER OWN, WITHOUT ANY HELP.
AND MY BROTHER'S WIFE TAKES VERY GOOD CARE OF HER ALSO. YOU MAY KNOW MY BROTHER TOOK OVER AS HEAD OF HOUSEHOLD? THERE IS NO NEED TO WORRY ABOUT MY MOTHER.
GOOD...
IS NAMIE STILL THE WAY SHE ALWAYS WAS? I WAS OFTEN SCOLDED BY HER WHEN I WAS SMALL.
YES, SHE REMAINS THE SAME. SHE IS A STRICT WOMAN, WITH HERSELF AS WITH OTHERS.
I RECALL THAT SHE WAS TERRIBLY RUDE TO YOUR MOTHER, LADY JITSUJO-IN, ON COUNTLESS OCCASIONS... I SHUDDER AT THE MEMORY.
I REMEMBER! IT WAS BECAUSE I WAS ALREADY SO FOND OF SWEET THINGS AS A CHILD...

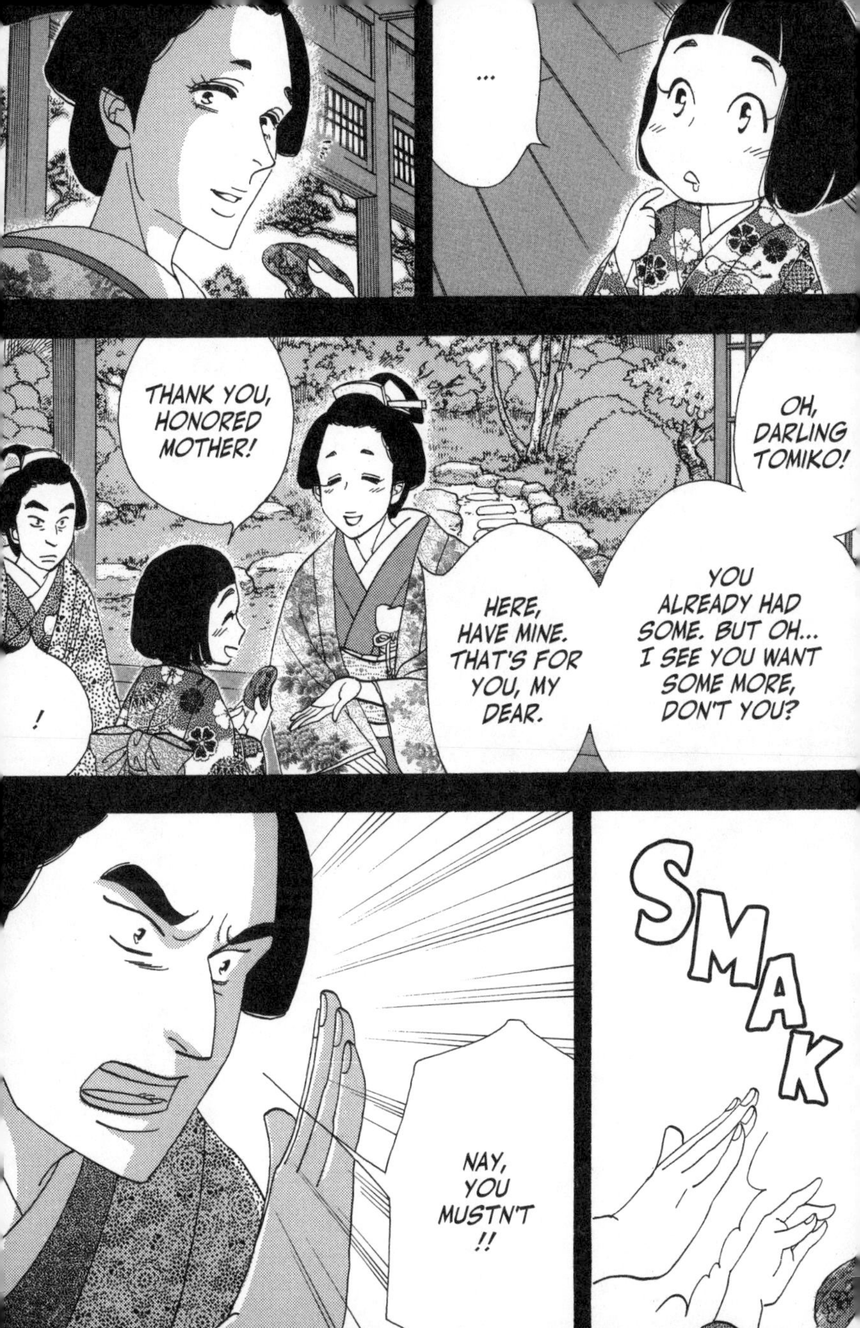
...
OH, DARLING TOMIKO!
YOU ALREADY HAD SOME. BUT OH... I SEE YOU WANT SOME MORE, DON'T YOU?
HERE, HAVE MINE. THAT'S FOR YOU, MY DEAR.
THANK YOU, HONORED MOTHER!
!
SMAK
NAY, YOU MUSTN'T !!

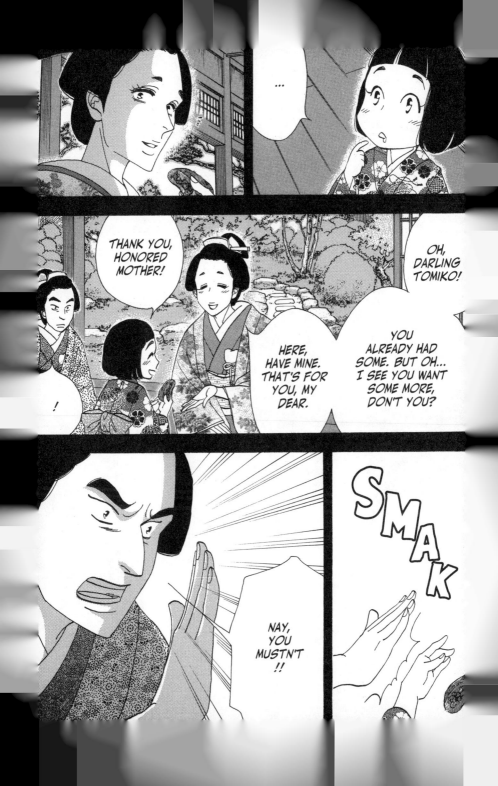

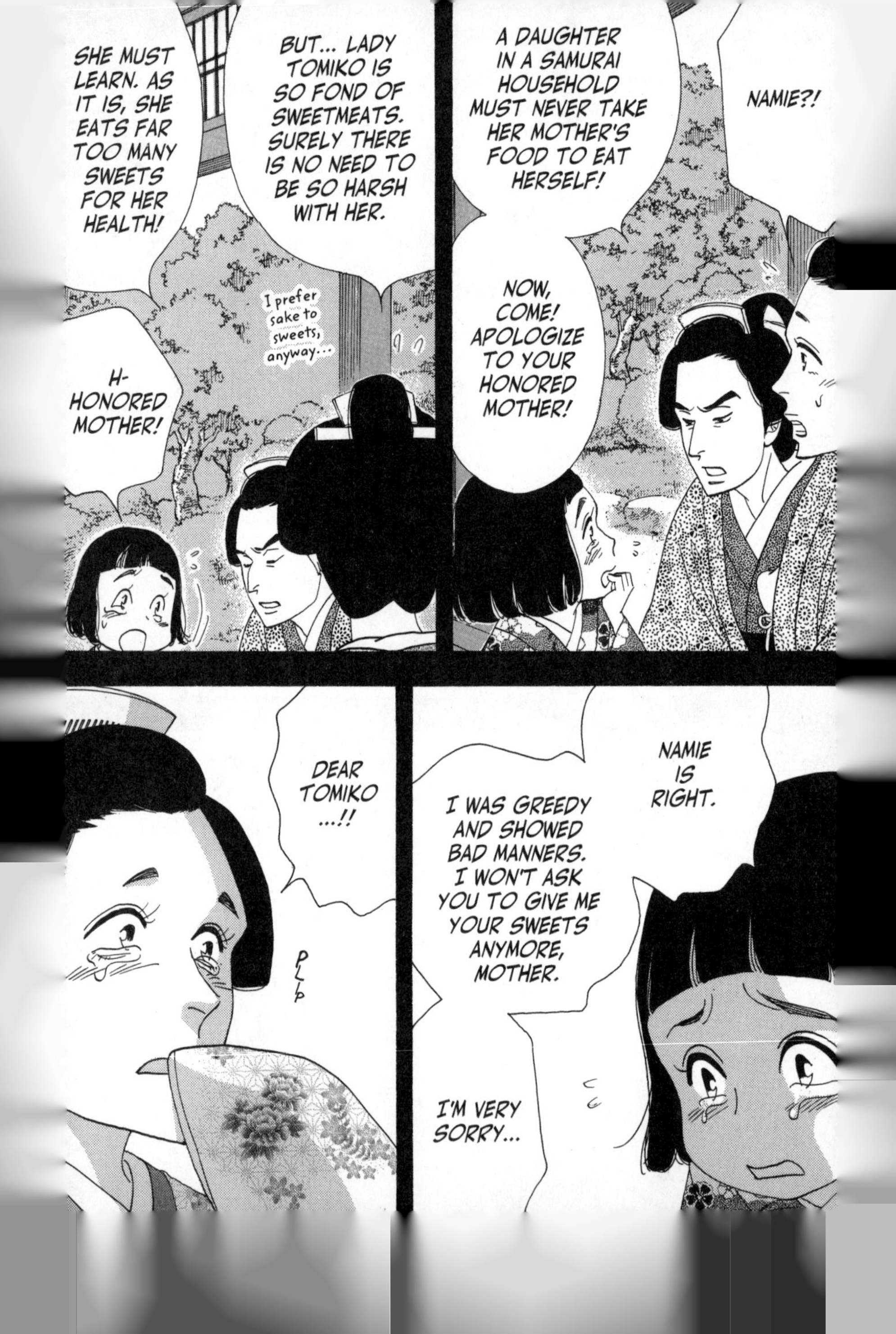
NAMIE?!
A DAUGHTER IN A SAMURAI HOUSEHOLD MUST NEVER TAKE HER MOTHER'S FOOD TO EAT HERSELF!
NOW, COME! APOLOGIZE TO YOUR HONORED MOTHER!
BUT... LADY TOMIKO IS SO FOND OF SWEETMEATS. SURELY THERE IS NO NEED TO BE SO HARSH WITH HER.
SHE MUST LEARN. AS IT IS, SHE EATS FAR TOO MANY SWEETS FOR HER HEALTH!
I prefer sake to sweets, anyway...
H- HONORED MOTHER!
NAMIE IS RIGHT.
I WAS GREEDY AND SHOWED BAD MANNERS. I WON'T ASK YOU TO GIVE ME YOUR SWEETS ANYMORE, MOTHER.
I'M VERY SORRY...
DEAR TOMIKO ...!!
PLP

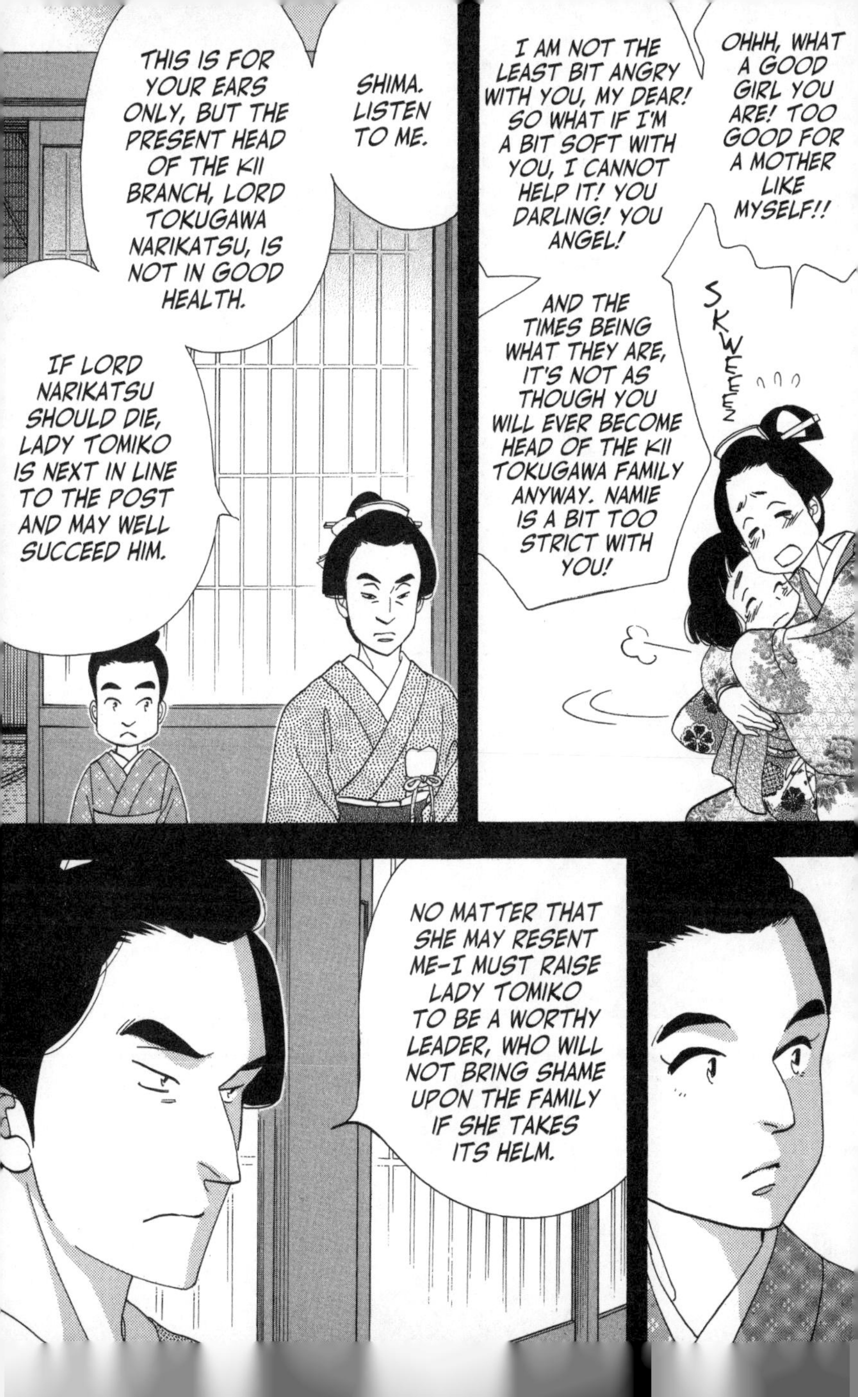
OHHH, WHAT A GOOD GIRL YOU ARE! TOO GOOD FOR A MOTHER LIKE MYSELF!!
I AM NOT THE LEAST BIT ANGRY WITH YOU, MY DEAR! SO WHAT IF I'M A BIT SOFT WITH YOU, I CANNOT HELP IT! YOU DARLING! YOU ANGEL!
AND THE TIMES BEING WHAT THEY ARE, IT'S NOT AS THOUGH YOU WILL EVER BECOME HEAD OF THE KII TOKUGAWA FAMILY ANYWAY. NAMIE IS A BIT TOO STRICT WITH YOU!
SKWEEEN
SHIMA. LISTEN TO ME.
THIS IS FOR YOUR EARS ONLY, BUT THE PRESENT HEAD OF THE KII BRANCH, LORD TOKUGAWA NARIKATSU, IS NOT IN GOOD HEALTH.
IF LORD NARIKATSU SHOULD DIE, LADY TOMIKO IS NEXT IN LINE TO THE POST AND MAY WELL SUCCEED HIM.
NO MATTER THAT SHE MAY RESENT ME—I MUST RAISE LADY TOMIKO TO BE A WORTHY LEADER, WHO WILL NOT BRING SHAME UPON THE FAMILY IF SHE TAKES ITS HELM.

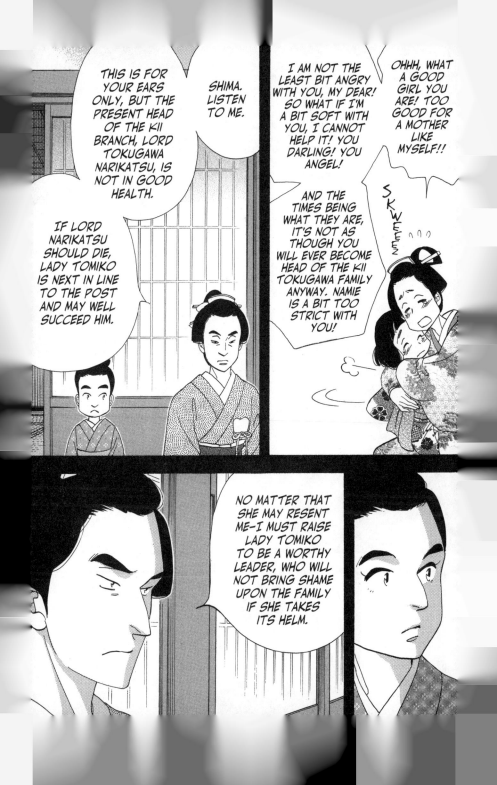

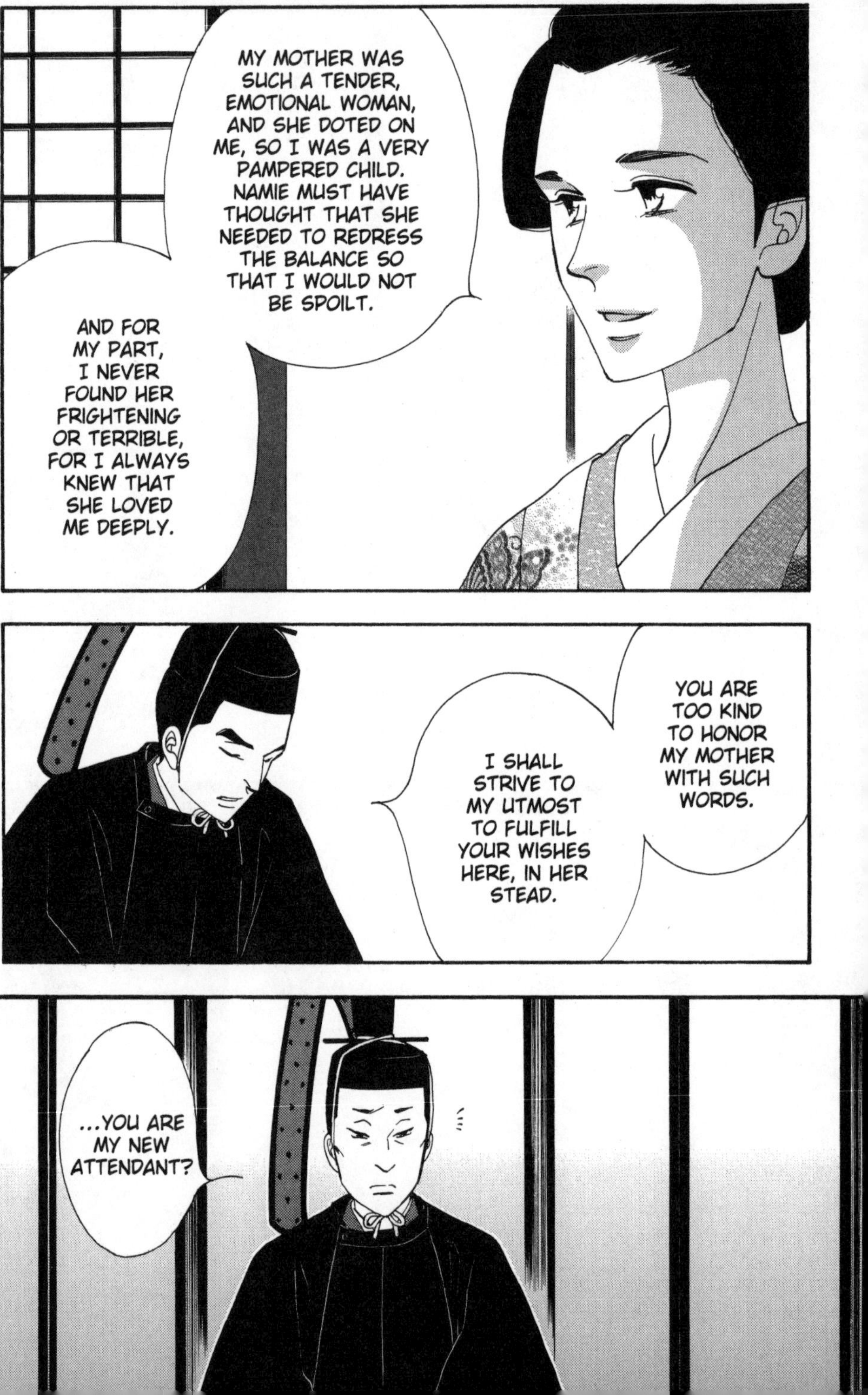
MY MOTHER WAS SUCH A TENDER, EMOTIONAL WOMAN, AND SHE DOTED ON ME, SO I WAS A VERY PAMPERED CHILD. NAMIE MUST HAVE THOUGHT THAT SHE NEEDED TO REDRESS THE BALANCE SO THAT I WOULD NOT BE SPOILT.
AND FOR MY PART, I NEVER FOUND HER FRIGHTENING OR TERRIBLE, FOR I ALWAYS KNEW THAT SHE LOVED ME DEEPLY.
YOU ARE TOO KIND TO HONOR MY MOTHER WITH SUCH WORDS.
I SHALL STRIVE TO MY UTMOST TO FULFILL YOUR WISHES HERE, IN HER STEAD.
...YOU ARE MY NEW ATTENDANT?

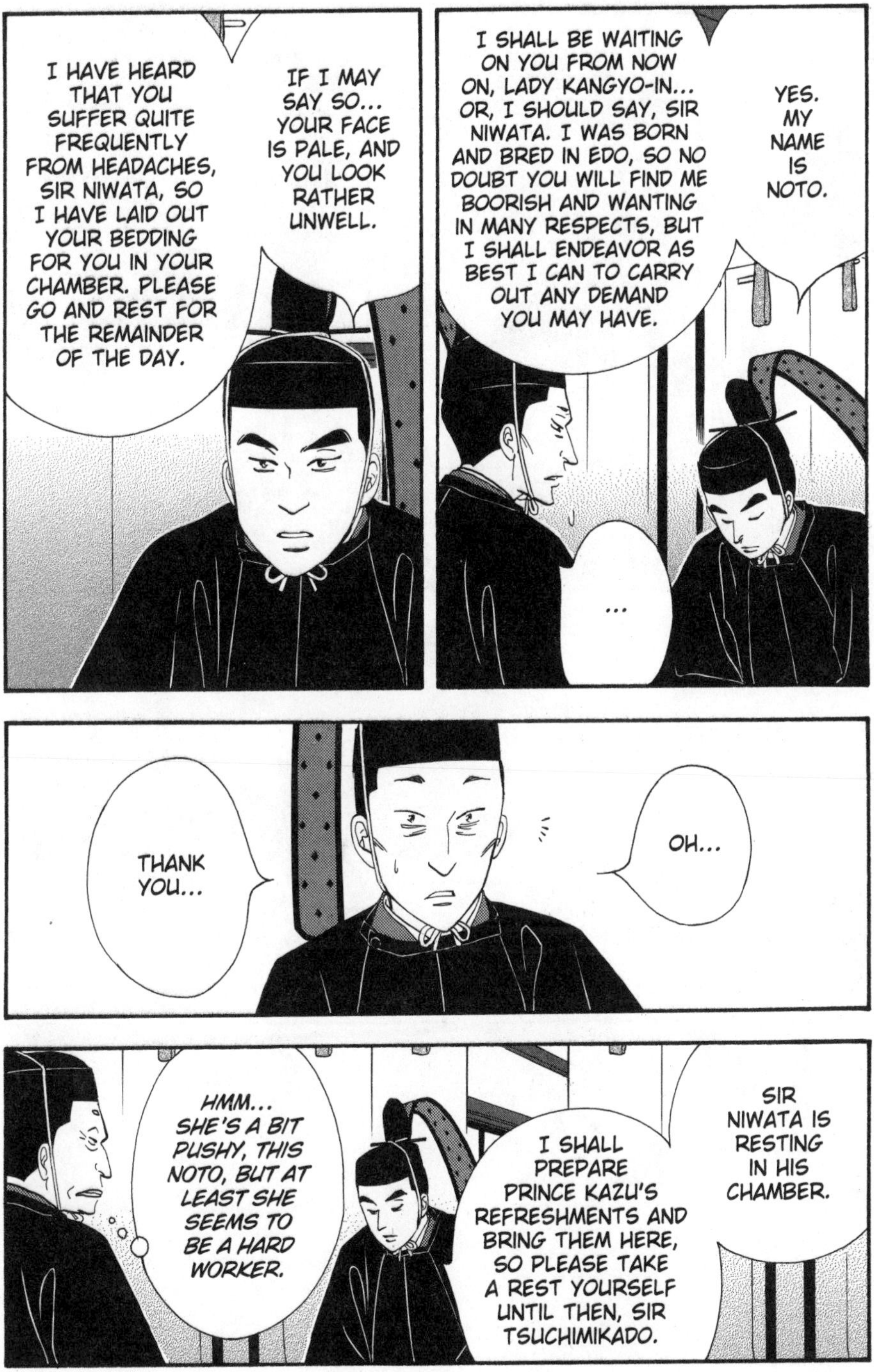
YES. MY NAME IS NOTO.
I SHALL BE WAITING ON YOU FROM NOW ON, LADY KANGYO-IN... OR, I SHOULD SAY, SIR NIWATA. I WAS BORN AND BRED IN EDO, SO NO DOUBT YOU WILL FIND ME BOORISH AND WANTING IN MANY RESPECTS, BUT I SHALL ENDEAVOR AS BEST I CAN TO CARRY OUT ANY DEMAND YOU MAY HAVE.
...
IF I MAY SAY SO... YOUR FACE IS PALE, AND YOU LOOK RATHER UNWELL.
I HAVE HEARD THAT YOU SUFFER QUITE FREQUENTLY FROM HEADACHES, SIR NIWATA, SO I HAVE LAID OUT YOUR BEDDING FOR YOU IN YOUR CHAMBER. PLEASE GO AND REST FOR THE REMAINDER OF THE DAY.
OH...
THANK YOU...
SIR NIWATA IS RESTING IN HIS CHAMBER.
I SHALL PREPARE PRINCE KAZU'S REFRESHMENTS AND BRING THEM HERE, SO PLEASE TAKE A REST YOURSELF UNTIL THEN, SIR TSUCHIMIKADO.
HMM... SHE'S A BIT PUSHY, THIS NOTO, BUT AT LEAST SHE SEEMS TO BE A HARD WORKER.

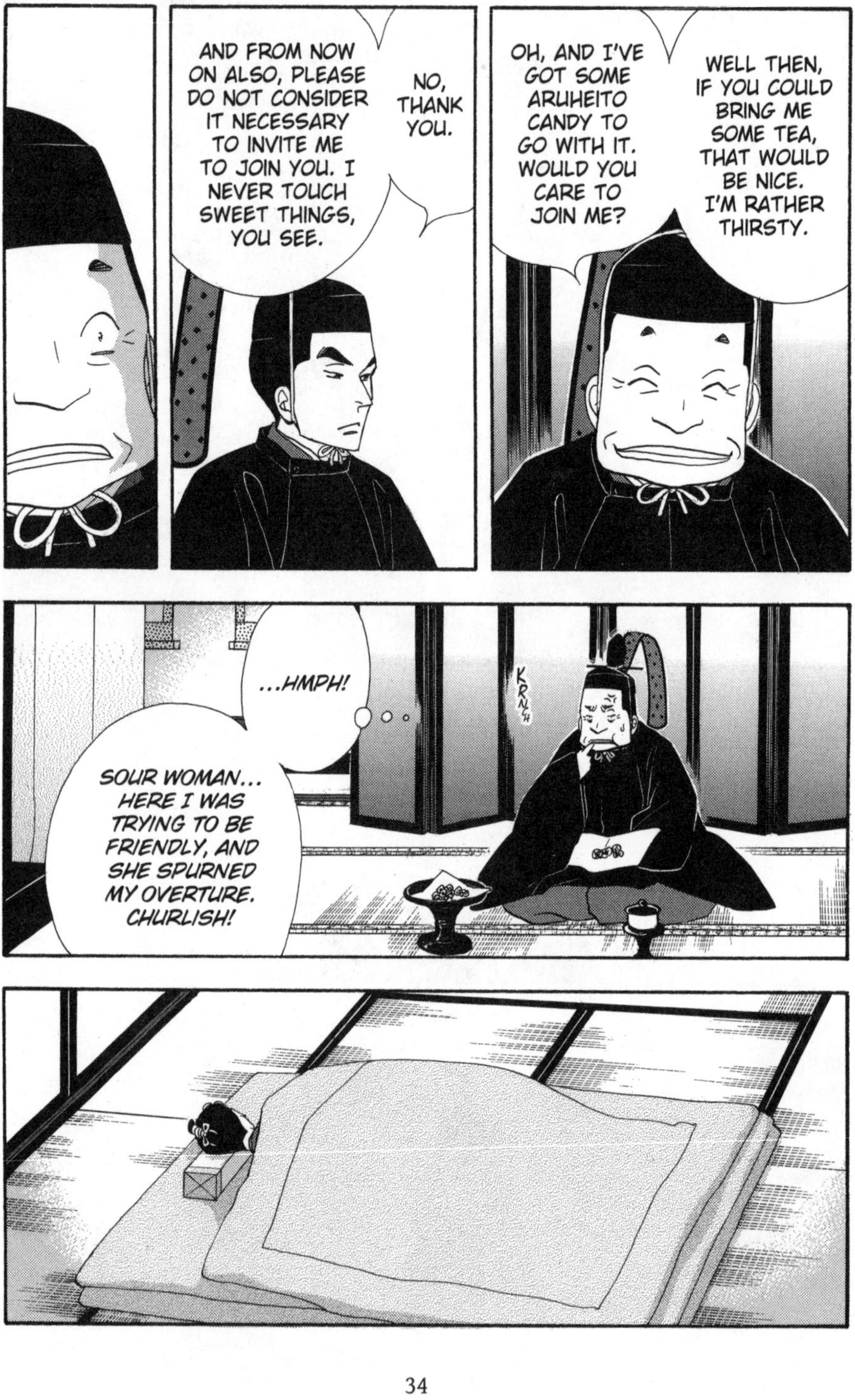
WELL THEN, IF YOU COULD BRING ME SOME TEA, THAT WOULD BE NICE. I'M RATHER THIRSTY.
OH, AND I'VE GOT SOME ARUHEITO CANDY TO GO WITH IT. WOULD YOU CARE TO JOIN ME?
NO, THANK YOU.
AND FROM NOW ON ALSO, PLEASE DO NOT CONSIDER IT NECESSARY TO INVITE ME TO JOIN YOU. I NEVER TOUCH SWEET THINGS, YOU SEE.
KRNCH
...HMPH!
SOUR WOMAN... HERE I WAS TRYING TO BE FRIENDLY, AND SHE SPURNED MY OVERTURE. CHURLISH!

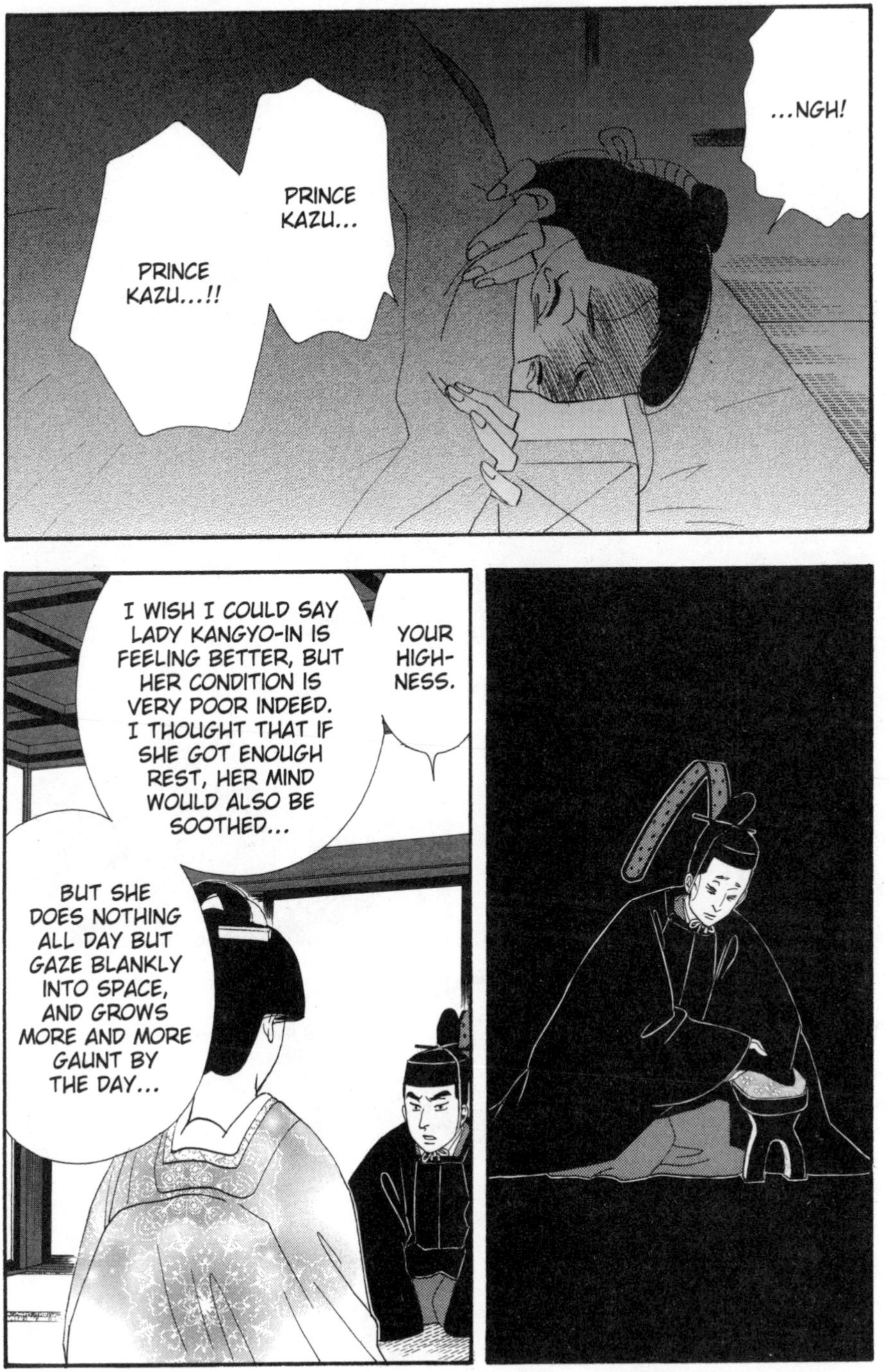
...NGH!
PRINCE KAZU...
PRINCE KAZU...!!
YOUR HIGH-NESS.
I WISH I COULD SAY LADY KANGYO-IN IS FEELING BETTER, BUT HER CONDITION IS VERY POOR INDEED. I THOUGHT THAT IF SHE GOT ENOUGH REST, HER MIND WOULD ALSO BE SOOTHED...
BUT SHE DOES NOTHING ALL DAY BUT GAZE BLANKLY INTO SPACE, AND GROWS MORE AND MORE GAUNT BY THE DAY...

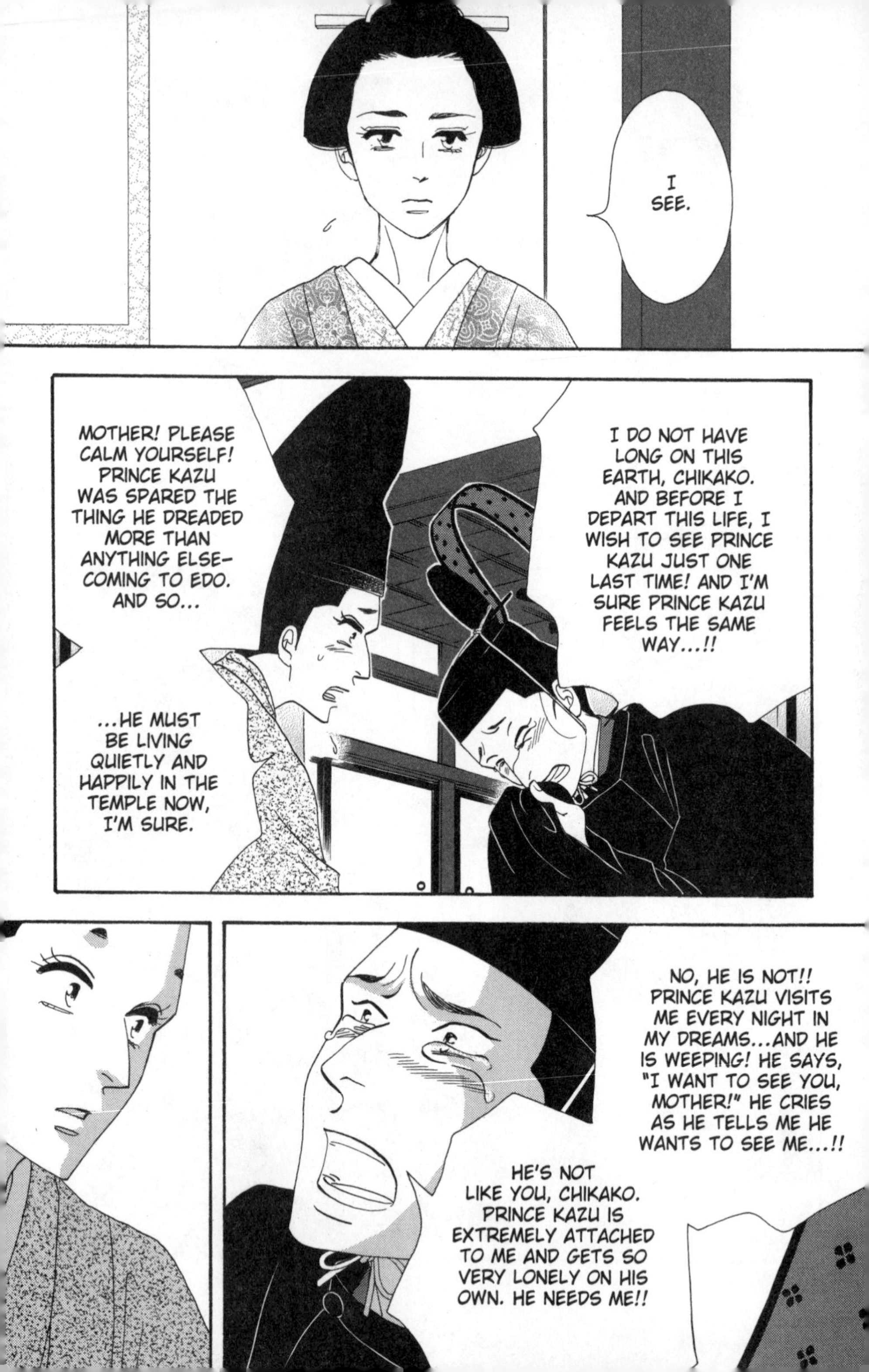
I SEE.
I DO NOT HAVE LONG ON THIS EARTH, CHIKAKO. AND BEFORE I DEPART THIS LIFE, I WISH TO SEE PRINCE KAZU JUST ONE LAST TIME! AND I'M SURE PRINCE KAZU FEELS THE SAME WAY...!!
MOTHER! PLEASE CALM YOURSELF! PRINCE KAZU WAS SPARED THE THING HE DREADED MORE THAN ANYTHING ELSE-COMING TO EDO. AND SO...
...HE MUST BE LIVING QUIETLY AND HAPPILY IN THE TEMPLE NOW, I'M SURE.
NO, HE IS NOT!! PRINCE KAZU VISITS ME EVERY NIGHT IN MY DREAMS...AND HE IS WEEPING! HE SAYS, "I WANT TO SEE YOU, MOTHER!" HE CRIES AS HE TELLS ME HE WANTS TO SEE ME...!!
HE'S NOT LIKE YOU, CHIKAKO. PRINCE KAZU IS EXTREMELY ATTACHED TO ME AND GETS SO VERY LONELY ON HIS OWN. HE NEEDS ME!!

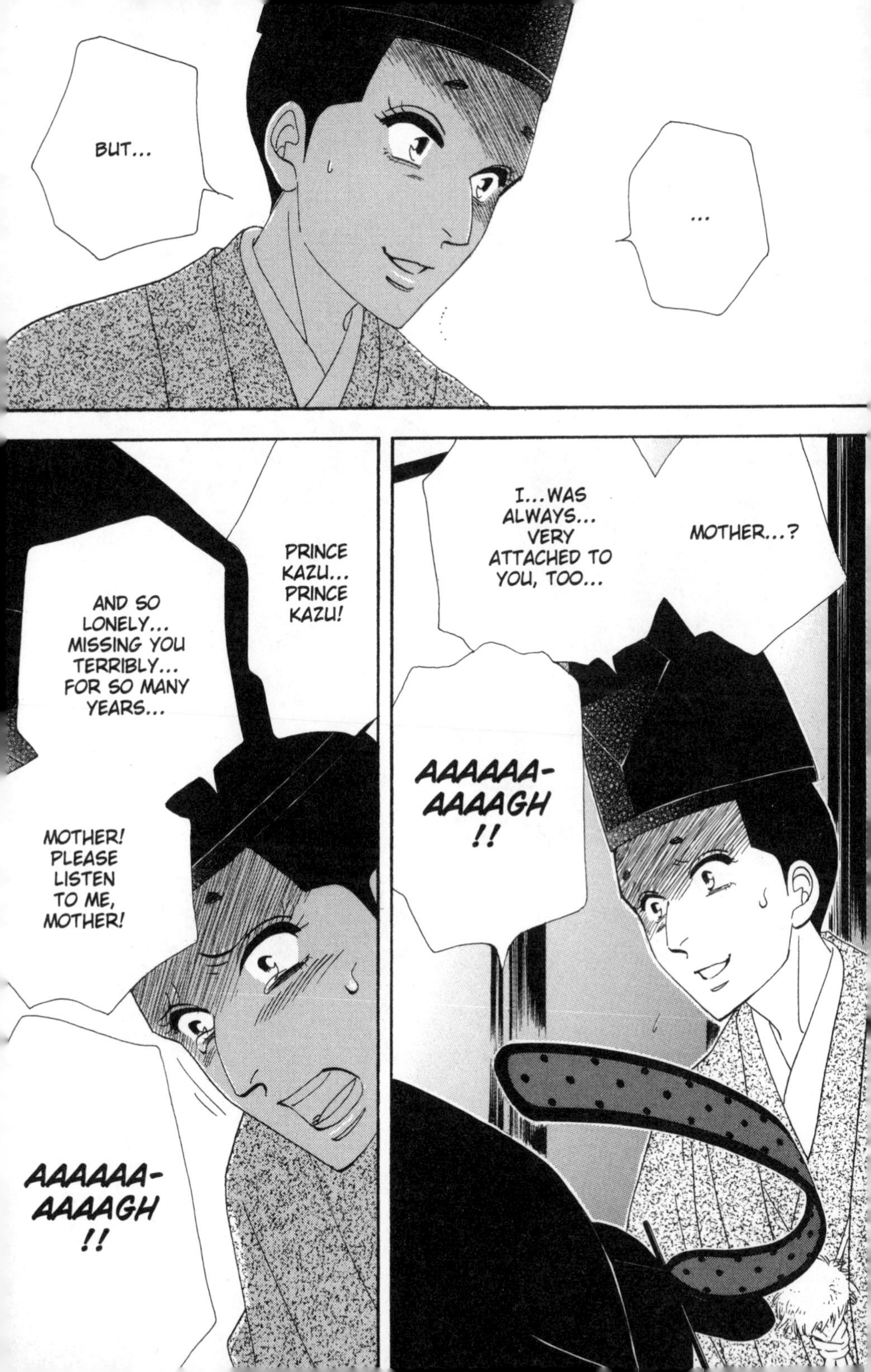
BUT...
...
MOTHER...?
I...WAS ALWAYS... VERY ATTACHED TO YOU, TOO...
AAAAAA-AAAAGH!!
PRINCE KAZU... PRINCE KAZU!
AND SO LONELY... MISSING YOU TERRIBLY... FOR SO MANY YEARS...
MOTHER! PLEASE LISTEN TO ME, MOTHER!
AAAAAA-AAAAGH!!

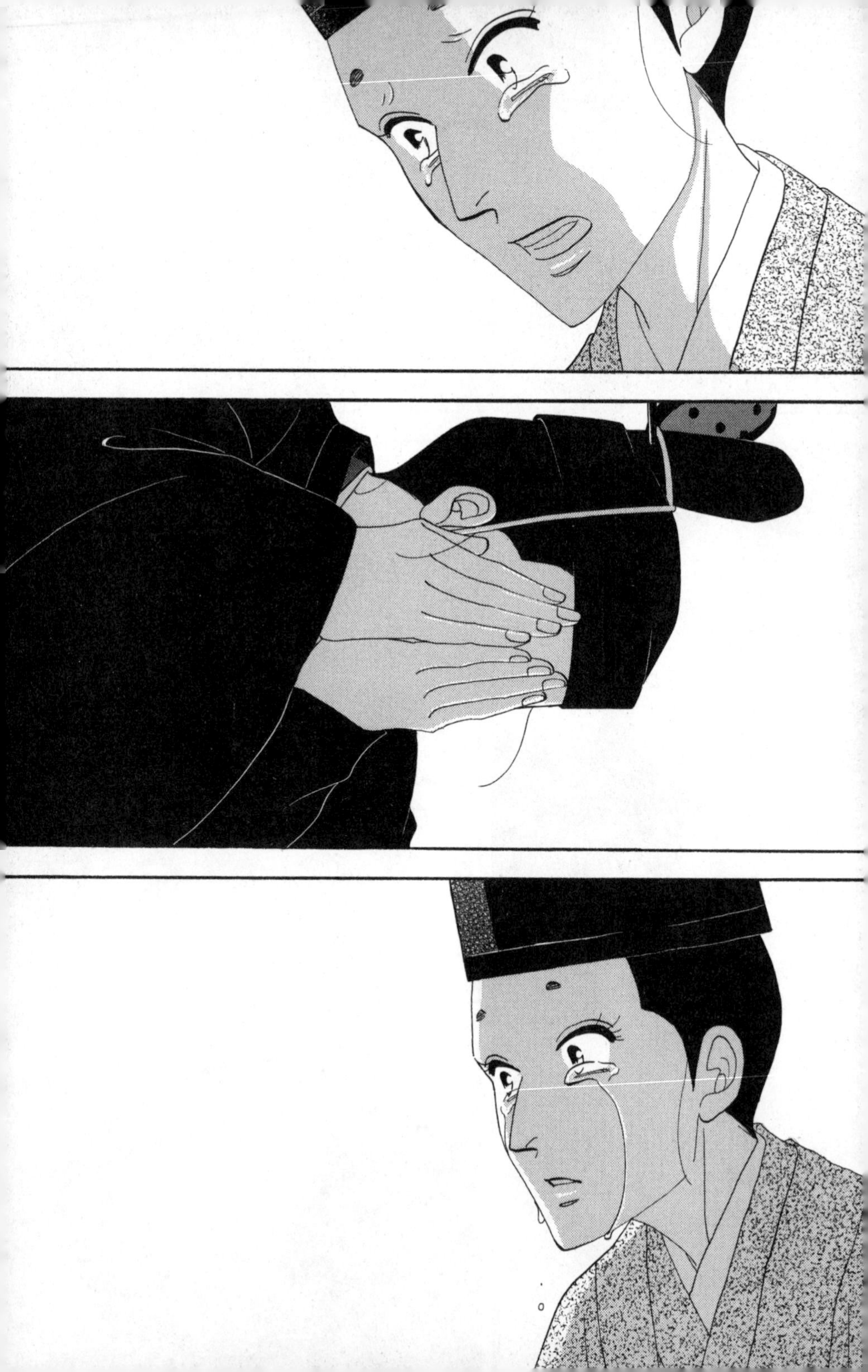

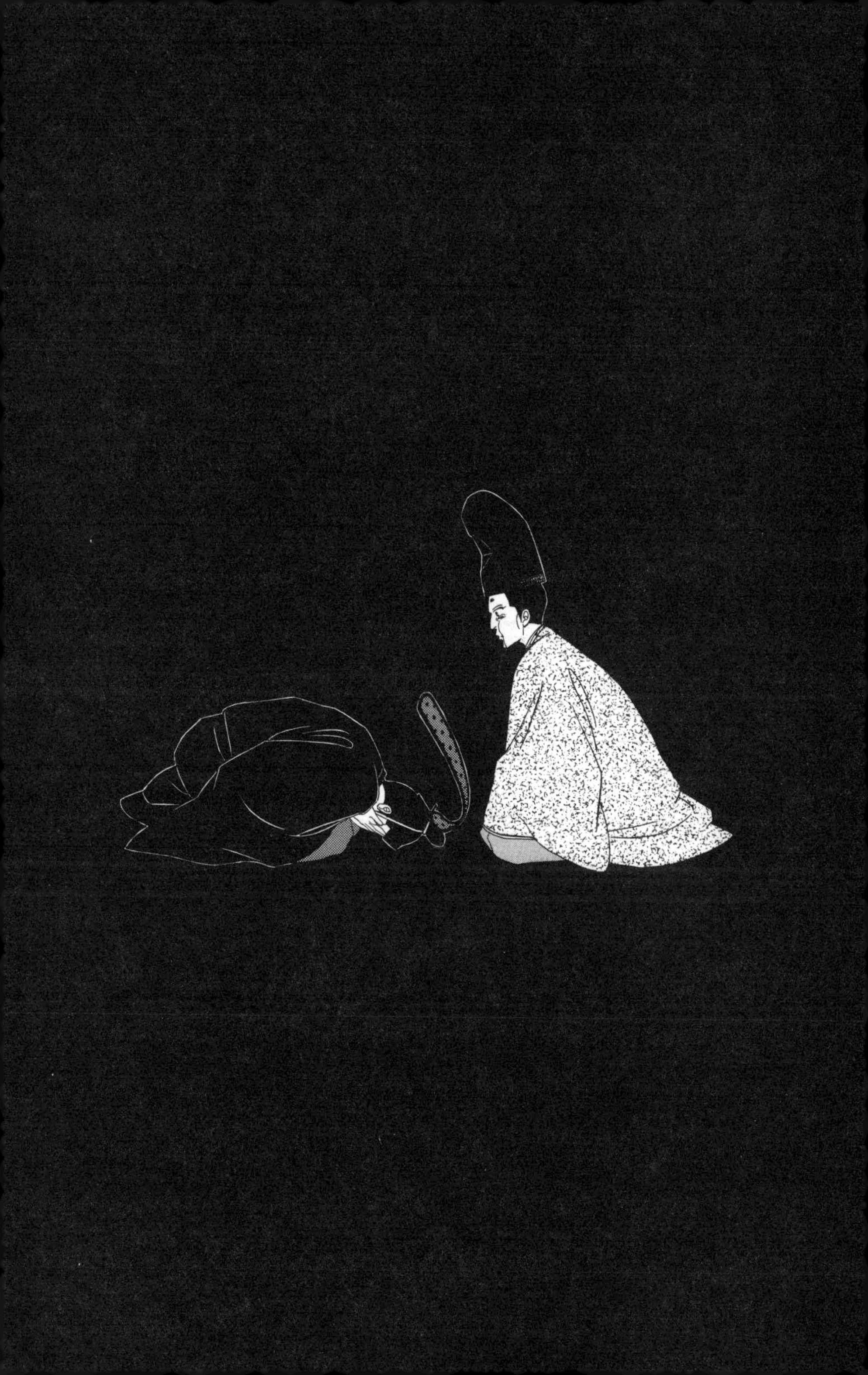

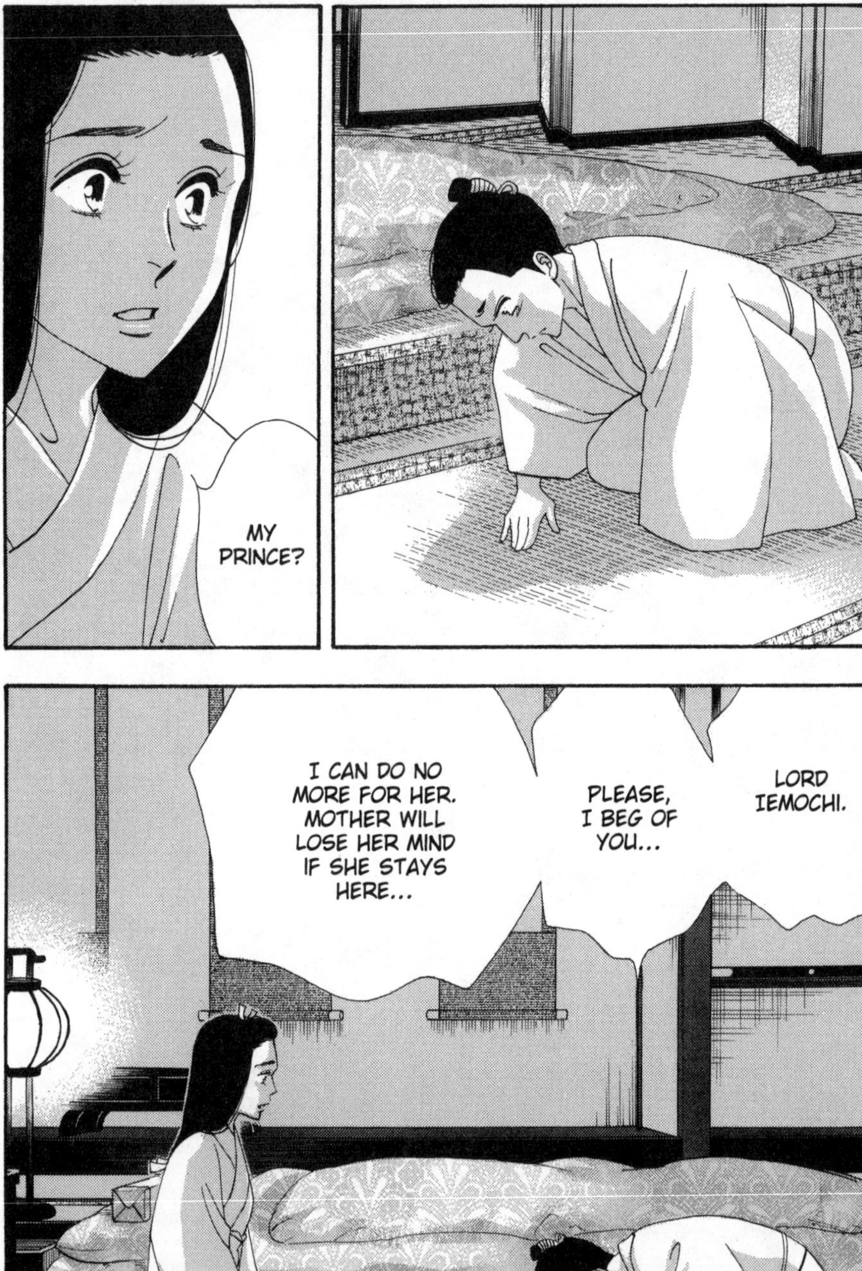
MY PRINCE?
LORD IEMOCHI.
PLEASE, I BEG OF YOU...
I CAN DO NO MORE FOR HER. MOTHER WILL LOSE HER MIND IF SHE STAYS HERE...

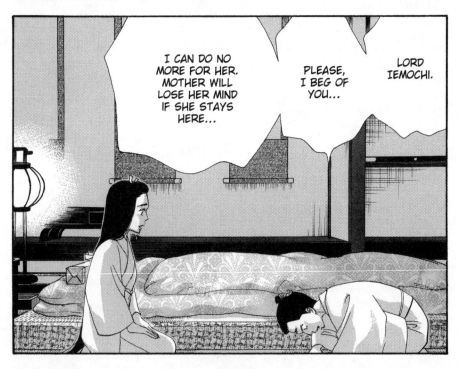

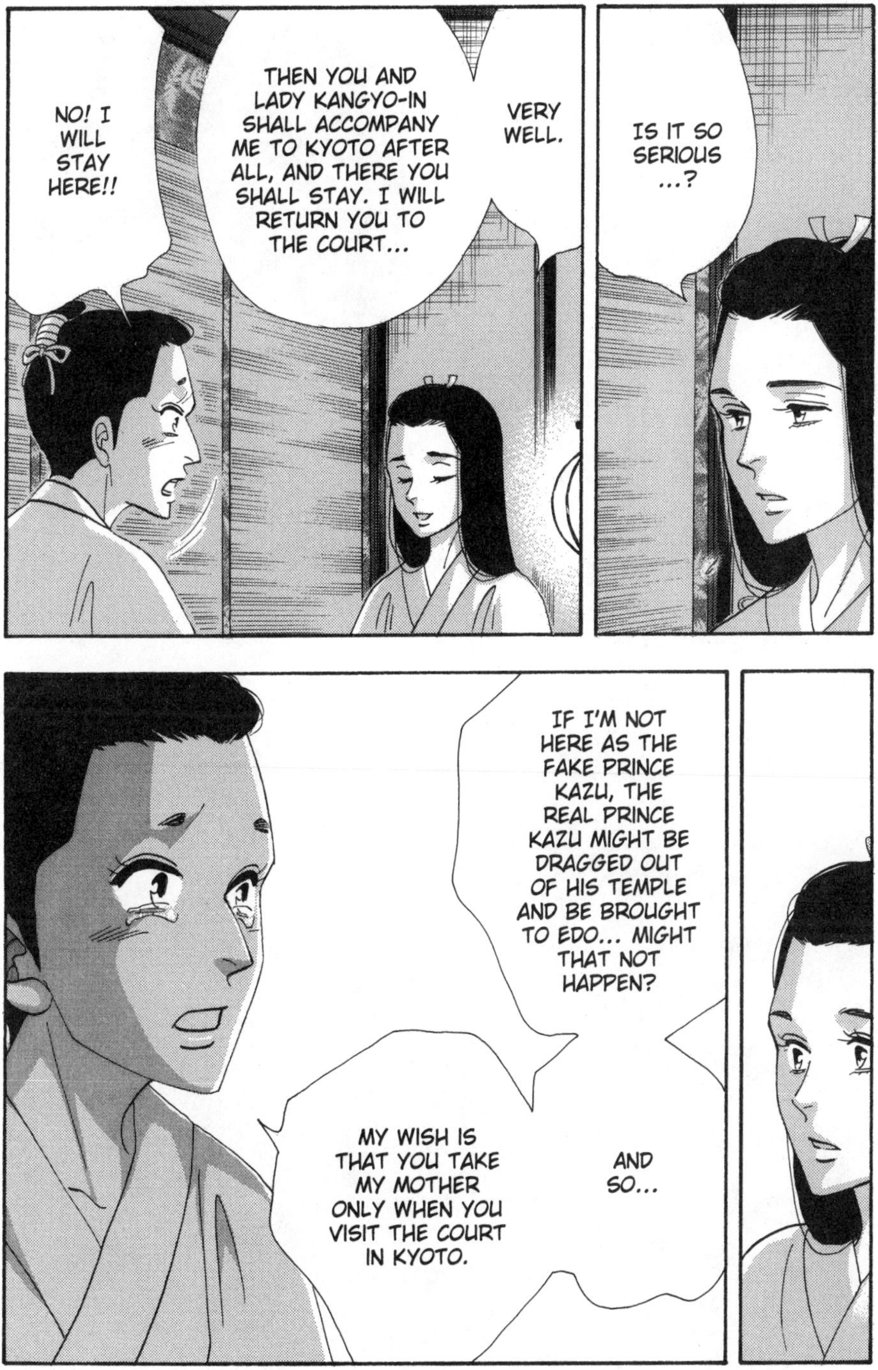
IS IT SO SERIOUS ...?
VERY WELL.
THEN YOU AND LADY KANGYO-IN SHALL ACCOMPANY ME TO KYOTO AFTER ALL, AND THERE YOU SHALL STAY. I WILL RETURN YOU TO THE COURT...
NO! I WILL STAY HERE!!
IF I'M NOT HERE AS THE FAKE PRINCE KAZU, THE REAL PRINCE KAZU MIGHT BE DRAGGED OUT OF HIS TEMPLE AND BE BROUGHT TO EDO... MIGHT THAT NOT HAPPEN?
AND SO...
MY WISH IS THAT YOU TAKE MY MOTHER ONLY WHEN YOU VISIT THE COURT IN KYOTO.

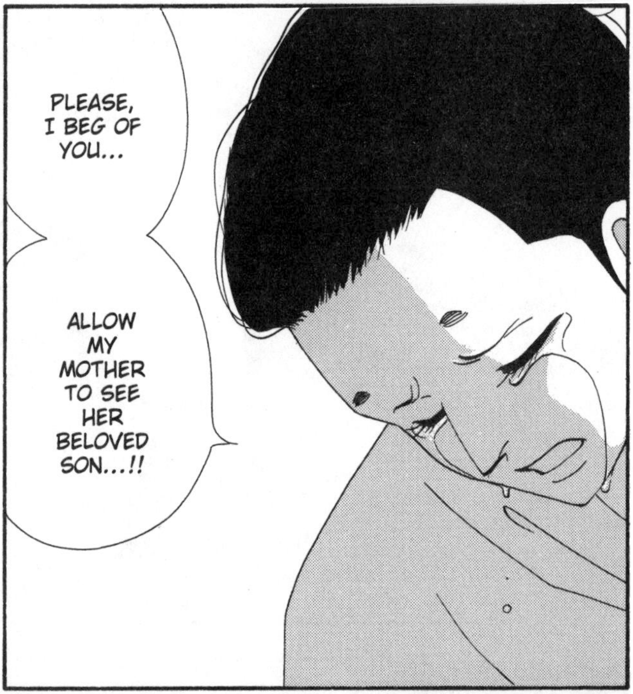
PLEASE, I BEG OF YOU...
ALLOW MY MOTHER TO SEE HER BELOVED SON...!!
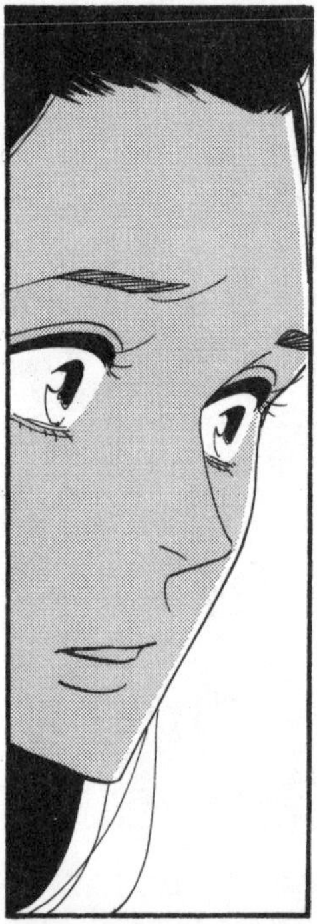
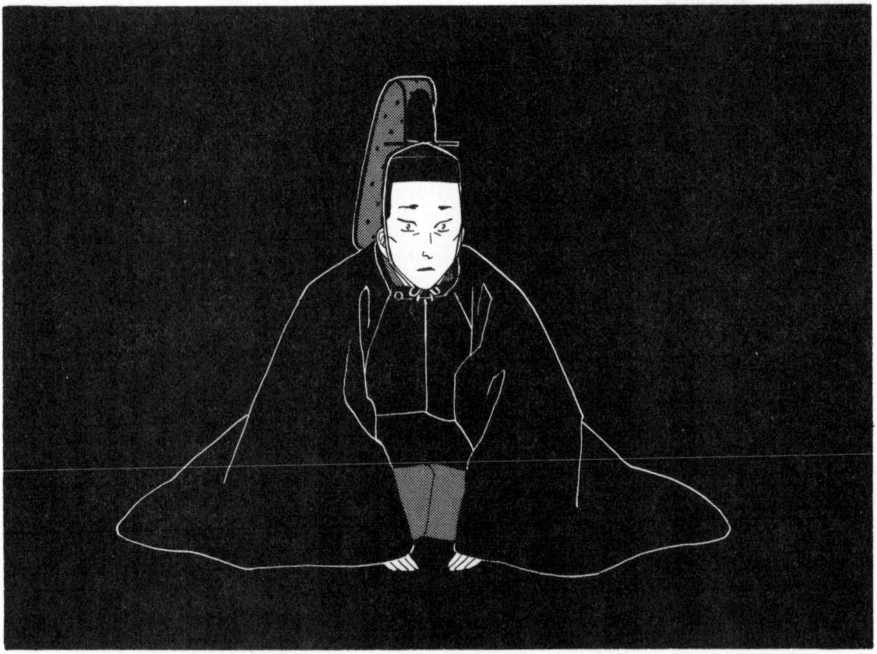

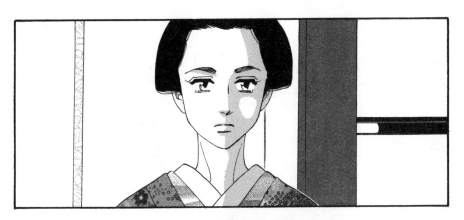

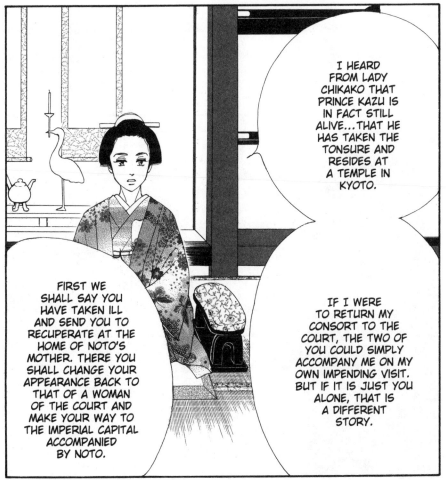

I HEARD FROM LADY CHIKAKO THAT PRINCE KAZU IS IN FACT STILL ALIVE...THAT HE HAS TAKEN THE TONSURE AND RESIDES AT A TEMPLE IN KYOTO.
IF I WERE TO RETURN MY CONSORT TO THE COURT, THE TWO OF YOU COULD SIMPLY ACCOMPANY ME ON MY OWN IMPENDING VISIT. BUT IF IT IS JUST YOU ALONE, THAT IS A DIFFERENT STORY.
FIRST WE SHALL SAY YOU HAVE TAKEN ILL AND SEND YOU TO RECUPERATE AT THE HOME OF NOTO'S MOTHER. THERE YOU SHALL CHANGE YOUR APPEARANCE BACK TO THAT OF A WOMAN OF THE COURT AND MAKE YOUR WAY TO THE IMPERIAL CAPITAL ACCOMPANIED BY NOTO.

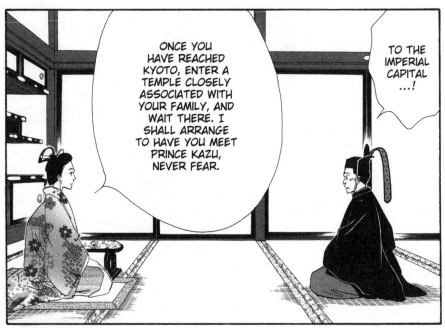

TO THE IMPERIAL CAPITAL ...!
ONCE YOU HAVE REACHED KYOTO, ENTER A TEMPLE CLOSELY ASSOCIATED WITH YOUR FAMILY, AND WAIT THERE. I SHALL ARRANGE TO HAVE YOU MEET PRINCE KAZU, NEVER FEAR.
NOW THAT PRINCE KAZU IS A MONK, YOU WILL NOT BE ABLE TO RESIDE TOGETHER AS YOU ONCE DID. IS THAT ACCEPTABLE TO YOU?
...!!
O-OF COURSE IT IS...!! IF I CAN ASCERTAIN WITH MY OWN EYES THAT PRINCE KAZU IS HEALTHY... IF I CAN MEET HIM AGAIN, EVEN JUST ONE TIME...I WOULD BE...
...GH!

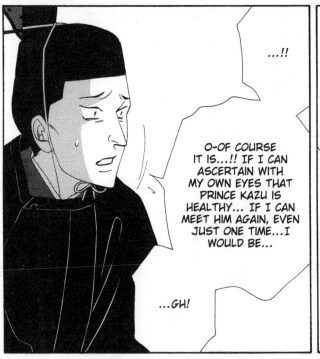

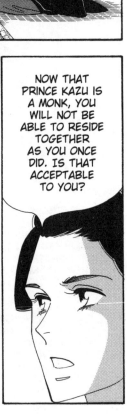

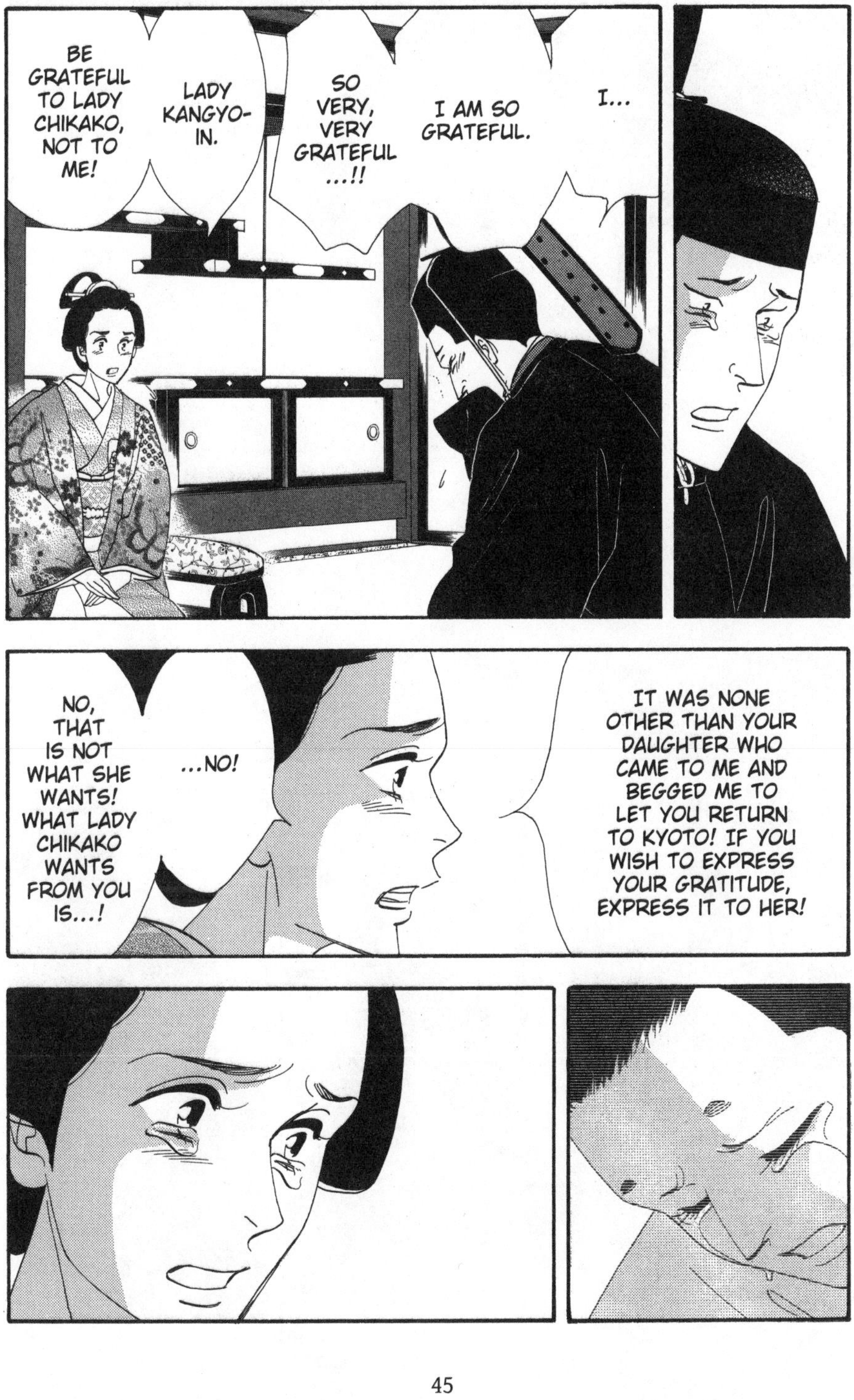
I...
I AM SO GRATEFUL.
SO VERY, VERY GRATEFUL ...!!
LADY KANGYO-IN.
BE GRATEFUL TO LADY CHIKAKO, NOT TO ME!
IT WAS NONE OTHER THAN YOUR DAUGHTER WHO CAME TO ME AND BEGGED ME TO LET YOU RETURN TO KYOTO! IF YOU WISH TO EXPRESS YOUR GRATITUDE, EXPRESS IT TO HER!
...NO!
NO, THAT IS NOT WHAT SHE WANTS! WHAT LADY CHIKAKO WANTS FROM YOU IS...!

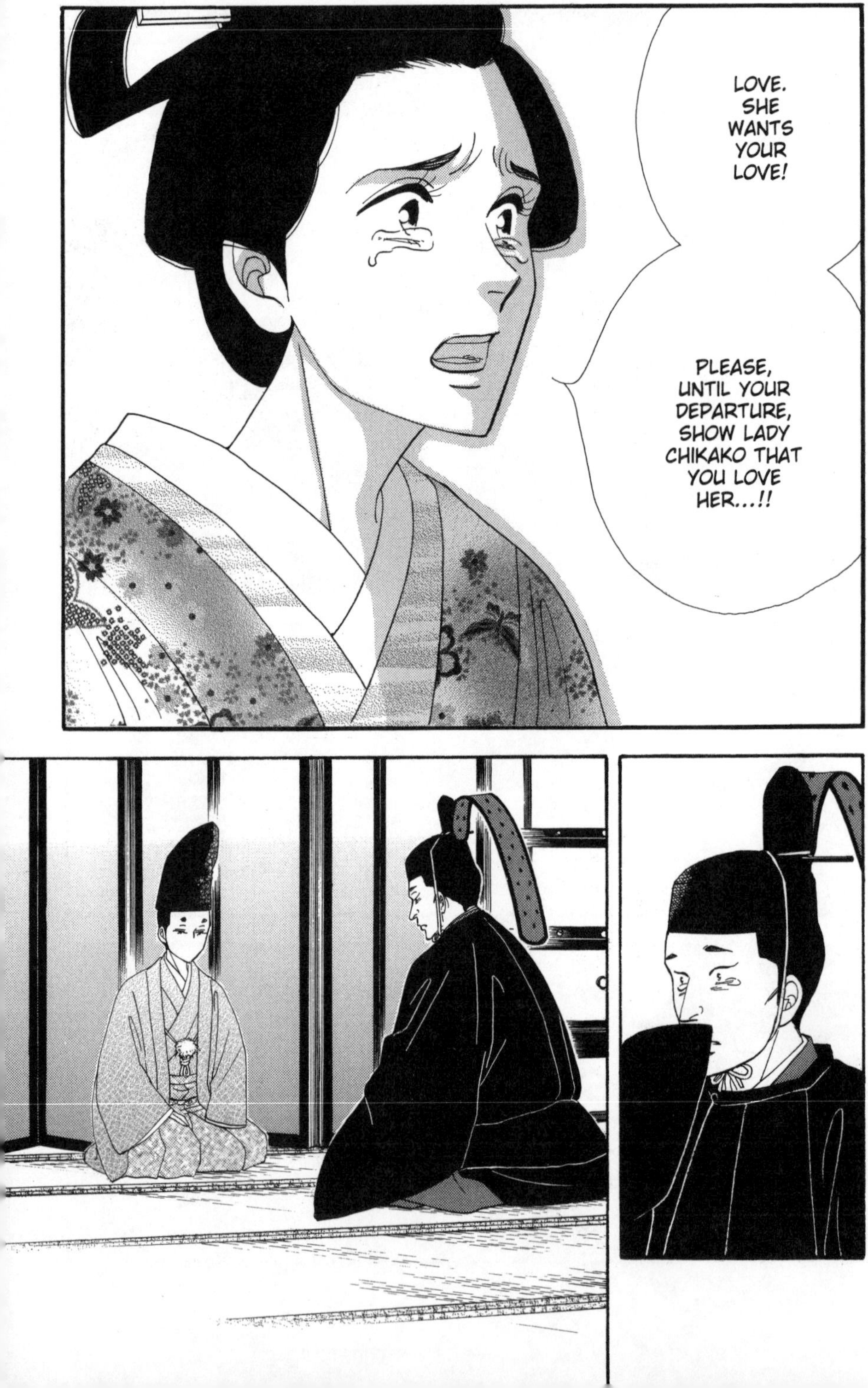
LOVE. SHE WANTS YOUR LOVE!
PLEASE, UNTIL YOUR DEPARTURE, SHOW LADY CHIKAKO THAT YOU LOVE HER...!!

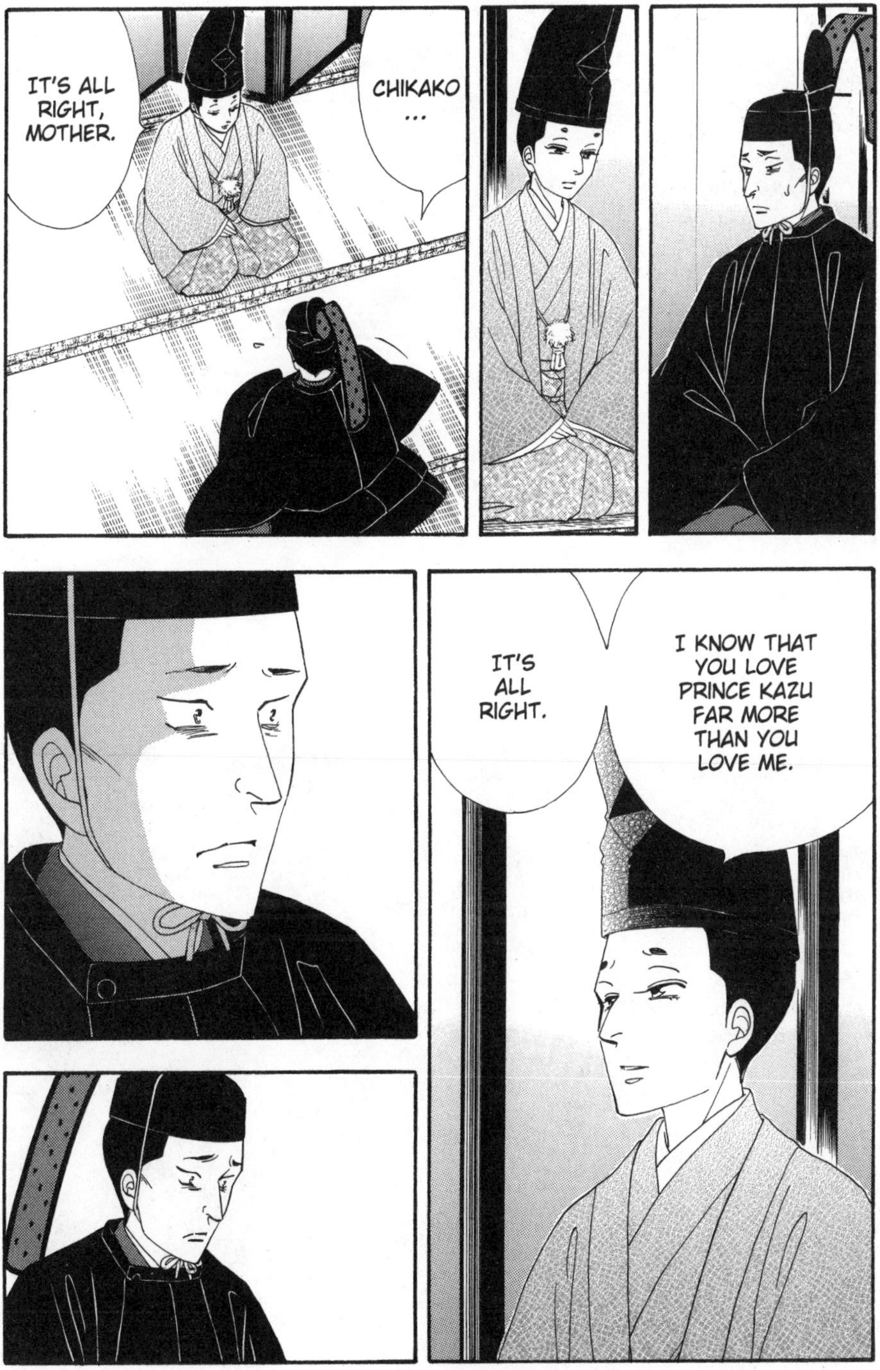
CHIKAKO ...
IT'S ALL RIGHT, MOTHER.
I KNOW THAT YOU LOVE PRINCE KAZU FAR MORE THAN YOU LOVE ME.
IT'S ALL RIGHT.

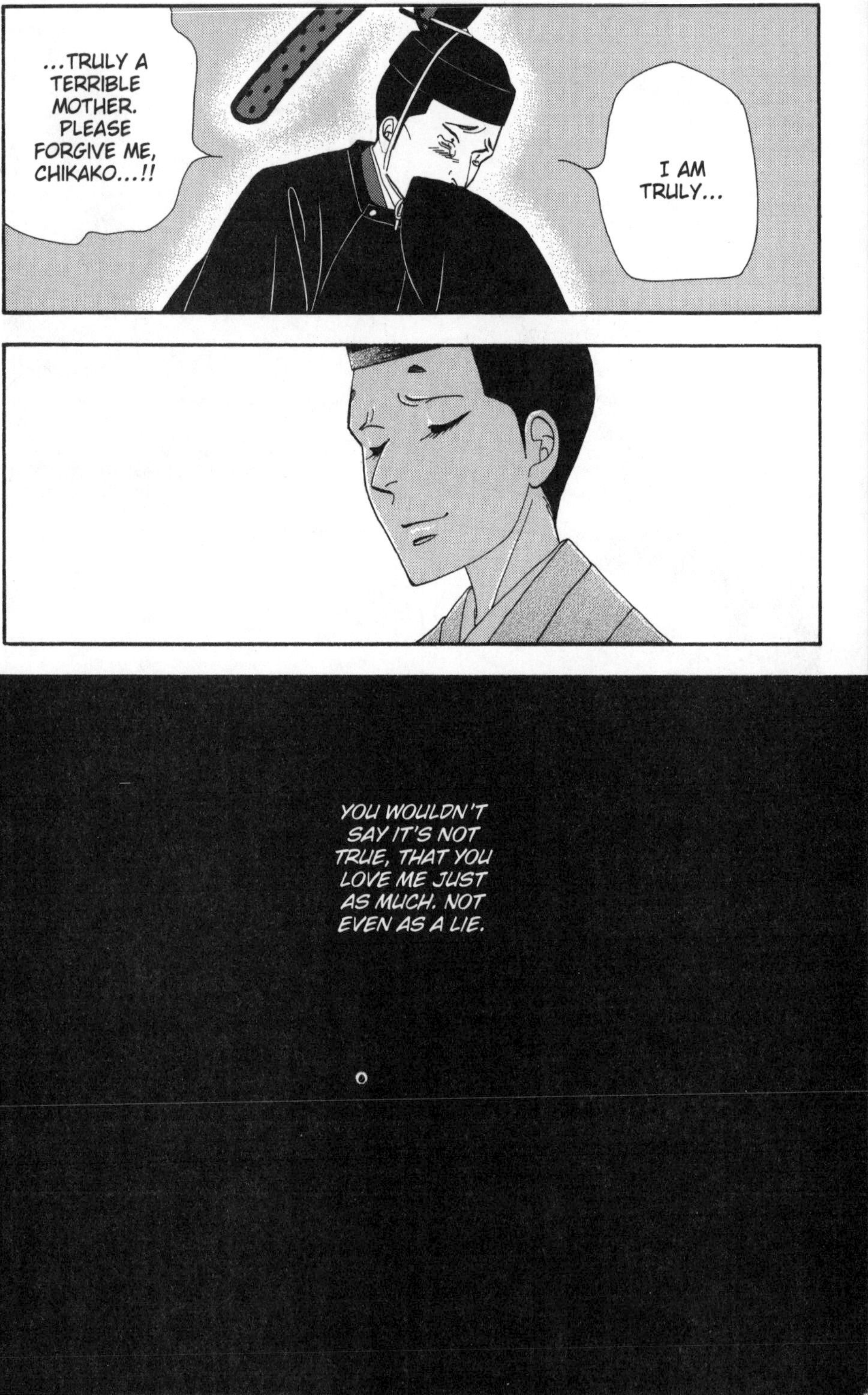
I AM TRULY...
...TRULY A TERRIBLE MOTHER. PLEASE FORGIVE ME, CHIKAKO...!!
YOU WOULDN'T SAY IT'S NOT TRUE, THAT YOU LOVE ME JUST AS MUCH. NOT EVEN AS A LIE.

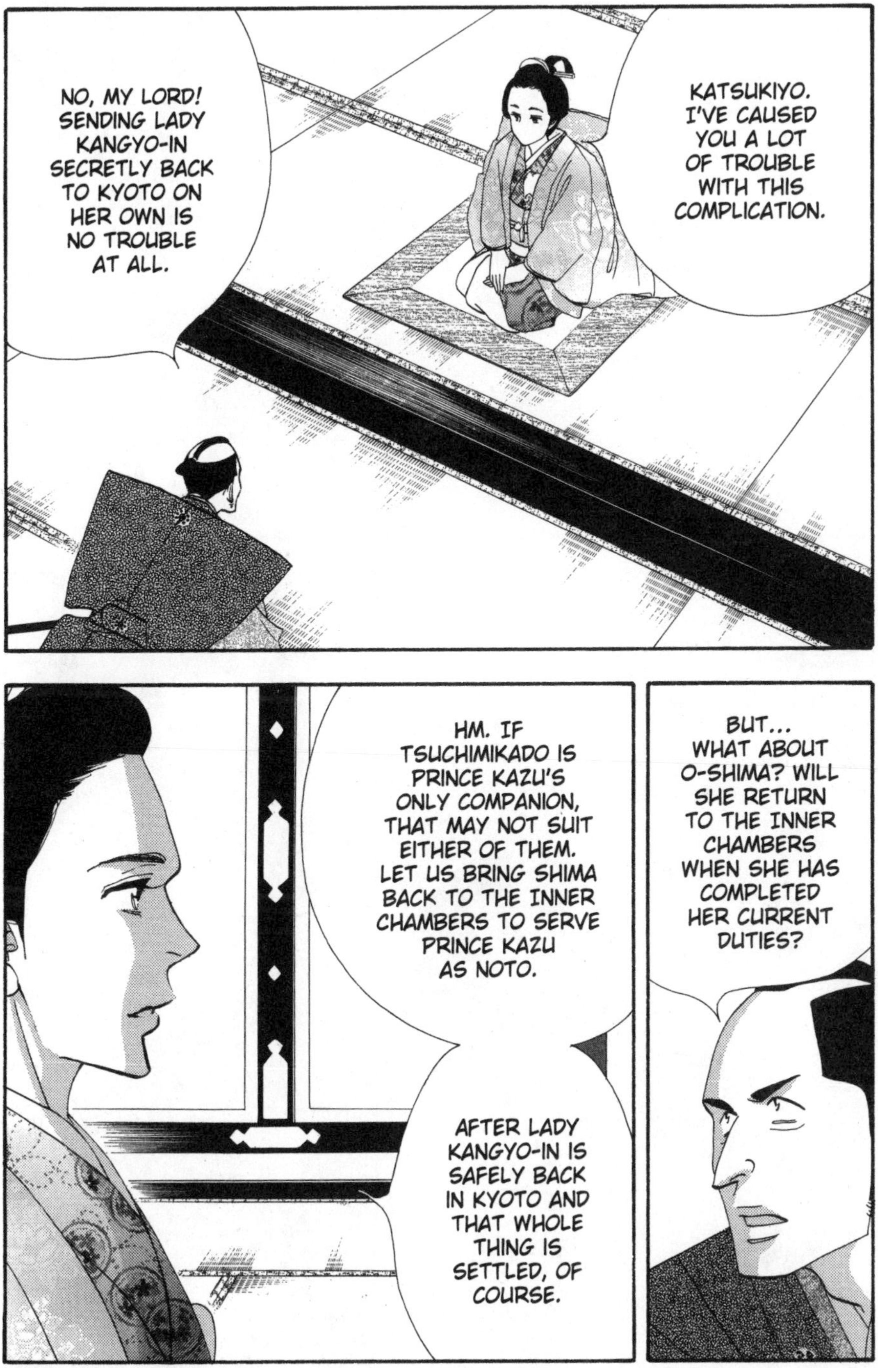
KATSUKIYO. I'VE CAUSED YOU A LOT OF TROUBLE WITH THIS COMPLICATION.
NO, MY LORD! SENDING LADY KANGYO-IN SECRETLY BACK TO KYOTO ON HER OWN IS NO TROUBLE AT ALL.
BUT... WHAT ABOUT O-SHIMA? WILL SHE RETURN TO THE INNER CHAMBERS WHEN SHE HAS COMPLETED HER CURRENT DUTIES?
HM. IF TSUCHIMIKADO IS PRINCE KAZU'S ONLY COMPANION, THAT MAY NOT SUIT EITHER OF THEM. LET US BRING SHIMA BACK TO THE INNER CHAMBERS TO SERVE PRINCE KAZU AS NOTO.
AFTER LADY KANGYO-IN IS SAFELY BACK IN KYOTO AND THAT WHOLE THING IS SETTLED, OF COURSE.

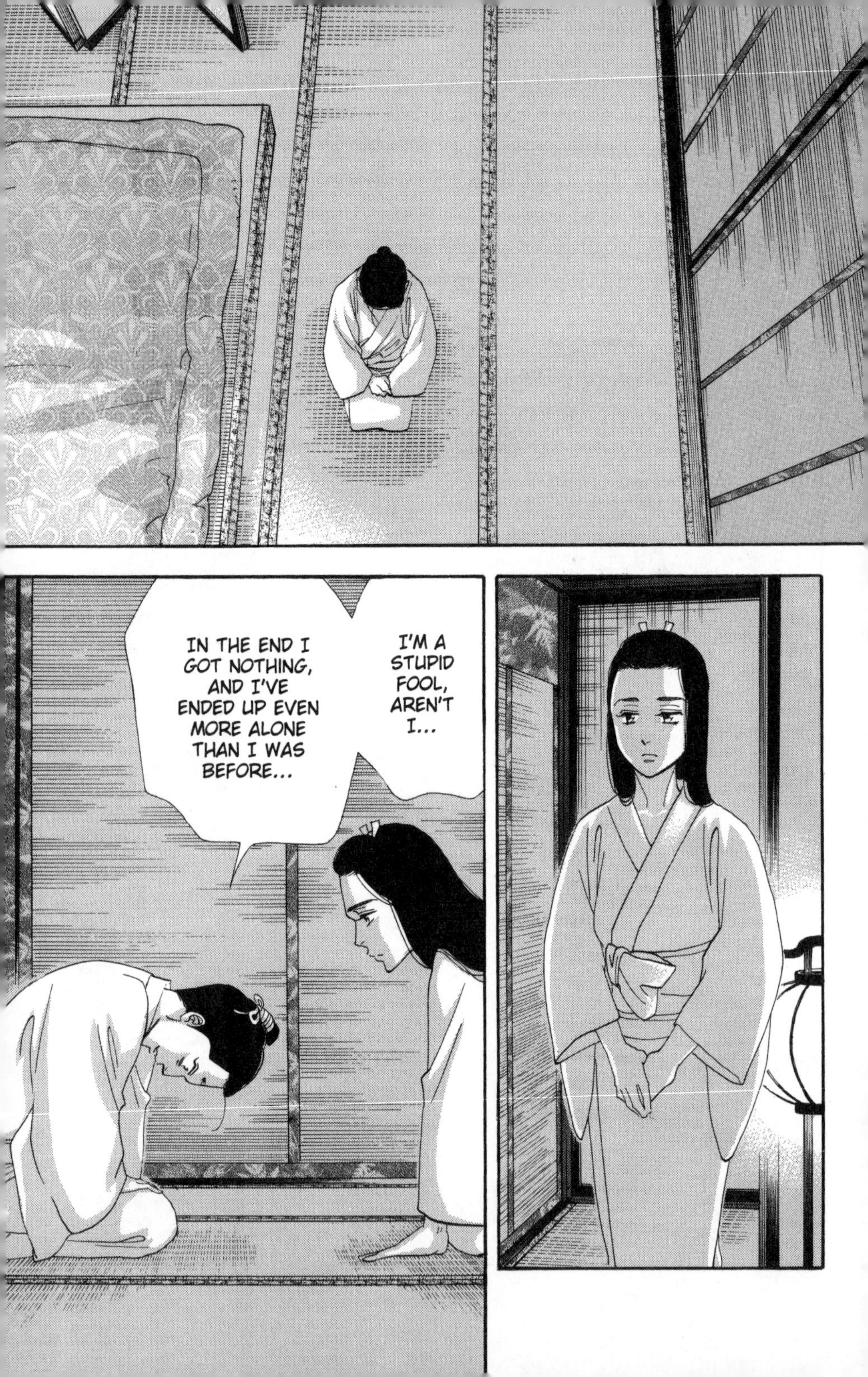
I'M A STUPID FOOL, AREN'T I...
IN THE END I GOT NOTHING, AND I'VE ENDED UP EVEN MORE ALONE THAN I WAS BEFORE...

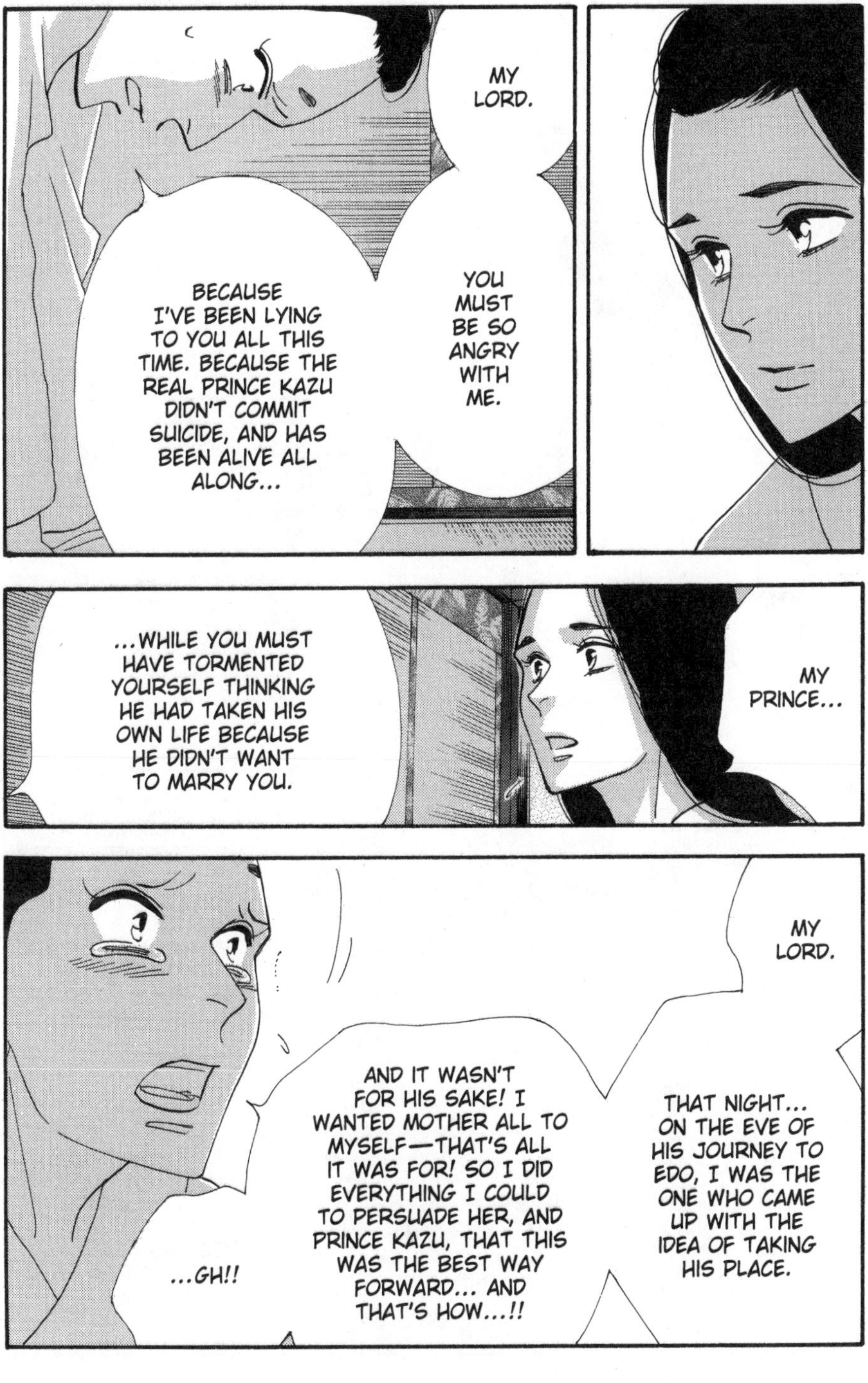
MY LORD.
YOU MUST BE SO ANGRY WITH ME.
BECAUSE I'VE BEEN LYING TO YOU ALL THIS TIME. BECAUSE THE REAL PRINCE KAZU DIDN'T COMMIT SUICIDE, AND HAS BEEN ALIVE ALL ALONG...
MY PRINCE...
...WHILE YOU MUST HAVE TORMENTED YOURSELF THINKING HE HAD TAKEN HIS OWN LIFE BECAUSE HE DIDN'T WANT TO MARRY YOU.
MY LORD.
THAT NIGHT... ON THE EVE OF HIS JOURNEY TO EDO, I WAS THE ONE WHO CAME UP WITH THE IDEA OF TAKING HIS PLACE.
AND IT WASN'T FOR HIS SAKE! I WANTED MOTHER ALL TO MYSELF—THAT'S ALL IT WAS FOR! SO I DID EVERYTHING I COULD TO PERSUADE HER, AND PRINCE KAZU, THAT THIS WAS THE BEST WAY FORWARD... AND THAT'S HOW...!!
...GH!!

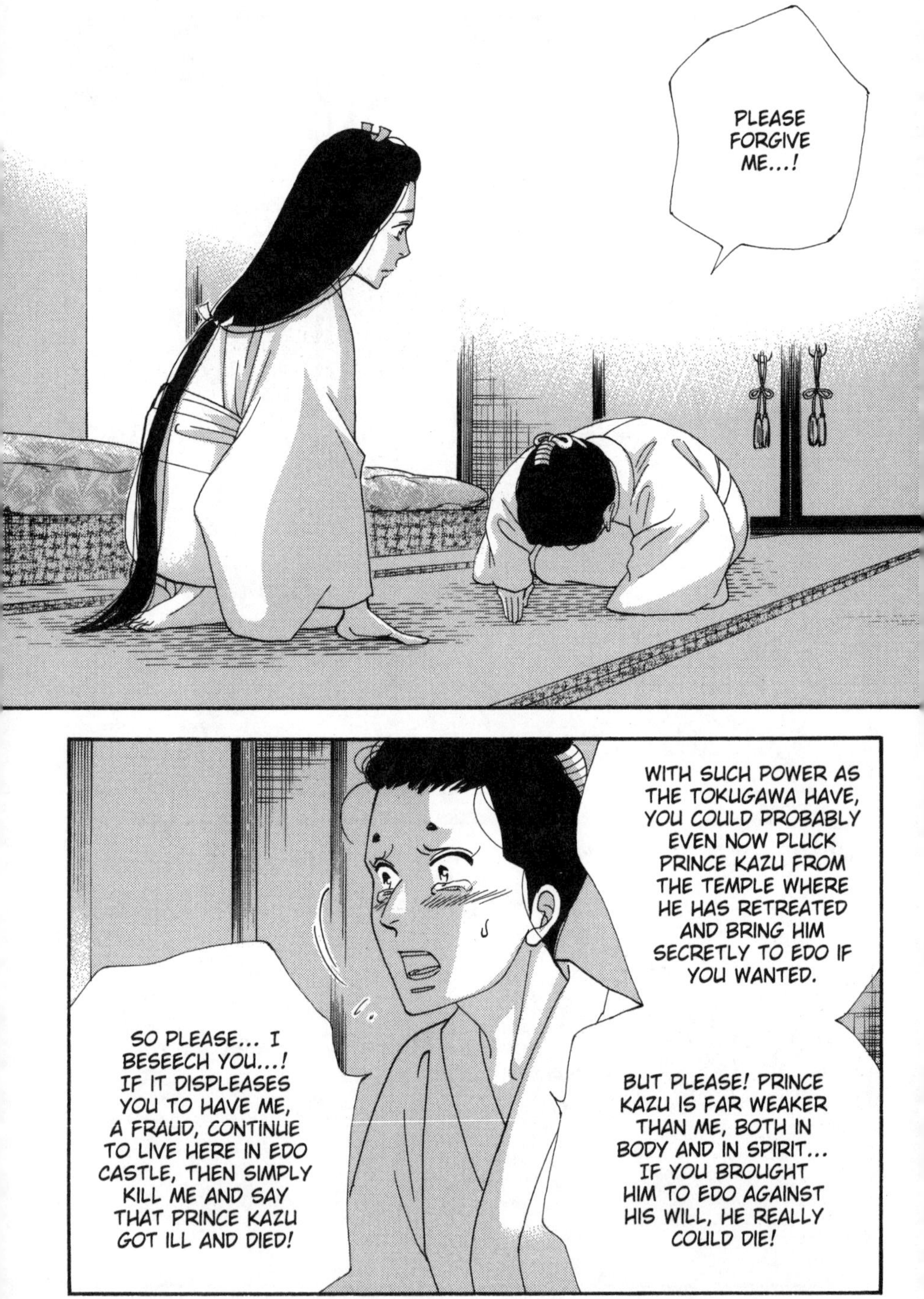
PLEASE FORGIVE ME...!
WITH SUCH POWER AS THE TOKUGAWA HAVE, YOU COULD PROBABLY EVEN NOW PLUCK PRINCE KAZU FROM THE TEMPLE WHERE HE HAS RETREATED AND BRING HIM SECRETLY TO EDO IF YOU WANTED.
BUT PLEASE! PRINCE KAZU IS FAR WEAKER THAN ME, BOTH IN BODY AND IN SPIRIT... IF YOU BROUGHT HIM TO EDO AGAINST HIS WILL, HE REALLY COULD DIE!
SO PLEASE... I BESEECH YOU...! IF IT DISPLEASES YOU TO HAVE ME, A FRAUD, CONTINUE TO LIVE HERE IN EDO CASTLE, THEN SIMPLY KILL ME AND SAY THAT PRINCE KAZU GOT ILL AND DIED!

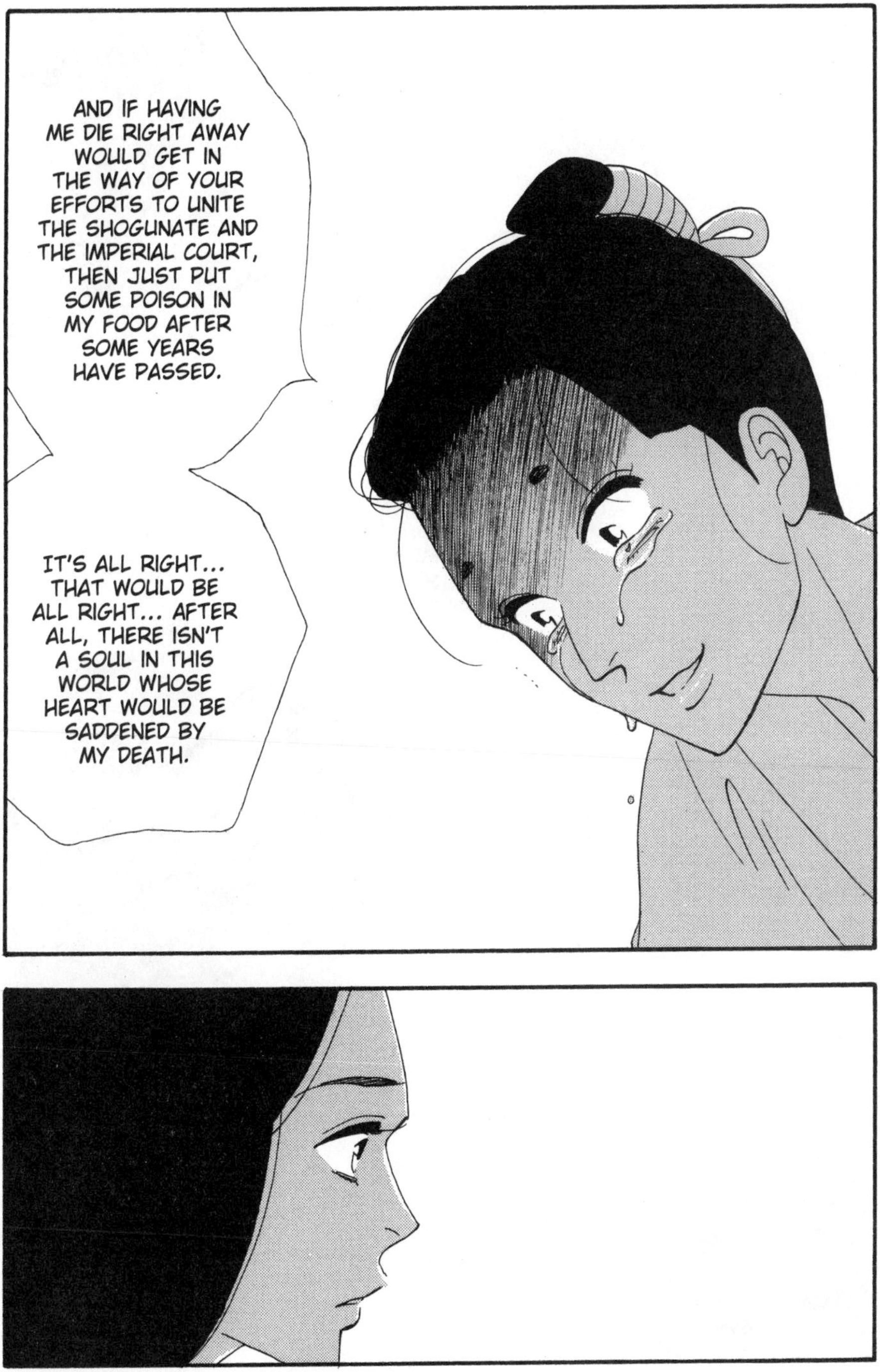
AND IF HAVING ME DIE RIGHT AWAY WOULD GET IN THE WAY OF YOUR EFFORTS TO UNITE THE SHOGUNATE AND THE IMPERIAL COURT, THEN JUST PUT SOME POISON IN MY FOOD AFTER SOME YEARS HAVE PASSED.
IT'S ALL RIGHT... THAT WOULD BE ALL RIGHT... AFTER ALL, THERE ISN'T A SOUL IN THIS WORLD WHOSE HEART WOULD BE SADDENED BY MY DEATH.

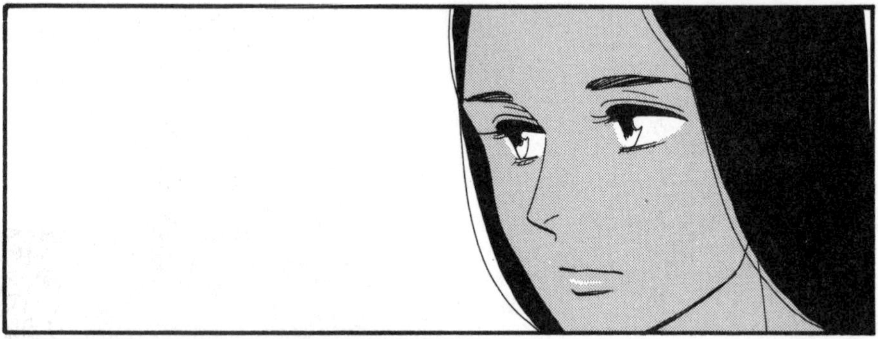

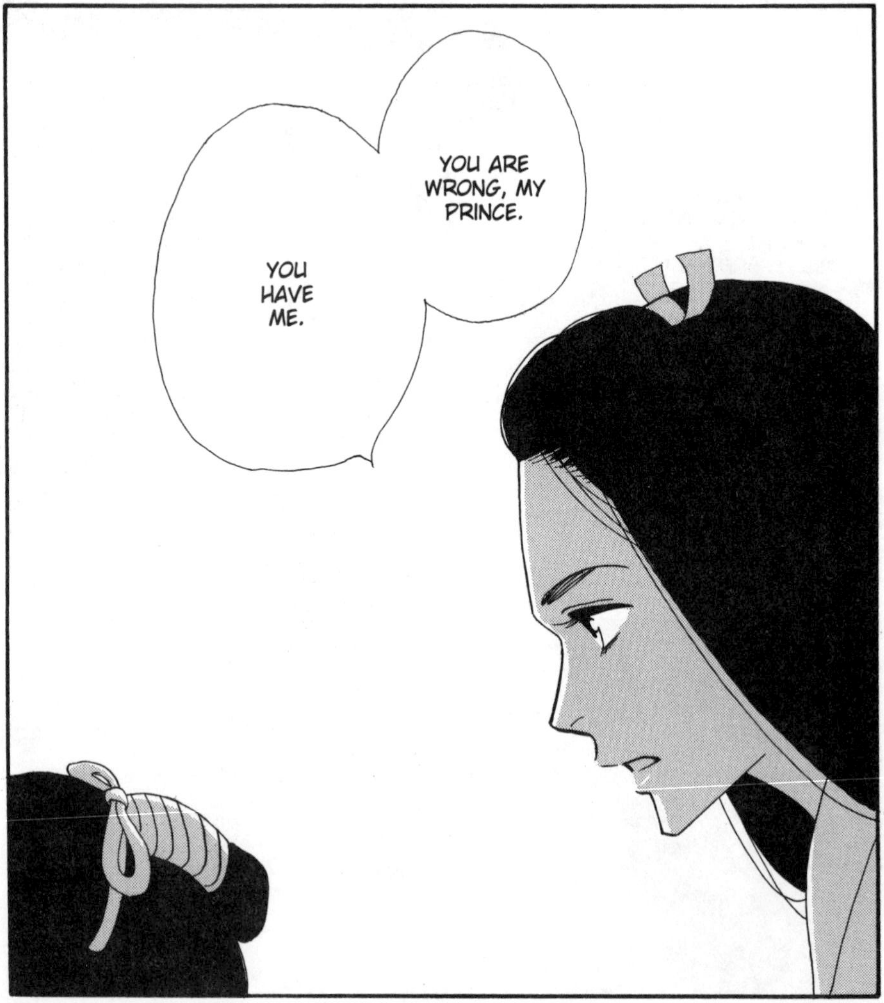
YOU ARE WRONG, MY PRINCE.
YOU HAVE ME.

WE AREN'T EVEN TRULY A COUPLE.

YOU HAVE *ME.*

EVEN SO, YOU HAVE ME.

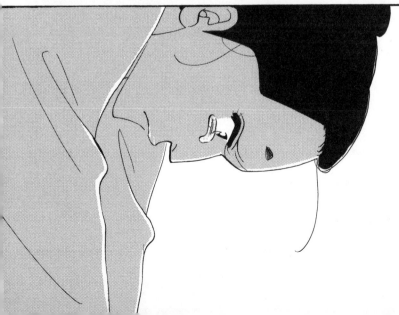

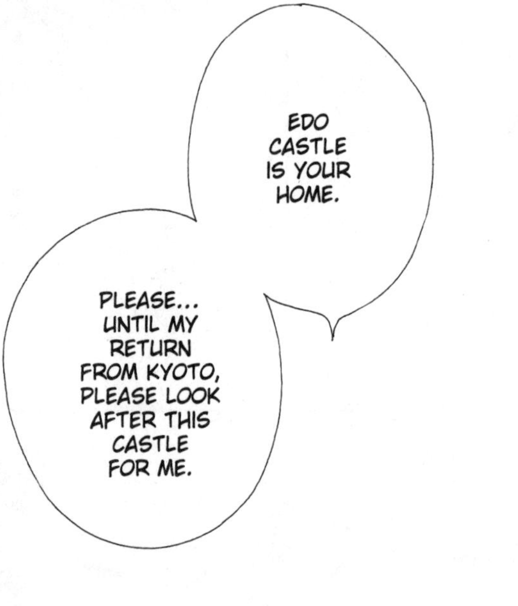
EDO CASTLE IS YOUR HOME.
PLEASE... UNTIL MY RETURN FROM KYOTO, PLEASE LOOK AFTER THIS CASTLE FOR ME.

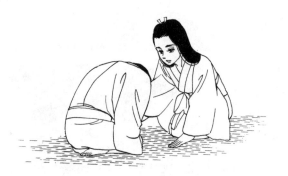

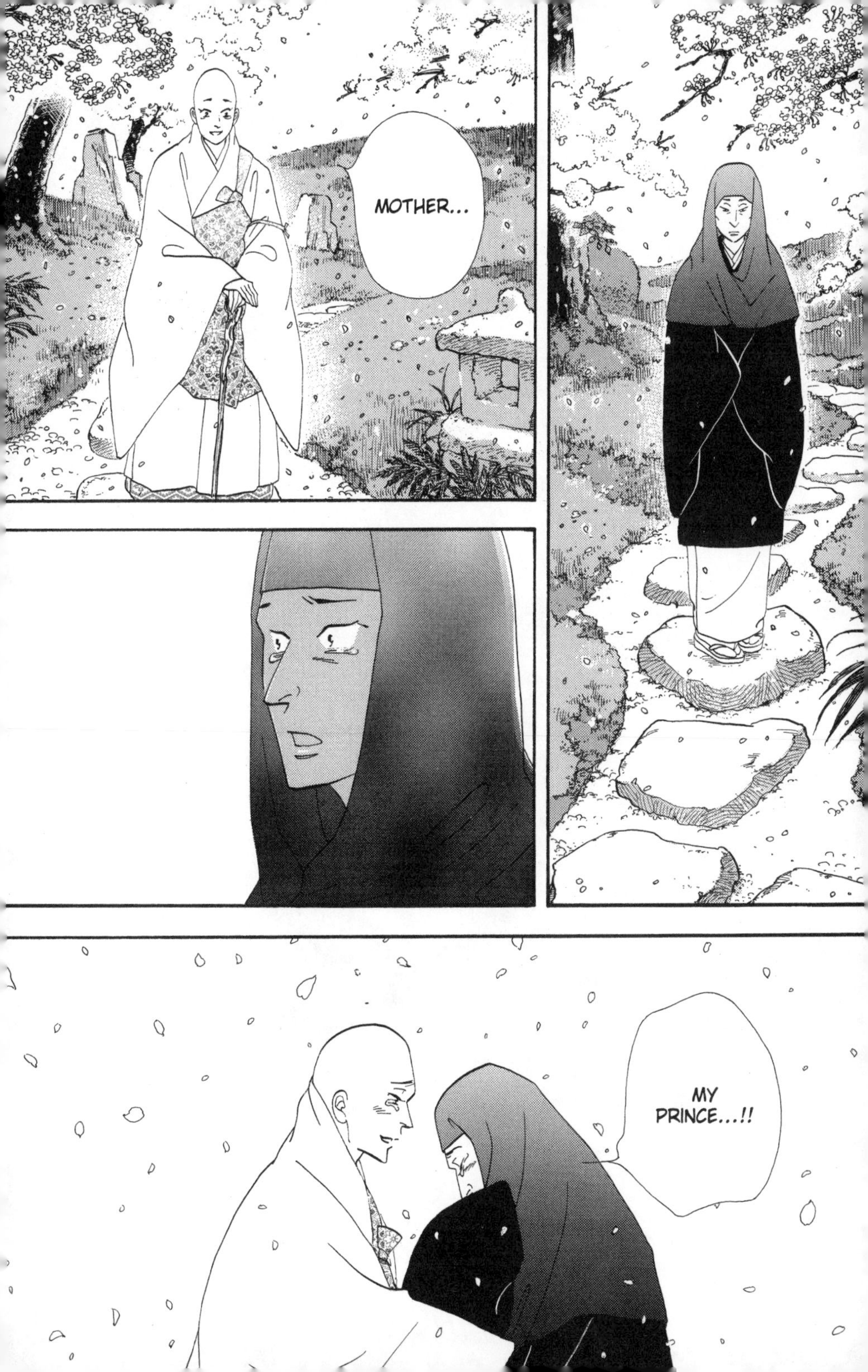
MOTHER...
MY PRINCE...!!

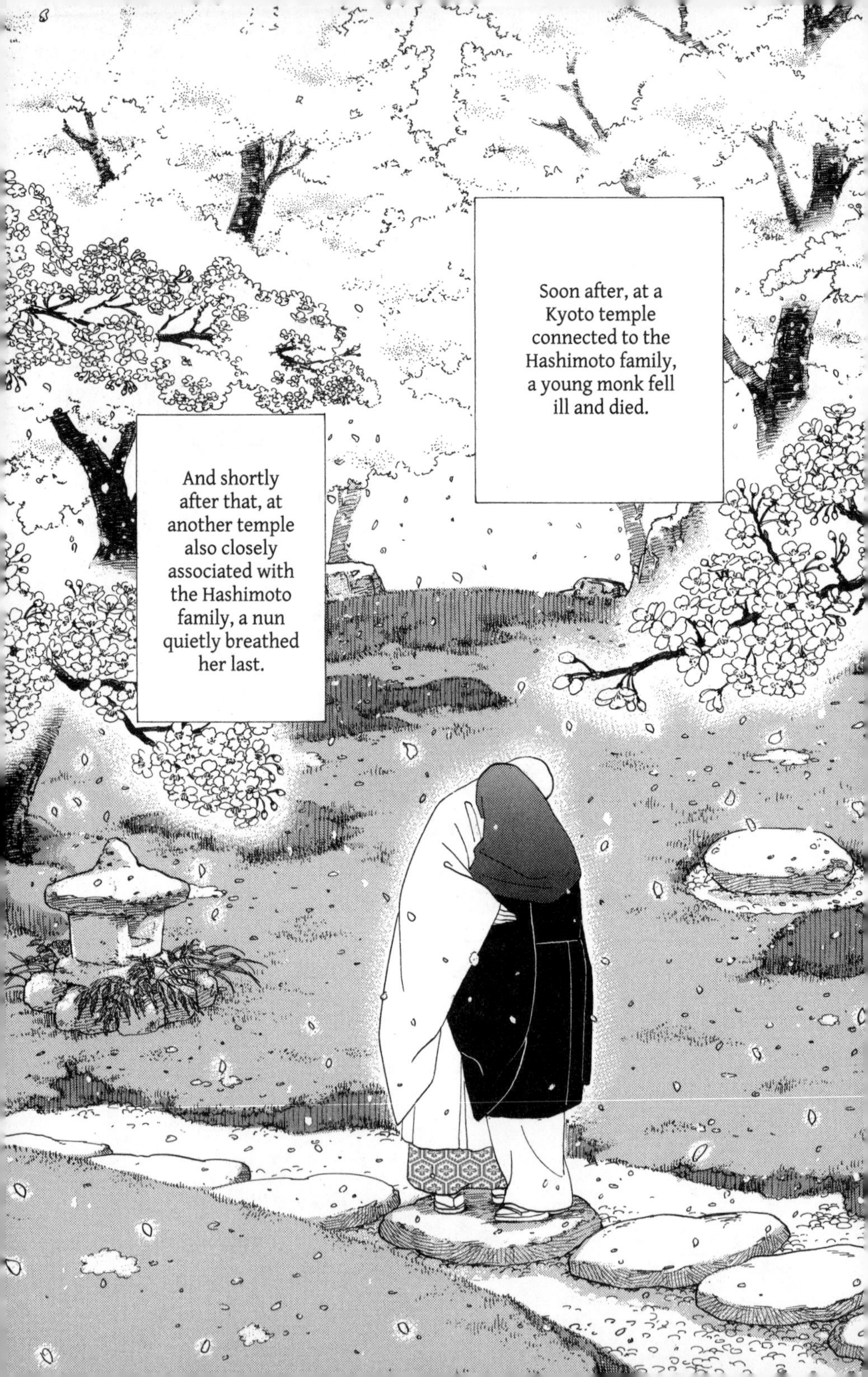
Soon after, at a Kyoto temple connected to the Hashimoto family, a young monk fell ill and died.
And shortly after that, at another temple also closely associated with the Hashimoto family, a nun quietly breathed her last.

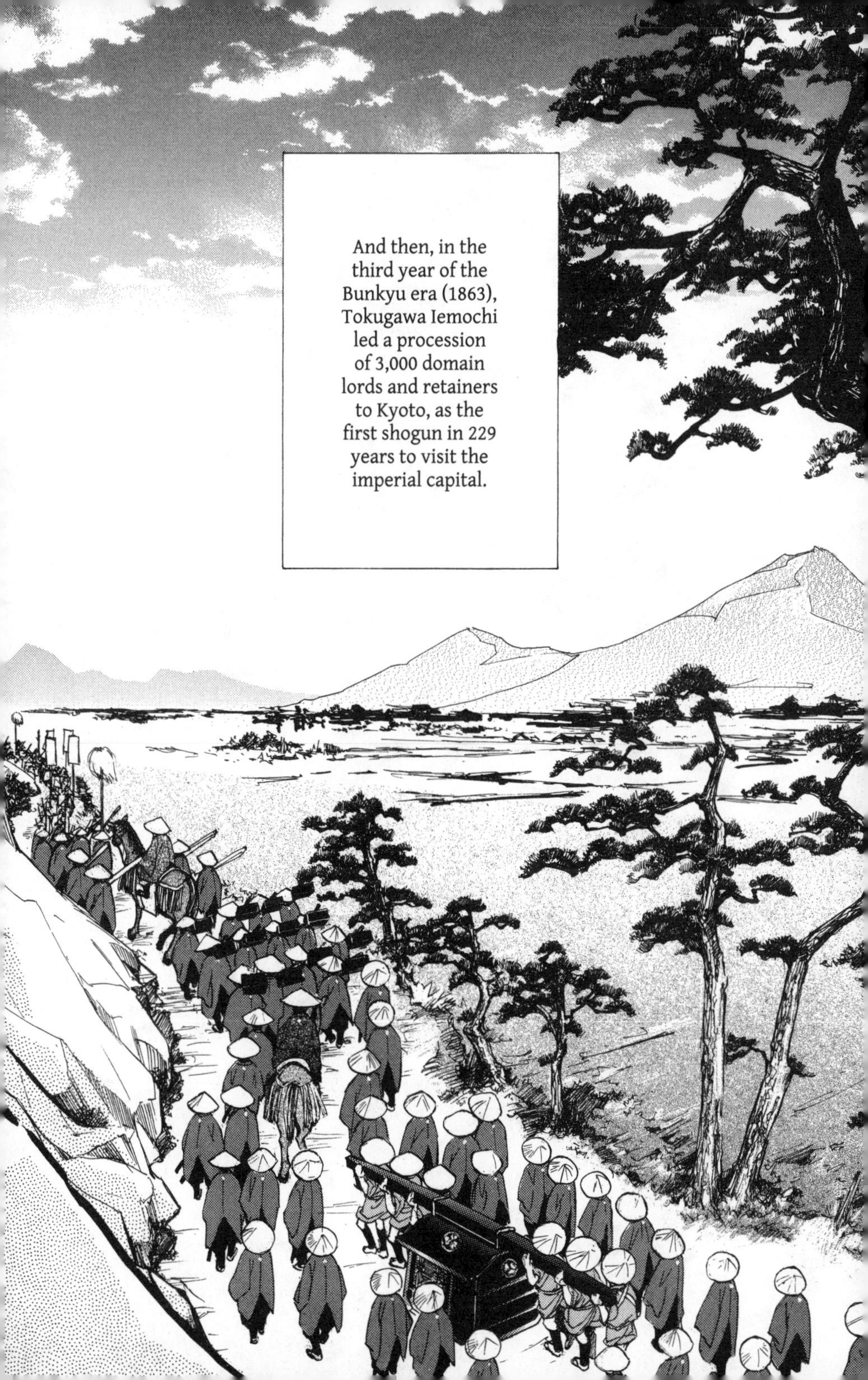
And then, in the third year of the Bunkyu era (1863), Tokugawa Iemochi led a procession of 3,000 domain lords and retainers to Kyoto, as the first shogun in 229 years to visit the imperial capital.

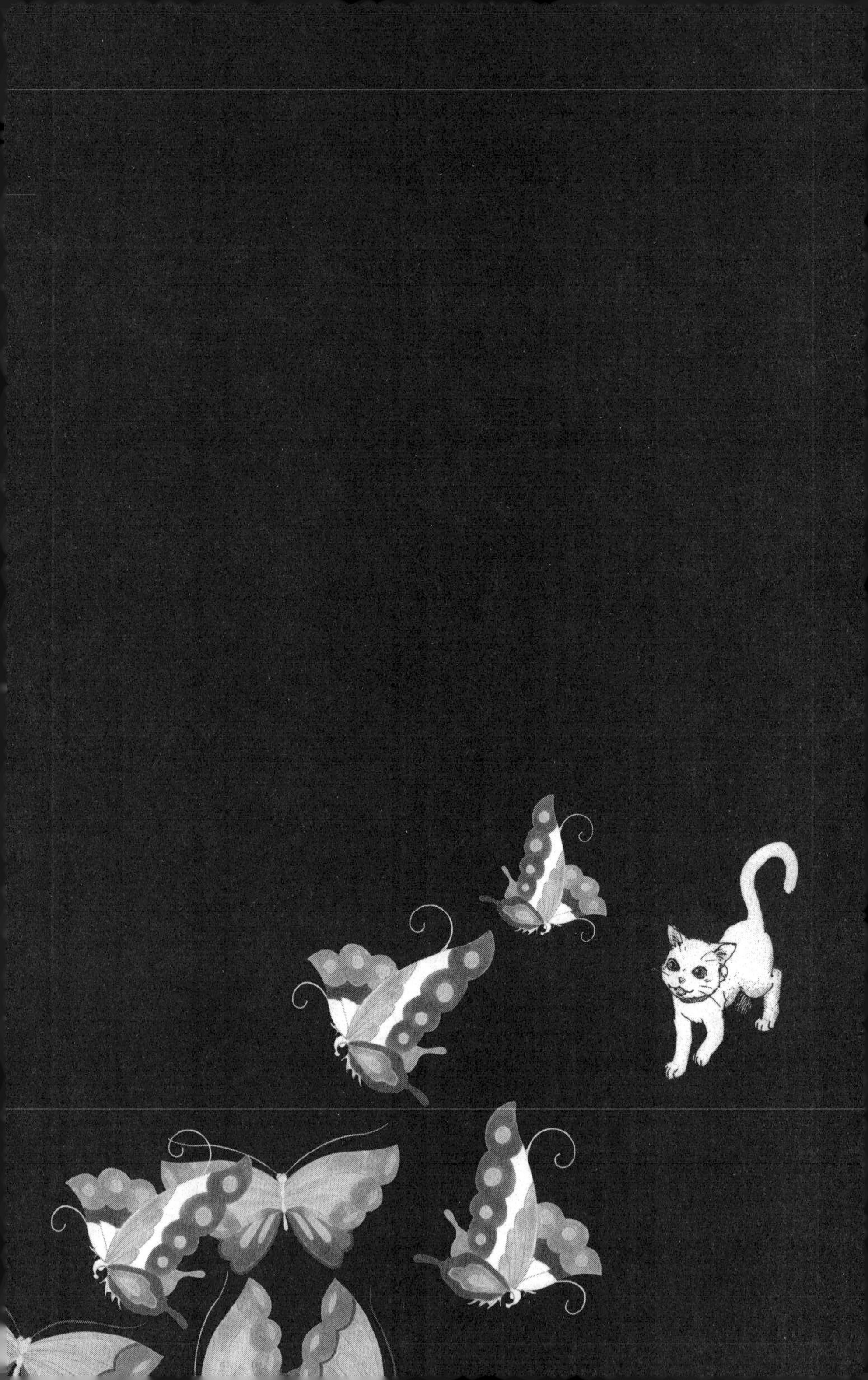

Ōoku

THE INNER CHAMBERS

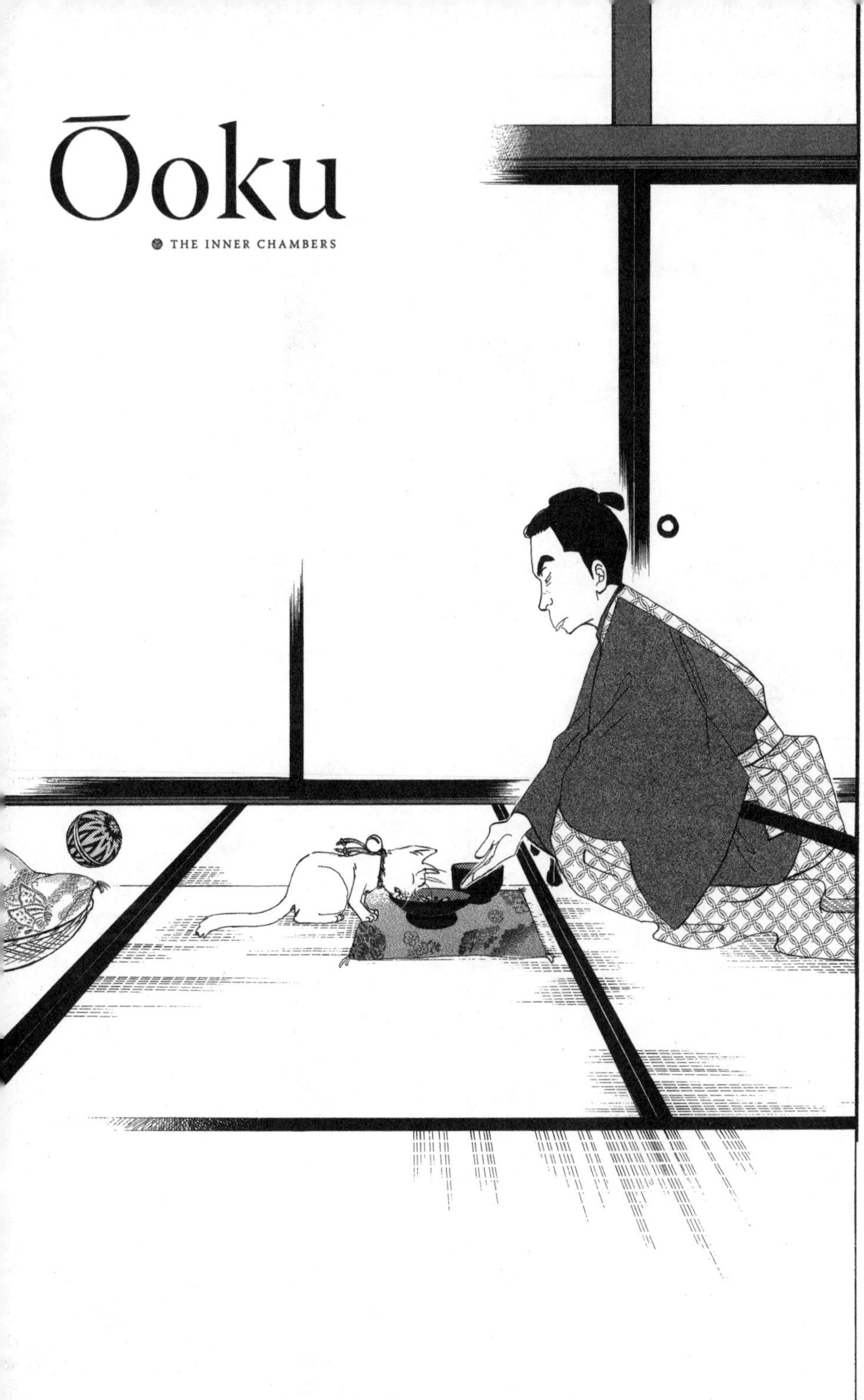

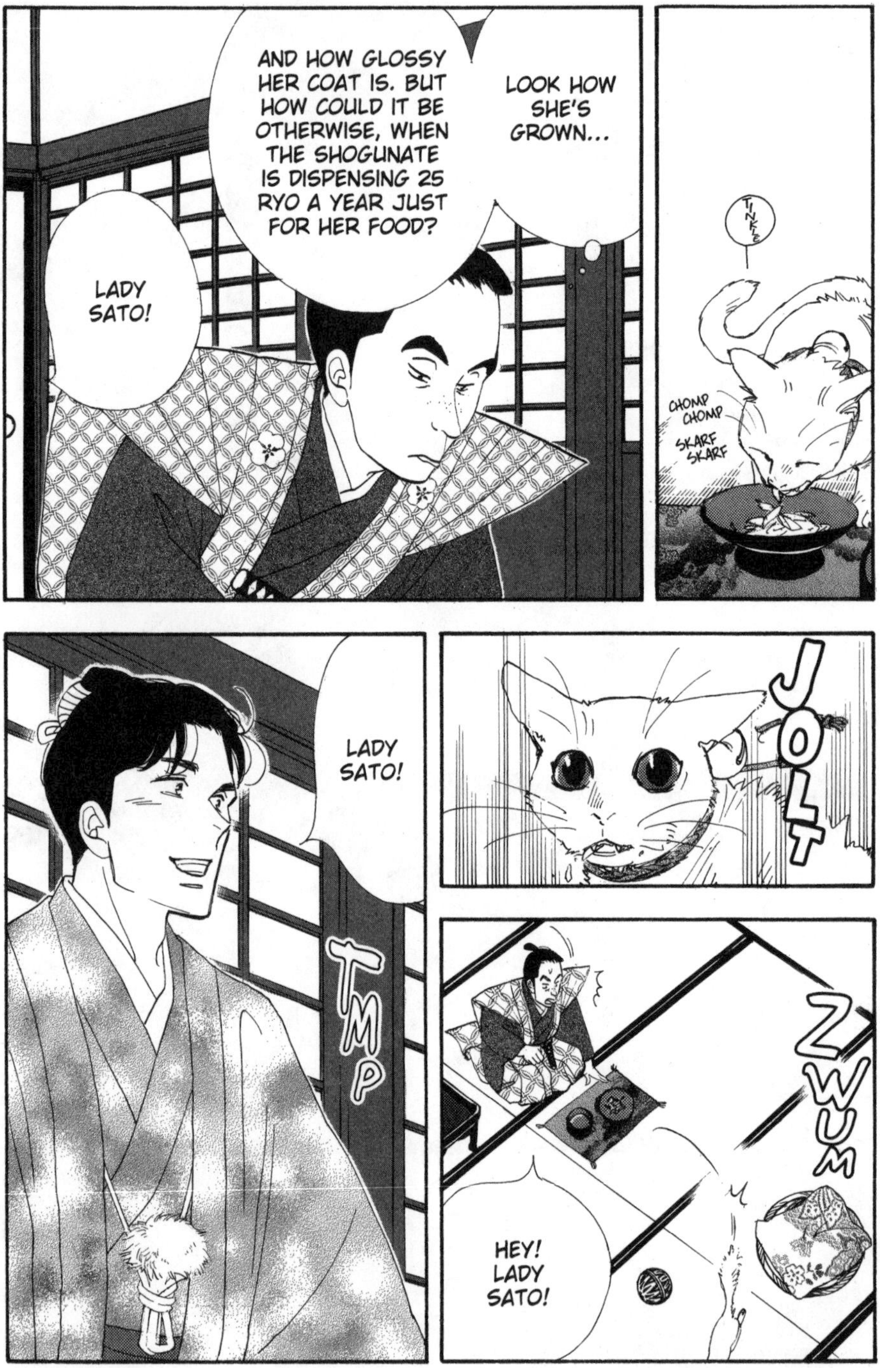
TINKLE
CHOMP CHOMP
SKARF SKARF
LOOK HOW SHE'S GROWN...
AND HOW GLOSSY HER COAT IS. BUT HOW COULD IT BE OTHERWISE, WHEN THE SHOGUNATE IS DISPENSING 25 RYO A YEAR JUST FOR HER FOOD?
LADY SATO!
JOLT
ZWUM
HEY! LADY SATO!
LADY SATO!
TMP

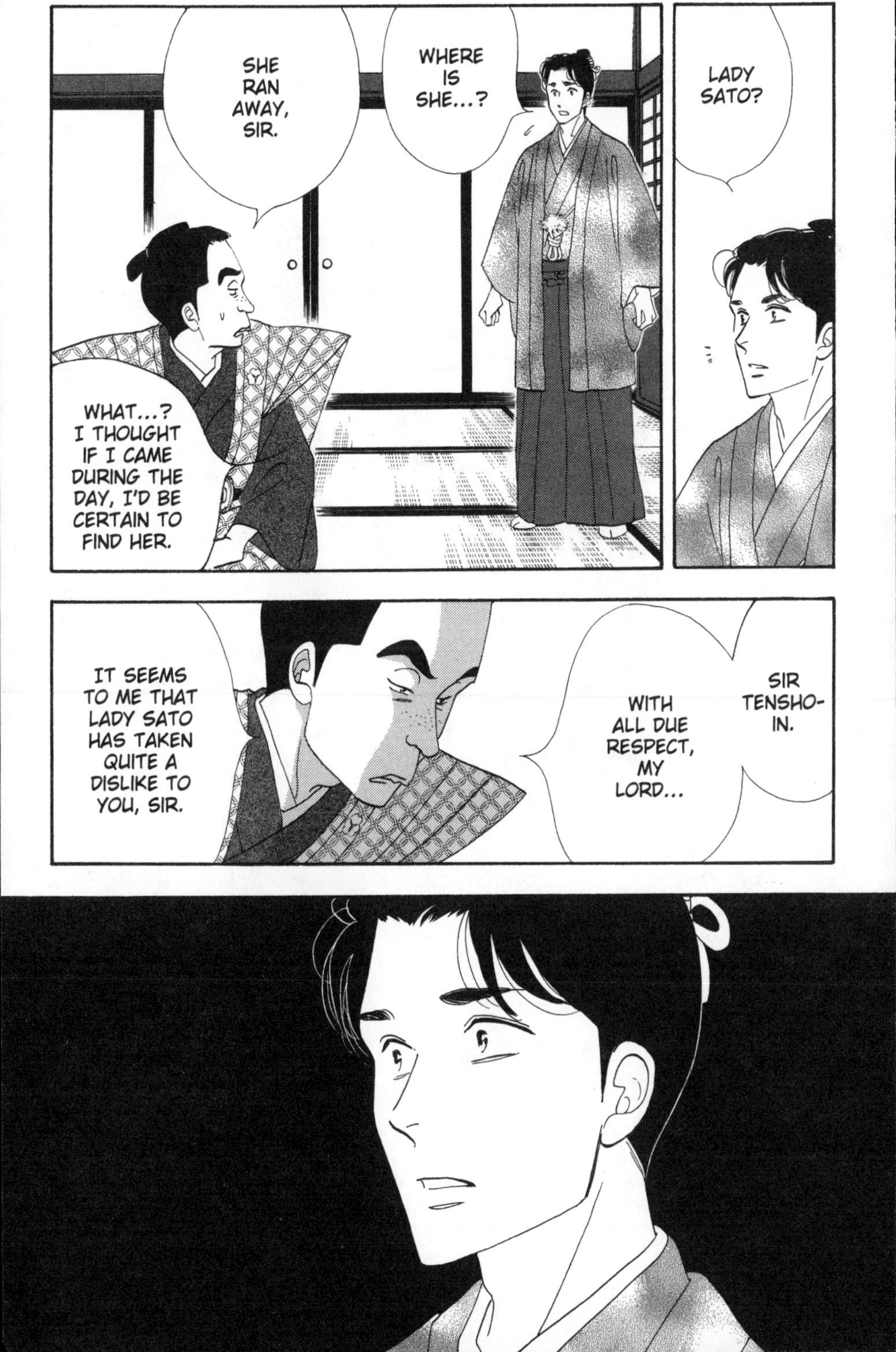
LADY SATO?
WHERE IS SHE...?
SHE RAN AWAY, SIR.
WHAT...? I THOUGHT IF I CAME DURING THE DAY, I'D BE CERTAIN TO FIND HER.
SIR TENSHO-IN.
WITH ALL DUE RESPECT, MY LORD...
IT SEEMS TO ME THAT LADY SATO HAS TAKEN QUITE A DISLIKE TO YOU, SIR.

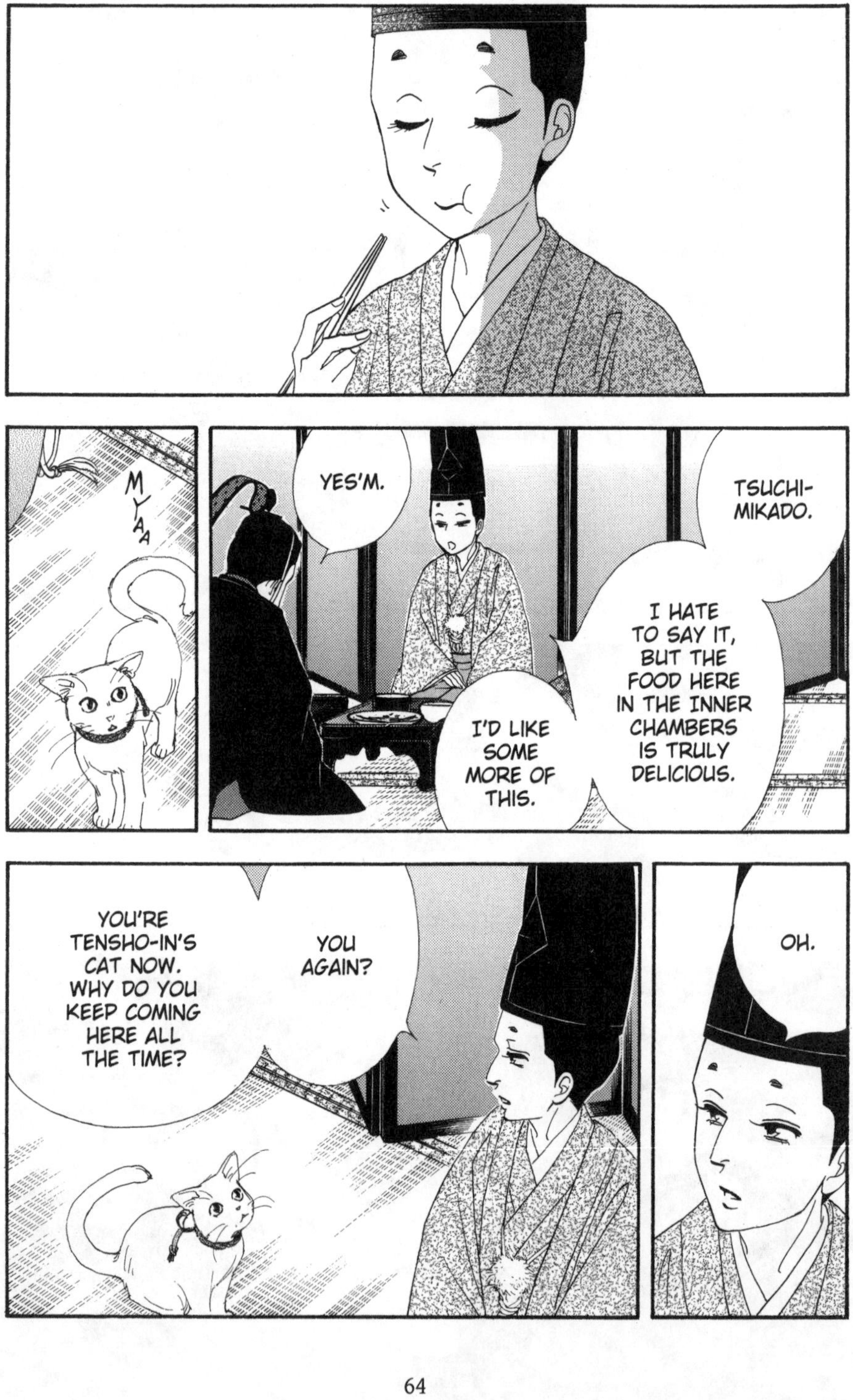
TSUCHI-MIKADO.
I HATE TO SAY IT, BUT THE FOOD HERE IN THE INNER CHAMBERS IS TRULY DELICIOUS.
I'D LIKE SOME MORE OF THIS.
YES'M.
MYAA
OH.
YOU AGAIN?
YOU'RE TENSHO-IN'S CAT NOW. WHY DO YOU KEEP COMING HERE ALL THE TIME?

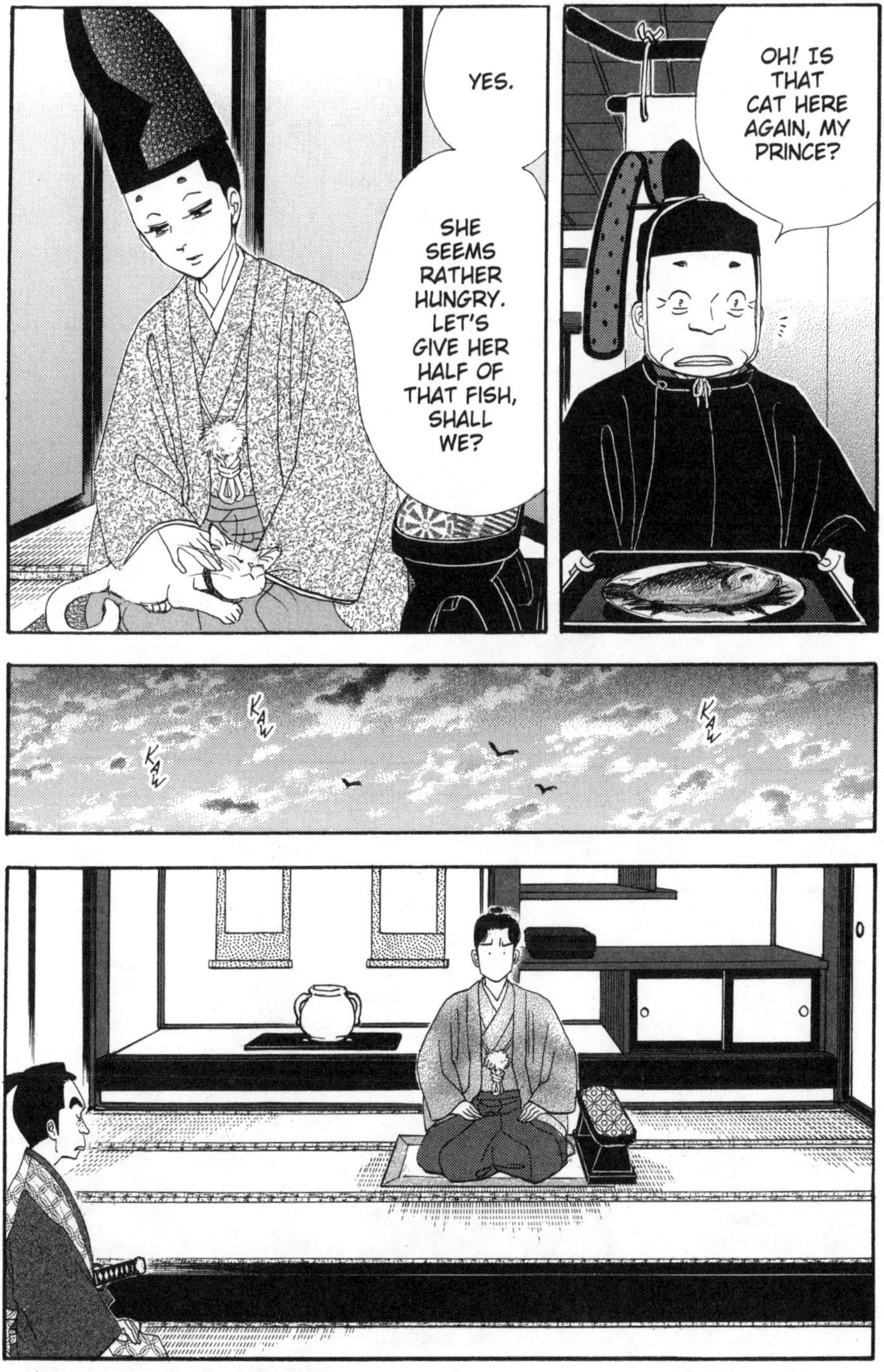
OH! IS THAT CAT HERE AGAIN, MY PRINCE?
YES.
SHE SEEMS RATHER HUNGRY. LET'S GIVE HER HALF OF THAT FISH, SHALL WE?
KAW
KAW
KAW

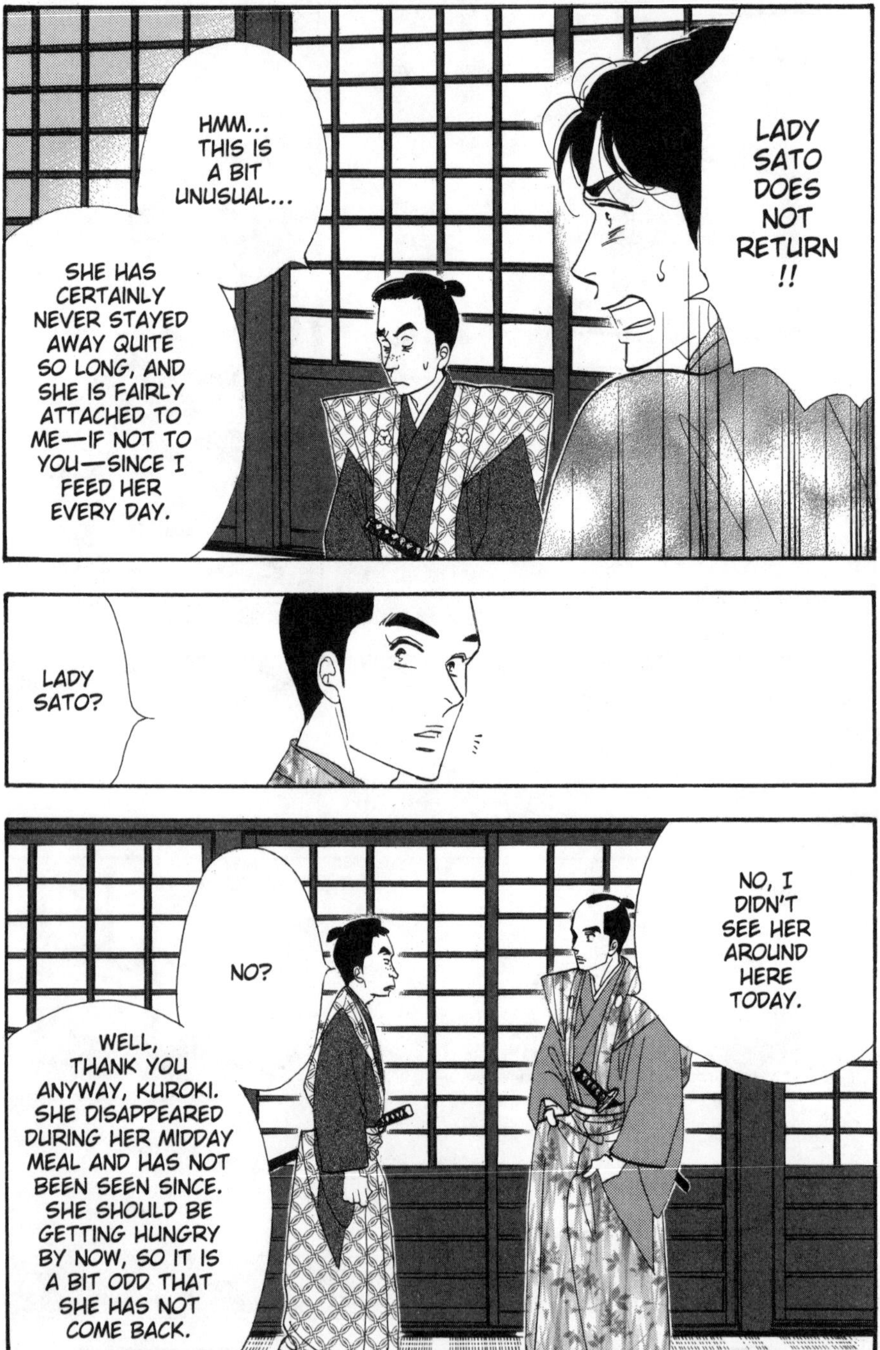
LADY SATO DOES NOT RETURN!!
HMM... THIS IS A BIT UNUSUAL...
SHE HAS CERTAINLY NEVER STAYED AWAY QUITE SO LONG, AND SHE IS FAIRLY ATTACHED TO ME—IF NOT TO YOU—SINCE I FEED HER EVERY DAY.
LADY SATO?
NO, I DIDN'T SEE HER AROUND HERE TODAY.
NO?
WELL, THANK YOU ANYWAY, KUROKI. SHE DISAPPEARED DURING HER MIDDAY MEAL AND HAS NOT BEEN SEEN SINCE. SHE SHOULD BE GETTING HUNGRY BY NOW, SO IT IS A BIT ODD THAT SHE HAS NOT COME BACK.

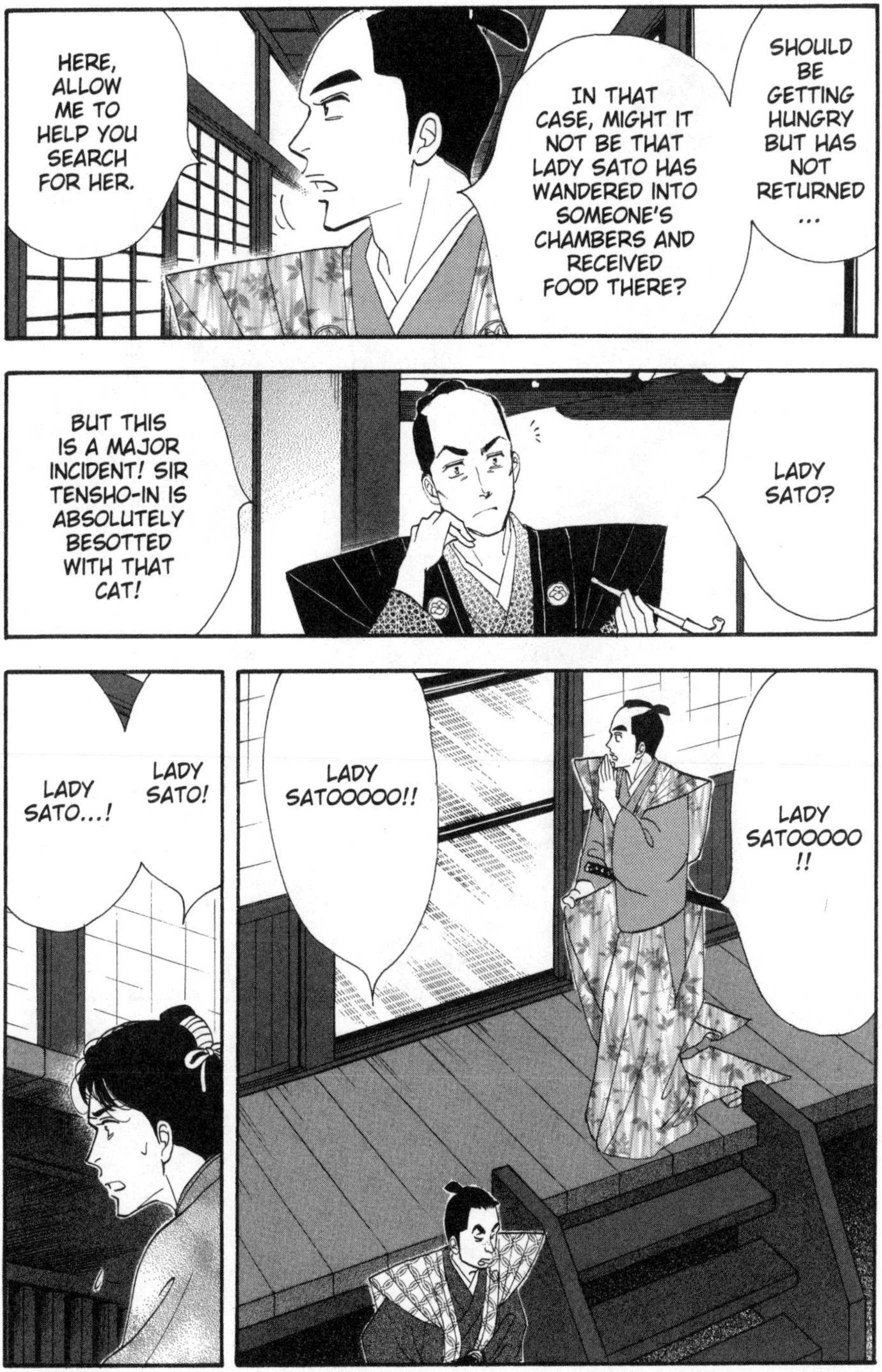
SHOULD BE GETTING HUNGRY BUT HAS NOT RETURNED ...
IN THAT CASE, MIGHT IT NOT BE THAT LADY SATO HAS WANDERED INTO SOMEONE'S CHAMBERS AND RECEIVED FOOD THERE?
HERE, ALLOW ME TO HELP YOU SEARCH FOR HER.
LADY SATO?
BUT THIS IS A MAJOR INCIDENT! SIR TENSHO-IN IS ABSOLUTELY BESOTTED WITH THAT CAT!
LADY SATOOOOOO !!
LADY SATOOOOOO!!
LADY SATO!
LADY SATO...!

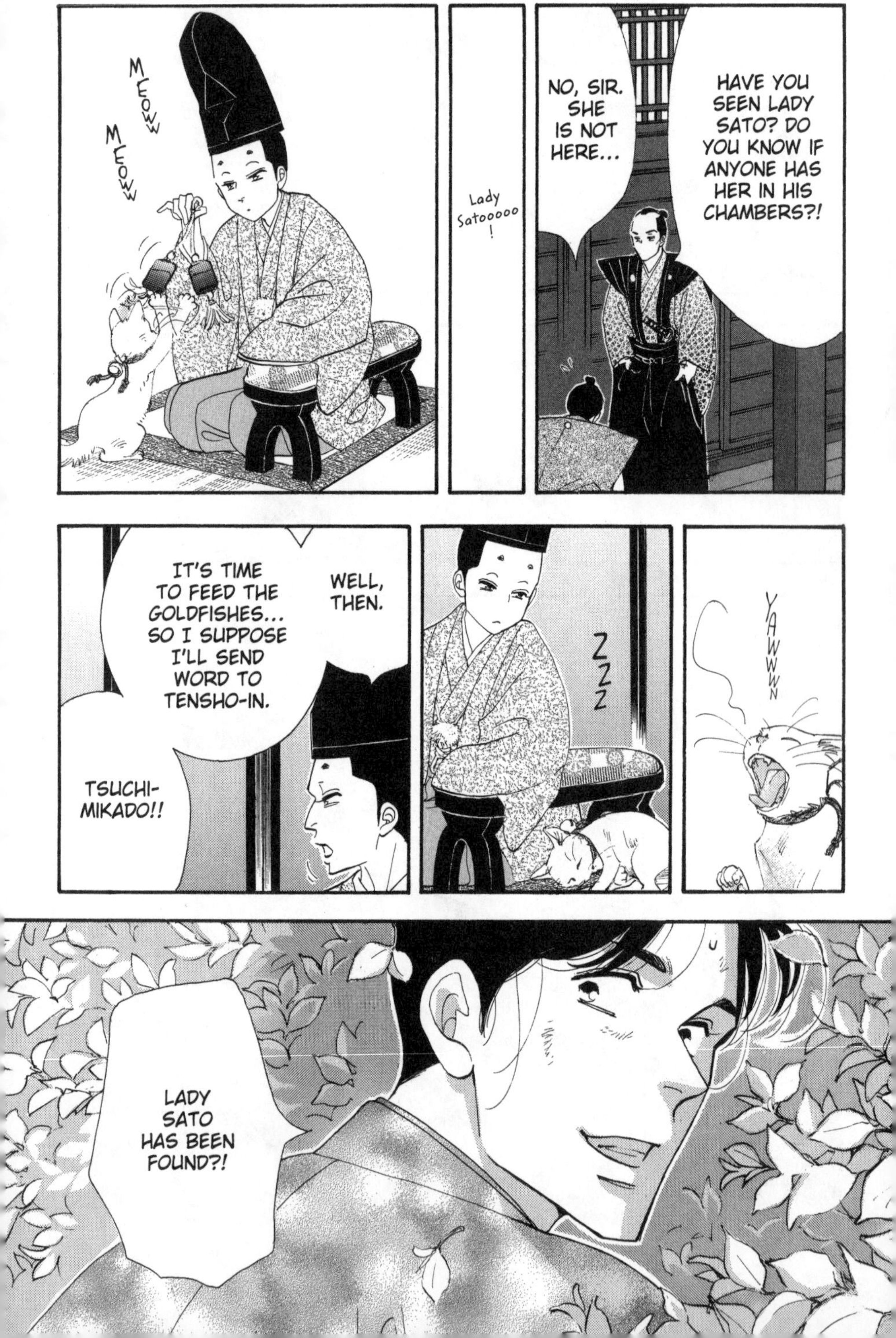
HAVE YOU SEEN LADY SATO? DO YOU KNOW IF ANYONE HAS HER IN HIS CHAMBERS?!
NO, SIR. SHE IS NOT HERE...
Lady Satoooooo!
MEOWW
MEOWW
YAWWWN
ZZZ
WELL, THEN.
IT'S TIME TO FEED THE GOLDFISHES... SO I SUPPOSE I'LL SEND WORD TO TENSHO-IN.
TSUCHI-MIKADO!!
LADY SATO HAS BEEN FOUND?!

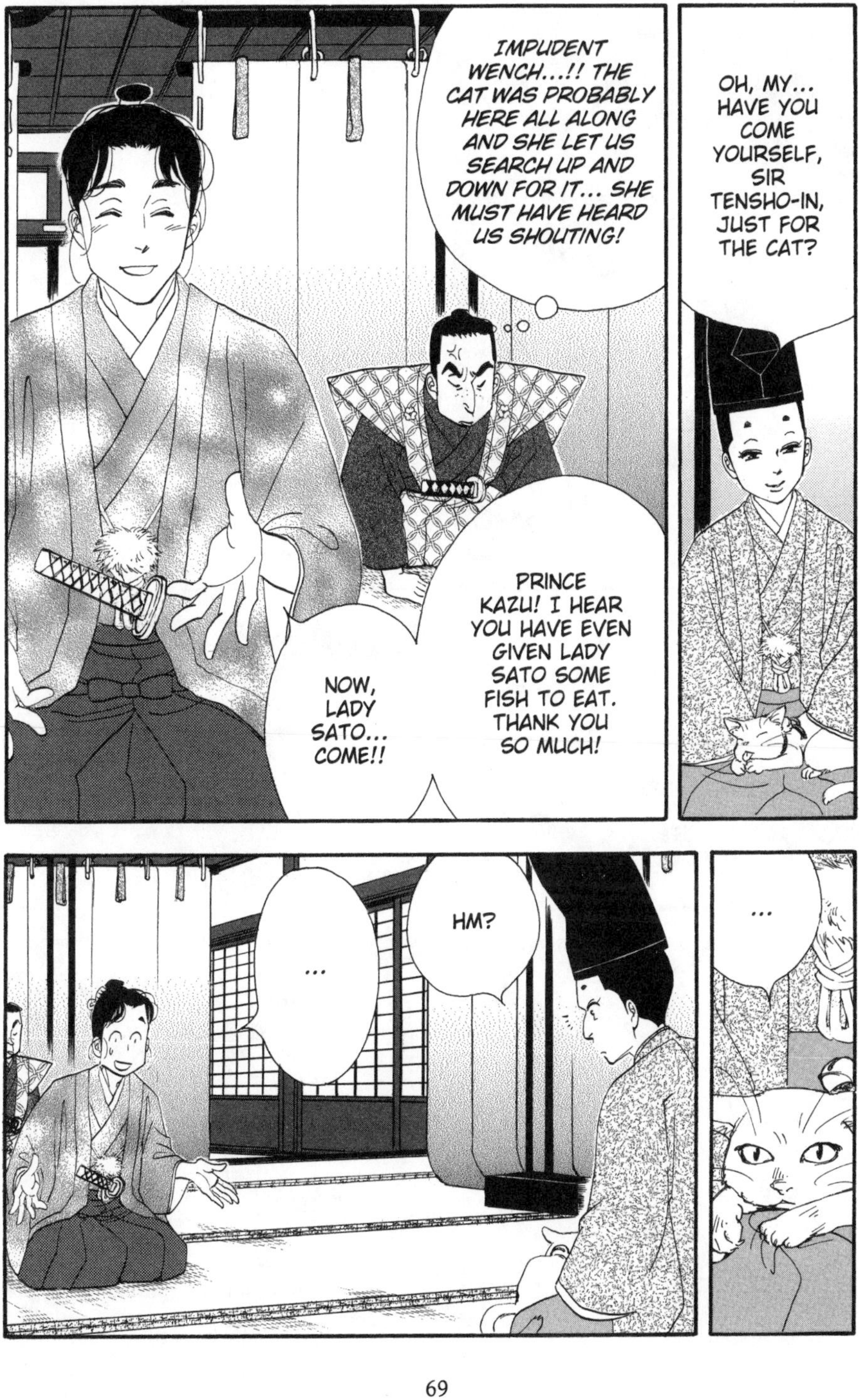
OH, MY... HAVE YOU COME YOURSELF, SIR TENSHO-IN, JUST FOR THE CAT?
IMPUDENT WENCH...!! THE CAT WAS PROBABLY HERE ALL ALONG AND SHE LET US SEARCH UP AND DOWN FOR IT... SHE MUST HAVE HEARD US SHOUTING!
PRINCE KAZU! I HEAR YOU HAVE EVEN GIVEN LADY SATO SOME FISH TO EAT. THANK YOU SO MUCH!
NOW, LADY SATO... COME!!
...
HM?
...

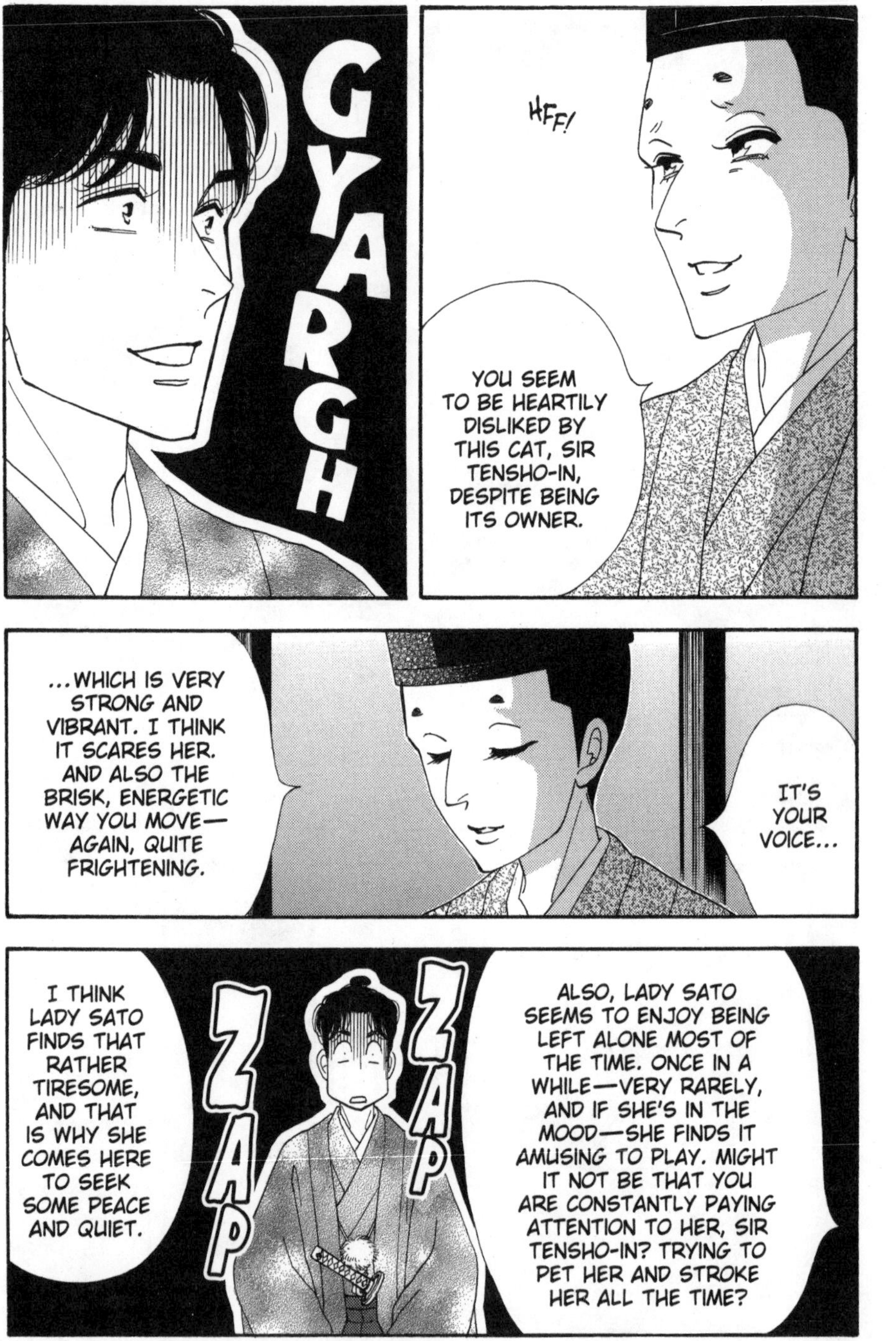
HFF!
YOU SEEM TO BE HEARTILY DISLIKED BY THIS CAT, SIR TENSHO-IN, DESPITE BEING ITS OWNER.
GYARGH
IT'S YOUR VOICE...
...WHICH IS VERY STRONG AND VIBRANT. I THINK IT SCARES HER. AND ALSO THE BRISK, ENERGETIC WAY YOU MOVE—AGAIN, QUITE FRIGHTENING.
ALSO, LADY SATO SEEMS TO ENJOY BEING LEFT ALONE MOST OF THE TIME. ONCE IN A WHILE—VERY RARELY, AND IF SHE'S IN THE MOOD—SHE FINDS IT AMUSING TO PLAY. MIGHT IT NOT BE THAT YOU ARE CONSTANTLY PAYING ATTENTION TO HER, SIR TENSHO-IN? TRYING TO PET HER AND STROKE HER ALL THE TIME?
ZAP
ZAP
I THINK LADY SATO FINDS THAT RATHER TIRESOME, AND THAT IS WHY SHE COMES HERE TO SEEK SOME PEACE AND QUIET.

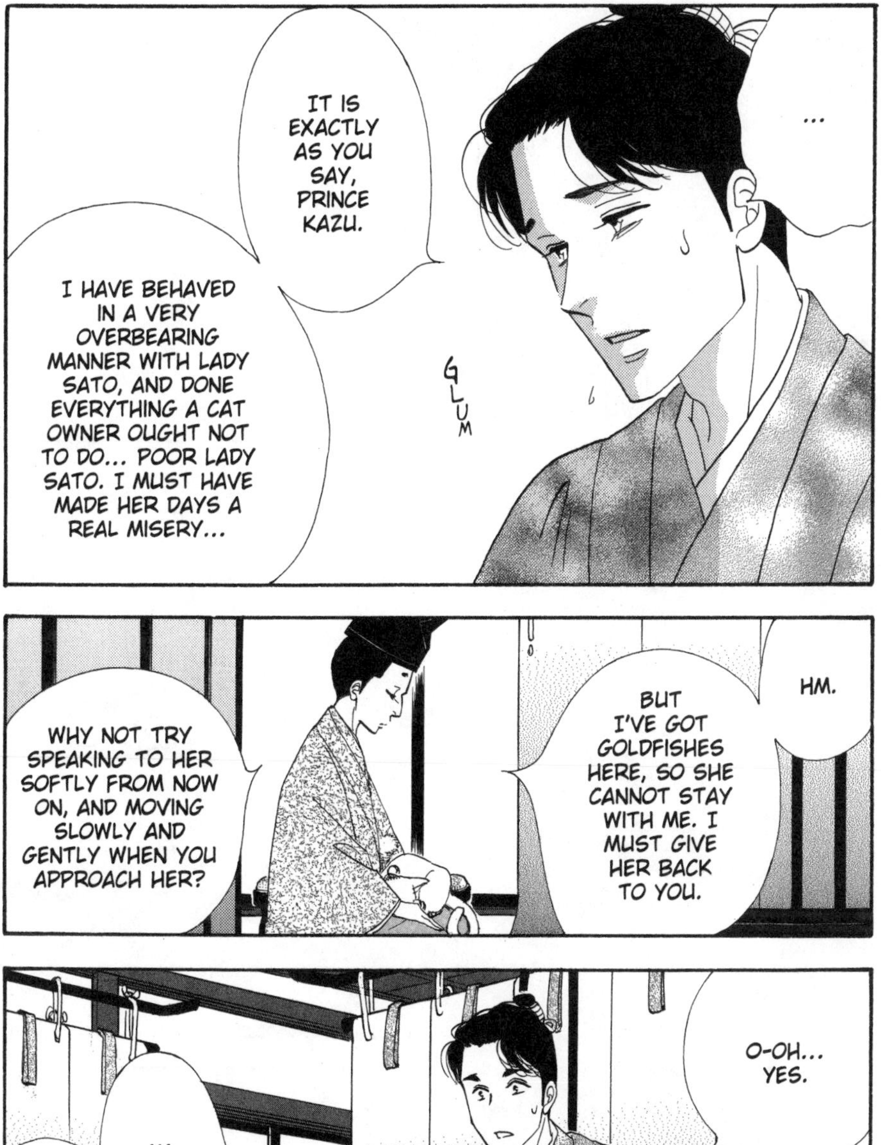
...
IT IS EXACTLY AS YOU SAY, PRINCE KAZU.
GLUM
I HAVE BEHAVED IN A VERY OVERBEARING MANNER WITH LADY SATO, AND DONE EVERYTHING A CAT OWNER OUGHT NOT TO DO... POOR LADY SATO. I MUST HAVE MADE HER DAYS A REAL MISERY...
HM.
BUT I'VE GOT GOLDFISHES HERE, SO SHE CANNOT STAY WITH ME. I MUST GIVE HER BACK TO YOU.
WHY NOT TRY SPEAKING TO HER SOFTLY FROM NOW ON, AND MOVING SLOWLY AND GENTLY WHEN YOU APPROACH HER?
O-OH... YES.
...
LADY SATO...

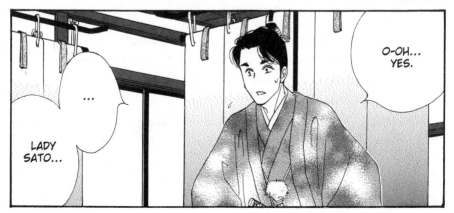

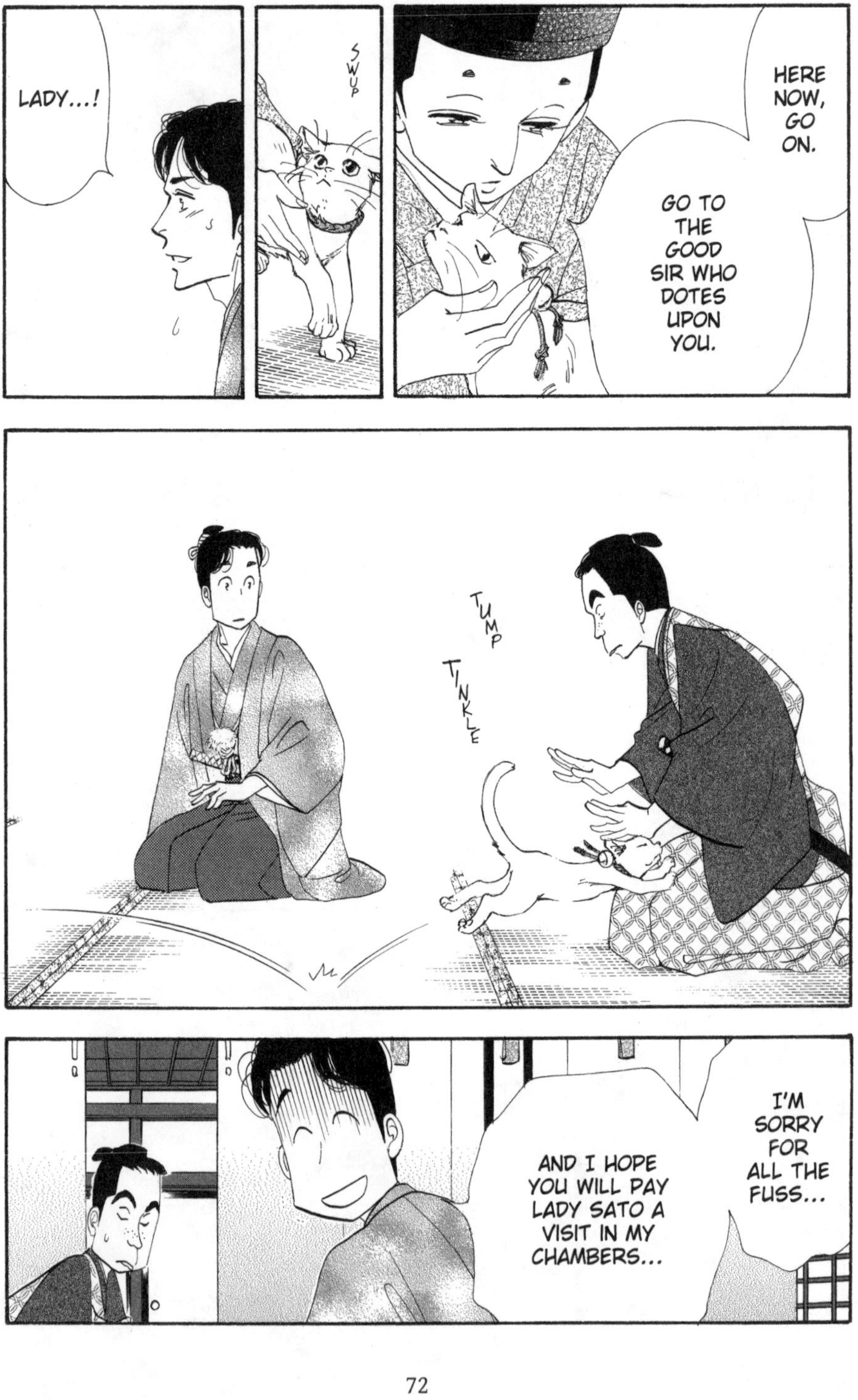
HERE NOW, GO ON.
GO TO THE GOOD SIR WHO DOTES UPON YOU.
SWUP
LADY...!
TUMP
TINKLE
I'M SORRY FOR ALL THE FUSS...
AND I HOPE YOU WILL PAY LADY SATO A VISIT IN MY CHAMBERS...

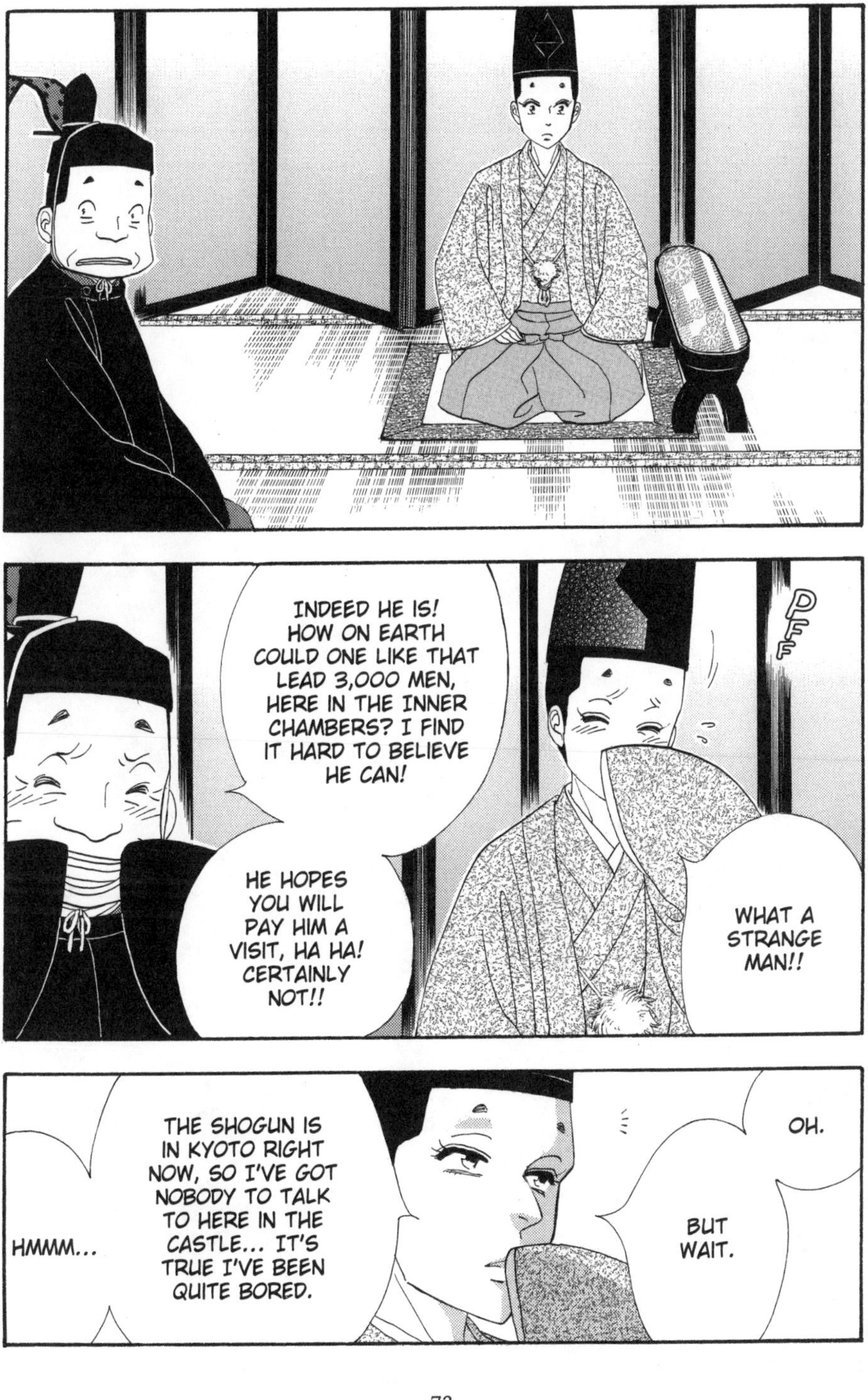
PFF
WHAT A STRANGE MAN!!
INDEED HE IS! HOW ON EARTH COULD ONE LIKE THAT LEAD 3,000 MEN, HERE IN THE INNER CHAMBERS? I FIND IT HARD TO BELIEVE HE CAN!
HE HOPES YOU WILL PAY HIM A VISIT, HA HA! CERTAINLY NOT!!
OH.
BUT WAIT.
THE SHOGUN IS IN KYOTO RIGHT NOW, SO I'VE GOT NOBODY TO TALK TO HERE IN THE CASTLE... IT'S TRUE I'VE BEEN QUITE BORED.
HMMM...

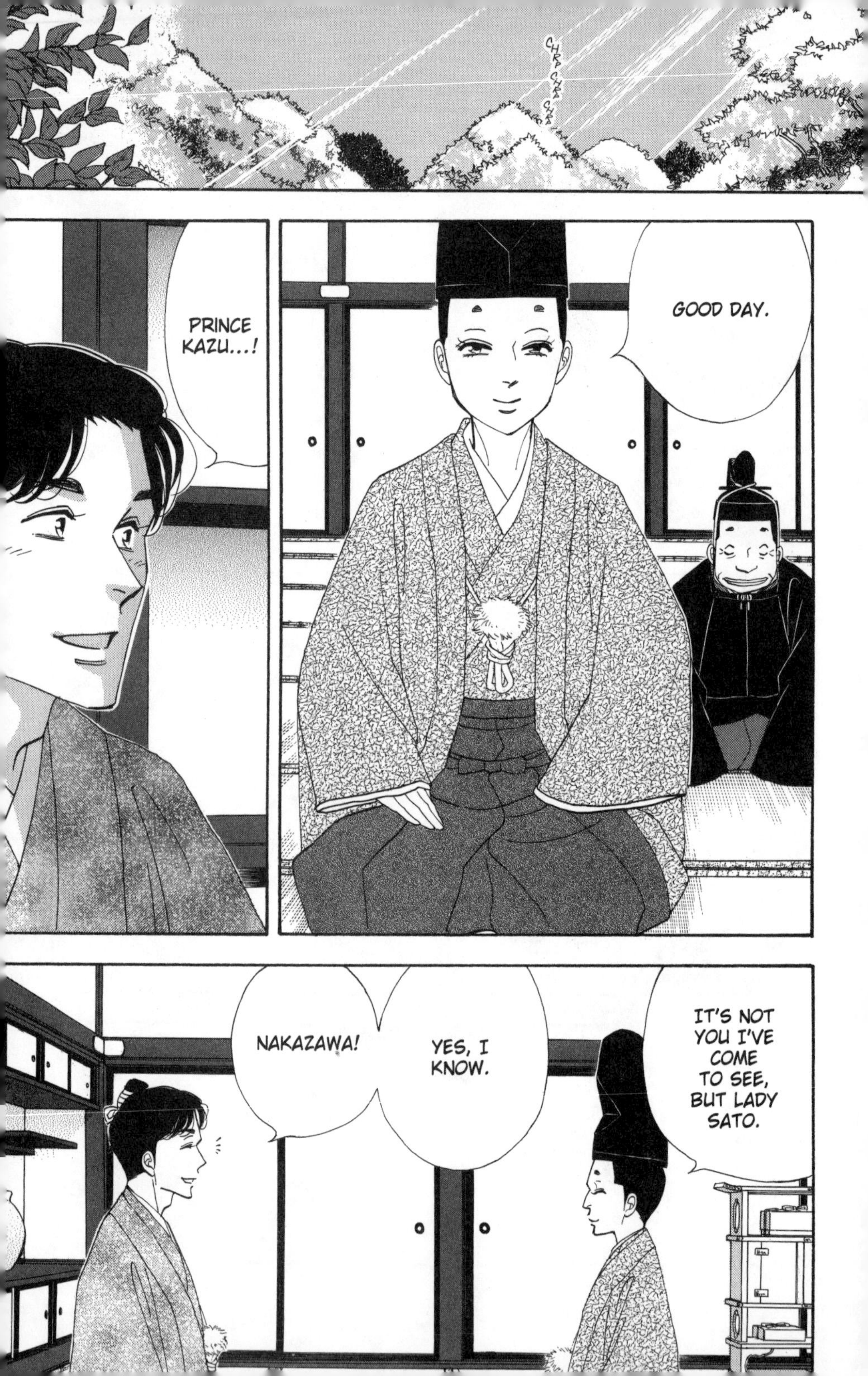
CHRP CHRP CHRP
GOOD DAY.
PRINCE KAZU...!
IT'S NOT YOU I'VE COME TO SEE, BUT LADY SATO.
YES, I KNOW.
NAKAZAWA!

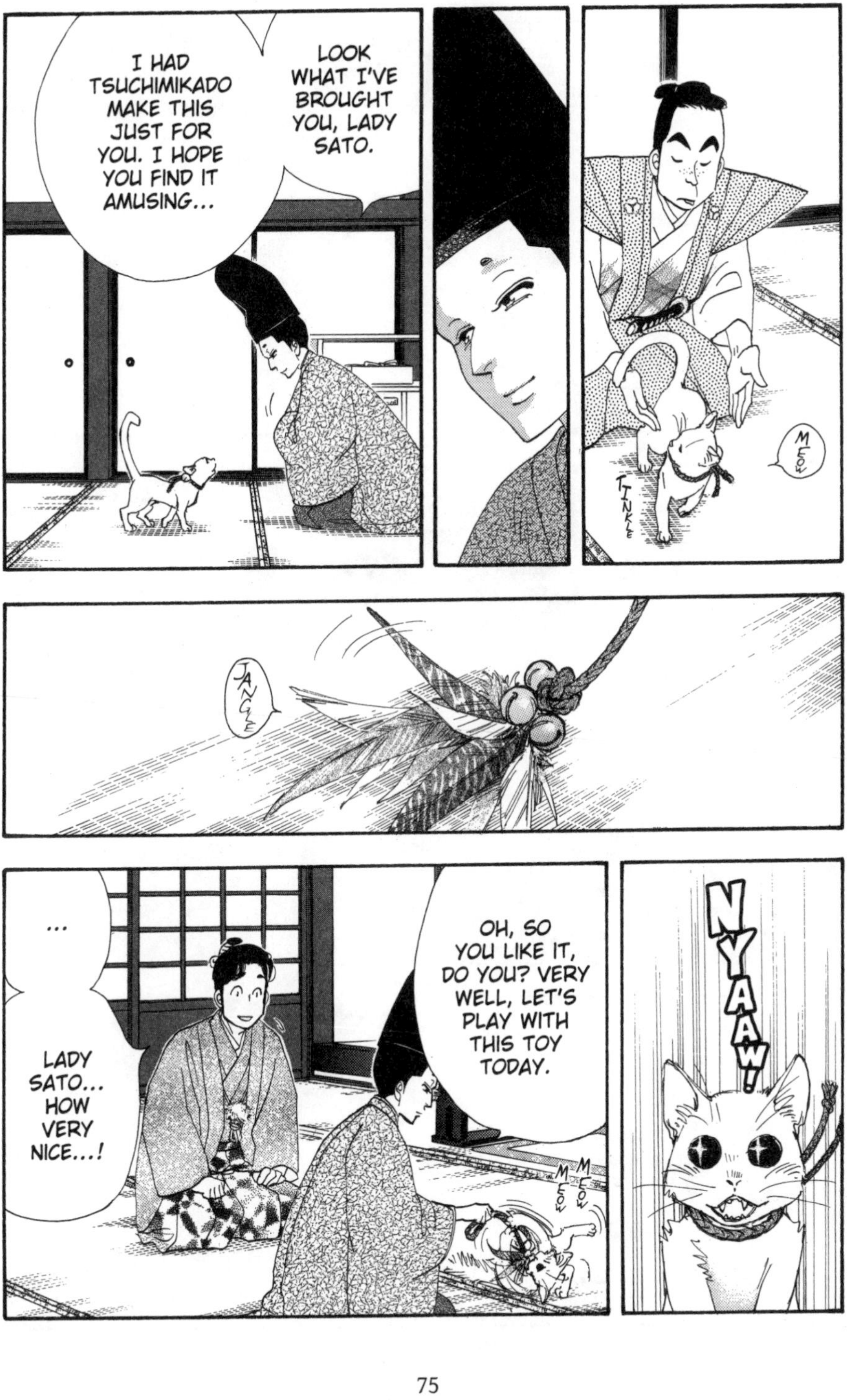
MEOW
TINKLE
LOOK WHAT I'VE BROUGHT YOU, LADY SATO.
I HAD TSUCHIMIKADO MAKE THIS JUST FOR YOU. I HOPE YOU FIND IT AMUSING...
JANGLE
NYAAAW!
OH, SO YOU LIKE IT, DO YOU? VERY WELL, LET'S PLAY WITH THIS TOY TODAY.
MEOW
MEOW
...
LADY SATO... HOW VERY NICE...!

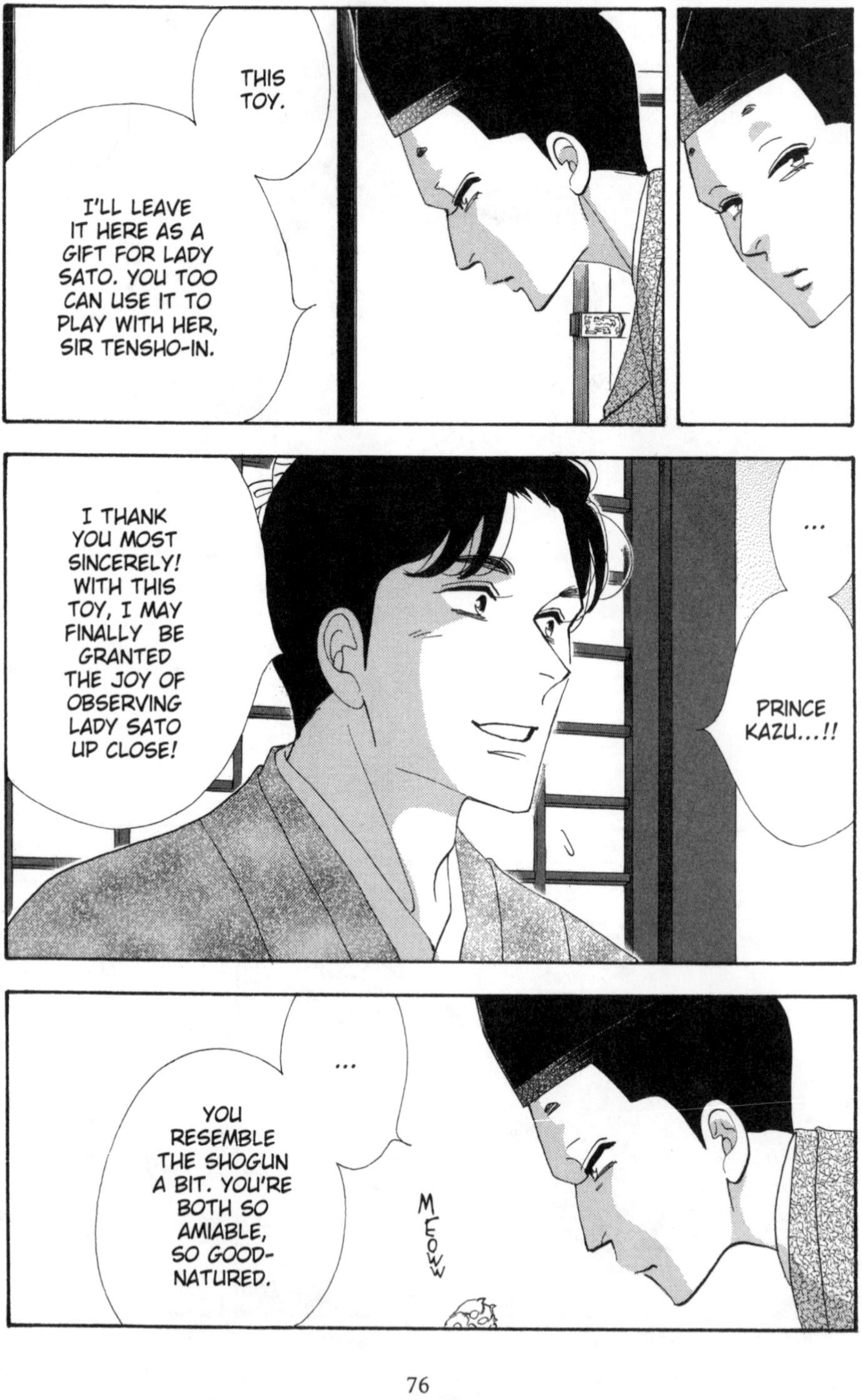
THIS TOY.
I'LL LEAVE IT HERE AS A GIFT FOR LADY SATO. YOU TOO CAN USE IT TO PLAY WITH HER, SIR TENSHO-IN.
... PRINCE KAZU...!!
I THANK YOU MOST SINCERELY! WITH THIS TOY, I MAY FINALLY BE GRANTED THE JOY OF OBSERVING LADY SATO UP CLOSE!
... YOU RESEMBLE THE SHOGUN A BIT. YOU'RE BOTH SO AMIABLE, SO GOOD-NATURED.
MEOWW

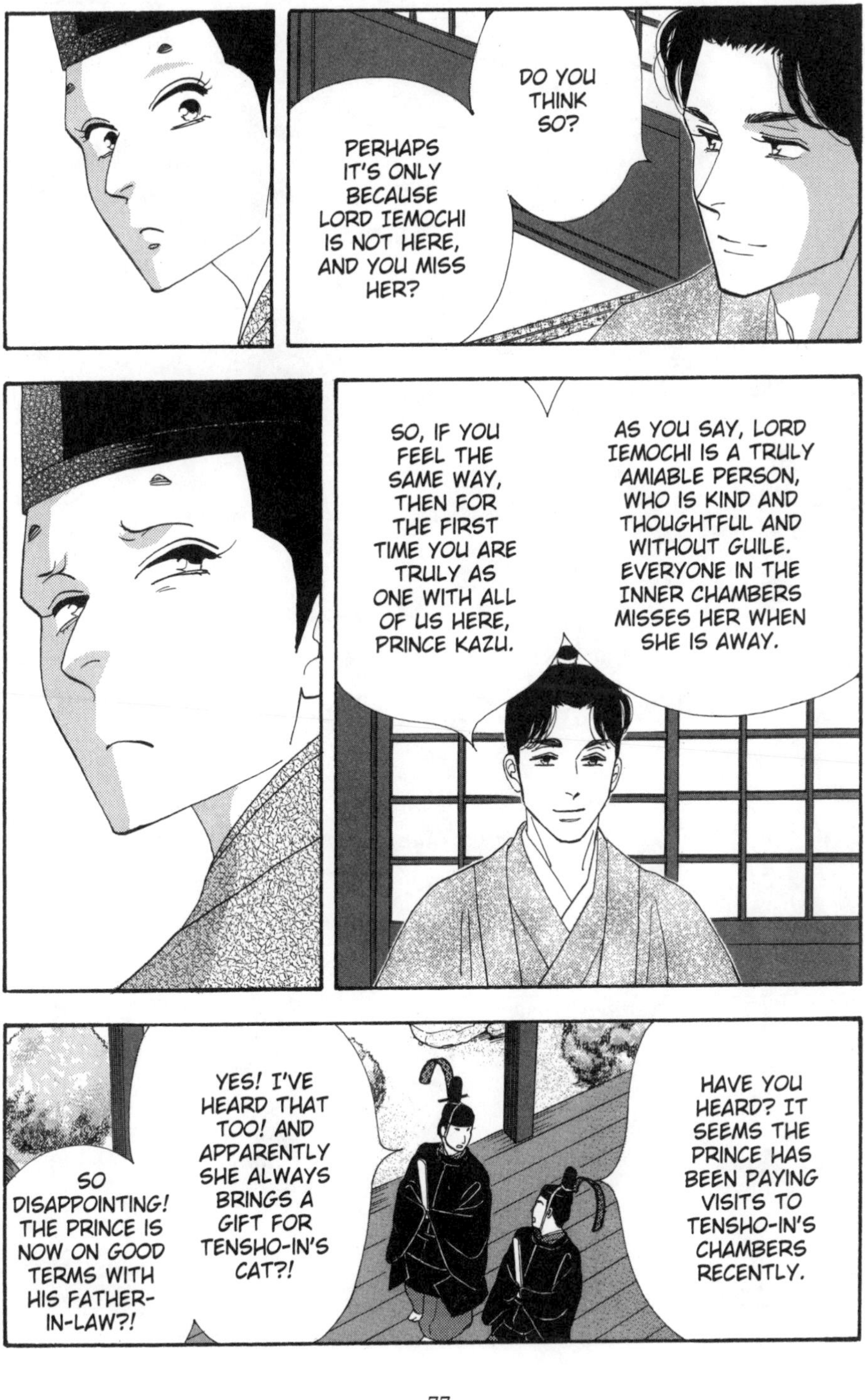
DO YOU THINK SO?
PERHAPS IT'S ONLY BECAUSE LORD IEMOCHI IS NOT HERE, AND YOU MISS HER?
AS YOU SAY, LORD IEMOCHI IS A TRULY AMIABLE PERSON, WHO IS KIND AND THOUGHTFUL AND WITHOUT GUILE. EVERYONE IN THE INNER CHAMBERS MISSES HER WHEN SHE IS AWAY.
SO, IF YOU FEEL THE SAME WAY, THEN FOR THE FIRST TIME YOU ARE TRULY AS ONE WITH ALL OF US HERE, PRINCE KAZU.
HAVE YOU HEARD? IT SEEMS THE PRINCE HAS BEEN PAYING VISITS TO TENSHO-IN'S CHAMBERS RECENTLY.
YES! I'VE HEARD THAT TOO! AND APPARENTLY SHE ALWAYS BRINGS A GIFT FOR TENSHO-IN'S CAT?!
SO DISAPPOINTING! THE PRINCE IS NOW ON GOOD TERMS WITH HIS FATHER-IN-LAW?!

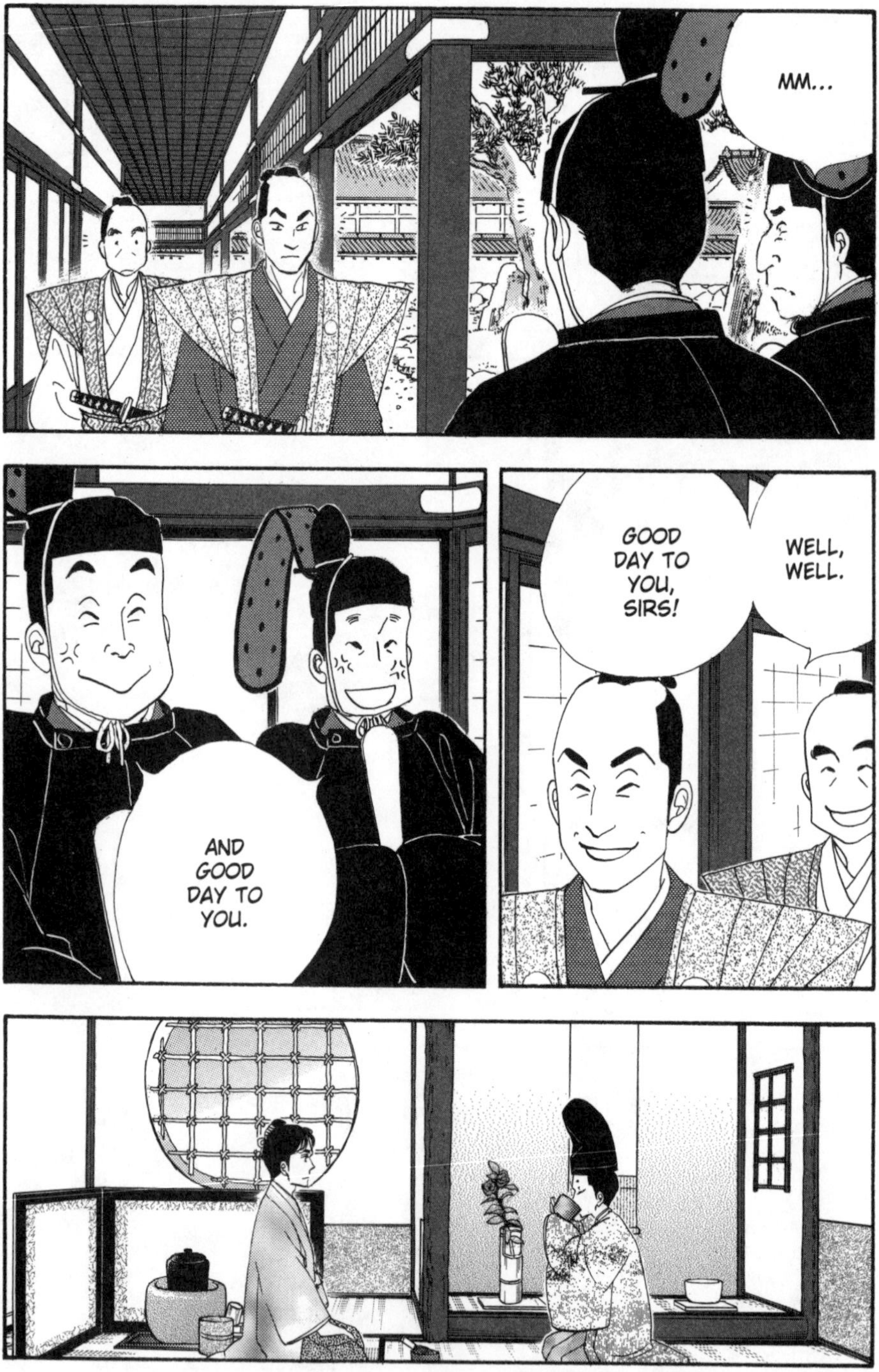
MM...
WELL, WELL.
GOOD DAY TO YOU, SIRS!
AND GOOD DAY TO YOU.

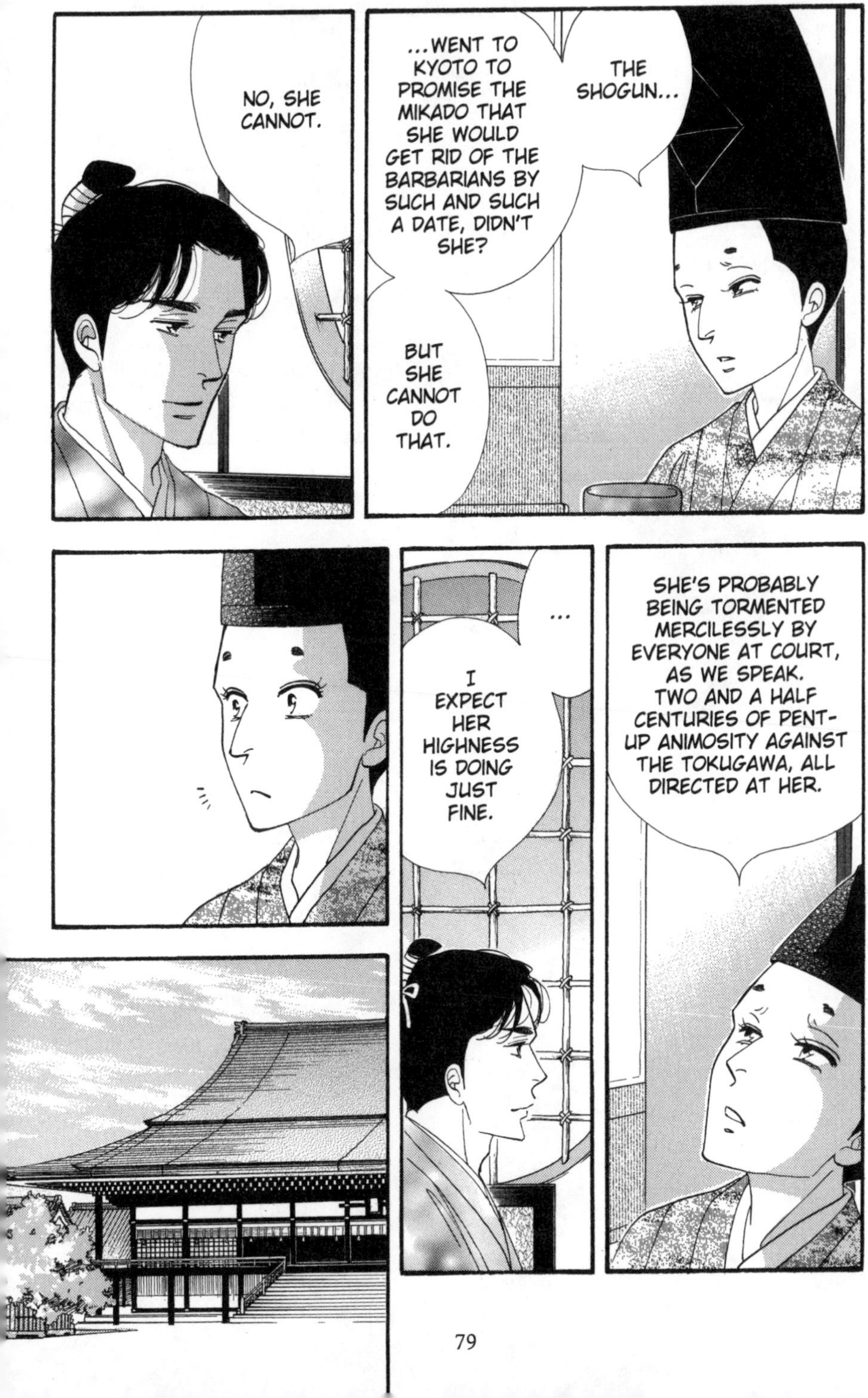
THE SHOGUN...
...WENT TO KYOTO TO PROMISE THE MIKADO THAT SHE WOULD GET RID OF THE BARBARIANS BY SUCH AND SUCH A DATE, DIDN'T SHE?
BUT SHE CANNOT DO THAT.
NO, SHE CANNOT.
SHE'S PROBABLY BEING TORMENTED MERCILESSLY BY EVERYONE AT COURT, AS WE SPEAK. TWO AND A HALF CENTURIES OF PENT-UP ANIMOSITY AGAINST THE TOKUGAWA, ALL DIRECTED AT HER.
...
I EXPECT HER HIGHNESS IS DOING JUST FINE.

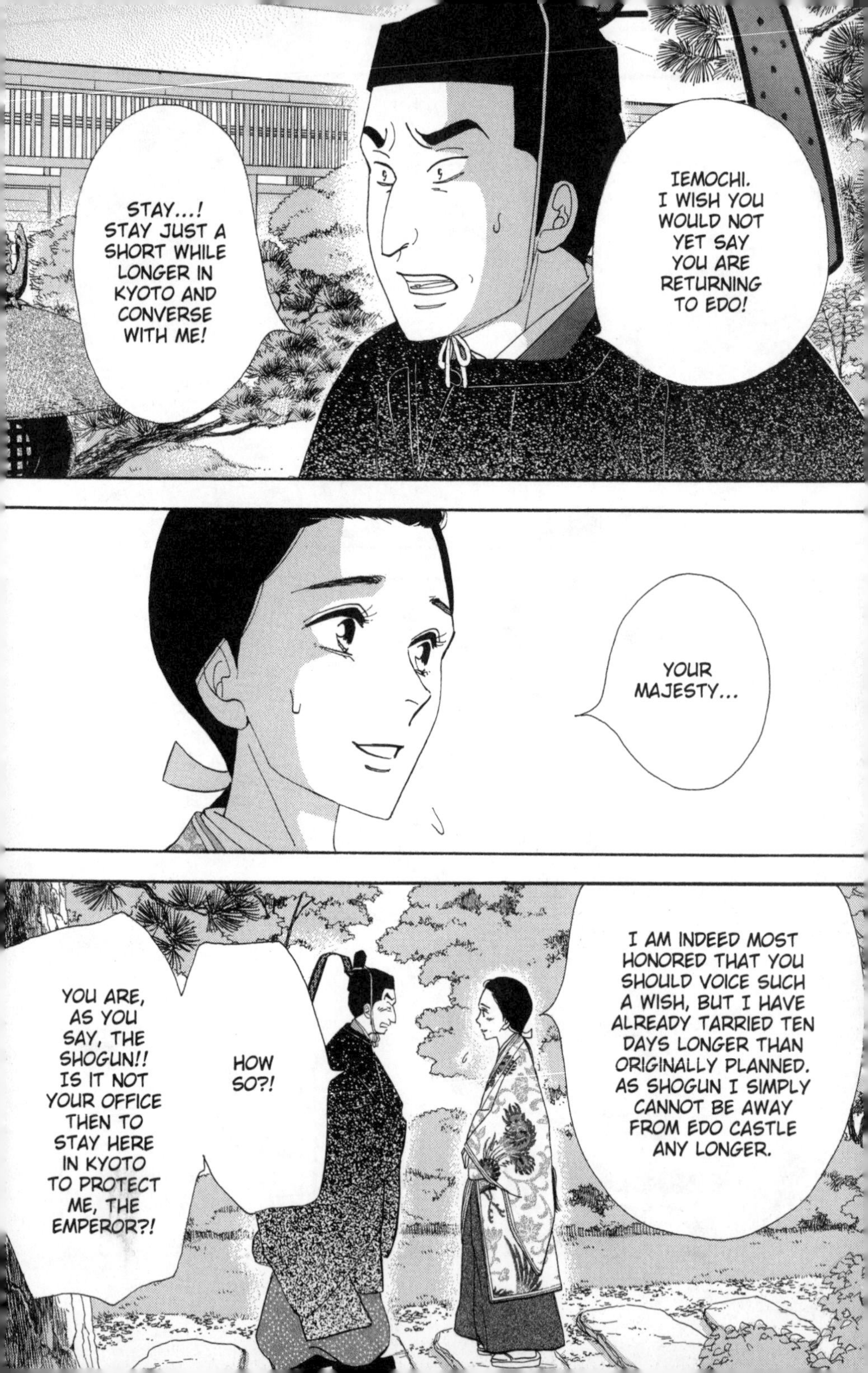
IEMOCHI. I WISH YOU WOULD NOT YET SAY YOU ARE RETURNING TO EDO!
STAY...! STAY JUST A SHORT WHILE LONGER IN KYOTO AND CONVERSE WITH ME!
YOUR MAJESTY...
I AM INDEED MOST HONORED THAT YOU SHOULD VOICE SUCH A WISH, BUT I HAVE ALREADY TARRIED TEN DAYS LONGER THAN ORIGINALLY PLANNED. AS SHOGUN I SIMPLY CANNOT BE AWAY FROM EDO CASTLE ANY LONGER.
HOW SO?!
YOU ARE, AS YOU SAY, THE SHOGUN!! IS IT NOT YOUR OFFICE THEN TO STAY HERE IN KYOTO TO PROTECT ME, THE EMPEROR?!

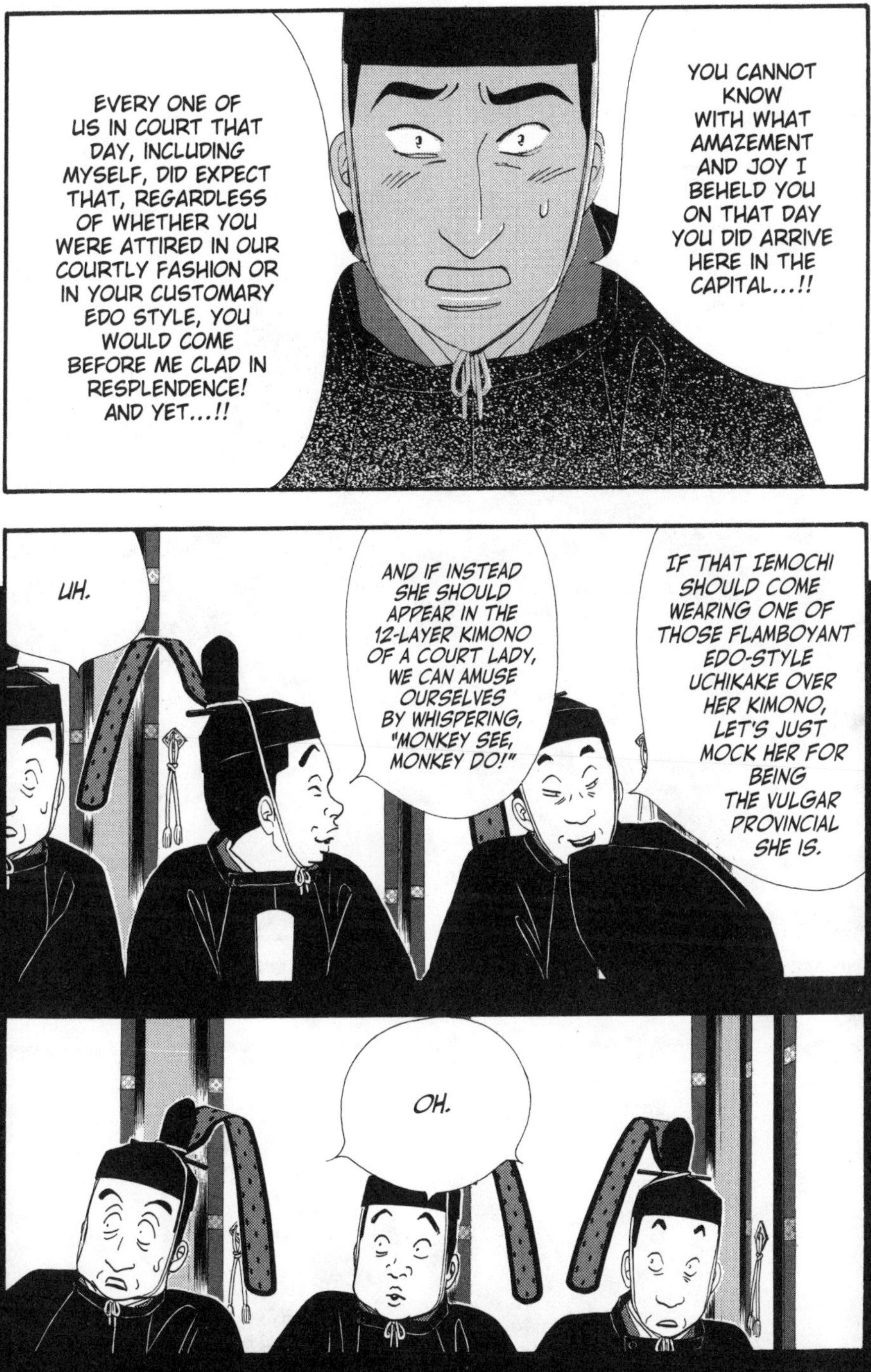
YOU CANNOT KNOW WITH WHAT AMAZEMENT AND JOY I BEHELD YOU ON THAT DAY YOU DID ARRIVE HERE IN THE CAPITAL...!!
EVERY ONE OF US IN COURT THAT DAY, INCLUDING MYSELF, DID EXPECT THAT, REGARDLESS OF WHETHER YOU WERE ATTIRED IN OUR COURTLY FASHION OR IN YOUR CUSTOMARY EDO STYLE, YOU WOULD COME BEFORE ME CLAD IN RESPLENDENCE! AND YET...!!
IF THAT IEMOCHI SHOULD COME WEARING ONE OF THOSE FLAMBOYANT EDO-STYLE UCHIKAKE OVER HER KIMONO, LET'S JUST MOCK HER FOR BEING THE VULGAR PROVINCIAL SHE IS.
AND IF INSTEAD SHE SHOULD APPEAR IN THE 12-LAYER KIMONO OF A COURT LADY, WE CAN AMUSE OURSELVES BY WHISPERING, "MONKEY SEE, MONKEY DO!"
UH.
OH.

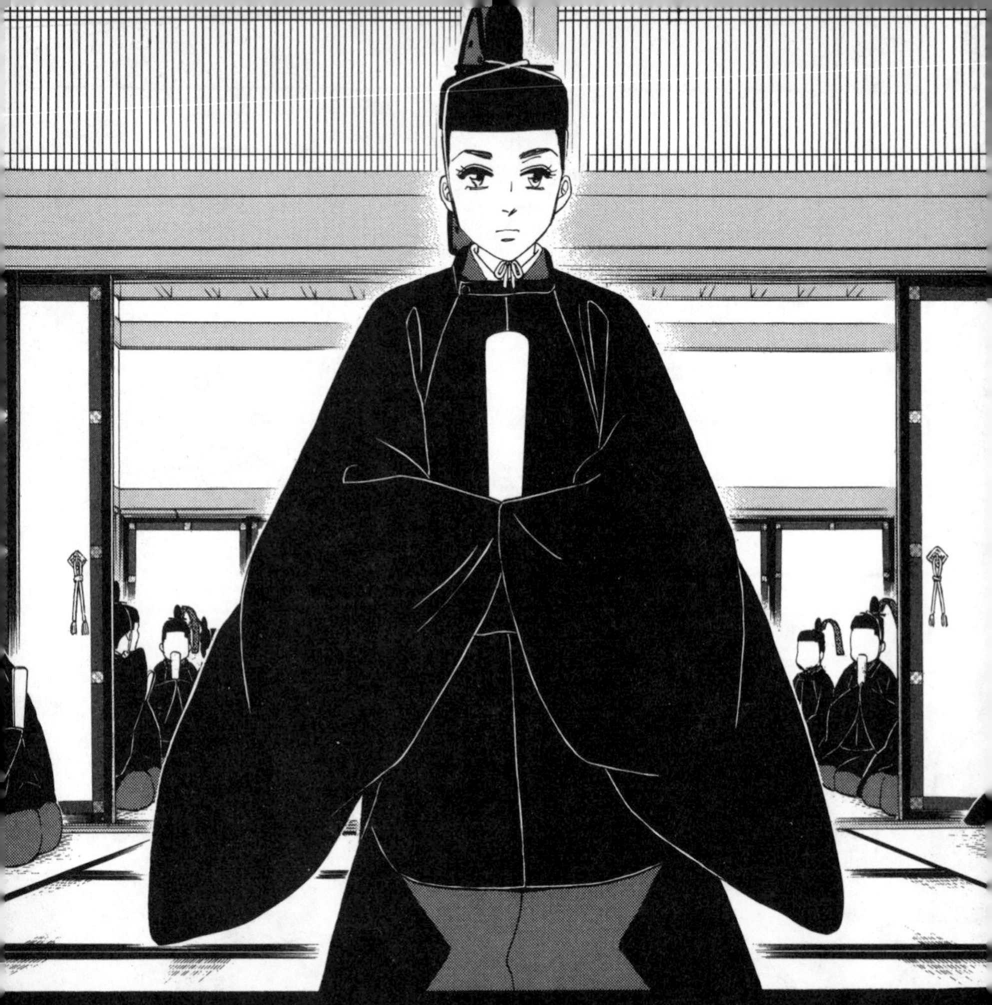
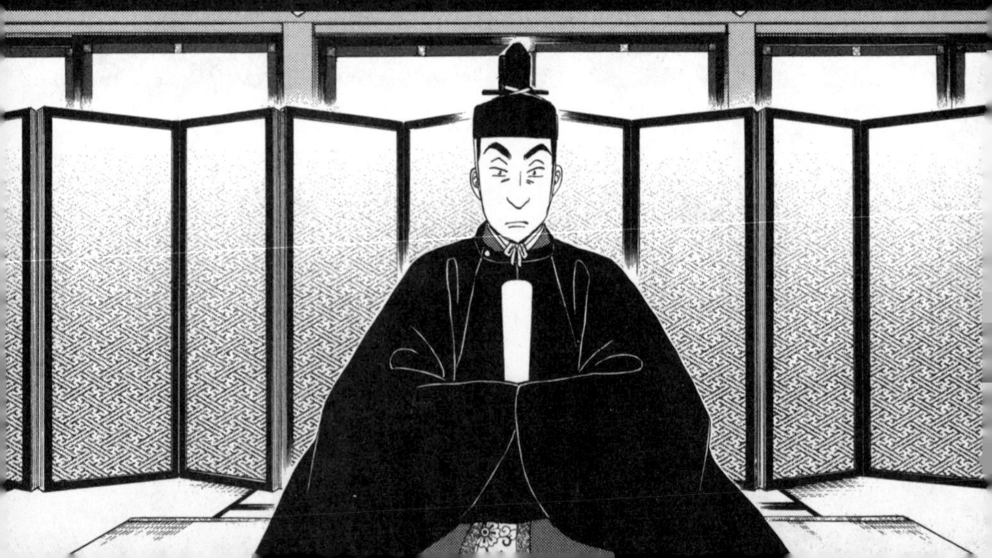

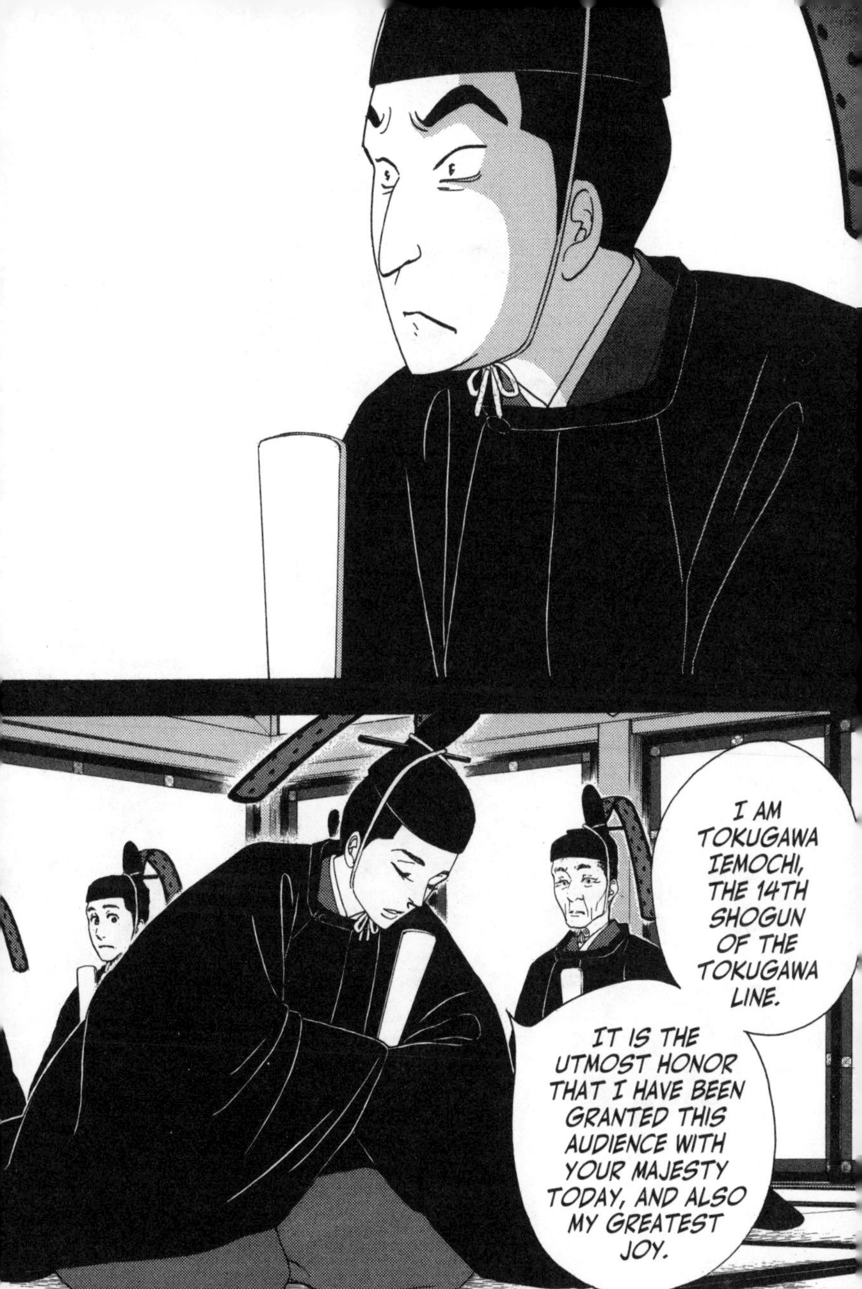
I AM TOKUGAWA IEMOCHI, THE 14TH SHOGUN OF THE TOKUGAWA LINE.
IT IS THE UTMOST HONOR THAT I HAVE BEEN GRANTED THIS AUDIENCE WITH YOUR MAJESTY TODAY, AND ALSO MY GREATEST JOY.

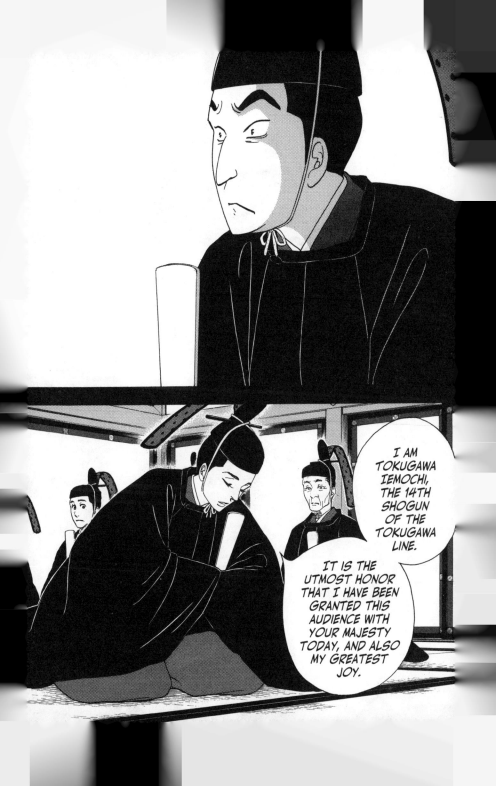

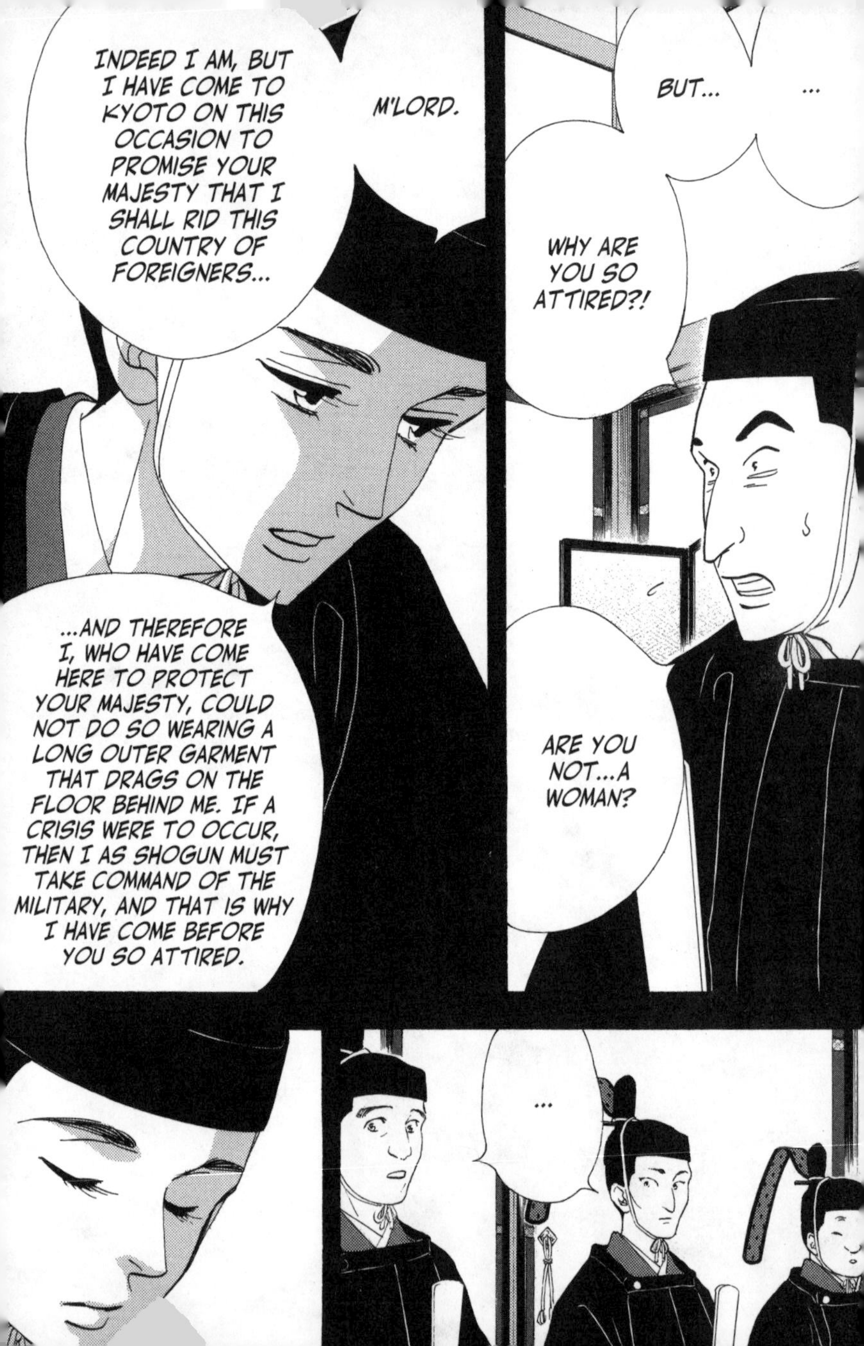
BUT...
...
WHY ARE YOU SO ATTIRED?!
ARE YOU NOT...A WOMAN?
M'LORD.
INDEED I AM, BUT I HAVE COME TO KYOTO ON THIS OCCASION TO PROMISE YOUR MAJESTY THAT I SHALL RID THIS COUNTRY OF FOREIGNERS...
...AND THEREFORE I, WHO HAVE COME HERE TO PROTECT YOUR MAJESTY, COULD NOT DO SO WEARING A LONG OUTER GARMENT THAT DRAGS ON THE FLOOR BEHIND ME. IF A CRISIS WERE TO OCCUR, THEN I AS SHOGUN MUST TAKE COMMAND OF THE MILITARY, AND THAT IS WHY I HAVE COME BEFORE YOU SO ATTIRED.
...

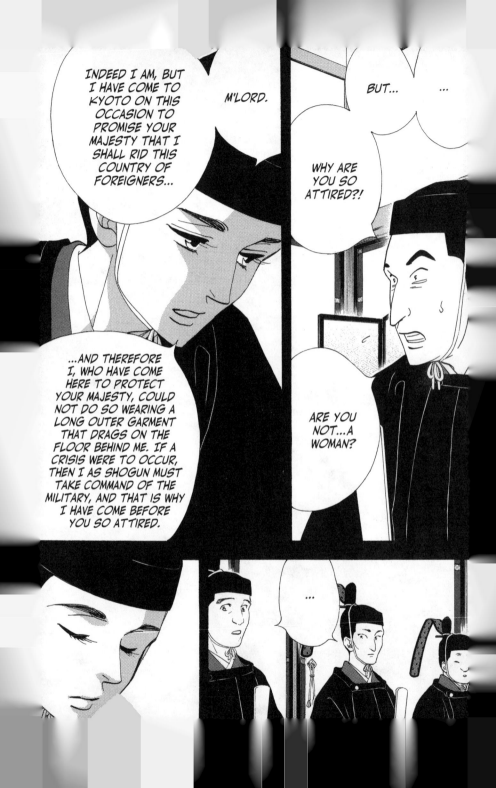

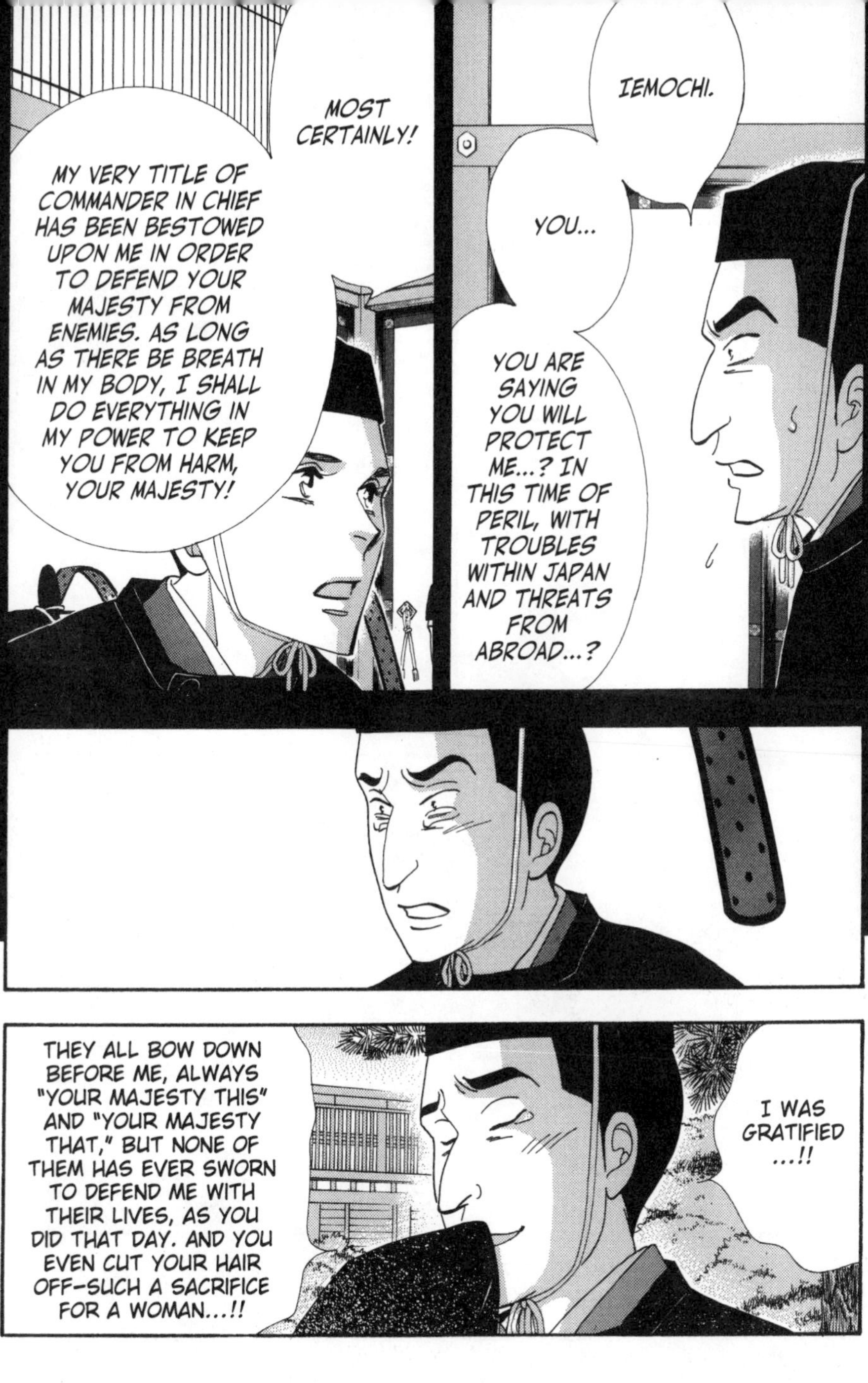
IEMOCHI.
YOU...
YOU ARE SAYING YOU WILL PROTECT ME...? IN THIS TIME OF PERIL, WITH TROUBLES WITHIN JAPAN AND THREATS FROM ABROAD...?
MOST CERTAINLY!
MY VERY TITLE OF COMMANDER IN CHIEF HAS BEEN BESTOWED UPON ME IN ORDER TO DEFEND YOUR MAJESTY FROM ENEMIES. AS LONG AS THERE BE BREATH IN MY BODY, I SHALL DO EVERYTHING IN MY POWER TO KEEP YOU FROM HARM, YOUR MAJESTY!
I WAS GRATIFIED ...!!
THEY ALL BOW DOWN BEFORE ME, ALWAYS "YOUR MAJESTY THIS" AND "YOUR MAJESTY THAT," BUT NONE OF THEM HAS EVER SWORN TO DEFEND ME WITH THEIR LIVES, AS YOU DID THAT DAY. AND YOU EVEN CUT YOUR HAIR OFF—SUCH A SACRIFICE FOR A WOMAN...!!

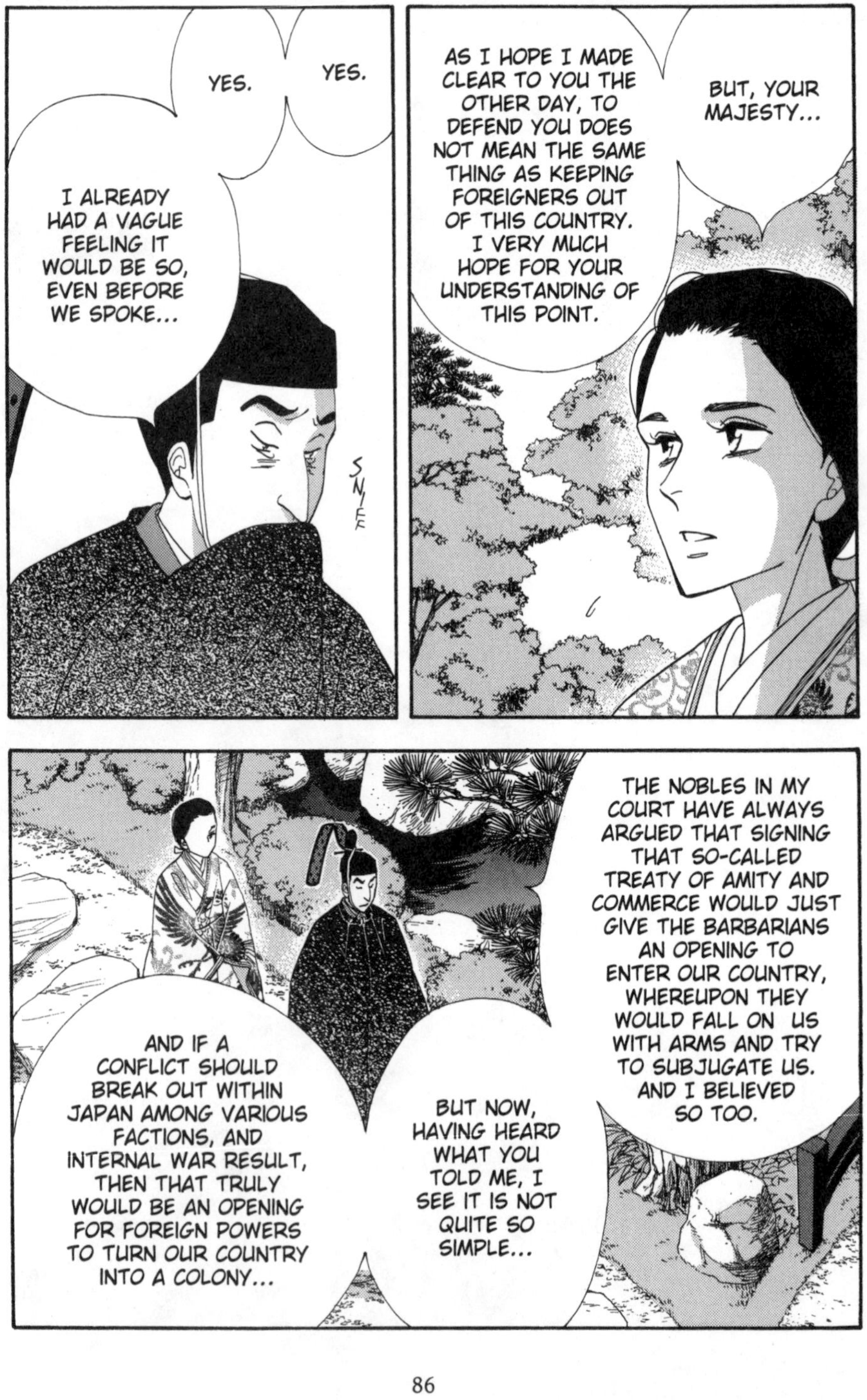
BUT, YOUR MAJESTY...
AS I HOPE I MADE CLEAR TO YOU THE OTHER DAY, TO DEFEND YOU DOES NOT MEAN THE SAME THING AS KEEPING FOREIGNERS OUT OF THIS COUNTRY. I VERY MUCH HOPE FOR YOUR UNDERSTANDING OF THIS POINT.
YES.
YES.
I ALREADY HAD A VAGUE FEELING IT WOULD BE SO, EVEN BEFORE WE SPOKE...
SNIFF
THE NOBLES IN MY COURT HAVE ALWAYS ARGUED THAT SIGNING THAT SO-CALLED TREATY OF AMITY AND COMMERCE WOULD JUST GIVE THE BARBARIANS AN OPENING TO ENTER OUR COUNTRY, WHEREUPON THEY WOULD FALL ON US WITH ARMS AND TRY TO SUBJUGATE US. AND I BELIEVED SO TOO.
BUT NOW, HAVING HEARD WHAT YOU TOLD ME, I SEE IT IS NOT QUITE SO SIMPLE...
AND IF A CONFLICT SHOULD BREAK OUT WITHIN JAPAN AMONG VARIOUS FACTIONS, AND INTERNAL WAR RESULT, THEN THAT TRULY WOULD BE AN OPENING FOR FOREIGN POWERS TO TURN OUR COUNTRY INTO A COLONY...

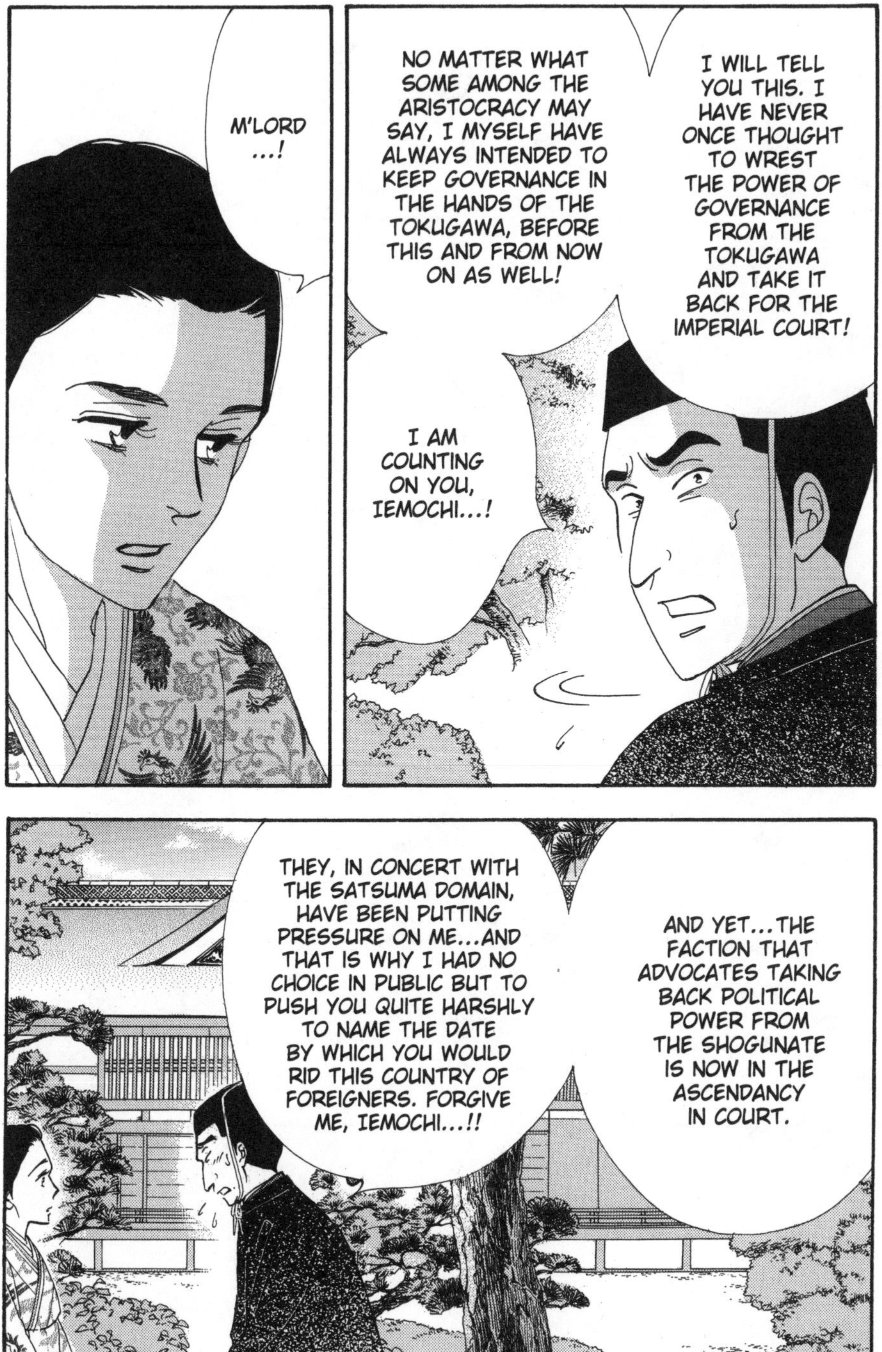
I WILL TELL YOU THIS. I HAVE NEVER ONCE THOUGHT TO WREST THE POWER OF GOVERNANCE FROM THE TOKUGAWA AND TAKE IT BACK FOR THE IMPERIAL COURT!
NO MATTER WHAT SOME AMONG THE ARISTOCRACY MAY SAY, I MYSELF HAVE ALWAYS INTENDED TO KEEP GOVERNANCE IN THE HANDS OF THE TOKUGAWA, BEFORE THIS AND FROM NOW ON AS WELL!
I AM COUNTING ON YOU, IEMOCHI...!
M'LORD ...!
AND YET...THE FACTION THAT ADVOCATES TAKING BACK POLITICAL POWER FROM THE SHOGUNATE IS NOW IN THE ASCENDANCY IN COURT.
THEY, IN CONCERT WITH THE SATSUMA DOMAIN, HAVE BEEN PUTTING PRESSURE ON ME...AND THAT IS WHY I HAD NO CHOICE IN PUBLIC BUT TO PUSH YOU QUITE HARSHLY TO NAME THE DATE BY WHICH YOU WOULD RID THIS COUNTRY OF FOREIGNERS. FORGIVE ME, IEMOCHI...!!

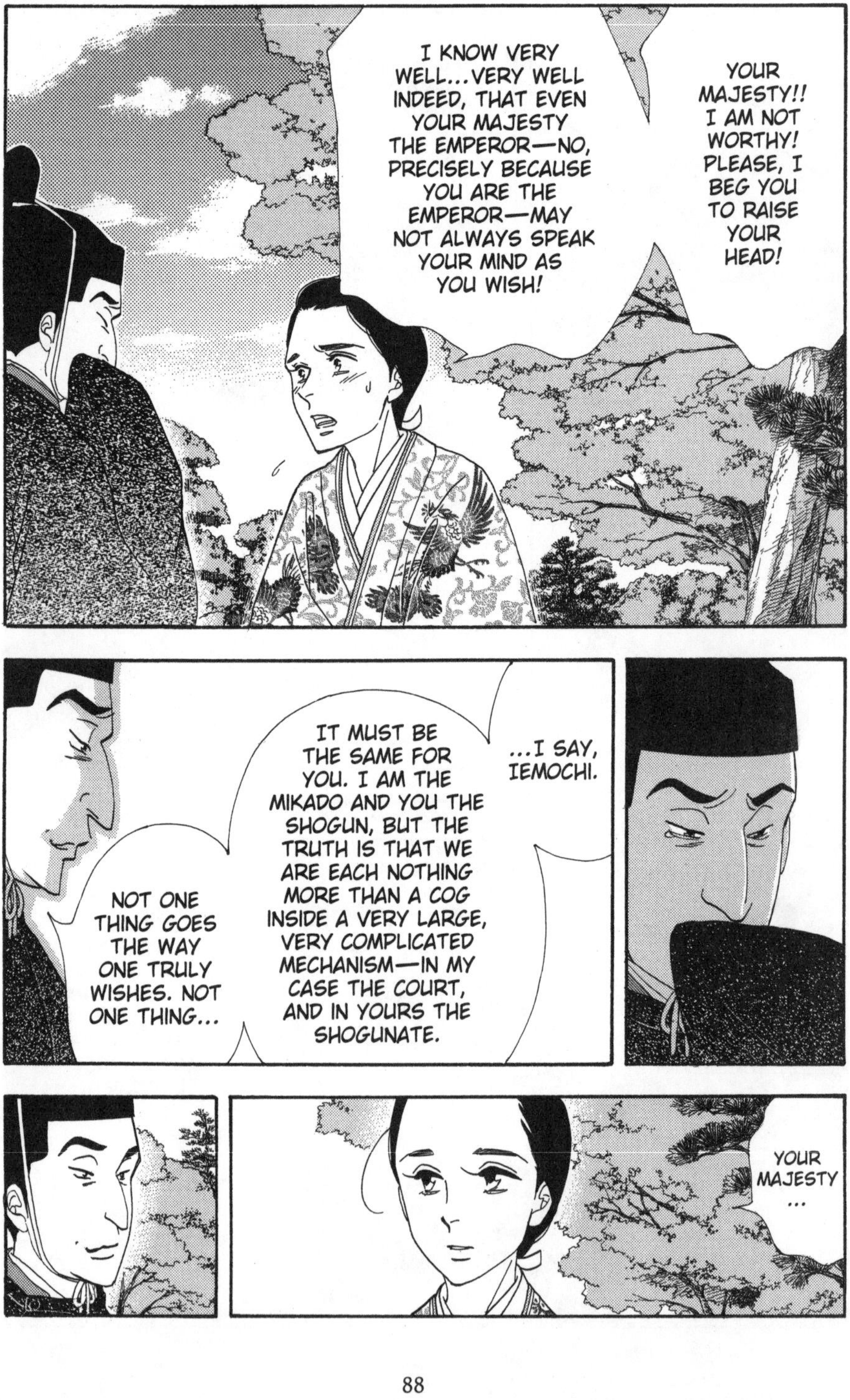
YOUR MAJESTY!! I AM NOT WORTHY! PLEASE, I BEG YOU TO RAISE YOUR HEAD!
I KNOW VERY WELL...VERY WELL INDEED, THAT EVEN YOUR MAJESTY THE EMPEROR—NO, PRECISELY BECAUSE YOU ARE THE EMPEROR—MAY NOT ALWAYS SPEAK YOUR MIND AS YOU WISH!
...I SAY, IEMOCHI.
IT MUST BE THE SAME FOR YOU. I AM THE MIKADO AND YOU THE SHOGUN, BUT THE TRUTH IS THAT WE ARE EACH NOTHING MORE THAN A COG INSIDE A VERY LARGE, VERY COMPLICATED MECHANISM—IN MY CASE THE COURT, AND IN YOURS THE SHOGUNATE.
NOT ONE THING GOES THE WAY ONE TRULY WISHES. NOT ONE THING...
YOUR MAJESTY...

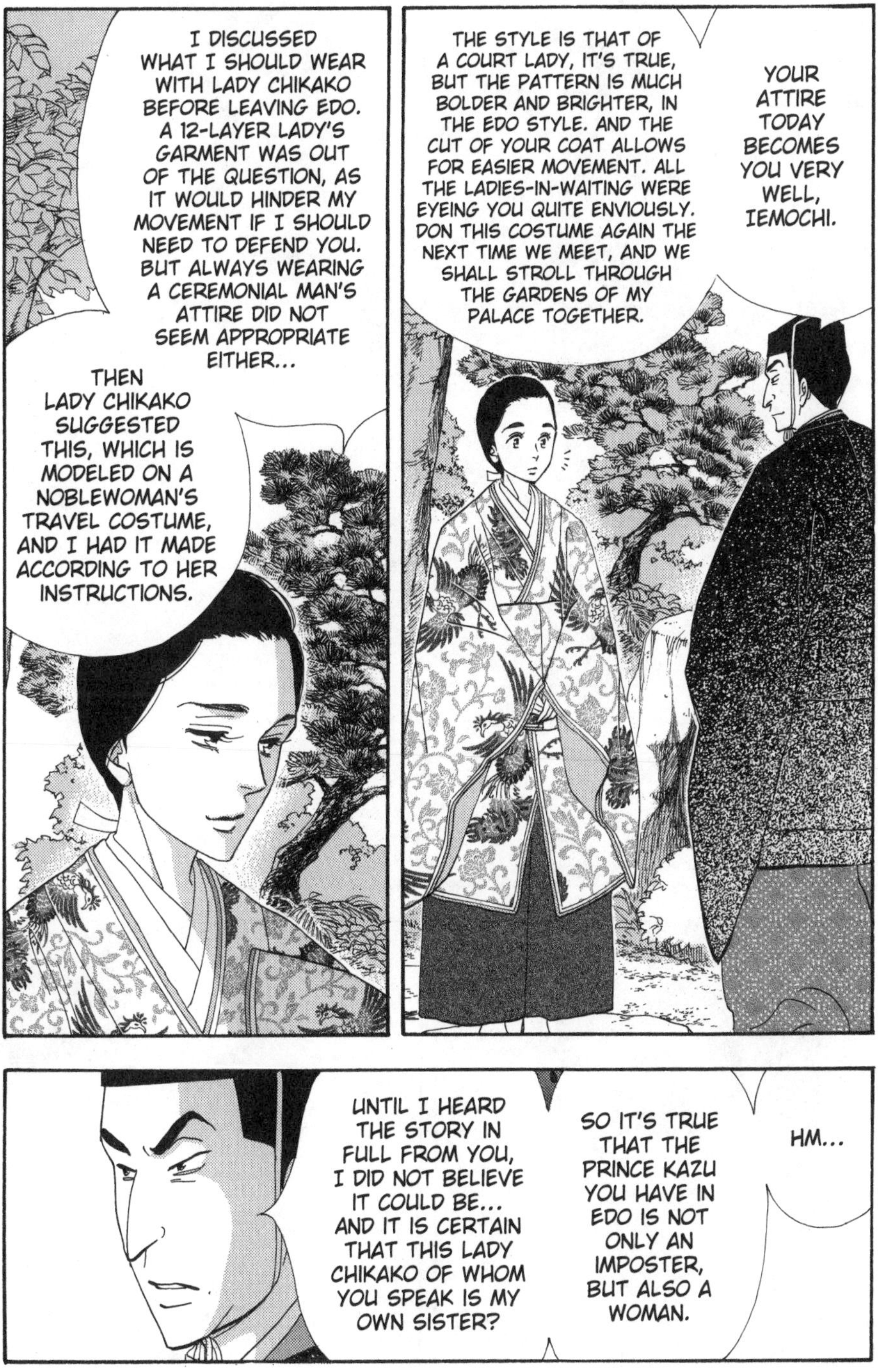
YOUR ATTIRE TODAY BECOMES YOU VERY WELL, IEMOCHI.
THE STYLE IS THAT OF A COURT LADY, IT'S TRUE, BUT THE PATTERN IS MUCH BOLDER AND BRIGHTER, IN THE EDO STYLE. AND THE CUT OF YOUR COAT ALLOWS FOR EASIER MOVEMENT. ALL THE LADIES-IN-WAITING WERE EYEING YOU QUITE ENVIOUSLY. DON THIS COSTUME AGAIN THE NEXT TIME WE MEET, AND WE SHALL STROLL THROUGH THE GARDENS OF MY PALACE TOGETHER.
I DISCUSSED WHAT I SHOULD WEAR WITH LADY CHIKAKO BEFORE LEAVING EDO. A 12-LAYER LADY'S GARMENT WAS OUT OF THE QUESTION, AS IT WOULD HINDER MY MOVEMENT IF I SHOULD NEED TO DEFEND YOU. BUT ALWAYS WEARING A CEREMONIAL MAN'S ATTIRE DID NOT SEEM APPROPRIATE EITHER...
THEN LADY CHIKAKO SUGGESTED THIS, WHICH IS MODELED ON A NOBLEWOMAN'S TRAVEL COSTUME, AND I HAD IT MADE ACCORDING TO HER INSTRUCTIONS.
HM...
SO IT'S TRUE THAT THE PRINCE KAZU YOU HAVE IN EDO IS NOT ONLY AN IMPOSTER, BUT ALSO A WOMAN.
UNTIL I HEARD THE STORY IN FULL FROM YOU, I DID NOT BELIEVE IT COULD BE... AND IT IS CERTAIN THAT THIS LADY CHIKAKO OF WHOM YOU SPEAK IS MY OWN SISTER?

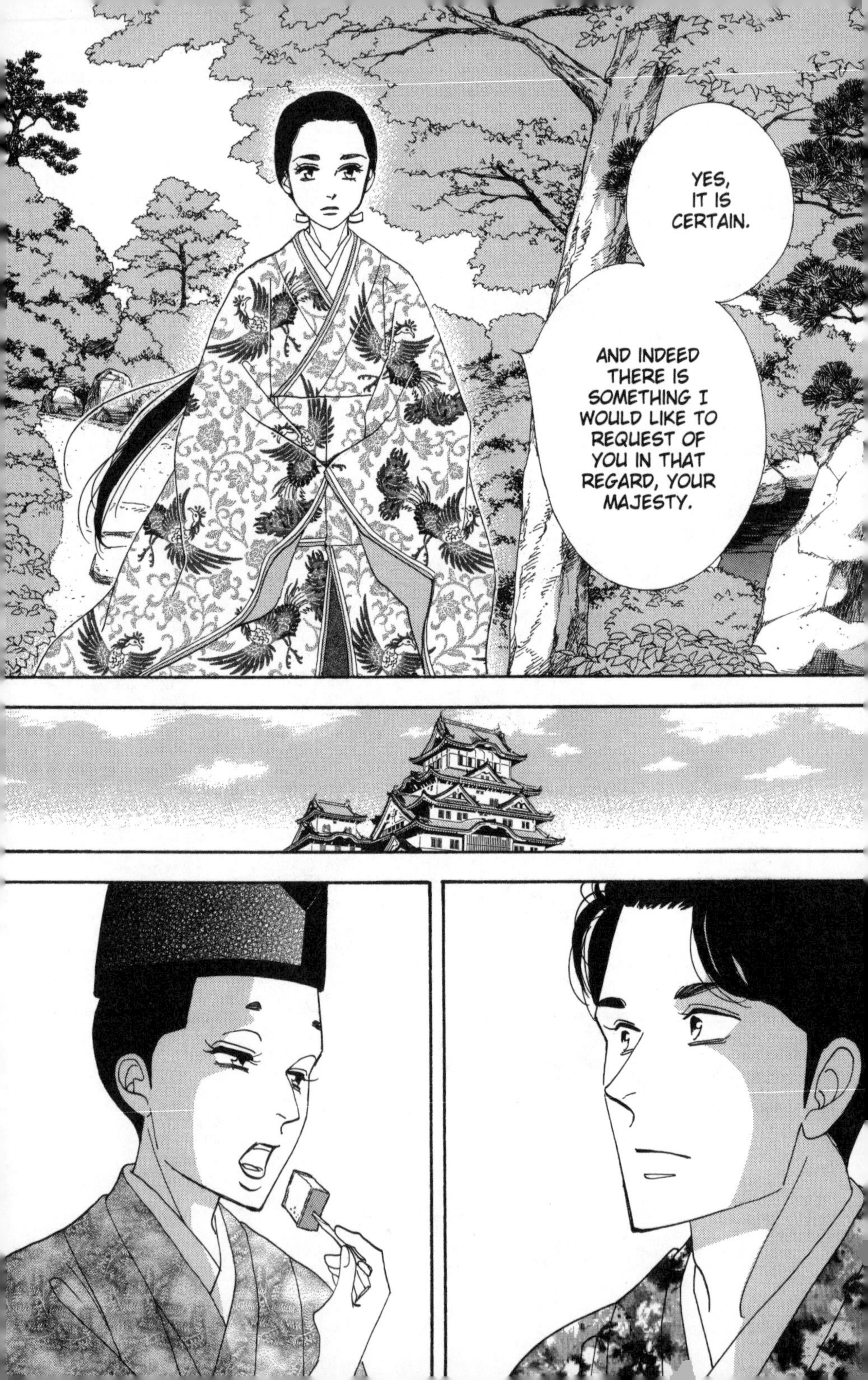
YES, IT IS CERTAIN.
AND INDEED THERE IS SOMETHING I WOULD LIKE TO REQUEST OF YOU IN THAT REGARD, YOUR MAJESTY.

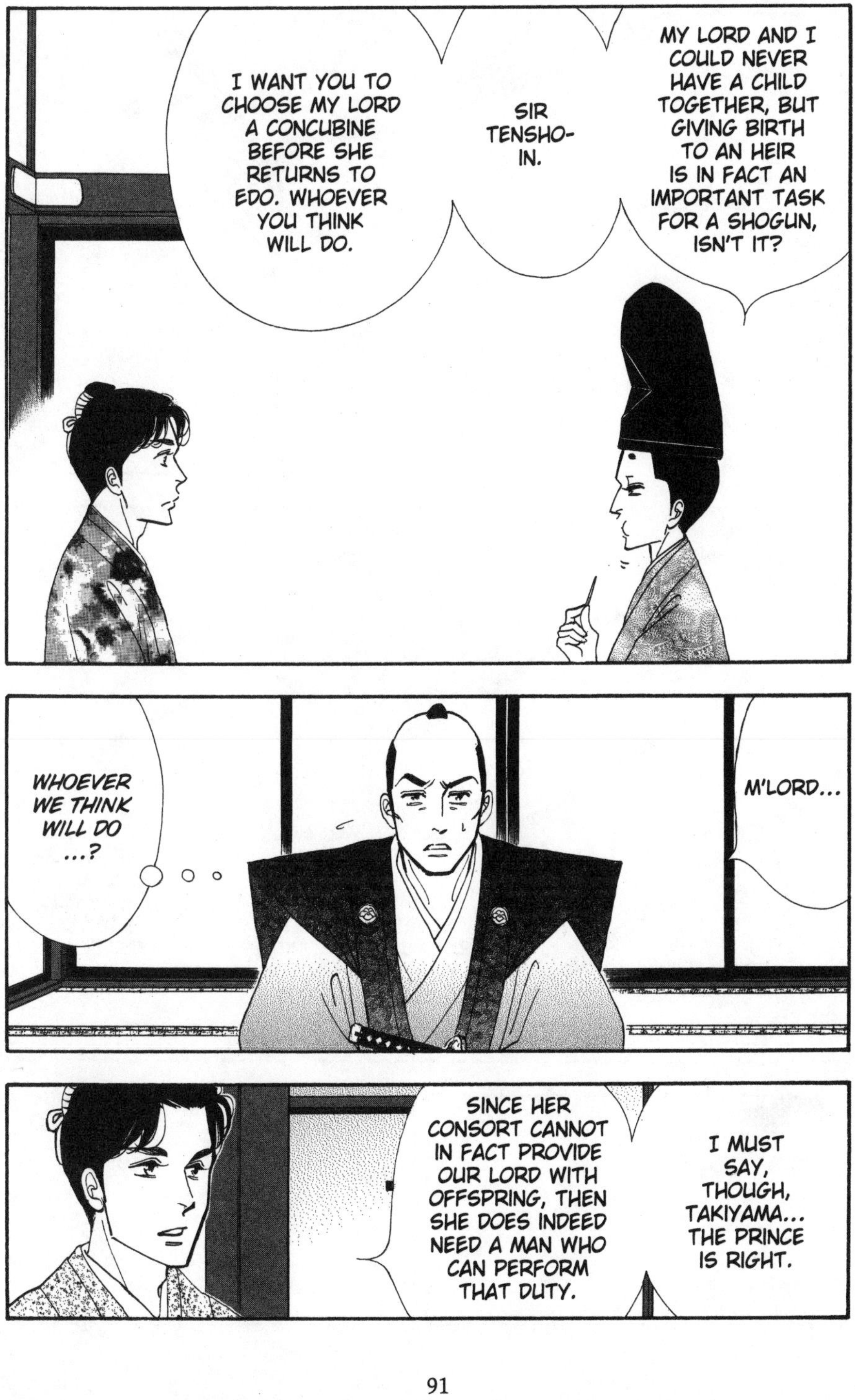
MY LORD AND I COULD NEVER HAVE A CHILD TOGETHER, BUT GIVING BIRTH TO AN HEIR IS IN FACT AN IMPORTANT TASK FOR A SHOGUN, ISN'T IT?
SIR TENSHO-IN.
I WANT YOU TO CHOOSE MY LORD A CONCUBINE BEFORE SHE RETURNS TO EDO. WHOEVER YOU THINK WILL DO.
M'LORD...
WHOEVER WE THINK WILL DO ...?
I MUST SAY, THOUGH, TAKIYAMA... THE PRINCE IS RIGHT.
SINCE HER CONSORT CANNOT IN FACT PROVIDE OUR LORD WITH OFFSPRING, THEN SHE DOES INDEED NEED A MAN WHO CAN PERFORM THAT DUTY.

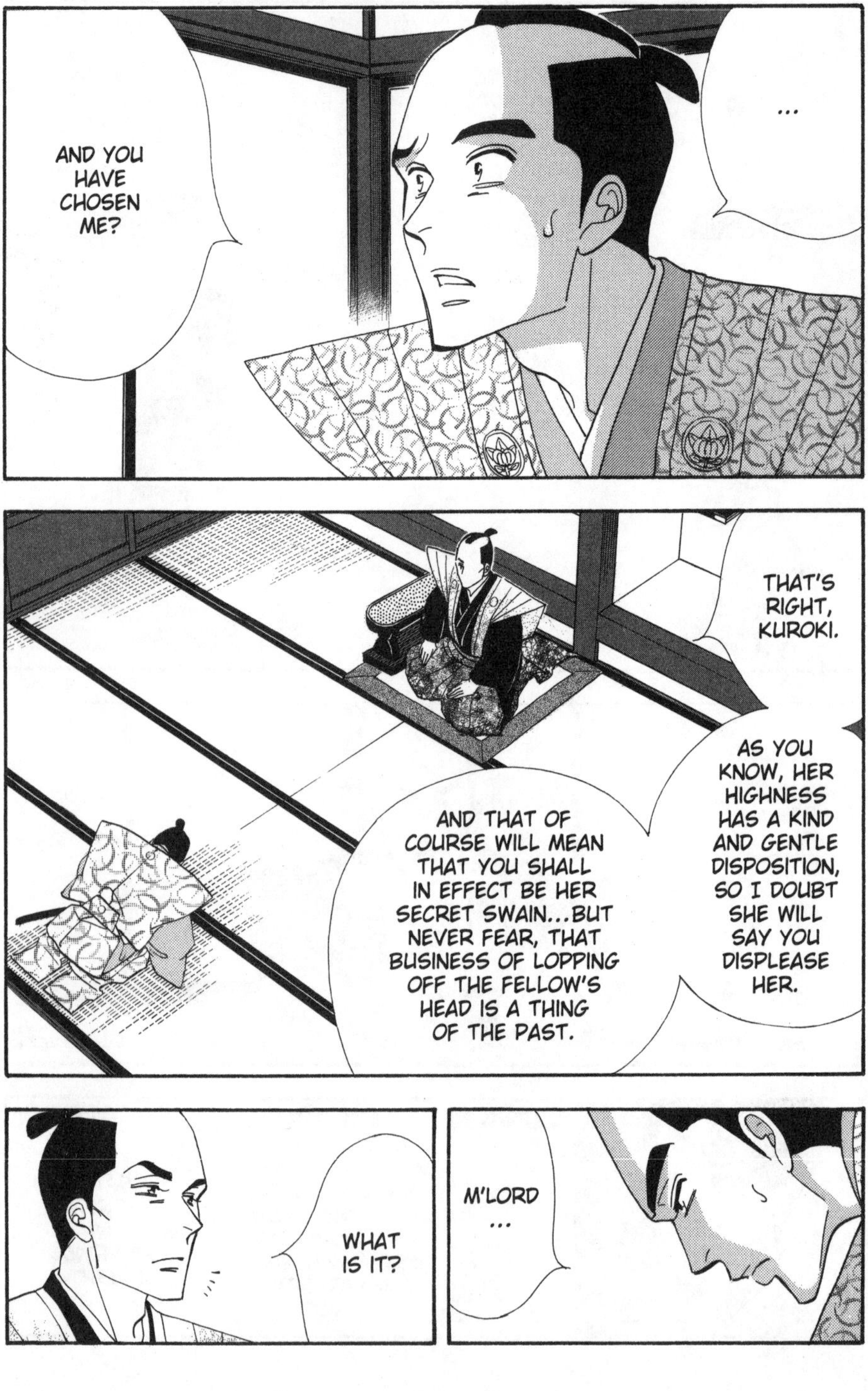
...
AND YOU HAVE CHOSEN ME?
THAT'S RIGHT, KUROKI.
AS YOU KNOW, HER HIGHNESS HAS A KIND AND GENTLE DISPOSITION, SO I DOUBT SHE WILL SAY YOU DISPLEASE HER.
AND THAT OF COURSE WILL MEAN THAT YOU SHALL IN EFFECT BE HER SECRET SWAIN...BUT NEVER FEAR, THAT BUSINESS OF LOPPING OFF THE FELLOW'S HEAD IS A THING OF THE PAST.
M'LORD ...
WHAT IS IT?

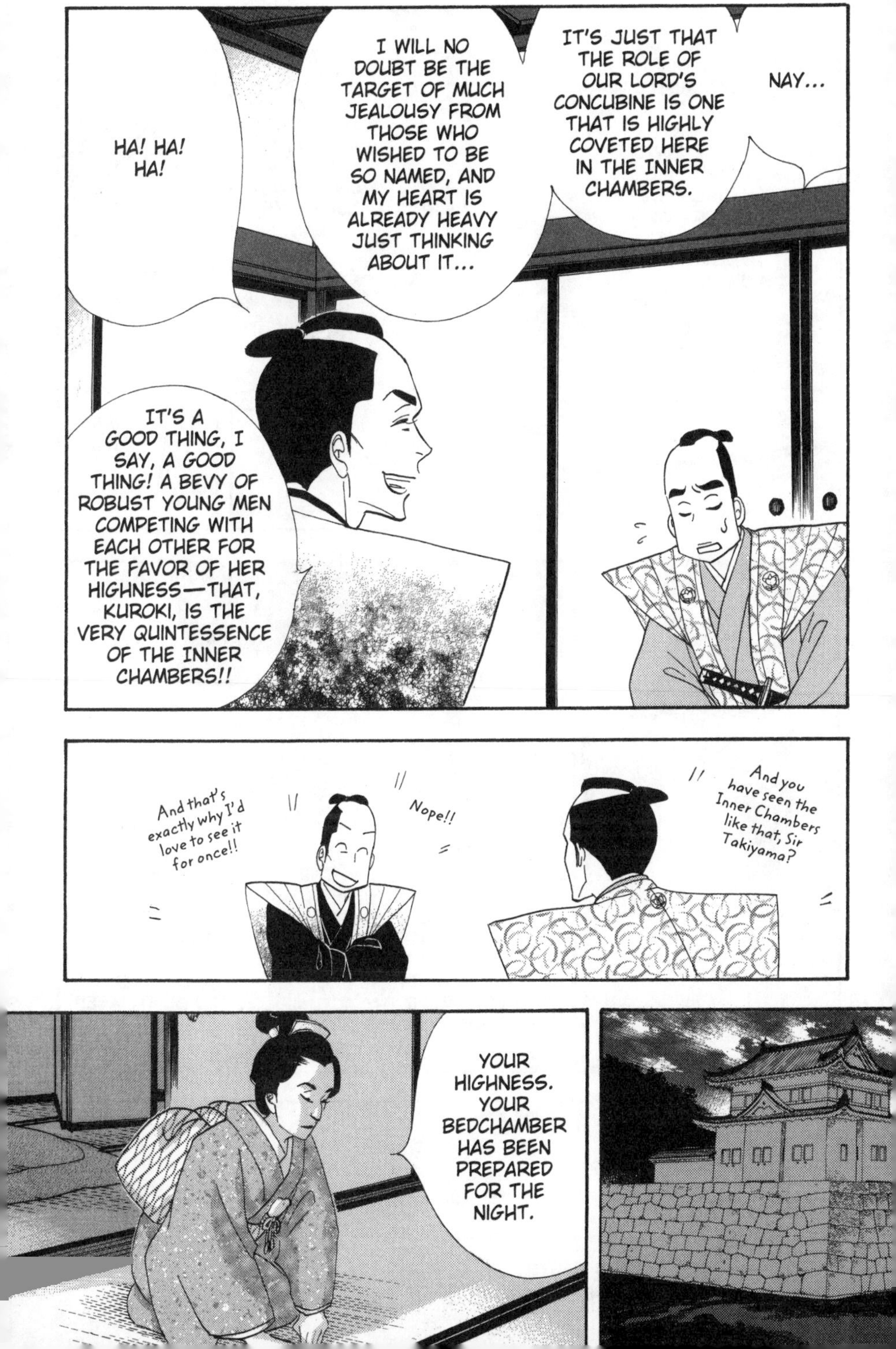
NAY...
IT'S JUST THAT THE ROLE OF OUR LORD'S CONCUBINE IS ONE THAT IS HIGHLY COVETED HERE IN THE INNER CHAMBERS.
I WILL NO DOUBT BE THE TARGET OF MUCH JEALOUSY FROM THOSE WHO WISHED TO BE SO NAMED, AND MY HEART IS ALREADY HEAVY JUST THINKING ABOUT IT...
HA! HA! HA!
IT'S A GOOD THING, I SAY, A GOOD THING! A BEVY OF ROBUST YOUNG MEN COMPETING WITH EACH OTHER FOR THE FAVOR OF HER HIGHNESS—THAT, KUROKI, IS THE VERY QUINTESSENCE OF THE INNER CHAMBERS!!
And you have seen the Inner Chambers like that, Sir Takiyama?
Nope!!
And that's exactly why I'd love to see it for once!!
YOUR HIGHNESS. YOUR BEDCHAMBER HAS BEEN PREPARED FOR THE NIGHT.

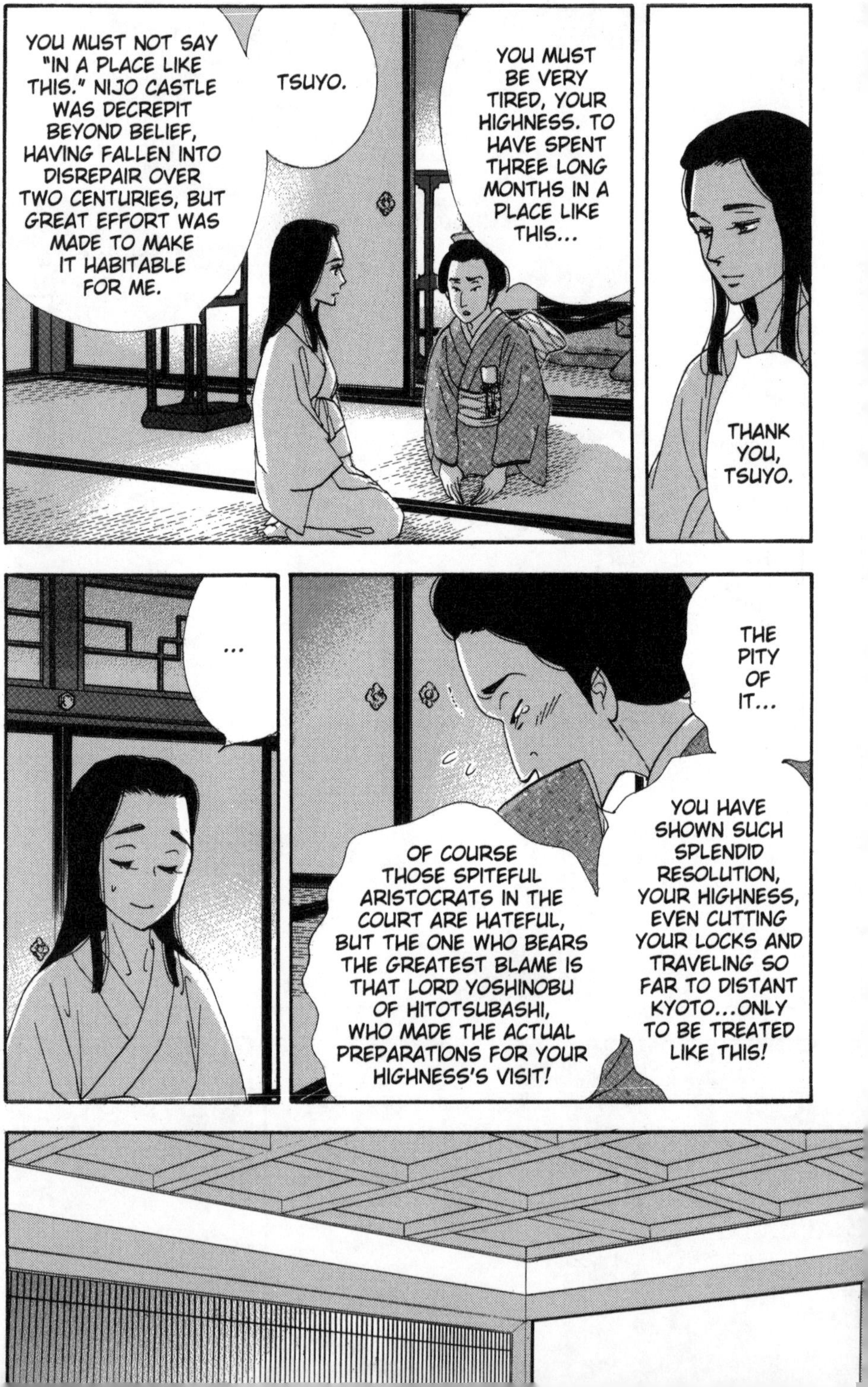
THANK YOU, TSUYO.
YOU MUST BE VERY TIRED, YOUR HIGHNESS. TO HAVE SPENT THREE LONG MONTHS IN A PLACE LIKE THIS...
TSUYO.
YOU MUST NOT SAY "IN A PLACE LIKE THIS." NIJO CASTLE WAS DECREPIT BEYOND BELIEF, HAVING FALLEN INTO DISREPAIR OVER TWO CENTURIES, BUT GREAT EFFORT WAS MADE TO MAKE IT HABITABLE FOR ME.
THE PITY OF IT...
YOU HAVE SHOWN SUCH SPLENDID RESOLUTION, YOUR HIGHNESS, EVEN CUTTING YOUR LOCKS AND TRAVELING SO FAR TO DISTANT KYOTO...ONLY TO BE TREATED LIKE THIS!
OF COURSE THOSE SPITEFUL ARISTOCRATS IN THE COURT ARE HATEFUL, BUT THE ONE WHO BEARS THE GREATEST BLAME IS THAT LORD YOSHINOBU OF HITOTSUBASHI, WHO MADE THE ACTUAL PREPARATIONS FOR YOUR HIGHNESS'S VISIT!
...

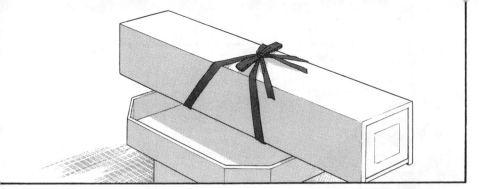

YOUR MAJESTY. IS THIS...?!

IT'S A MISSIVE, IN MY OWN HAND.

IT IS WRITTEN THERE THAT CHIKAKO, WHILE SHE IS NOT PRINCE KAZU, IS INDEED MY OWN SISTER, AND THEREFORE AN IMPERIAL PRINCESS.

I HOPE THAT IF, IN FUTURE, ANY UNFORESEEN SITUATION SHOULD ARISE IN EDO, IT WILL SERVE TO VOUCHSAFE HER SECURITY...

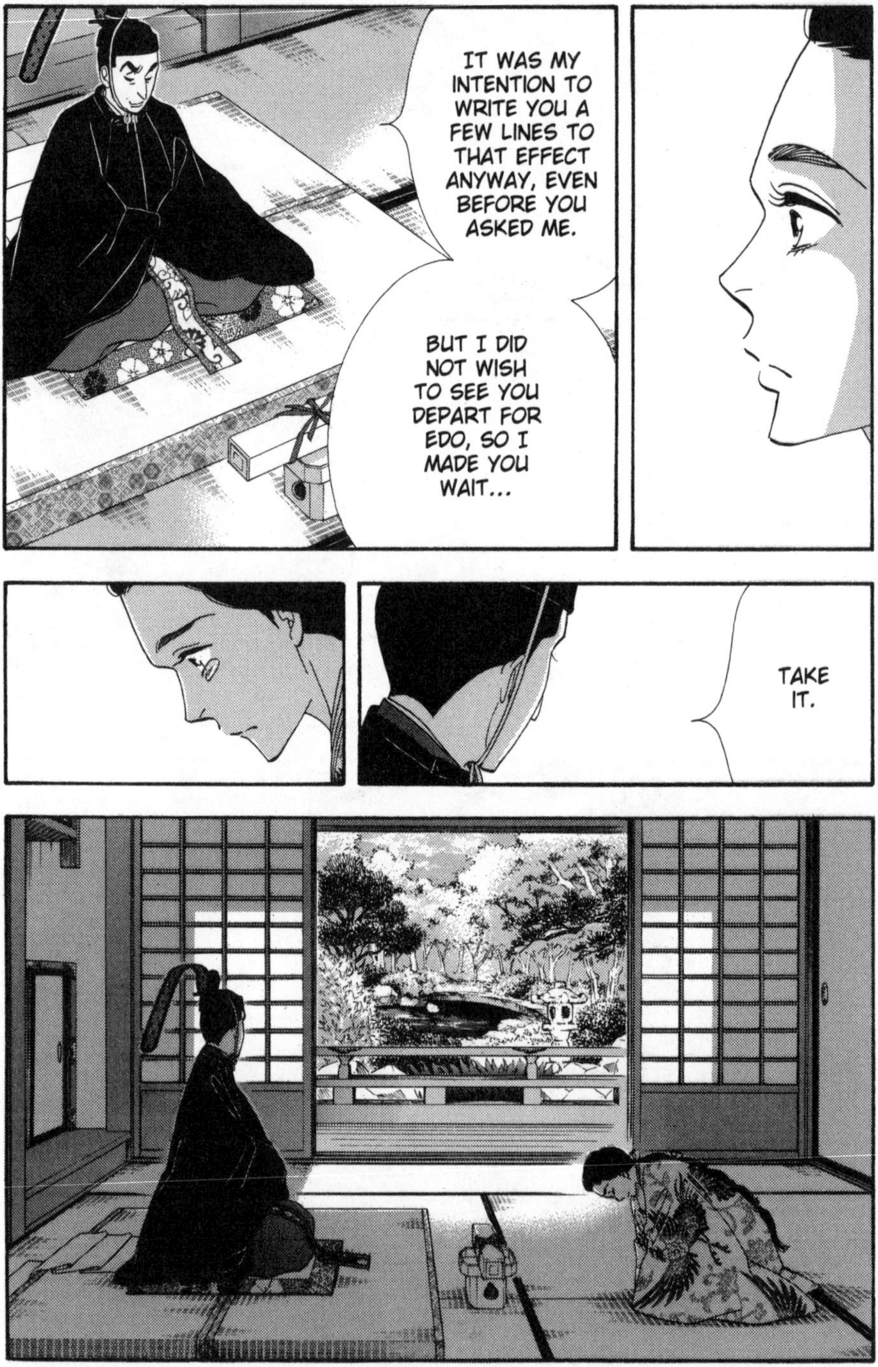
IT WAS MY INTENTION TO WRITE YOU A FEW LINES TO THAT EFFECT ANYWAY, EVEN BEFORE YOU ASKED ME.
BUT I DID NOT WISH TO SEE YOU DEPART FOR EDO, SO I MADE YOU WAIT...
TAKE IT.

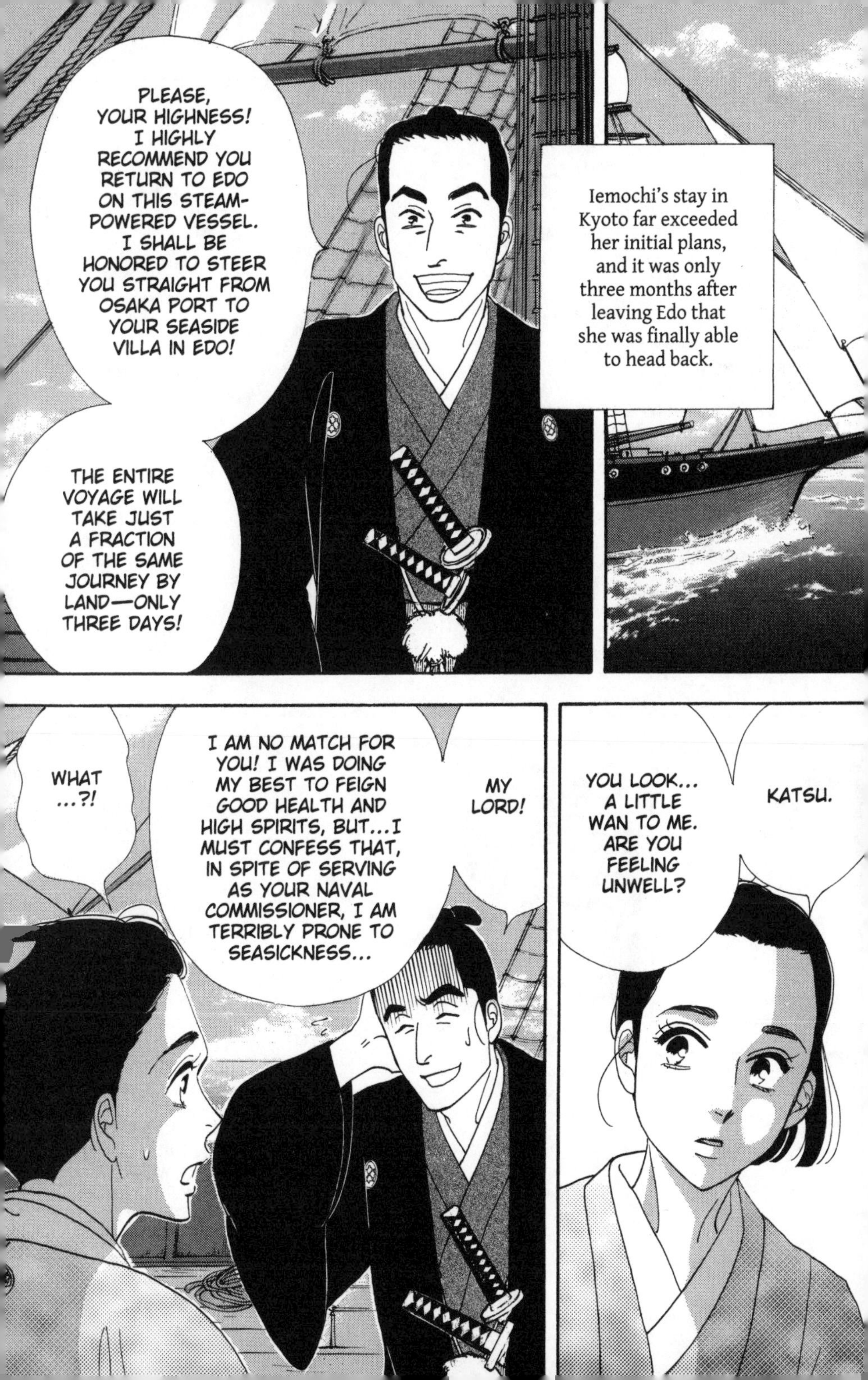
Iemochi's stay in Kyoto far exceeded her initial plans, and it was only three months after leaving Edo that she was finally able to head back.
PLEASE, YOUR HIGHNESS! I HIGHLY RECOMMEND YOU RETURN TO EDO ON THIS STEAM-POWERED VESSEL. I SHALL BE HONORED TO STEER YOU STRAIGHT FROM OSAKA PORT TO YOUR SEASIDE VILLA IN EDO!
THE ENTIRE VOYAGE WILL TAKE JUST A FRACTION OF THE SAME JOURNEY BY LAND—ONLY THREE DAYS!
KATSU.
YOU LOOK... A LITTLE WAN TO ME. ARE YOU FEELING UNWELL?
MY LORD!
I AM NO MATCH FOR YOU! I WAS DOING MY BEST TO FEIGN GOOD HEALTH AND HIGH SPIRITS, BUT...I MUST CONFESS THAT, IN SPITE OF SERVING AS YOUR NAVAL COMMISSIONER, I AM TERRIBLY PRONE TO SEASICKNESS...
WHAT...?!

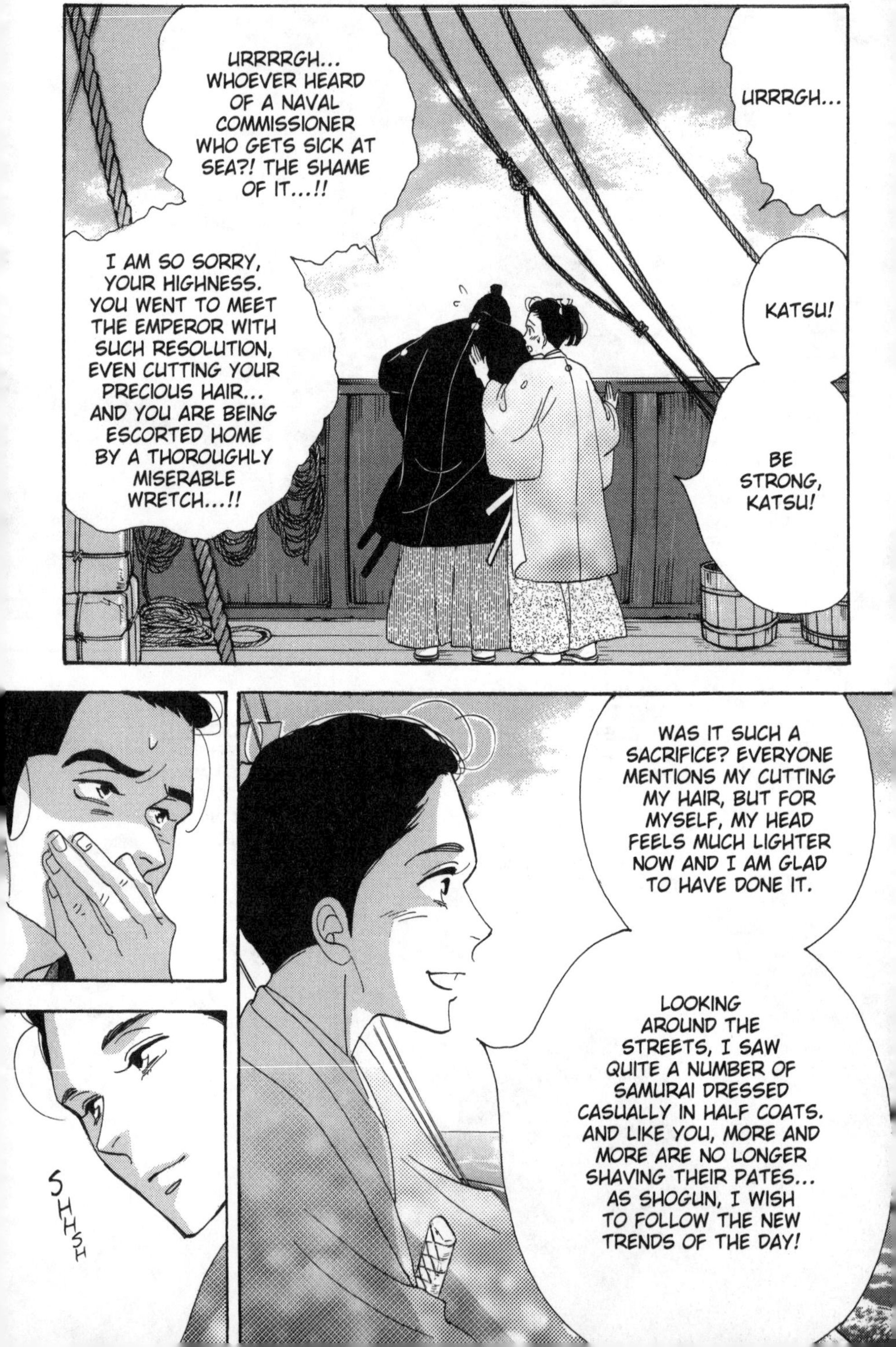
URRRGH...
URRRRGH... WHOEVER HEARD OF A NAVAL COMMISSIONER WHO GETS SICK AT SEA?! THE SHAME OF IT...!!
KATSU!
BE STRONG, KATSU!
I AM SO SORRY, YOUR HIGHNESS. YOU WENT TO MEET THE EMPEROR WITH SUCH RESOLUTION, EVEN CUTTING YOUR PRECIOUS HAIR... AND YOU ARE BEING ESCORTED HOME BY A THOROUGHLY MISERABLE WRETCH...!!
WAS IT SUCH A SACRIFICE? EVERYONE MENTIONS MY CUTTING MY HAIR, BUT FOR MYSELF, MY HEAD FEELS MUCH LIGHTER NOW AND I AM GLAD TO HAVE DONE IT.
LOOKING AROUND THE STREETS, I SAW QUITE A NUMBER OF SAMURAI DRESSED CASUALLY IN HALF COATS. AND LIKE YOU, MORE AND MORE ARE NO LONGER SHAVING THEIR PATES... AS SHOGUN, I WISH TO FOLLOW THE NEW TRENDS OF THE DAY!
SHHSH

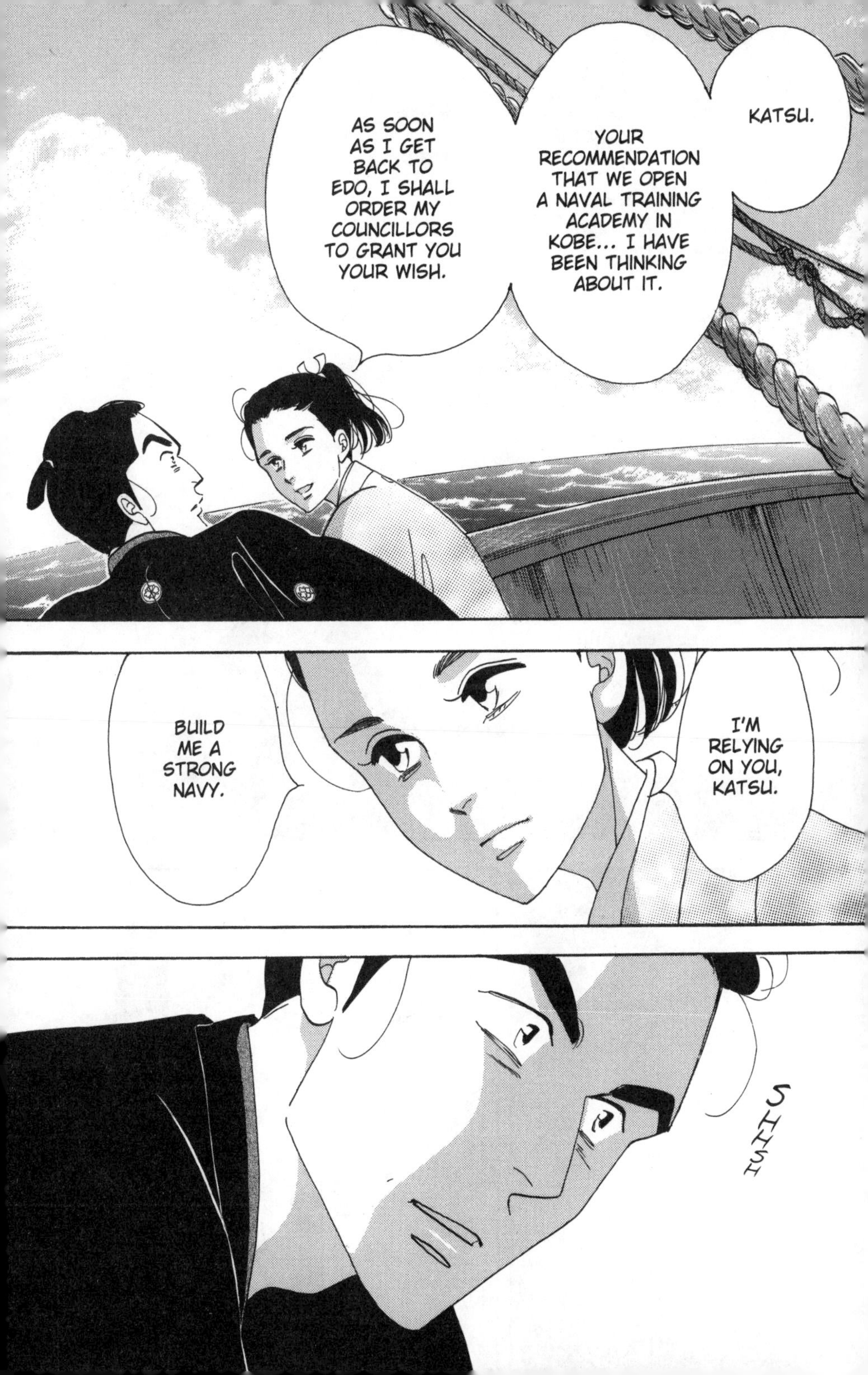
KATSU.
YOUR RECOMMENDATION THAT WE OPEN A NAVAL TRAINING ACADEMY IN KOBE... I HAVE BEEN THINKING ABOUT IT.
AS SOON AS I GET BACK TO EDO, I SHALL ORDER MY COUNCILLORS TO GRANT YOU YOUR WISH.
I'M RELYING ON YOU, KATSU.
BUILD ME A STRONG NAVY.
SHHSH

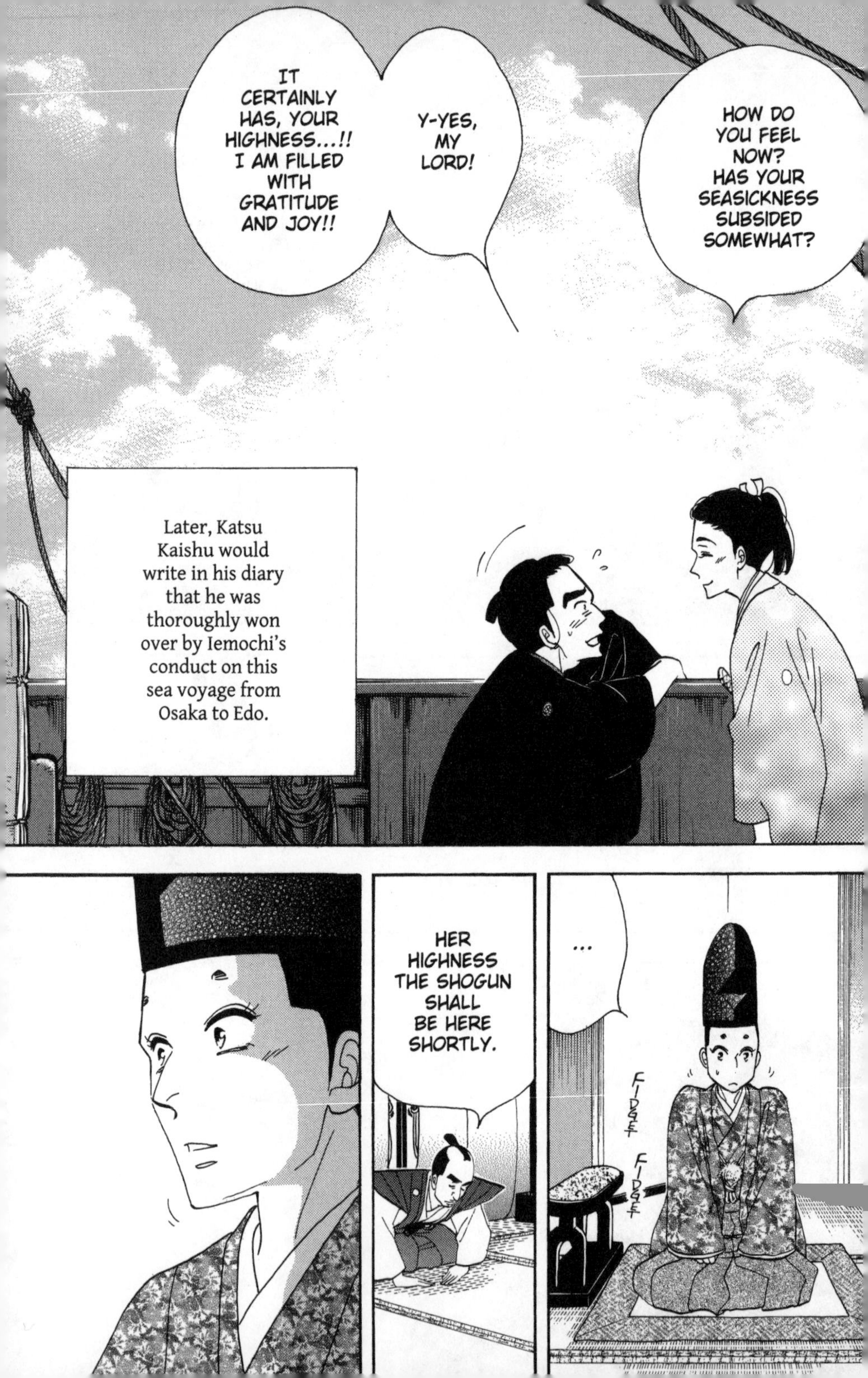
HOW DO YOU FEEL NOW? HAS YOUR SEASICKNESS SUBSIDED SOMEWHAT?
Y-YES, MY LORD!
IT CERTAINLY HAS, YOUR HIGHNESS...!! I AM FILLED WITH GRATITUDE AND JOY!!
Later, Katsu Kaishu would write in his diary that he was thoroughly won over by Iemochi's conduct on this sea voyage from Osaka to Edo.
...
FIDGET FIDGET
HER HIGHNESS THE SHOGUN SHALL BE HERE SHORTLY.

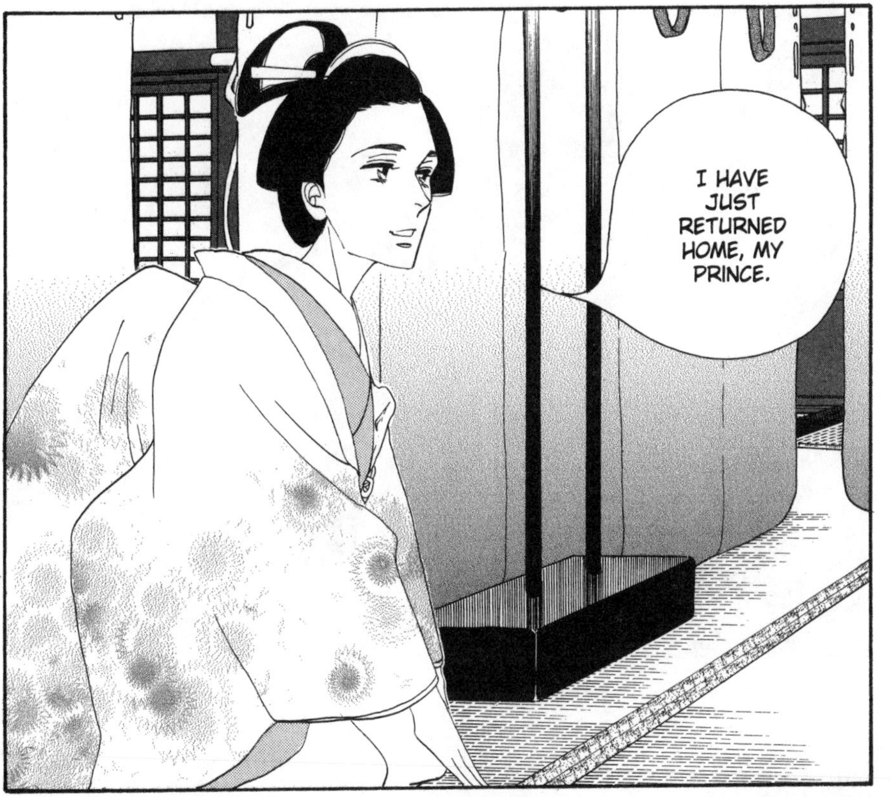
I HAVE JUST RETURNED HOME, MY PRINCE.

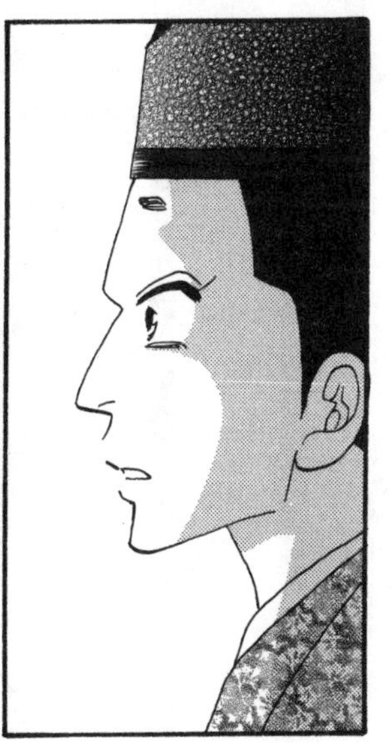

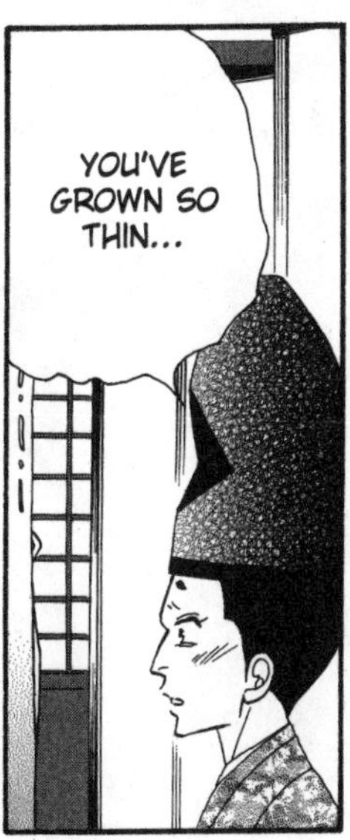
YOU'VE GROWN SO THIN...

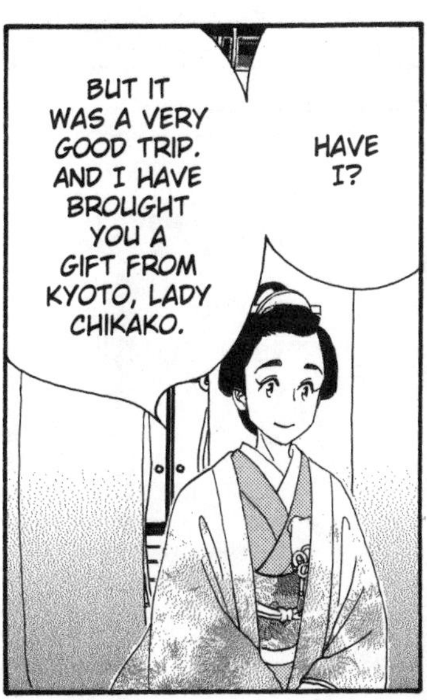
HAVE I?
BUT IT WAS A VERY GOOD TRIP. AND I HAVE BROUGHT YOU A GIFT FROM KYOTO, LADY CHIKAKO.

OH MY... WHAT A BEAUTIFULLY PATTERNED ROBE THIS IS!

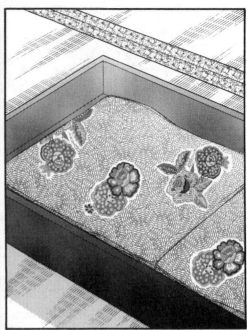

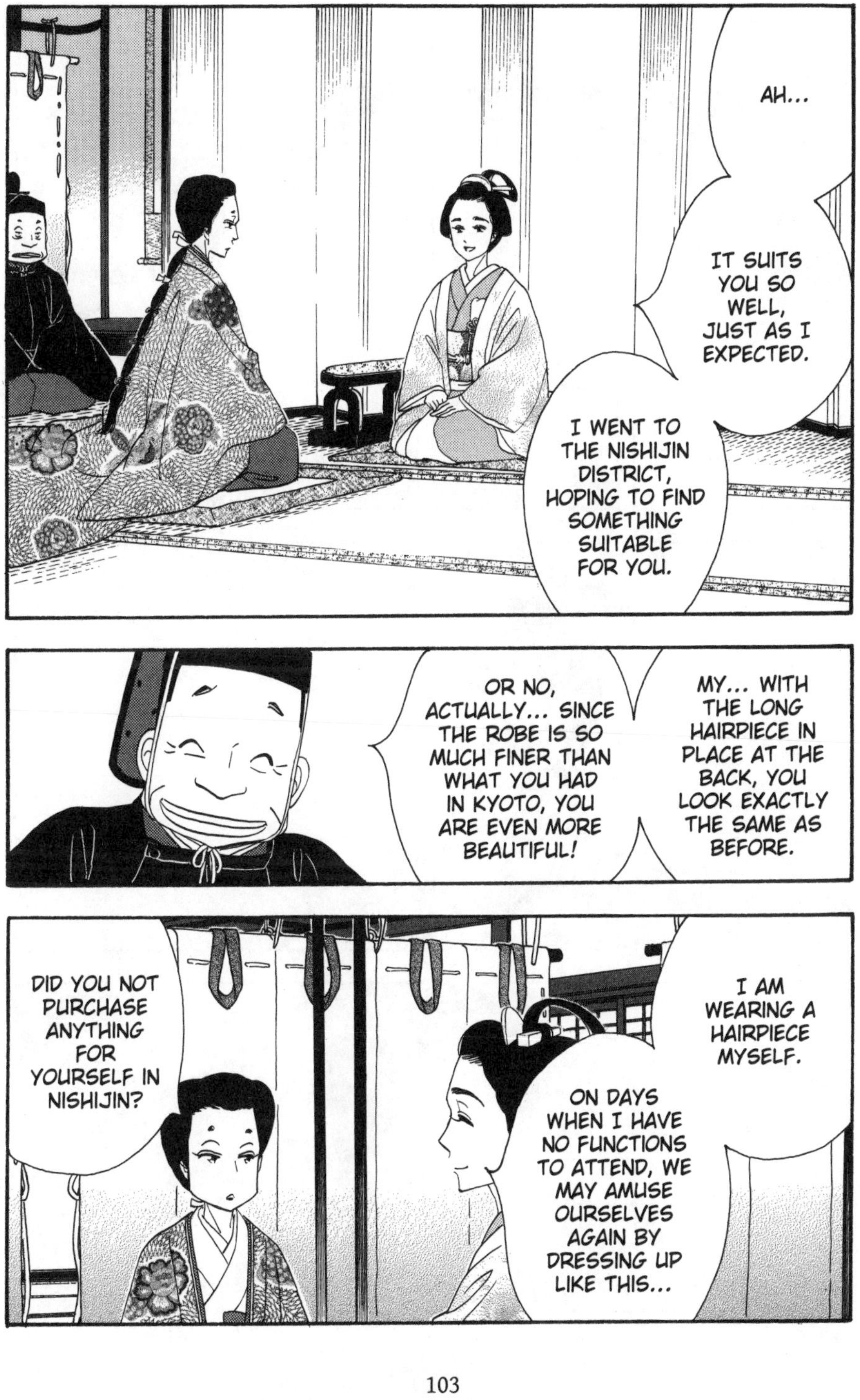
AH...
IT SUITS YOU SO WELL, JUST AS I EXPECTED.
I WENT TO THE NISHIJIN DISTRICT, HOPING TO FIND SOMETHING SUITABLE FOR YOU.
MY... WITH THE LONG HAIRPIECE IN PLACE AT THE BACK, YOU LOOK EXACTLY THE SAME AS BEFORE.
OR NO, ACTUALLY... SINCE THE ROBE IS SO MUCH FINER THAN WHAT YOU HAD IN KYOTO, YOU ARE EVEN MORE BEAUTIFUL!
I AM WEARING A HAIRPIECE MYSELF.
ON DAYS WHEN I HAVE NO FUNCTIONS TO ATTEND, WE MAY AMUSE OURSELVES AGAIN BY DRESSING UP LIKE THIS...
DID YOU NOT PURCHASE ANYTHING FOR YOURSELF IN NISHIJIN?

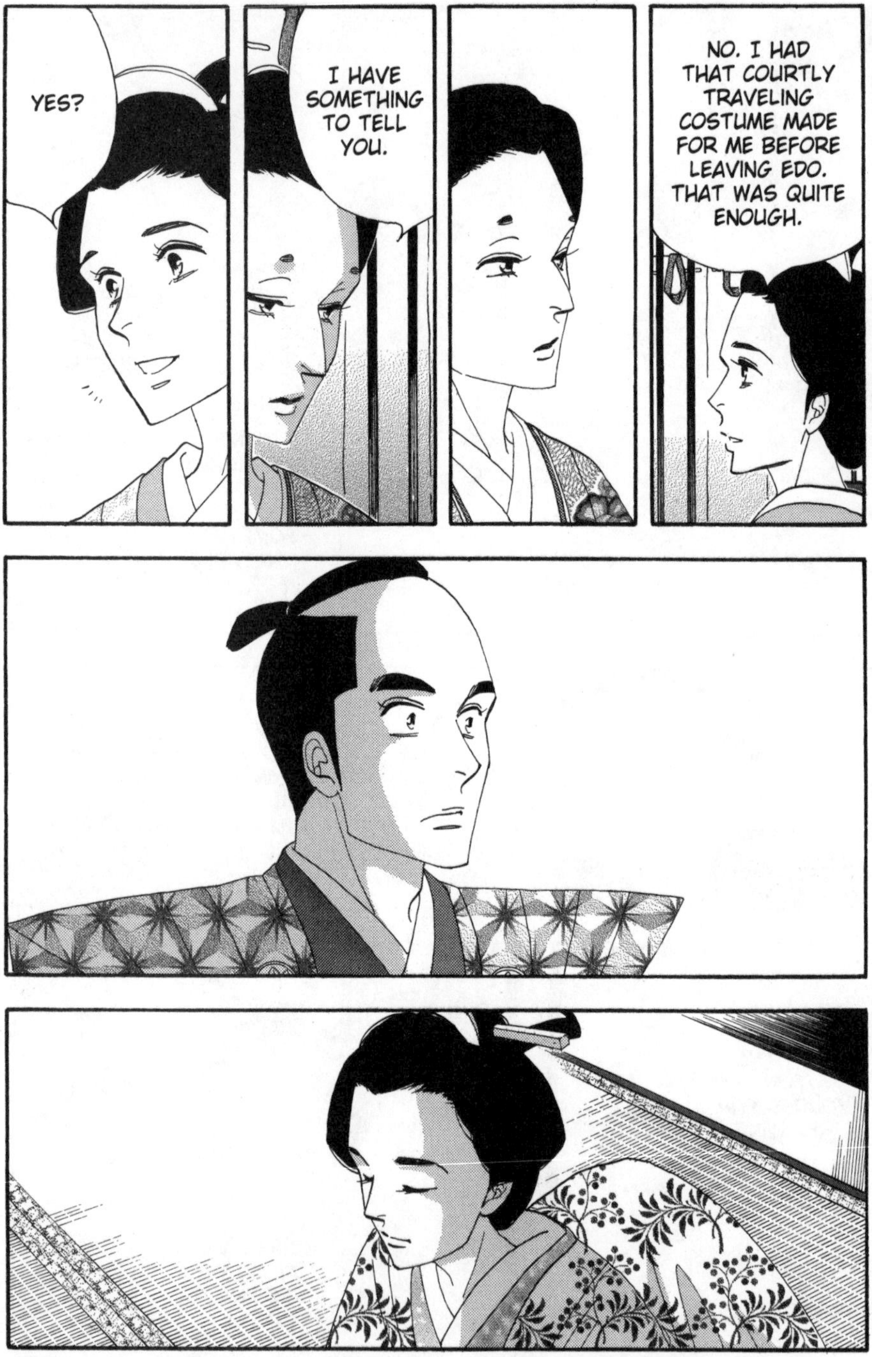
NO. I HAD THAT COURTLY TRAVELING COSTUME MADE FOR ME BEFORE LEAVING EDO. THAT WAS QUITE ENOUGH.
I HAVE SOMETHING TO TELL YOU.
YES?

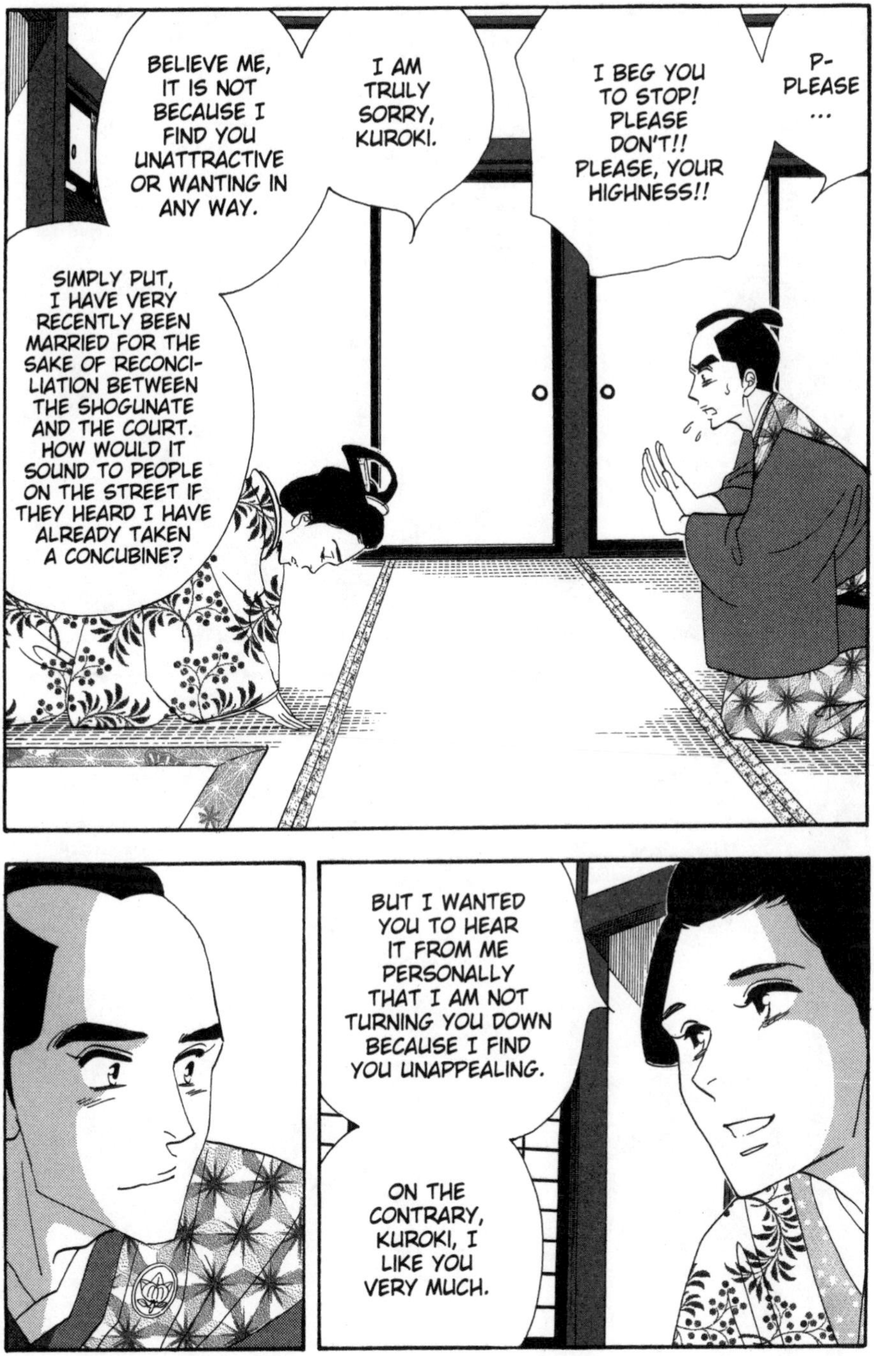
P-PLEASE ...
I BEG YOU TO STOP! PLEASE DON'T!! PLEASE, YOUR HIGHNESS!!
I AM TRULY SORRY, KUROKI.
BELIEVE ME, IT IS NOT BECAUSE I FIND YOU UNATTRACTIVE OR WANTING IN ANY WAY.
SIMPLY PUT, I HAVE VERY RECENTLY BEEN MARRIED FOR THE SAKE OF RECONCILIATION BETWEEN THE SHOGUNATE AND THE COURT. HOW WOULD IT SOUND TO PEOPLE ON THE STREET IF THEY HEARD I HAVE ALREADY TAKEN A CONCUBINE?
BUT I WANTED YOU TO HEAR IT FROM ME PERSONALLY THAT I AM NOT TURNING YOU DOWN BECAUSE I FIND YOU UNAPPEALING.
ON THE CONTRARY, KUROKI, I LIKE YOU VERY MUCH.

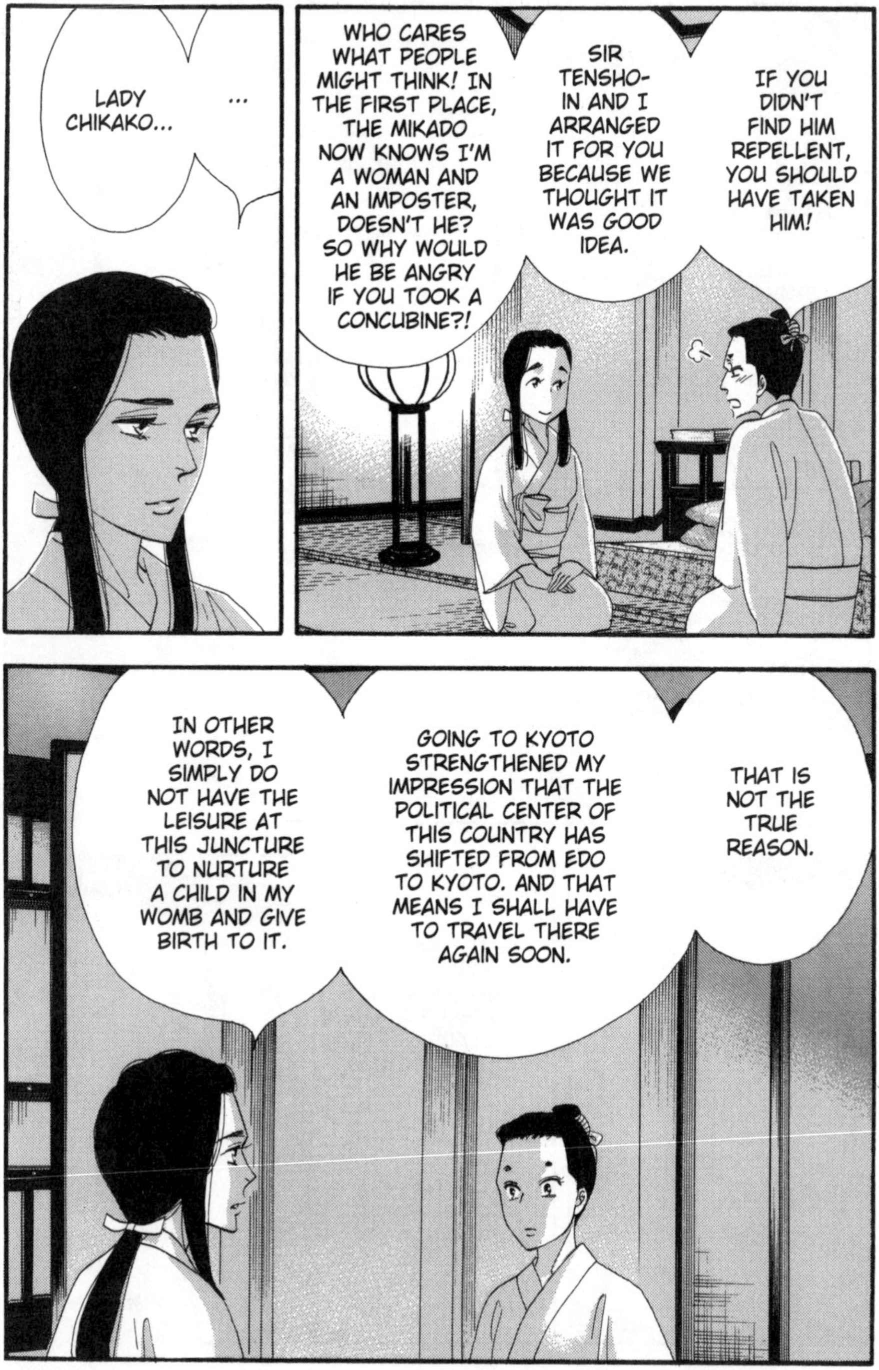
IF YOU DIDN'T FIND HIM REPELLENT, YOU SHOULD HAVE TAKEN HIM!
SIR TENSHO-IN AND I ARRANGED IT FOR YOU BECAUSE WE THOUGHT IT WAS GOOD IDEA.
WHO CARES WHAT PEOPLE MIGHT THINK! IN THE FIRST PLACE, THE MIKADO NOW KNOWS I'M A WOMAN AND AN IMPOSTER, DOESN'T HE? SO WHY WOULD HE BE ANGRY IF YOU TOOK A CONCUBINE?!
...
LADY CHIKAKO...
THAT IS NOT THE TRUE REASON.
GOING TO KYOTO STRENGTHENED MY IMPRESSION THAT THE POLITICAL CENTER OF THIS COUNTRY HAS SHIFTED FROM EDO TO KYOTO. AND THAT MEANS I SHALL HAVE TO TRAVEL THERE AGAIN SOON.
IN OTHER WORDS, I SIMPLY DO NOT HAVE THE LEISURE AT THIS JUNCTURE TO NURTURE A CHILD IN MY WOMB AND GIVE BIRTH TO IT.

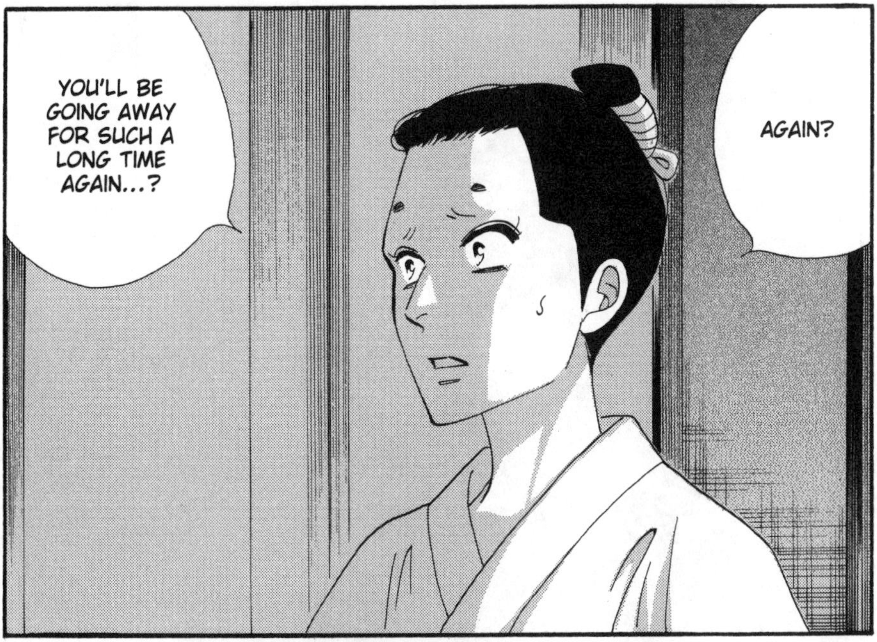
AGAIN?
YOU'LL BE GOING AWAY FOR SUCH A LONG TIME AGAIN...?

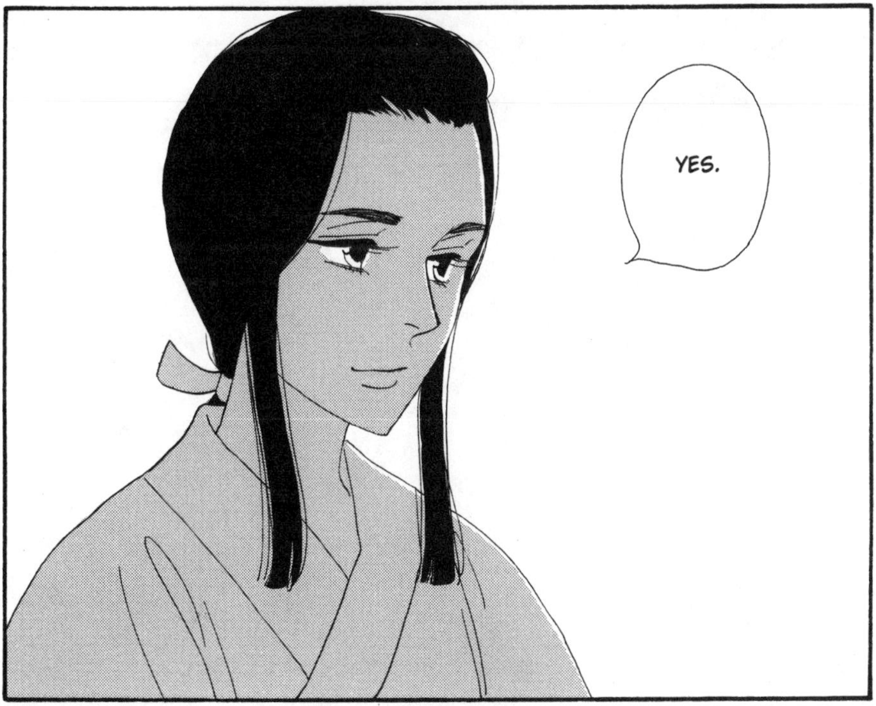
YES.

Ōoku

THE INNER CHAMBERS

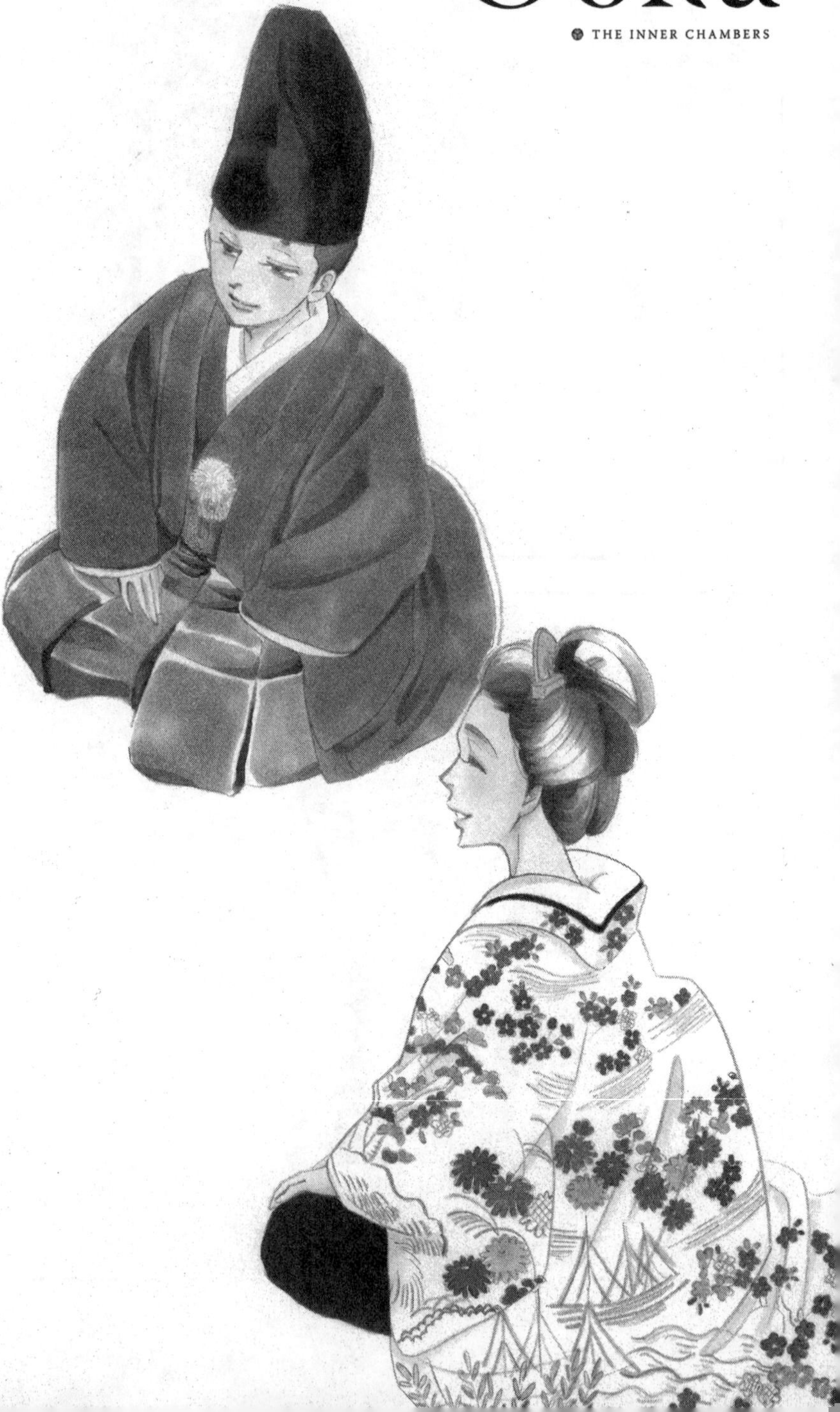

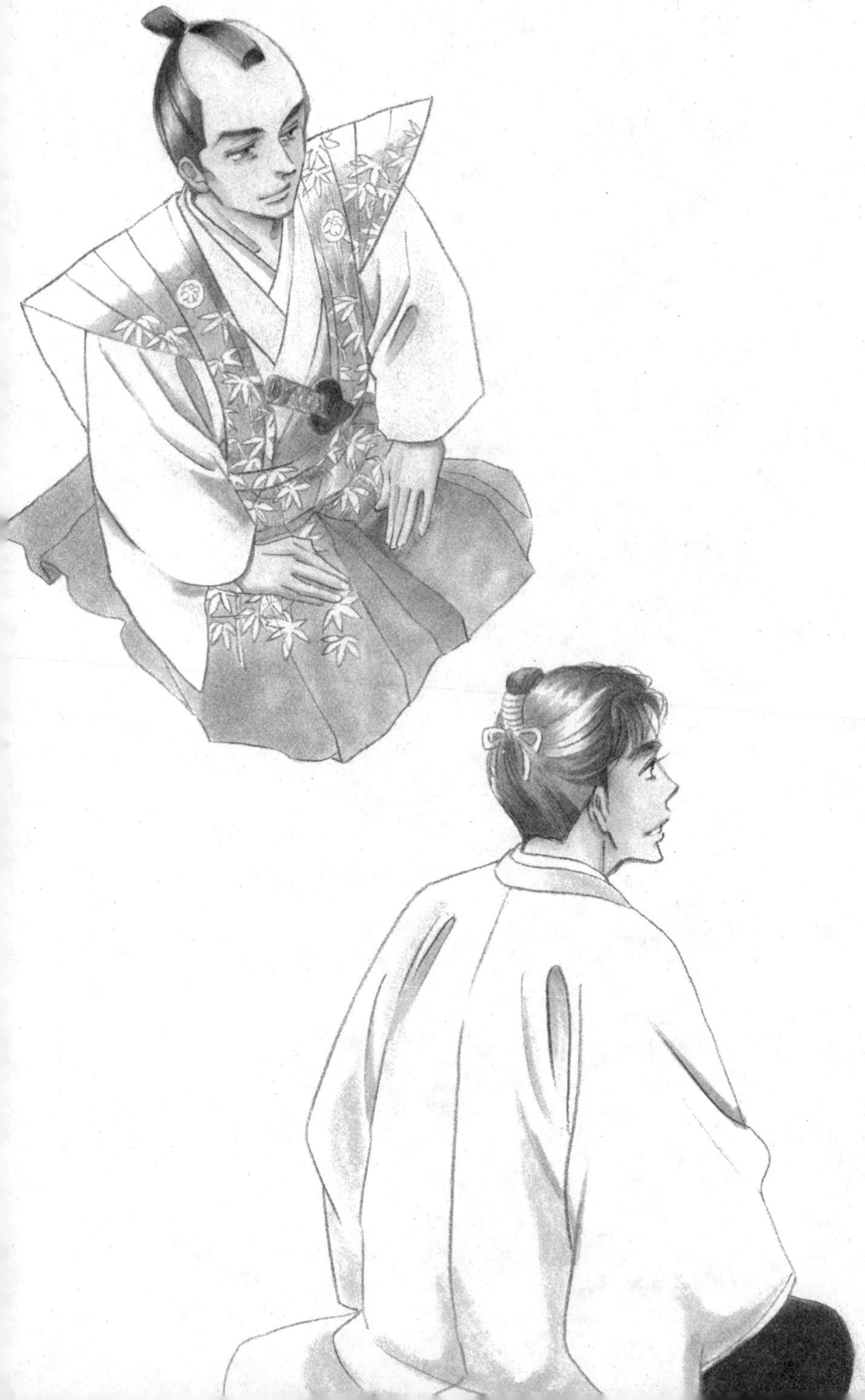

Ōoku

✤ THE INNER CHAMBERS

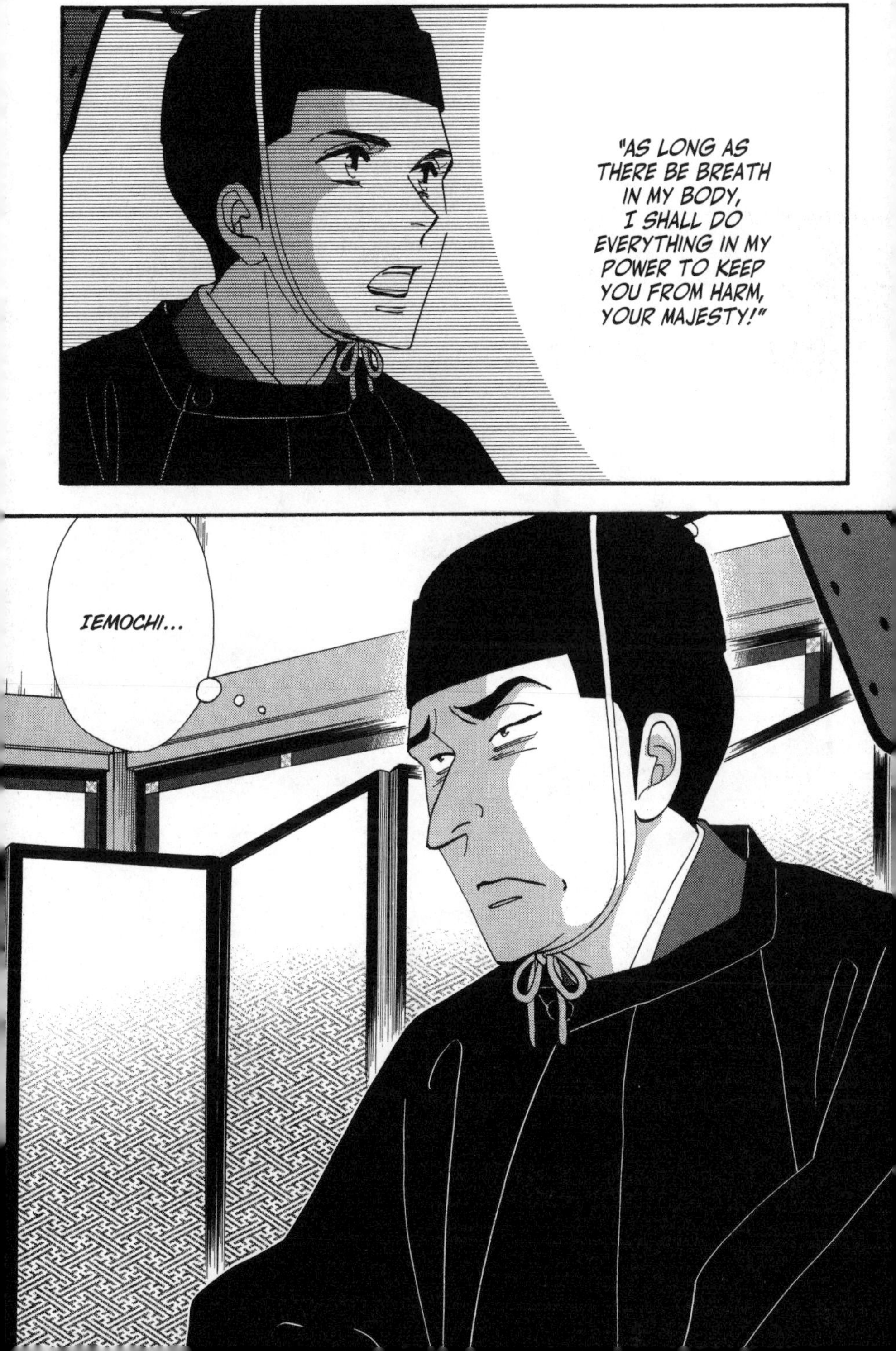
"AS LONG AS THERE BE BREATH IN MY BODY, I SHALL DO EVERYTHING IN MY POWER TO KEEP YOU FROM HARM, YOUR MAJESTY!"
IEMOCHI...

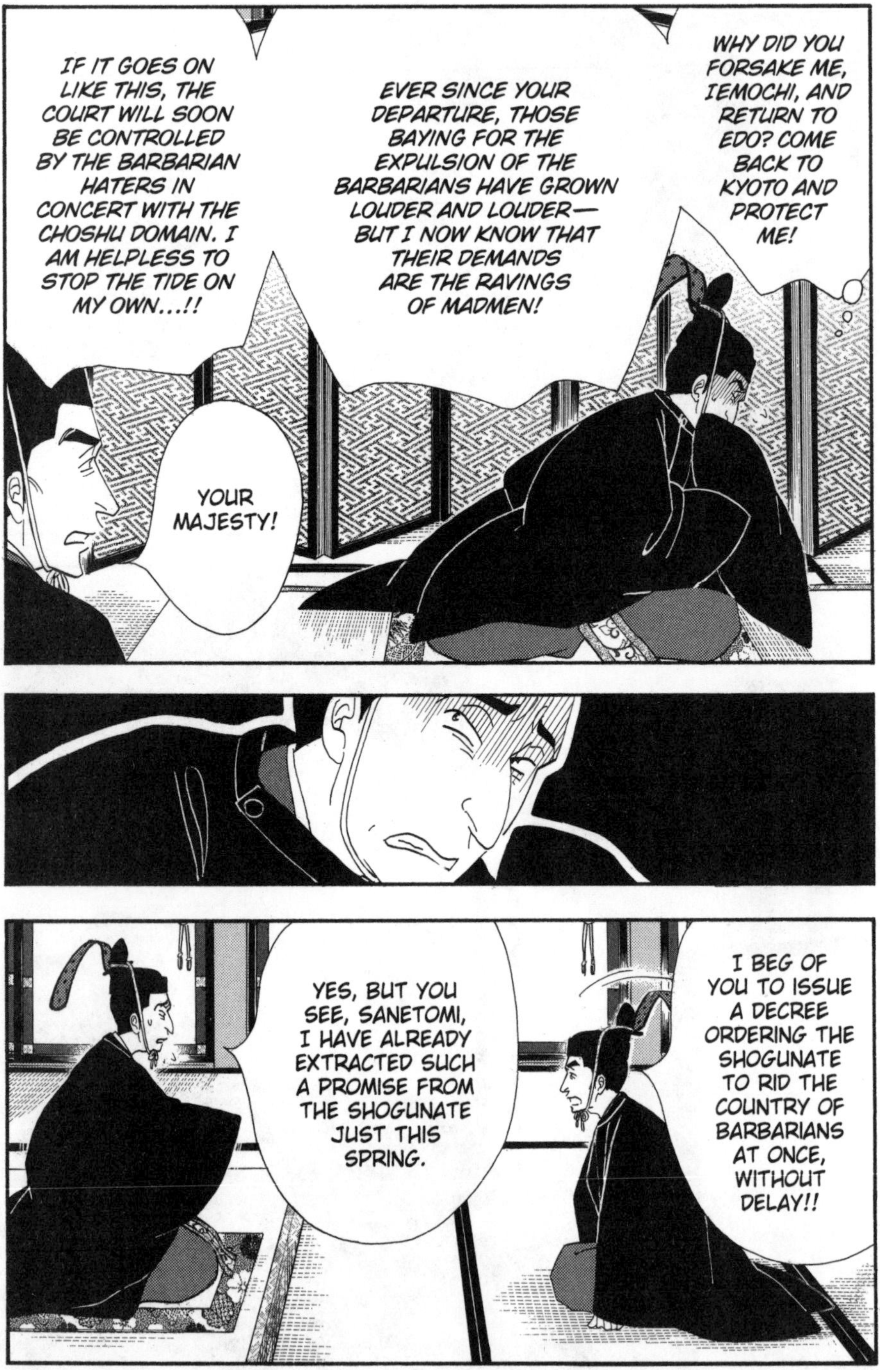
WHY DID YOU FORSAKE ME, IEMOCHI, AND RETURN TO EDO? COME BACK TO KYOTO AND PROTECT ME!
EVER SINCE YOUR DEPARTURE, THOSE BAYING FOR THE EXPULSION OF THE BARBARIANS HAVE GROWN LOUDER AND LOUDER—BUT I NOW KNOW THAT THEIR DEMANDS ARE THE RAVINGS OF MADMEN!
IF IT GOES ON LIKE THIS, THE COURT WILL SOON BE CONTROLLED BY THE BARBARIAN HATERS IN CONCERT WITH THE CHOSHU DOMAIN. I AM HELPLESS TO STOP THE TIDE ON MY OWN...!!
YOUR MAJESTY!
I BEG OF YOU TO ISSUE A DECREE ORDERING THE SHOGUNATE TO RID THE COUNTRY OF BARBARIANS AT ONCE, WITHOUT DELAY!!
YES, BUT YOU SEE, SANETOMI, I HAVE ALREADY EXTRACTED SUCH A PROMISE FROM THE SHOGUNATE JUST THIS SPRING.

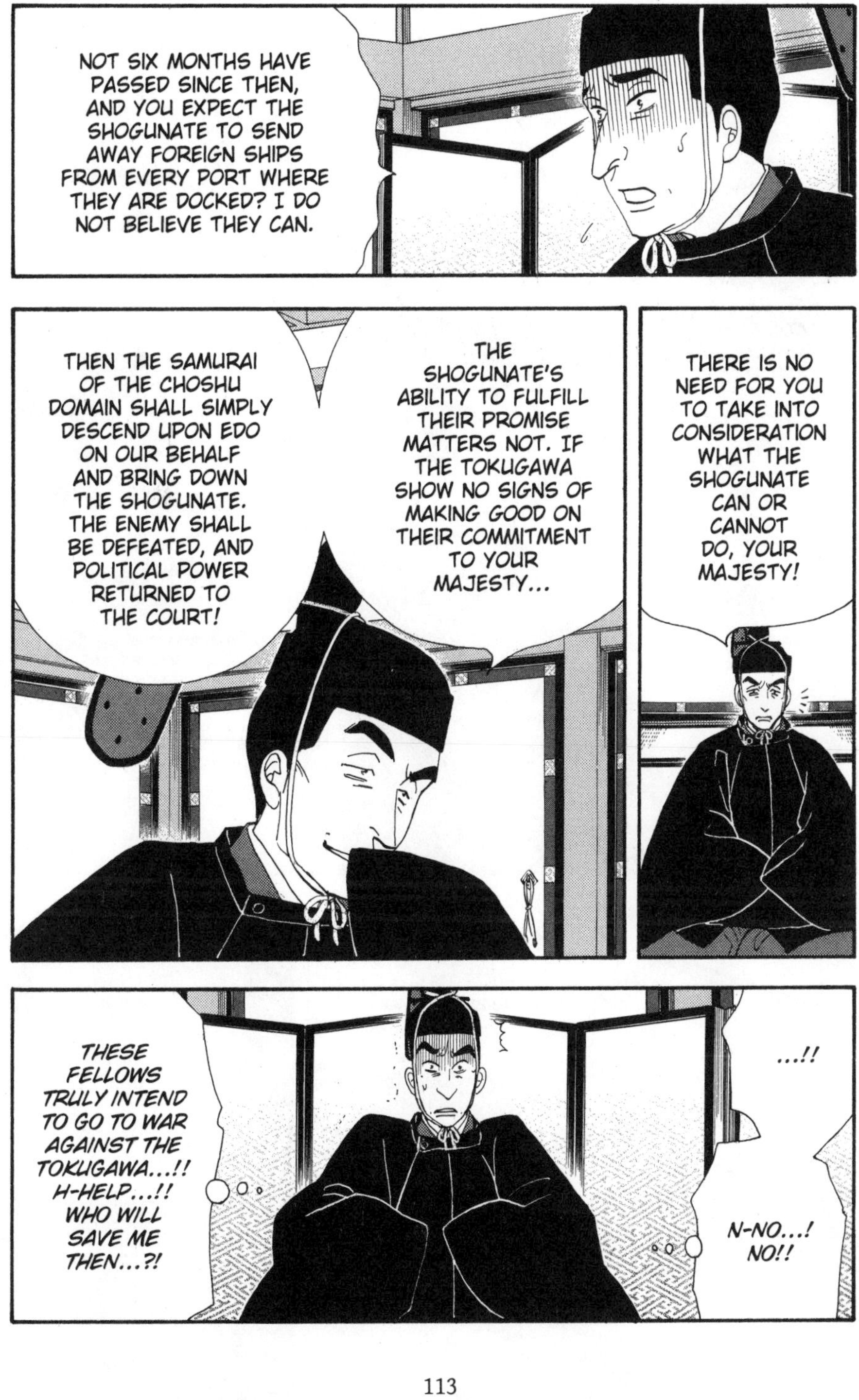
NOT SIX MONTHS HAVE PASSED SINCE THEN, AND YOU EXPECT THE SHOGUNATE TO SEND AWAY FOREIGN SHIPS FROM EVERY PORT WHERE THEY ARE DOCKED? I DO NOT BELIEVE THEY CAN.
THERE IS NO NEED FOR YOU TO TAKE INTO CONSIDERATION WHAT THE SHOGUNATE CAN OR CANNOT DO, YOUR MAJESTY!
THE SHOGUNATE'S ABILITY TO FULFILL THEIR PROMISE MATTERS NOT. IF THE TOKUGAWA SHOW NO SIGNS OF MAKING GOOD ON THEIR COMMITMENT TO YOUR MAJESTY...
THEN THE SAMURAI OF THE CHOSHU DOMAIN SHALL SIMPLY DESCEND UPON EDO ON OUR BEHALF AND BRING DOWN THE SHOGUNATE. THE ENEMY SHALL BE DEFEATED, AND POLITICAL POWER RETURNED TO THE COURT!
...!!
N-NO...! NO!!
THESE FELLOWS TRULY INTEND TO GO TO WAR AGAINST THE TOKUGAWA...!! H-HELP...!! WHO WILL SAVE ME THEN...?!

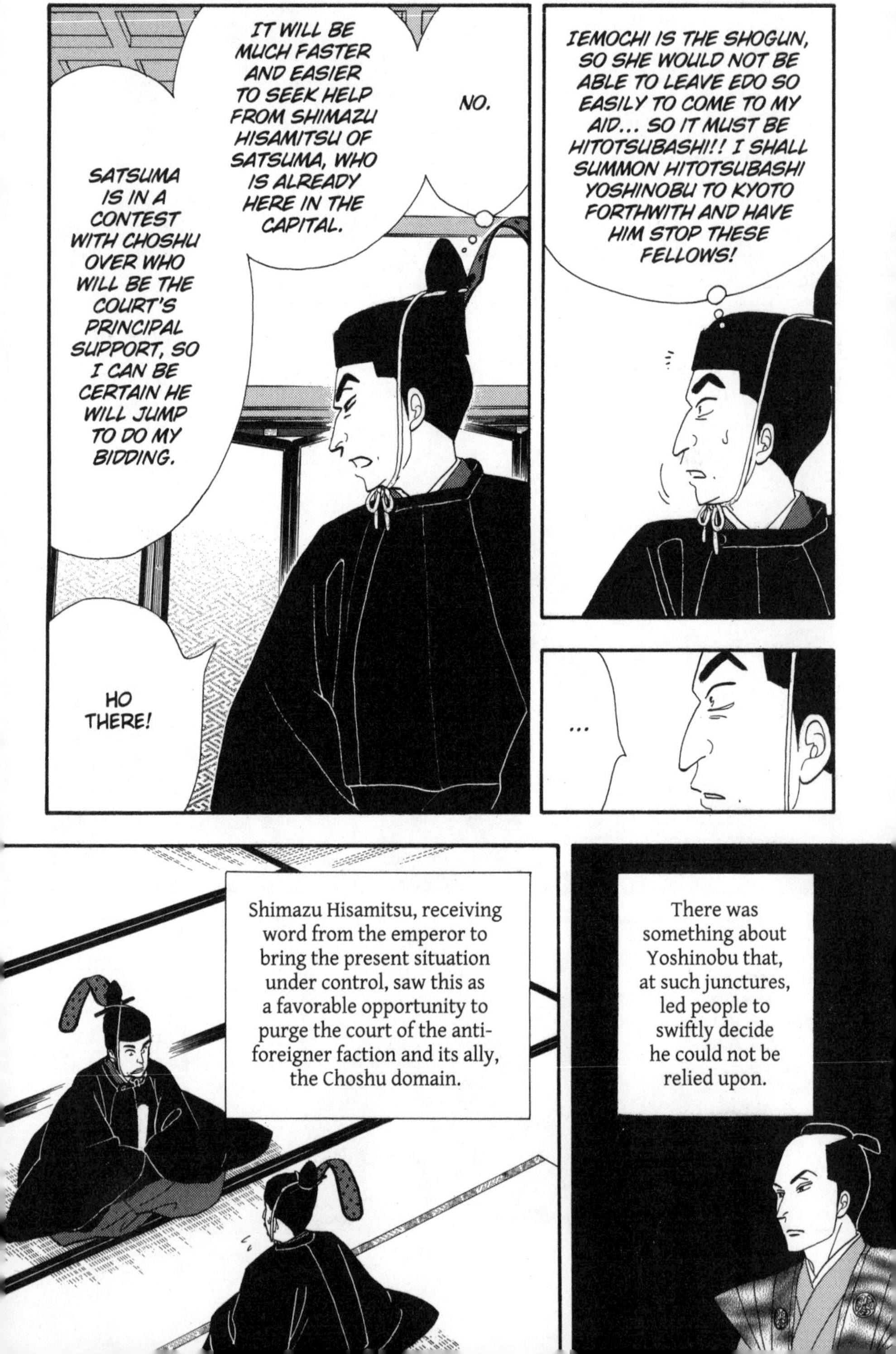
IEMOCHI IS THE SHOGUN, SO SHE WOULD NOT BE ABLE TO LEAVE EDO SO EASILY TO COME TO MY AID... SO IT MUST BE HITOTSUBASHI!! I SHALL SUMMON HITOTSUBASHI YOSHINOBU TO KYOTO FORTHWITH AND HAVE HIM STOP THESE FELLOWS!
...
NO.
IT WILL BE MUCH FASTER AND EASIER TO SEEK HELP FROM SHIMAZU HISAMITSU OF SATSUMA, WHO IS ALREADY HERE IN THE CAPITAL.
SATSUMA IS IN A CONTEST WITH CHOSHU OVER WHO WILL BE THE COURT'S PRINCIPAL SUPPORT, SO I CAN BE CERTAIN HE WILL JUMP TO DO MY BIDDING.
HO THERE!
There was something about Yoshinobu that, at such junctures, led people to swiftly decide he could not be relied upon.
Shimazu Hisamitsu, receiving word from the emperor to bring the present situation under control, saw this as a favorable opportunity to purge the court of the anti-foreigner faction and its ally, the Choshu domain.

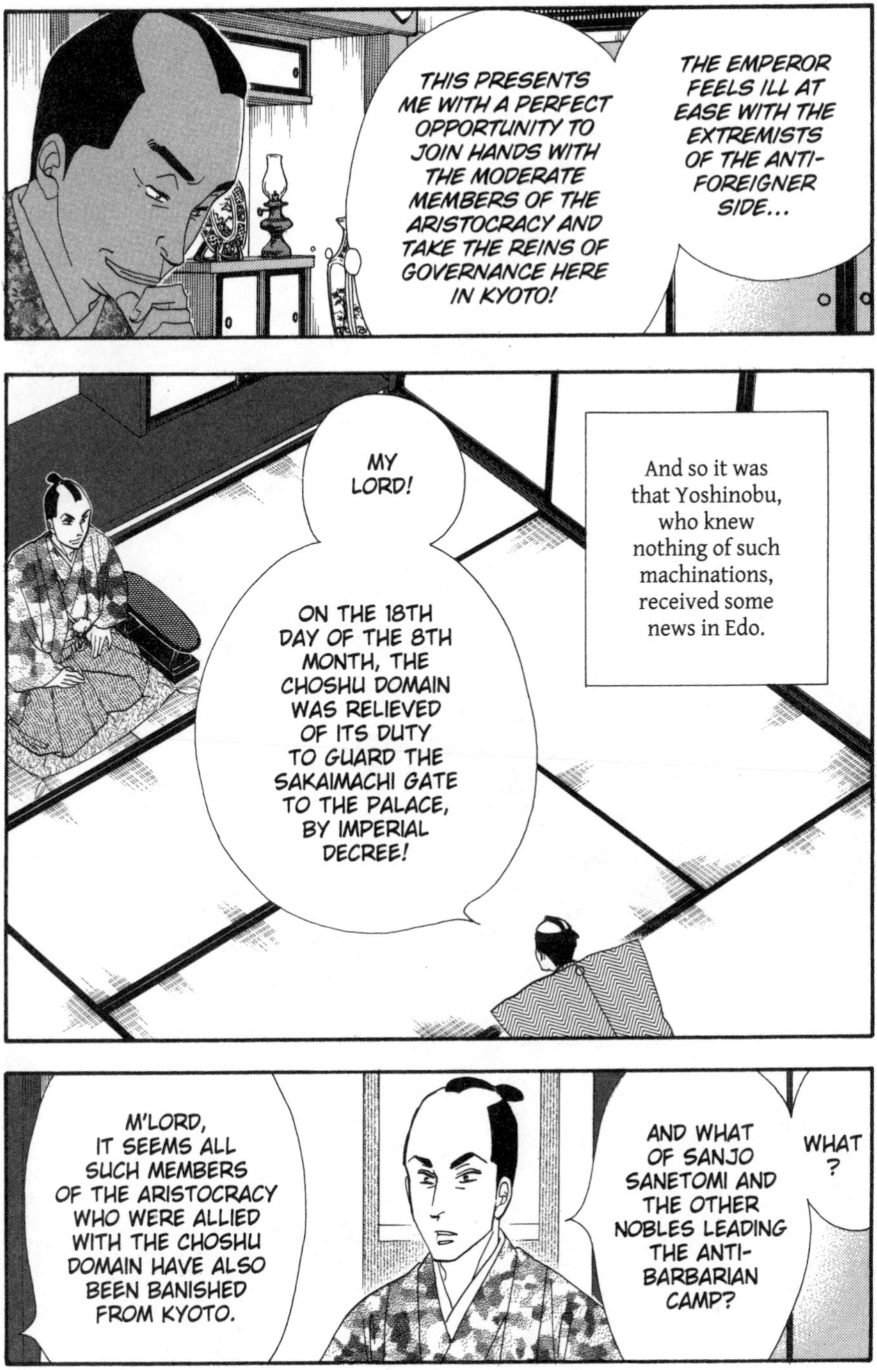
THE EMPEROR FEELS ILL AT EASE WITH THE EXTREMISTS OF THE ANTI-FOREIGNER SIDE...
THIS PRESENTS ME WITH A PERFECT OPPORTUNITY TO JOIN HANDS WITH THE MODERATE MEMBERS OF THE ARISTOCRACY AND TAKE THE REINS OF GOVERNANCE HERE IN KYOTO!
And so it was that Yoshinobu, who knew nothing of such machinations, received some news in Edo.
MY LORD!
ON THE 18TH DAY OF THE 8TH MONTH, THE CHOSHU DOMAIN WAS RELIEVED OF ITS DUTY TO GUARD THE SAKAIMACHI GATE TO THE PALACE, BY IMPERIAL DECREE!
WHAT?
AND WHAT OF SANJO SANETOMI AND THE OTHER NOBLES LEADING THE ANTI-BARBARIAN CAMP?
M'LORD, IT SEEMS ALL SUCH MEMBERS OF THE ARISTOCRACY WHO WERE ALLIED WITH THE CHOSHU DOMAIN HAVE ALSO BEEN BANISHED FROM KYOTO.

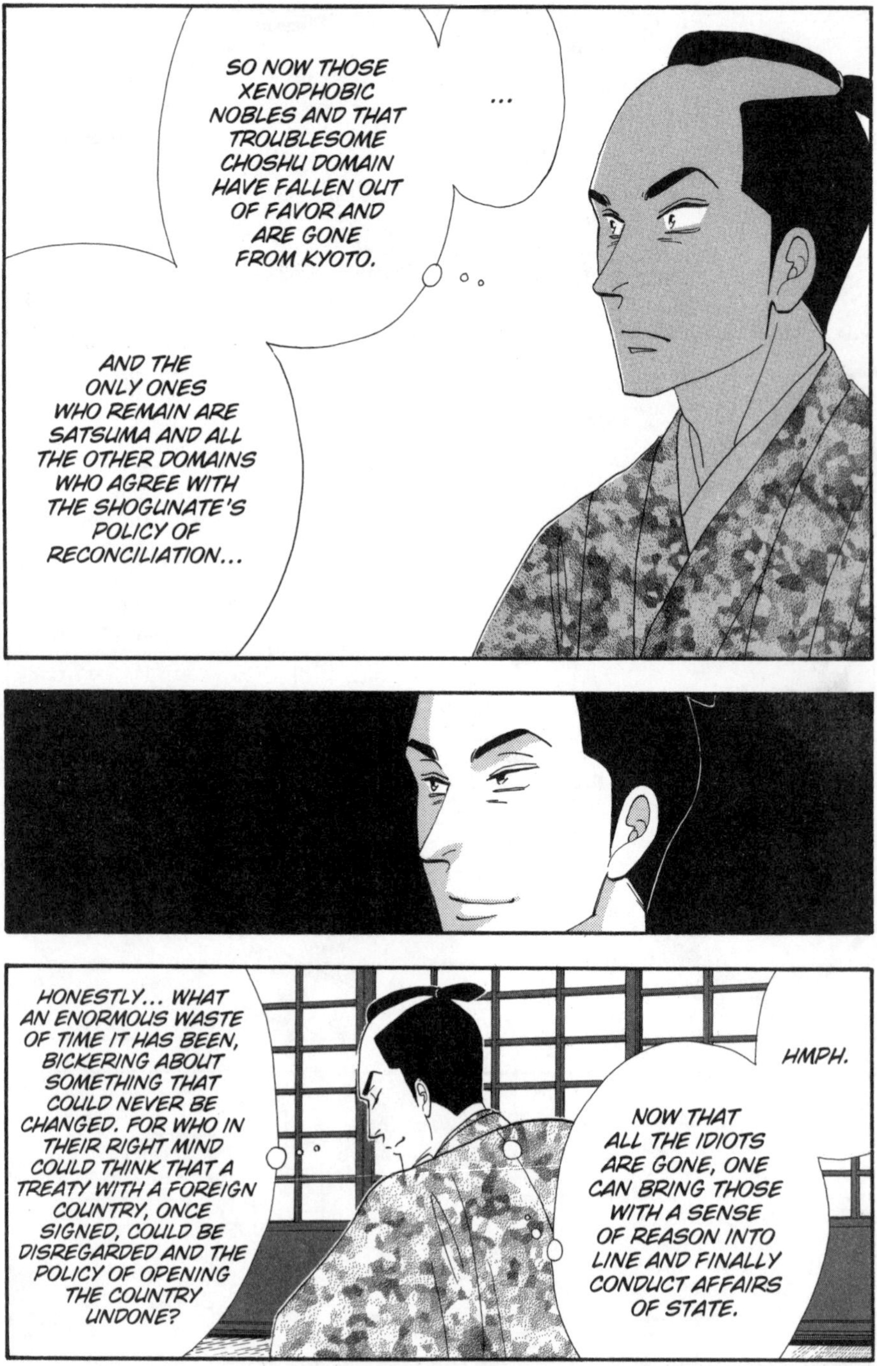
...
SO NOW THOSE XENOPHOBIC NOBLES AND THAT TROUBLESOME CHOSHU DOMAIN HAVE FALLEN OUT OF FAVOR AND ARE GONE FROM KYOTO.
AND THE ONLY ONES WHO REMAIN ARE SATSUMA AND ALL THE OTHER DOMAINS WHO AGREE WITH THE SHOGUNATE'S POLICY OF RECONCILIATION...
HMPH.
NOW THAT ALL THE IDIOTS ARE GONE, ONE CAN BRING THOSE WITH A SENSE OF REASON INTO LINE AND FINALLY CONDUCT AFFAIRS OF STATE.
HONESTLY... WHAT AN ENORMOUS WASTE OF TIME IT HAS BEEN, BICKERING ABOUT SOMETHING THAT COULD NEVER BE CHANGED. FOR WHO IN THEIR RIGHT MIND COULD THINK THAT A TREATY WITH A FOREIGN COUNTRY, ONCE SIGNED, COULD BE DISREGARDED AND THE POLICY OF OPENING THE COUNTRY UNDONE?

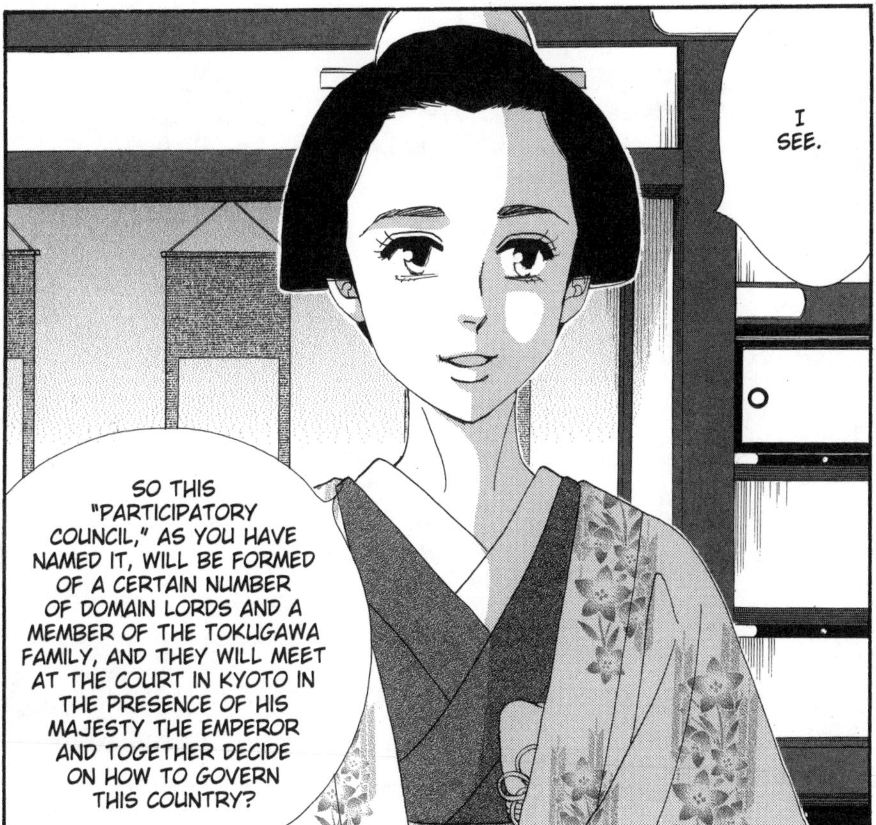
I SEE.
SO THIS "PARTICIPATORY COUNCIL," AS YOU HAVE NAMED IT, WILL BE FORMED OF A CERTAIN NUMBER OF DOMAIN LORDS AND A MEMBER OF THE TOKUGAWA FAMILY, AND THEY WILL MEET AT THE COURT IN KYOTO IN THE PRESENCE OF HIS MAJESTY THE EMPEROR AND TOGETHER DECIDE ON HOW TO GOVERN THIS COUNTRY?
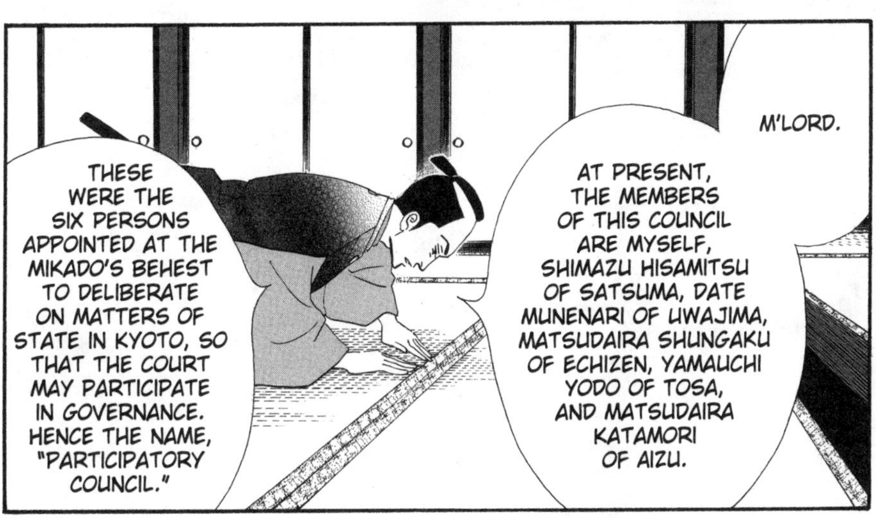
M'LORD.
AT PRESENT, THE MEMBERS OF THIS COUNCIL ARE MYSELF, SHIMAZU HISAMITSU OF SATSUMA, DATE MUNENARI OF UWAJIMA, MATSUDAIRA SHUNGAKU OF ECHIZEN, YAMAUCHI YODO OF TOSA, AND MATSUDAIRA KATAMORI OF AIZU.
THESE WERE THE SIX PERSONS APPOINTED AT THE MIKADO'S BEHEST TO DELIBERATE ON MATTERS OF STATE IN KYOTO, SO THAT THE COURT MAY PARTICIPATE IN GOVERNANCE. HENCE THE NAME, "PARTICIPATORY COUNCIL."

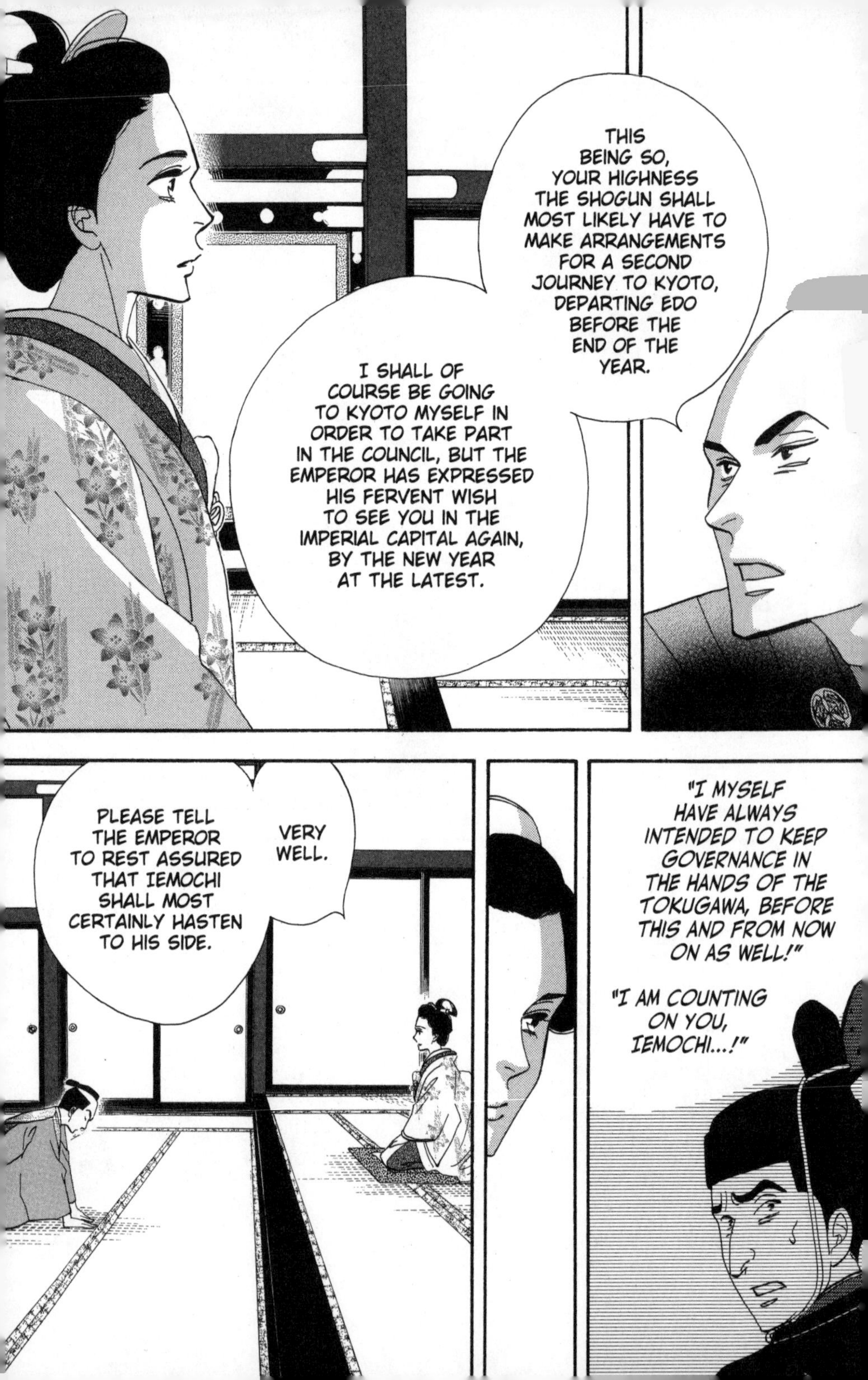
I SHALL OF COURSE BE GOING TO KYOTO MYSELF IN ORDER TO TAKE PART IN THE COUNCIL, BUT THE EMPEROR HAS EXPRESSED HIS FERVENT WISH TO SEE YOU IN THE IMPERIAL CAPITAL AGAIN, BY THE NEW YEAR AT THE LATEST.
THIS BEING SO, YOUR HIGHNESS THE SHOGUN SHALL MOST LIKELY HAVE TO MAKE ARRANGEMENTS FOR A SECOND JOURNEY TO KYOTO, DEPARTING EDO BEFORE THE END OF THE YEAR.
"I MYSELF HAVE ALWAYS INTENDED TO KEEP GOVERNANCE IN THE HANDS OF THE TOKUGAWA, BEFORE THIS AND FROM NOW ON AS WELL!"
"I AM COUNTING ON YOU, IEMOCHI...!"
VERY WELL.
PLEASE TELL THE EMPEROR TO REST ASSURED THAT IEMOCHI SHALL MOST CERTAINLY HASTEN TO HIS SIDE.

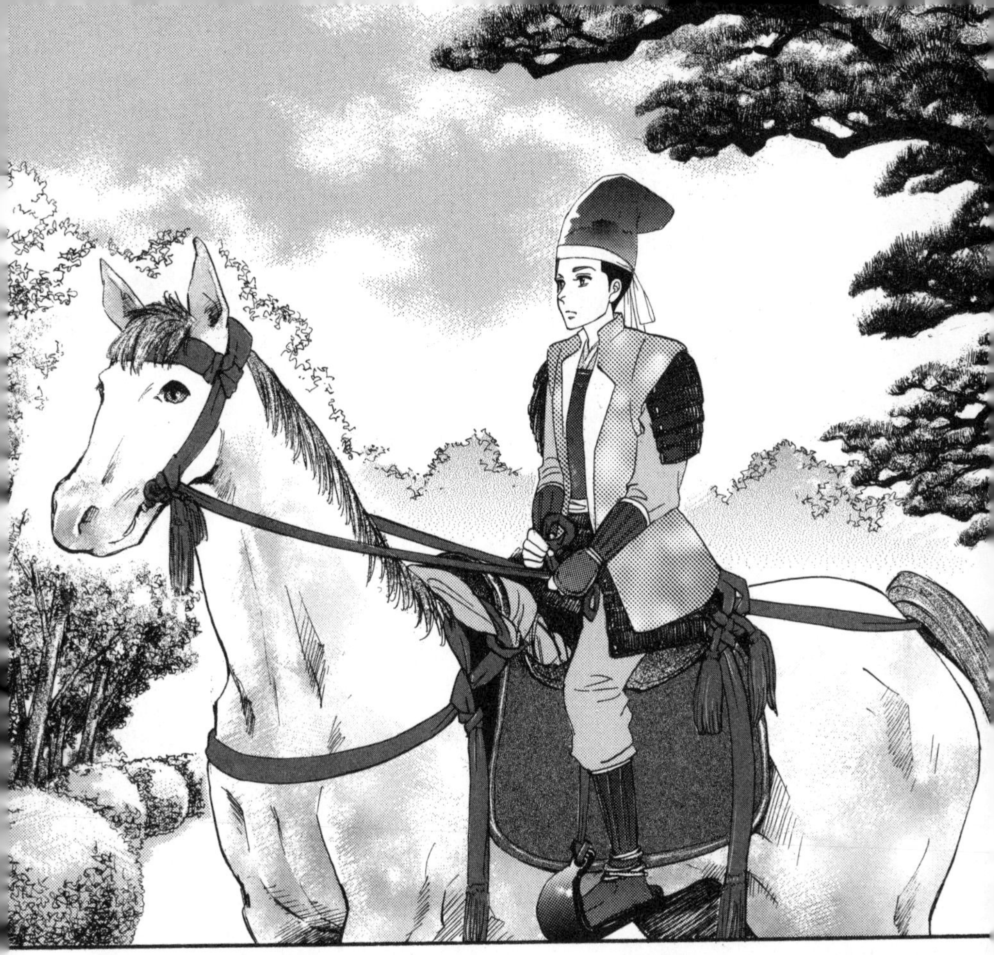

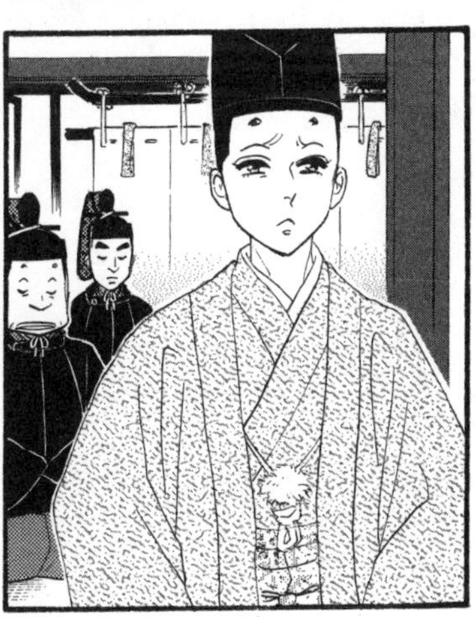

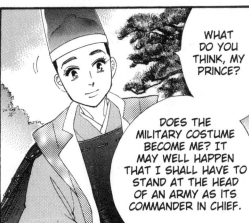

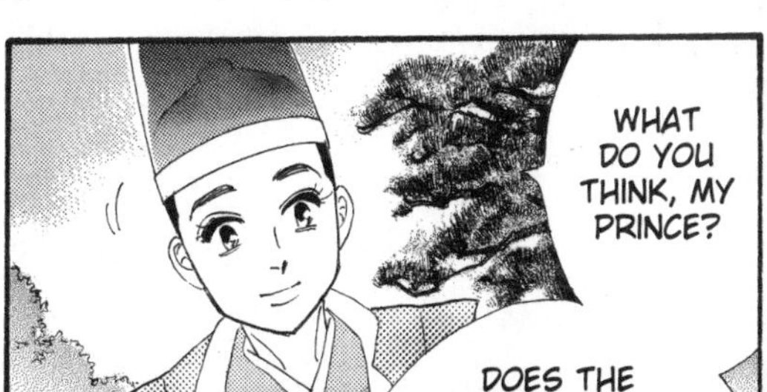
WHAT DO YOU THINK, MY PRINCE?
DOES THE MILITARY COSTUME BECOME ME? IT MAY WELL HAPPEN THAT I SHALL HAVE TO STAND AT THE HEAD OF AN ARMY AS ITS COMMANDER IN CHIEF.

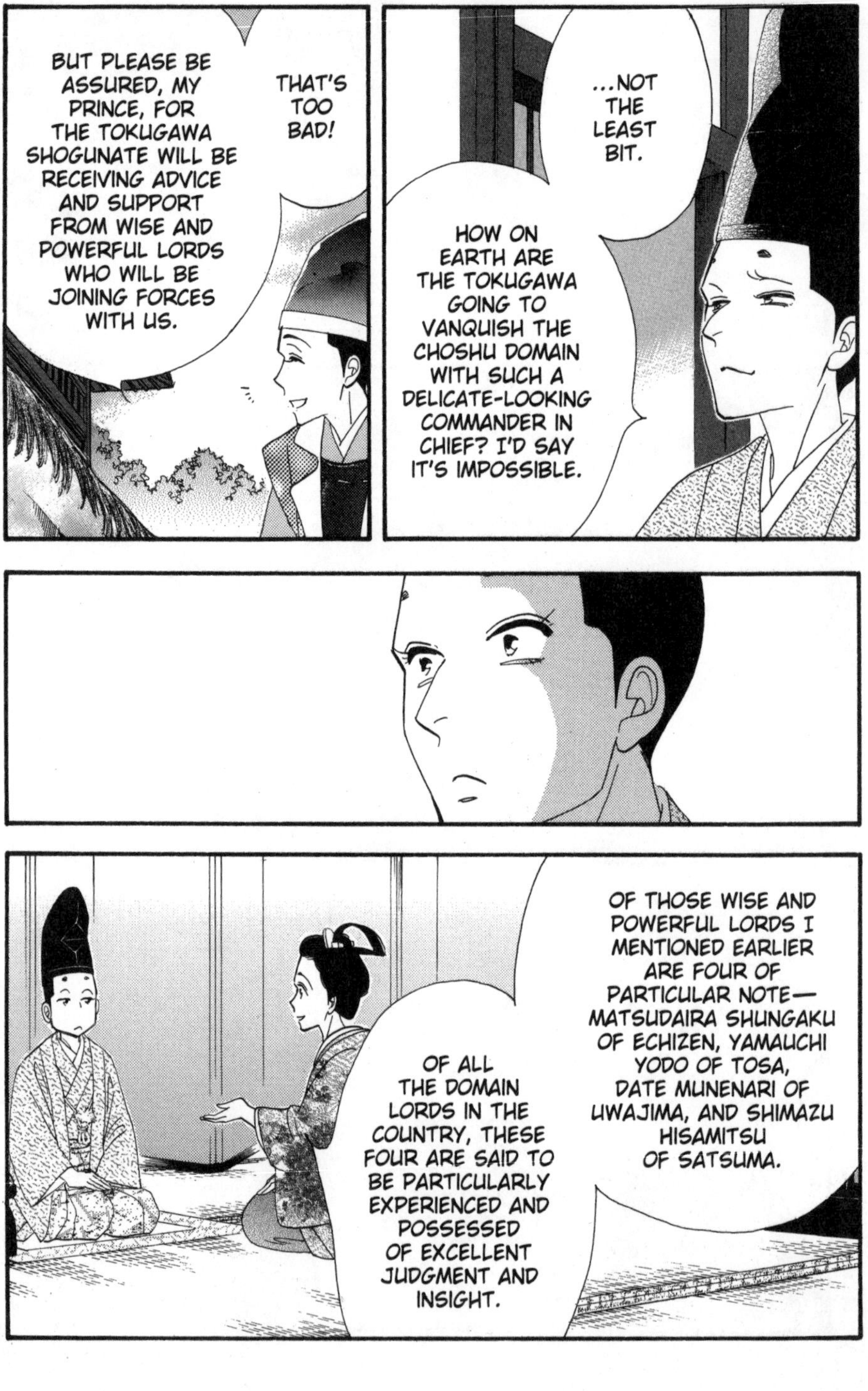
...NOT THE LEAST BIT.
HOW ON EARTH ARE THE TOKUGAWA GOING TO VANQUISH THE CHOSHU DOMAIN WITH SUCH A DELICATE-LOOKING COMMANDER IN CHIEF? I'D SAY IT'S IMPOSSIBLE.
THAT'S TOO BAD!
BUT PLEASE BE ASSURED, MY PRINCE, FOR THE TOKUGAWA SHOGUNATE WILL BE RECEIVING ADVICE AND SUPPORT FROM WISE AND POWERFUL LORDS WHO WILL BE JOINING FORCES WITH US.
OF THOSE WISE AND POWERFUL LORDS I MENTIONED EARLIER ARE FOUR OF PARTICULAR NOTE—MATSUDAIRA SHUNGAKU OF ECHIZEN, YAMAUCHI YODO OF TOSA, DATE MUNENARI OF UWAJIMA, AND SHIMAZU HISAMITSU OF SATSUMA.
OF ALL THE DOMAIN LORDS IN THE COUNTRY, THESE FOUR ARE SAID TO BE PARTICULARLY EXPERIENCED AND POSSESSED OF EXCELLENT JUDGMENT AND INSIGHT.

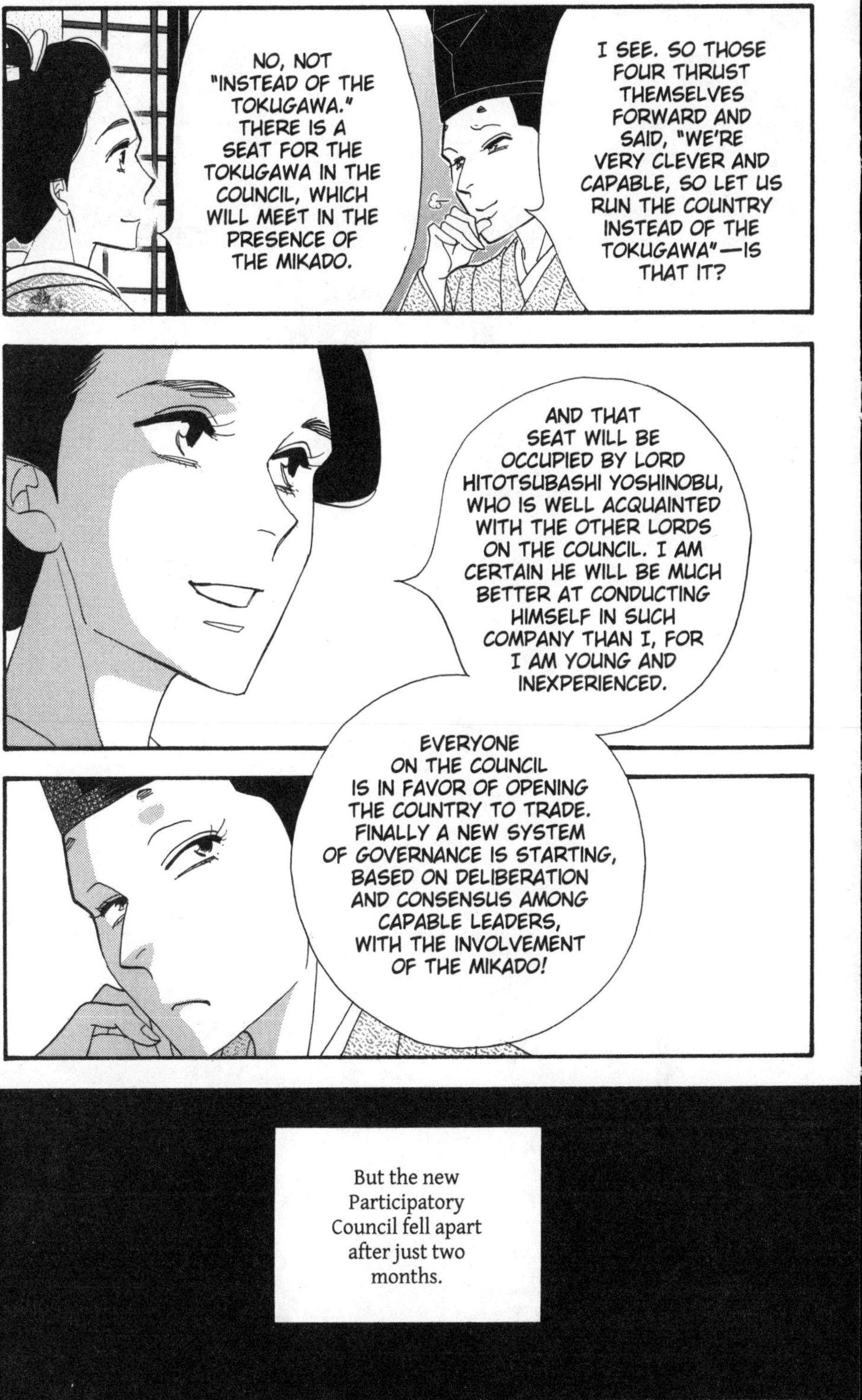
I SEE. SO THOSE FOUR THRUST THEMSELVES FORWARD AND SAID, "WE'RE VERY CLEVER AND CAPABLE, SO LET US RUN THE COUNTRY INSTEAD OF THE TOKUGAWA"—IS THAT IT?
NO, NOT "INSTEAD OF THE TOKUGAWA." THERE IS A SEAT FOR THE TOKUGAWA IN THE COUNCIL, WHICH WILL MEET IN THE PRESENCE OF THE MIKADO.
AND THAT SEAT WILL BE OCCUPIED BY LORD HITOTSUBASHI YOSHINOBU, WHO IS WELL ACQUAINTED WITH THE OTHER LORDS ON THE COUNCIL. I AM CERTAIN HE WILL BE MUCH BETTER AT CONDUCTING HIMSELF IN SUCH COMPANY THAN I, FOR I AM YOUNG AND INEXPERIENCED.
EVERYONE ON THE COUNCIL IS IN FAVOR OF OPENING THE COUNTRY TO TRADE. FINALLY A NEW SYSTEM OF GOVERNANCE IS STARTING, BASED ON DELIBERATION AND CONSENSUS AMONG CAPABLE LEADERS, WITH THE INVOLVEMENT OF THE MIKADO!
But the new Participatory Council fell apart after just two months.

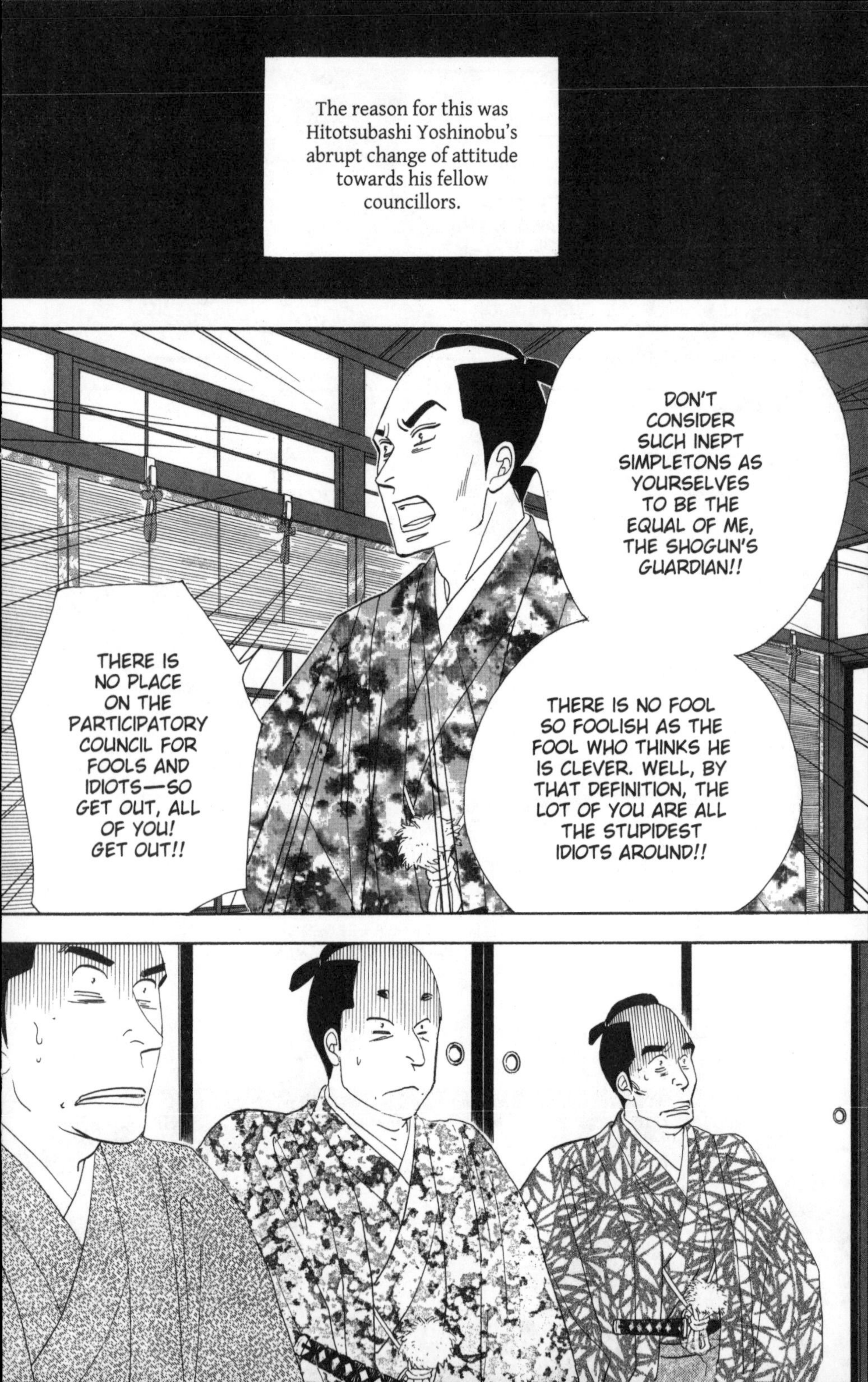
The reason for this was Hitotsubashi Yoshinobu's abrupt change of attitude towards his fellow councillors.
DON'T CONSIDER SUCH INEPT SIMPLETONS AS YOURSELVES TO BE THE EQUAL OF ME, THE SHOGUN'S GUARDIAN!!
THERE IS NO FOOL SO FOOLISH AS THE FOOL WHO THINKS HE IS CLEVER. WELL, BY THAT DEFINITION, THE LOT OF YOU ARE ALL THE STUPIDEST IDIOTS AROUND!!
THERE IS NO PLACE ON THE PARTICIPATORY COUNCIL FOR FOOLS AND IDIOTS—SO GET OUT, ALL OF YOU! GET OUT!!

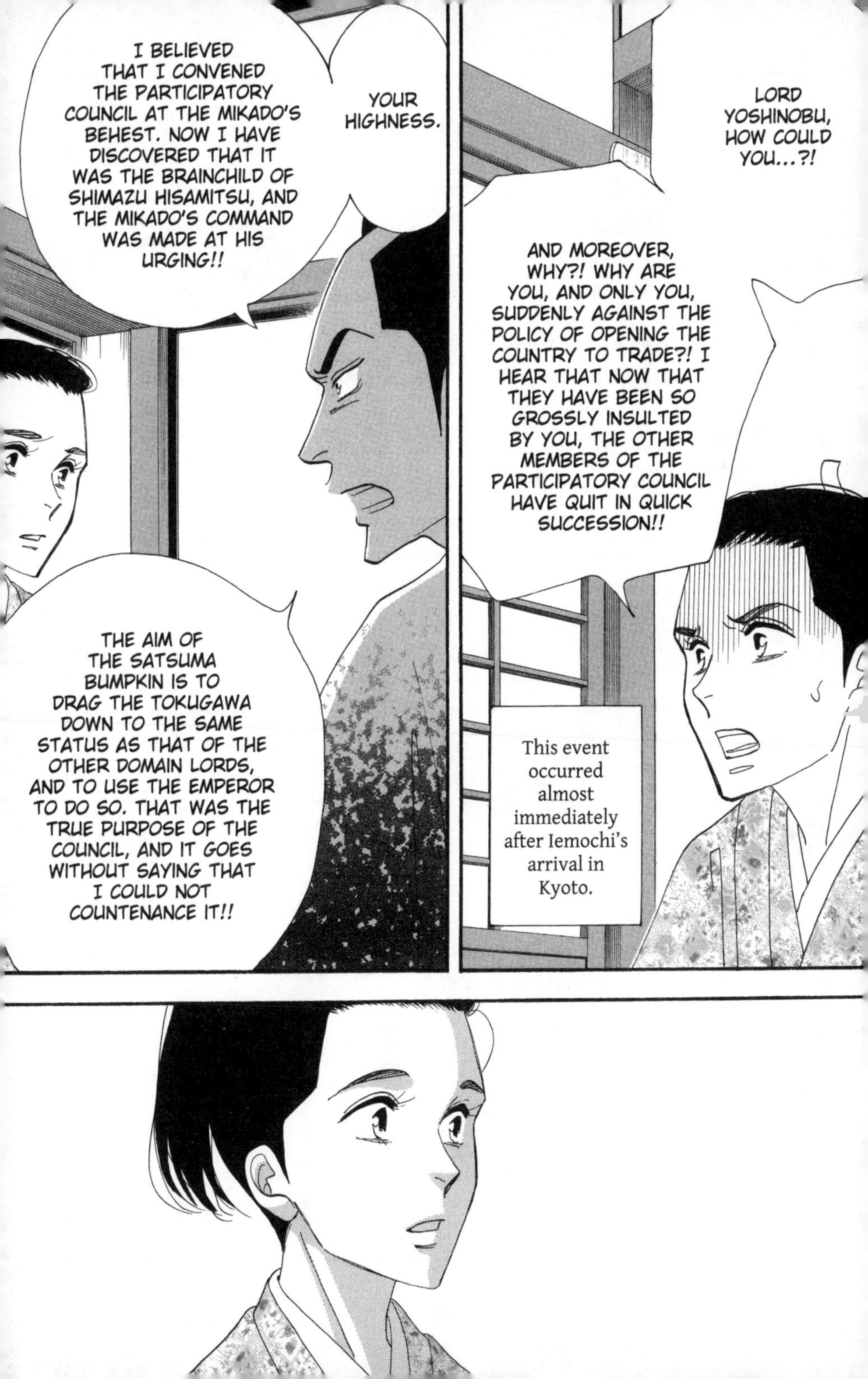
LORD YOSHINOBU, HOW COULD YOU...?!
AND MOREOVER, WHY?! WHY ARE YOU, AND ONLY YOU, SUDDENLY AGAINST THE POLICY OF OPENING THE COUNTRY TO TRADE?! I HEAR THAT NOW THAT THEY HAVE BEEN SO GROSSLY INSULTED BY YOU, THE OTHER MEMBERS OF THE PARTICIPATORY COUNCIL HAVE QUIT IN QUICK SUCCESSION!!
This event occurred almost immediately after Iemochi's arrival in Kyoto.
YOUR HIGHNESS.
I BELIEVED THAT I CONVENED THE PARTICIPATORY COUNCIL AT THE MIKADO'S BEHEST. NOW I HAVE DISCOVERED THAT IT WAS THE BRAINCHILD OF SHIMAZU HISAMITSU, AND THE MIKADO'S COMMAND WAS MADE AT HIS URGING!!
THE AIM OF THE SATSUMA BUMPKIN IS TO DRAG THE TOKUGAWA DOWN TO THE SAME STATUS AS THAT OF THE OTHER DOMAIN LORDS, AND TO USE THE EMPEROR TO DO SO. THAT WAS THE TRUE PURPOSE OF THE COUNCIL, AND IT GOES WITHOUT SAYING THAT I COULD NOT COUNTENANCE IT!!

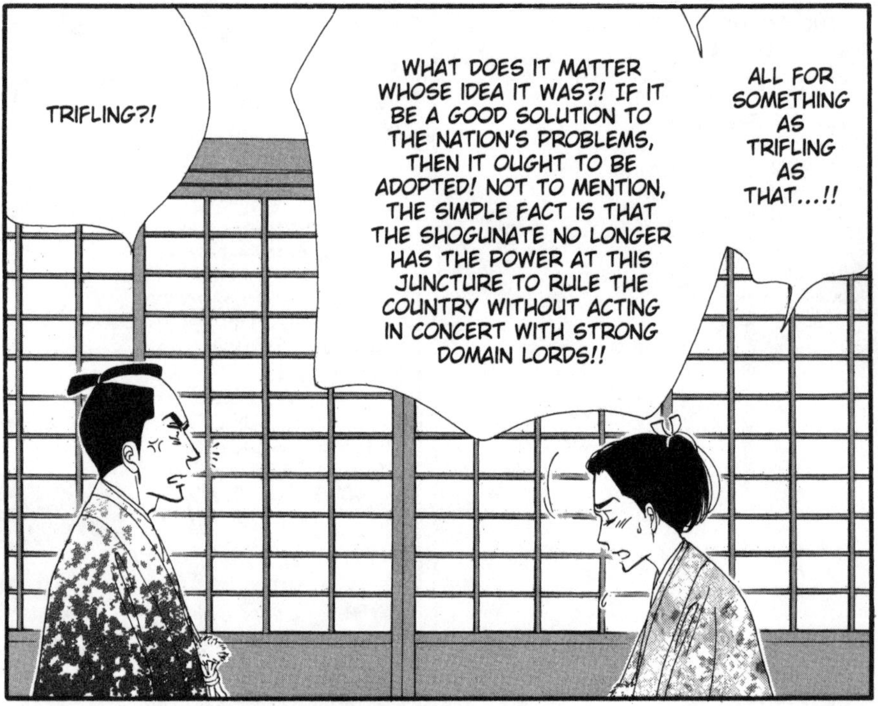
WHAT DOES IT MATTER WHOSE IDEA IT WAS?! IF IT BE A GOOD SOLUTION TO THE NATION'S PROBLEMS, THEN IT OUGHT TO BE ADOPTED! NOT TO MENTION, THE SIMPLE FACT IS THAT THE SHOGUNATE NO LONGER HAS THE POWER AT THIS JUNCTURE TO RULE THE COUNTRY WITHOUT ACTING IN CONCERT WITH STRONG DOMAIN LORDS!!
ALL FOR SOMETHING AS TRIFLING AS THAT...!!
TRIFLING?!

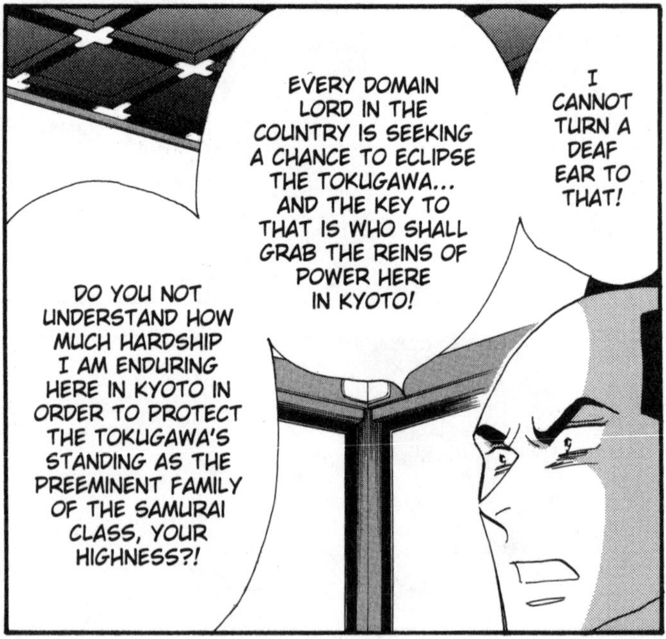
EVERY DOMAIN LORD IN THE COUNTRY IS SEEKING A CHANCE TO ECLIPSE THE TOKUGAWA... AND THE KEY TO THAT IS WHO SHALL GRAB THE REINS OF POWER HERE IN KYOTO!
I CANNOT TURN A DEAF EAR TO THAT!
DO YOU NOT UNDERSTAND HOW MUCH HARDSHIP I AM ENDURING HERE IN KYOTO IN ORDER TO PROTECT THE TOKUGAWA'S STANDING AS THE PREEMINENT FAMILY OF THE SAMURAI CLASS, YOUR HIGHNESS?!

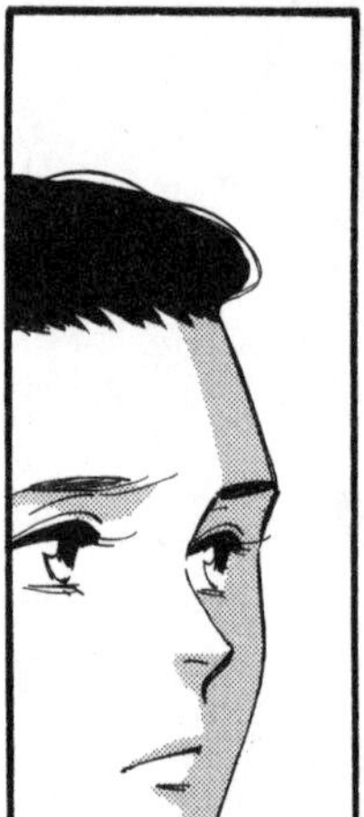

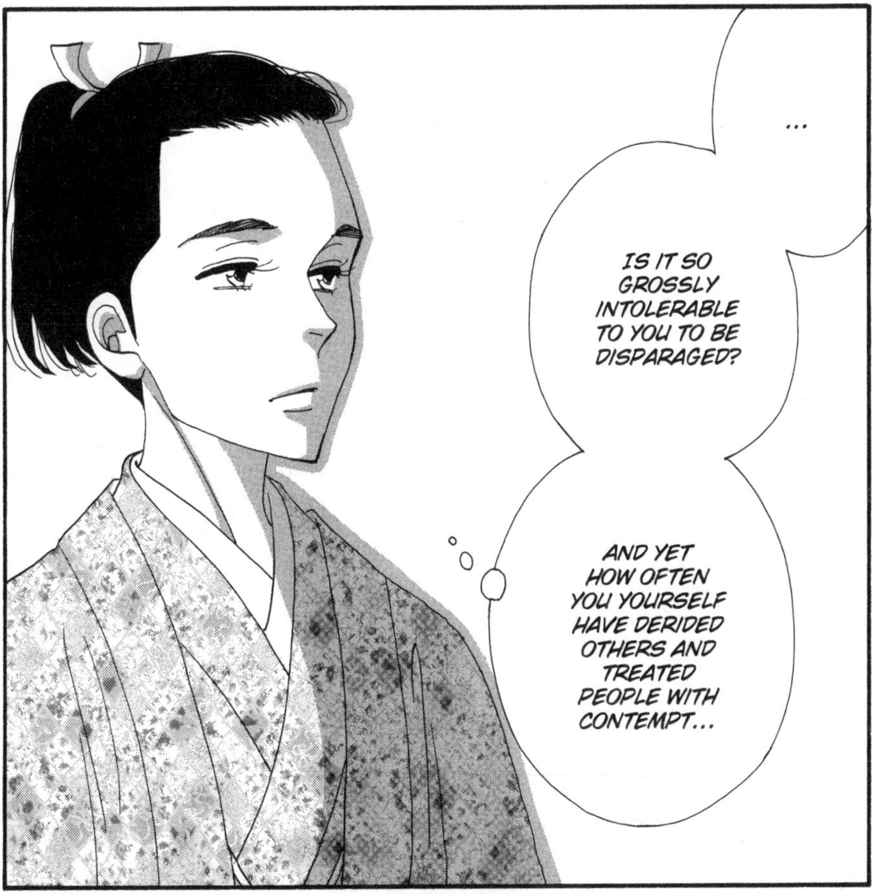
...
IS IT SO GROSSLY INTOLERABLE TO YOU TO BE DISPARAGED?
AND YET HOW OFTEN YOU YOURSELF HAVE DERIDED OTHERS AND TREATED PEOPLE WITH CONTEMPT...

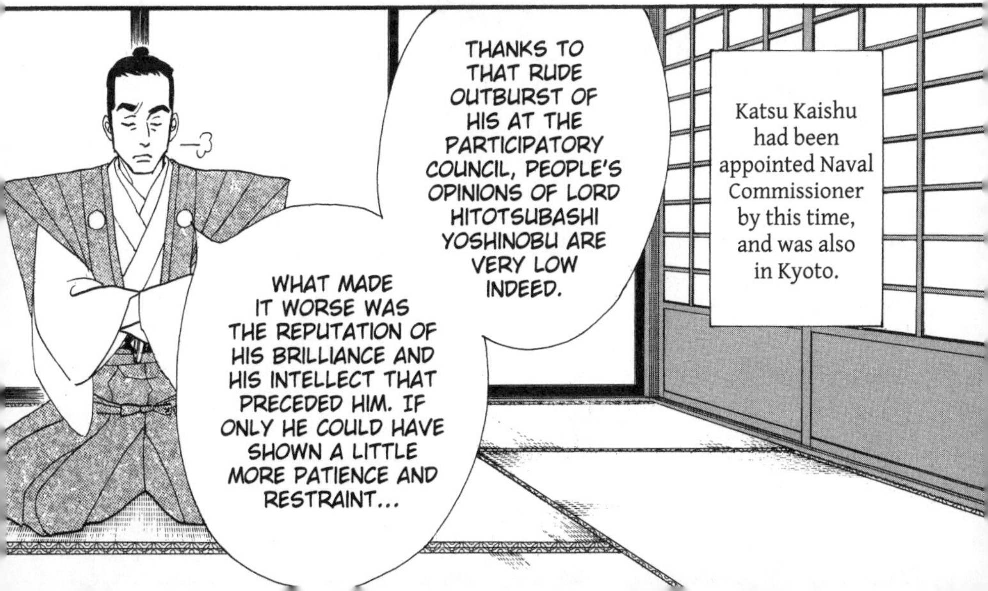
Katsu Kaishu had been appointed Naval Commissioner by this time, and was also in Kyoto.
THANKS TO THAT RUDE OUTBURST OF HIS AT THE PARTICIPATORY COUNCIL, PEOPLE'S OPINIONS OF LORD HITOTSUBASHI YOSHINOBU ARE VERY LOW INDEED.
WHAT MADE IT WORSE WAS THE REPUTATION OF HIS BRILLIANCE AND HIS INTELLECT THAT PRECEDED HIM. IF ONLY HE COULD HAVE SHOWN A LITTLE MORE PATIENCE AND RESTRAINT...

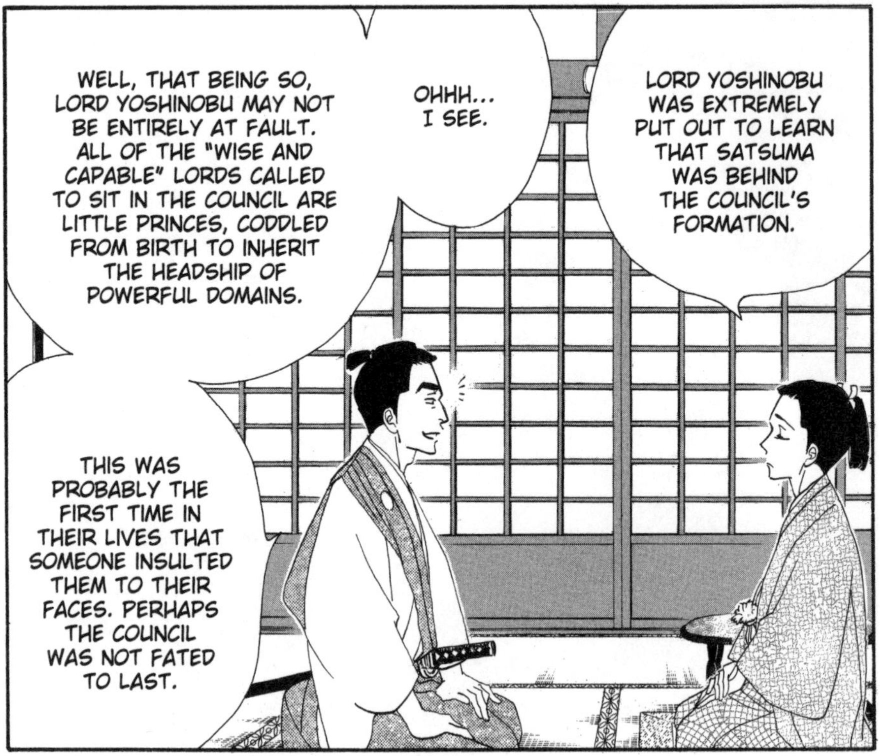
LORD YOSHINOBU WAS EXTREMELY PUT OUT TO LEARN THAT SATSUMA WAS BEHIND THE COUNCIL'S FORMATION.
OHHH... I SEE.
WELL, THAT BEING SO, LORD YOSHINOBU MAY NOT BE ENTIRELY AT FAULT. ALL OF THE "WISE AND CAPABLE" LORDS CALLED TO SIT IN THE COUNCIL ARE LITTLE PRINCES, CODDLED FROM BIRTH TO INHERIT THE HEADSHIP OF POWERFUL DOMAINS.
THIS WAS PROBABLY THE FIRST TIME IN THEIR LIVES THAT SOMEONE INSULTED THEM TO THEIR FACES. PERHAPS THE COUNCIL WAS NOT FATED TO LAST.
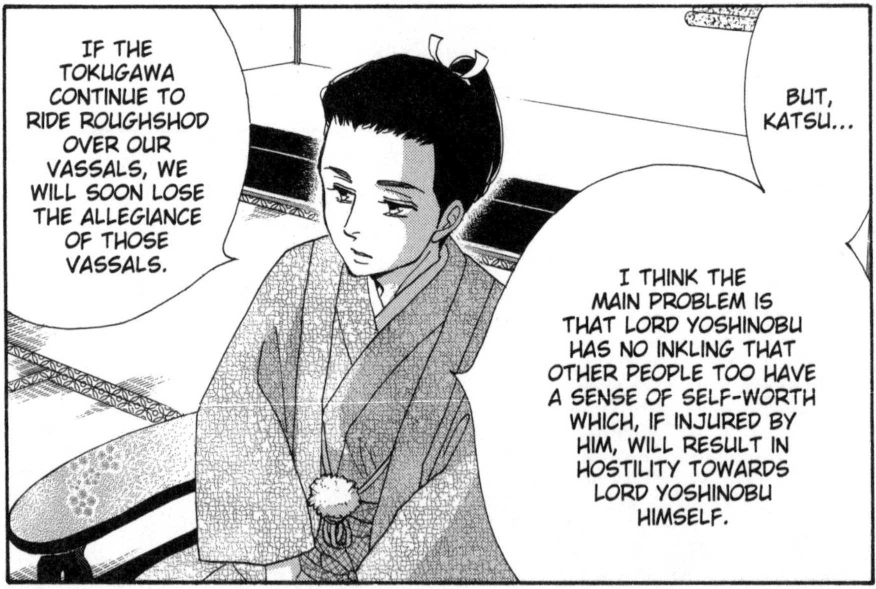
BUT, KATSU...
I THINK THE MAIN PROBLEM IS THAT LORD YOSHINOBU HAS NO INKLING THAT OTHER PEOPLE TOO HAVE A SENSE OF SELF-WORTH WHICH, IF INJURED BY HIM, WILL RESULT IN HOSTILITY TOWARDS LORD YOSHINOBU HIMSELF.
IF THE TOKUGAWA CONTINUE TO RIDE ROUGHSHOD OVER OUR VASSALS, WE WILL SOON LOSE THE ALLEGIANCE OF THOSE VASSALS.

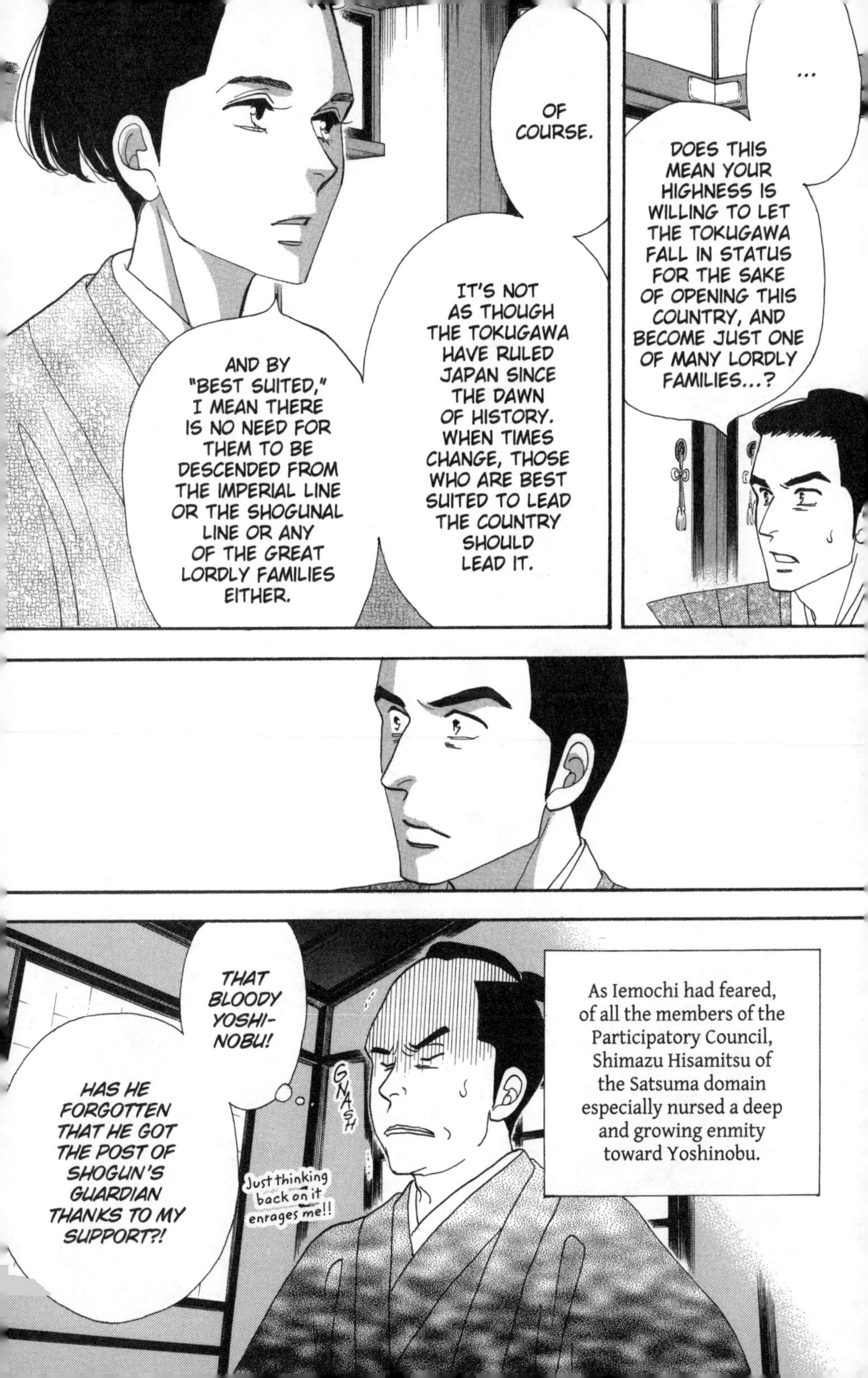
...
DOES THIS MEAN YOUR HIGHNESS IS WILLING TO LET THE TOKUGAWA FALL IN STATUS FOR THE SAKE OF OPENING THIS COUNTRY, AND BECOME JUST ONE OF MANY LORDLY FAMILIES...?
OF COURSE.
IT'S NOT AS THOUGH THE TOKUGAWA HAVE RULED JAPAN SINCE THE DAWN OF HISTORY. WHEN TIMES CHANGE, THOSE WHO ARE BEST SUITED TO LEAD THE COUNTRY SHOULD LEAD IT.
AND BY "BEST SUITED," I MEAN THERE IS NO NEED FOR THEM TO BE DESCENDED FROM THE IMPERIAL LINE OR THE SHOGUNAL LINE OR ANY OF THE GREAT LORDLY FAMILIES EITHER.
As Iemochi had feared, of all the members of the Participatory Council, Shimazu Hisamitsu of the Satsuma domain especially nursed a deep and growing enmity toward Yoshinobu.
THAT BLOODY YOSHI-NOBU!
GNASH
HAS HE FORGOTTEN THAT HE GOT THE POST OF SHOGUN'S GUARDIAN THANKS TO MY SUPPORT?!
Just thinking back on it enrages me!!

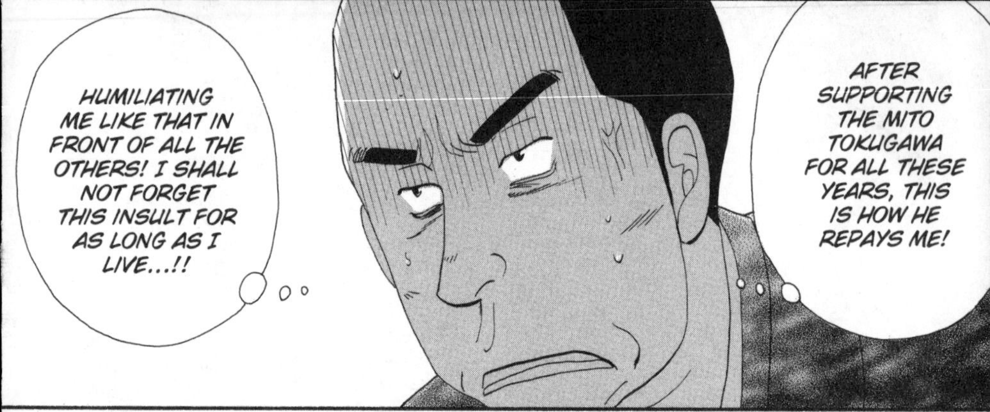
AFTER SUPPORTING THE MITO TOKUGAWA FOR ALL THESE YEARS, THIS IS HOW HE REPAYS ME!
HUMILIATING ME LIKE THAT IN FRONT OF ALL THE OTHERS! I SHALL NOT FORGET THIS INSULT FOR AS LONG AS I LIVE...!!

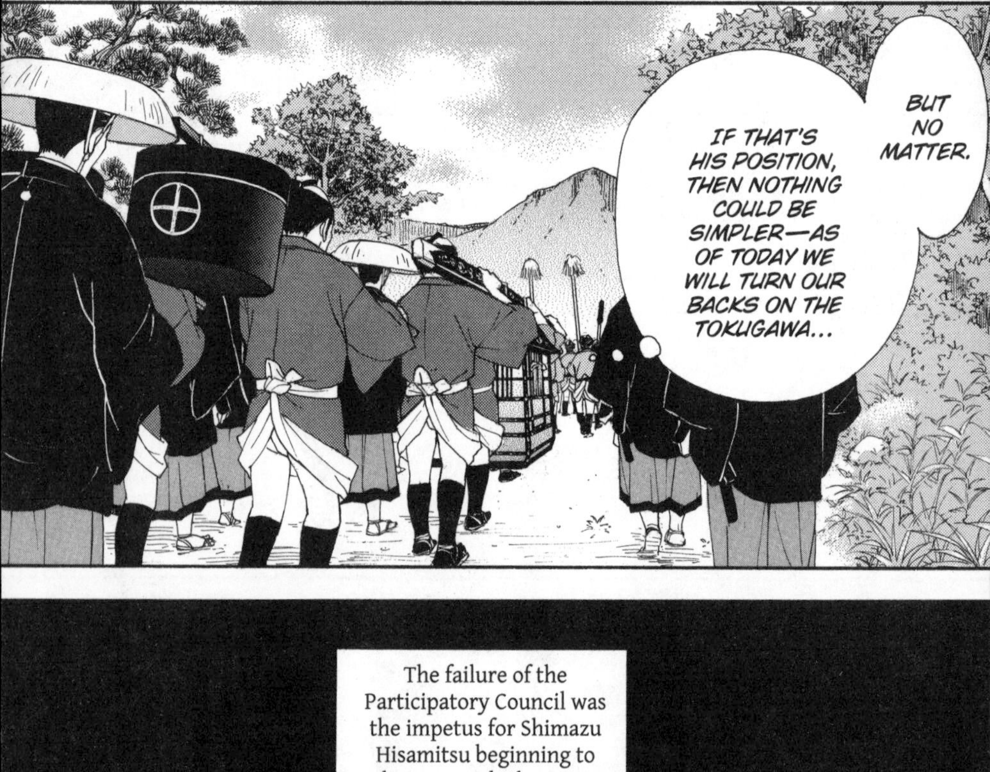
BUT NO MATTER.
IF THAT'S HIS POSITION, THEN NOTHING COULD BE SIMPLER—AS OF TODAY WE WILL TURN OUR BACKS ON THE TOKUGAWA...

The failure of the Participatory Council was the impetus for Shimazu Hisamitsu beginning to lean towards the anti-shogunate, revolutionary forces in the country. His change of heart was a first step towards Satsuma and Choshu later forging an alliance, which would eventually topple the Tokugawa shogunate.

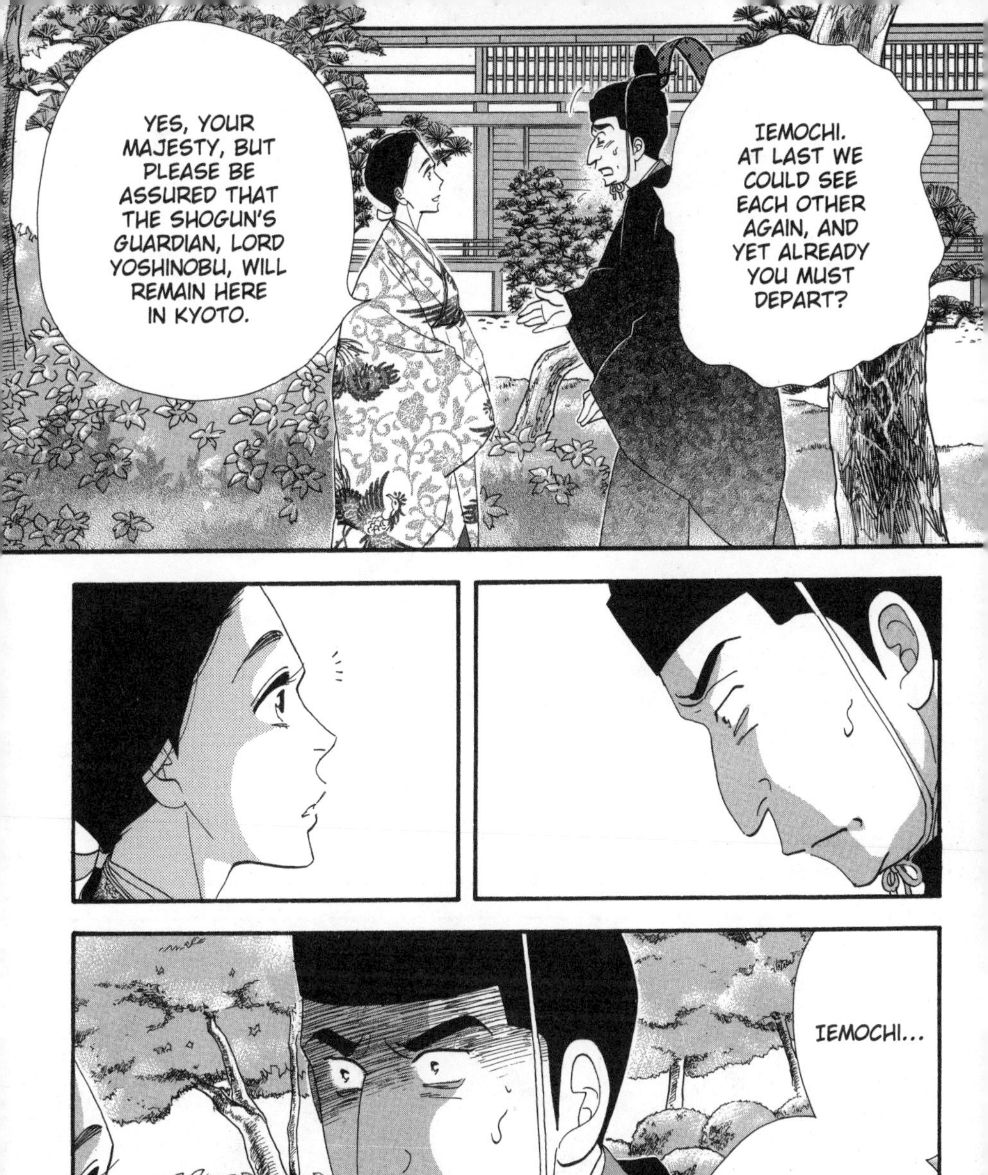
IEMOCHI. AT LAST WE COULD SEE EACH OTHER AGAIN, AND YET ALREADY YOU MUST DEPART?
YES, YOUR MAJESTY, BUT PLEASE BE ASSURED THAT THE SHOGUN'S GUARDIAN, LORD YOSHINOBU, WILL REMAIN HERE IN KYOTO.
IEMOCHI...
THAT HITOTSUBASHI YOSHINOBU! I HAVE NO CONFIDENCE IN THE MAN. I JUST KNOW—THAT MAN WILL NOT PROTECT ME TO THE LAST!!
SO PLEASE, IEMOCHI...COME BACK TO KYOTO AGAIN...!!

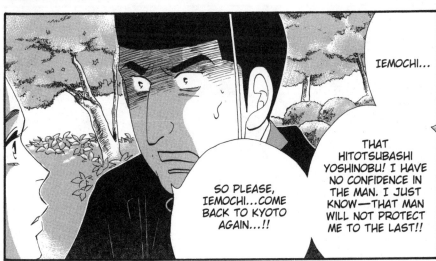

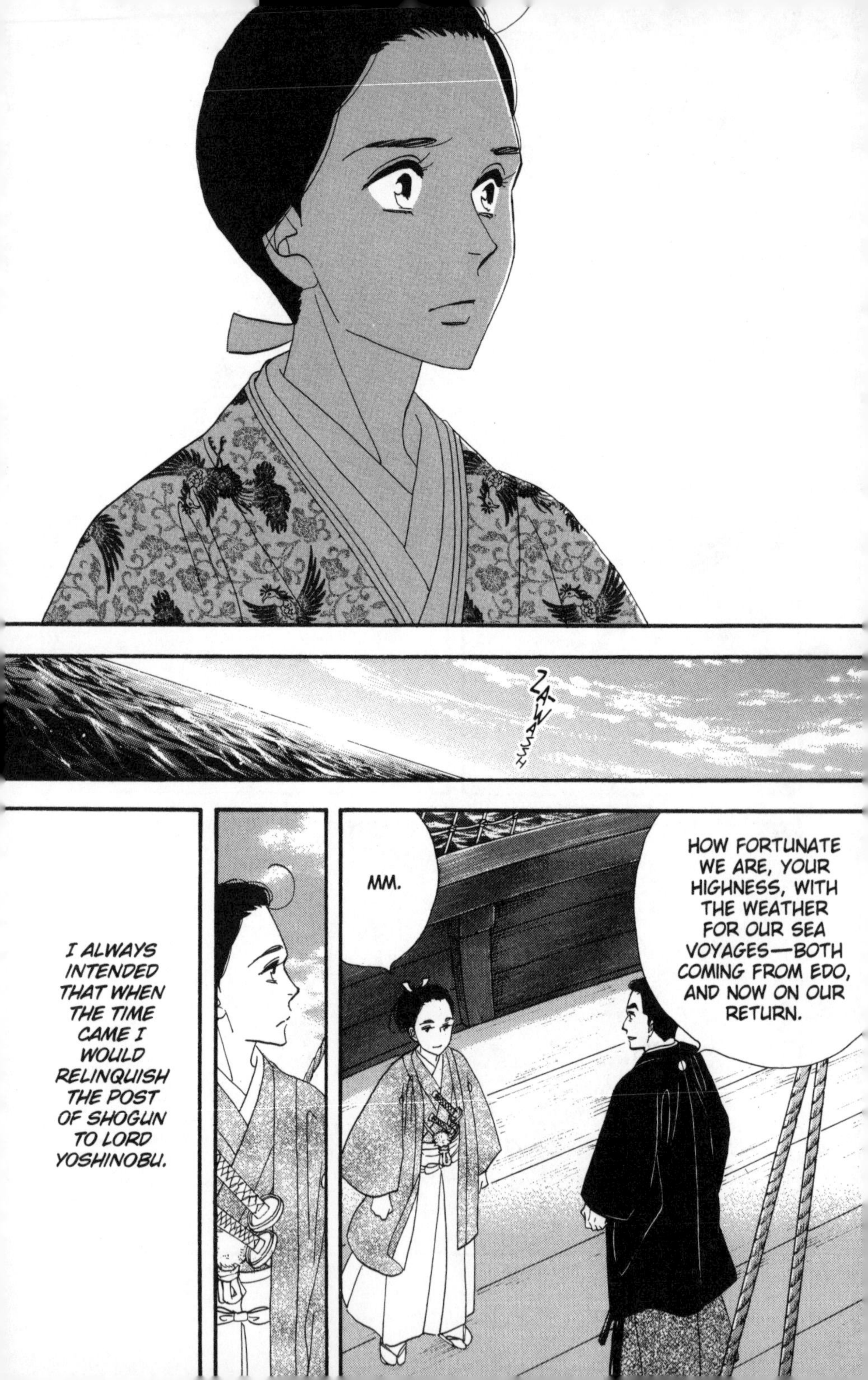
ZA-WASSH
HOW FORTUNATE WE ARE, YOUR HIGHNESS, WITH THE WEATHER FOR OUR SEA VOYAGES—BOTH COMING FROM EDO, AND NOW ON OUR RETURN.
MM.
I ALWAYS INTENDED THAT WHEN THE TIME CAME I WOULD RELINQUISH THE POST OF SHOGUN TO LORD YOSHINOBU.

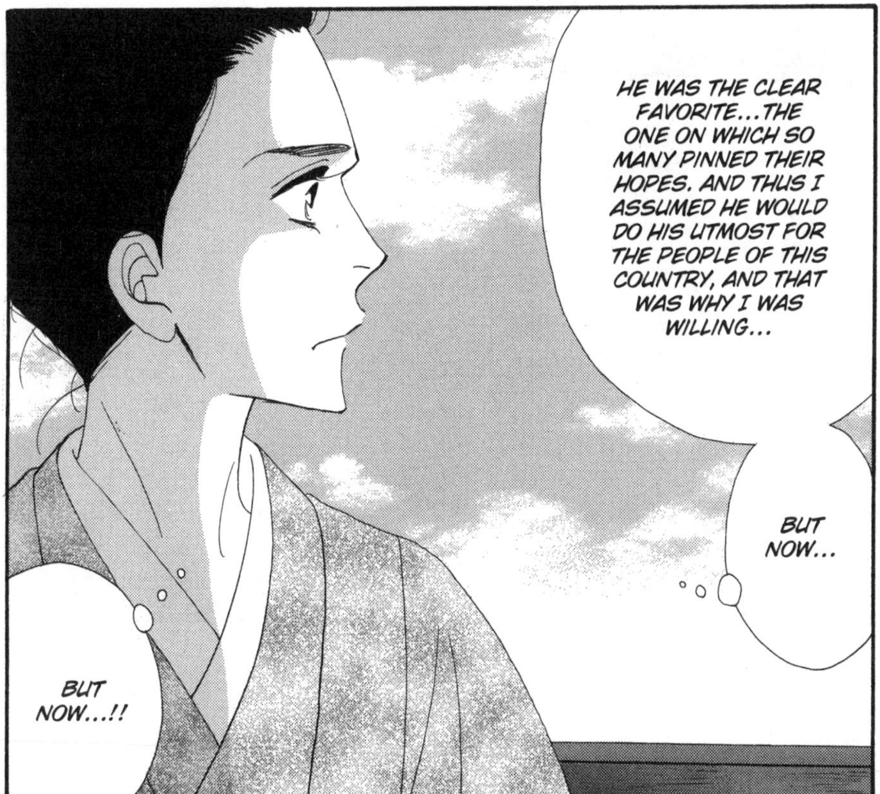
HE WAS THE CLEAR FAVORITE...THE ONE ON WHICH SO MANY PINNED THEIR HOPES. AND THUS I ASSUMED HE WOULD DO HIS UTMOST FOR THE PEOPLE OF THIS COUNTRY, AND THAT WAS WHY I WAS WILLING...
BUT NOW...
BUT NOW...!!

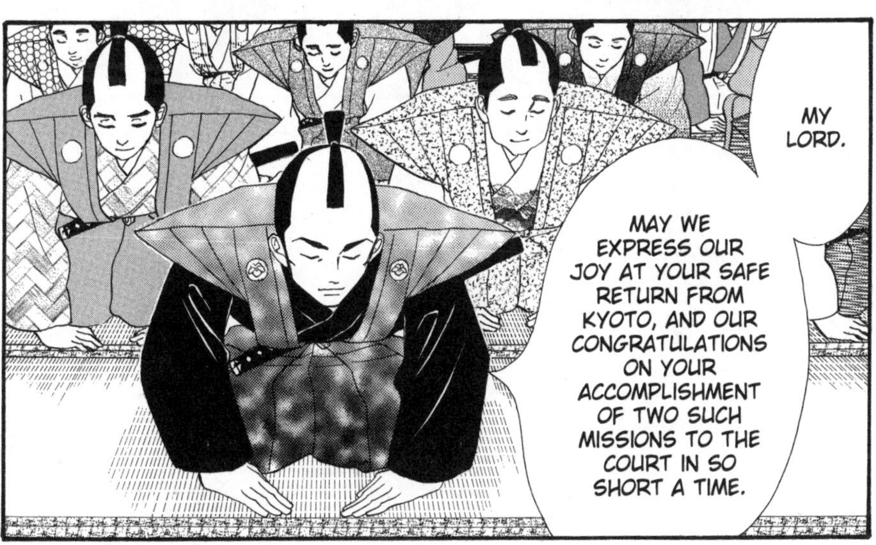
MY LORD.
MAY WE EXPRESS OUR JOY AT YOUR SAFE RETURN FROM KYOTO, AND OUR CONGRATULATIONS ON YOUR ACCOMPLISHMENT OF TWO SUCH MISSIONS TO THE COURT IN SO SHORT A TIME.

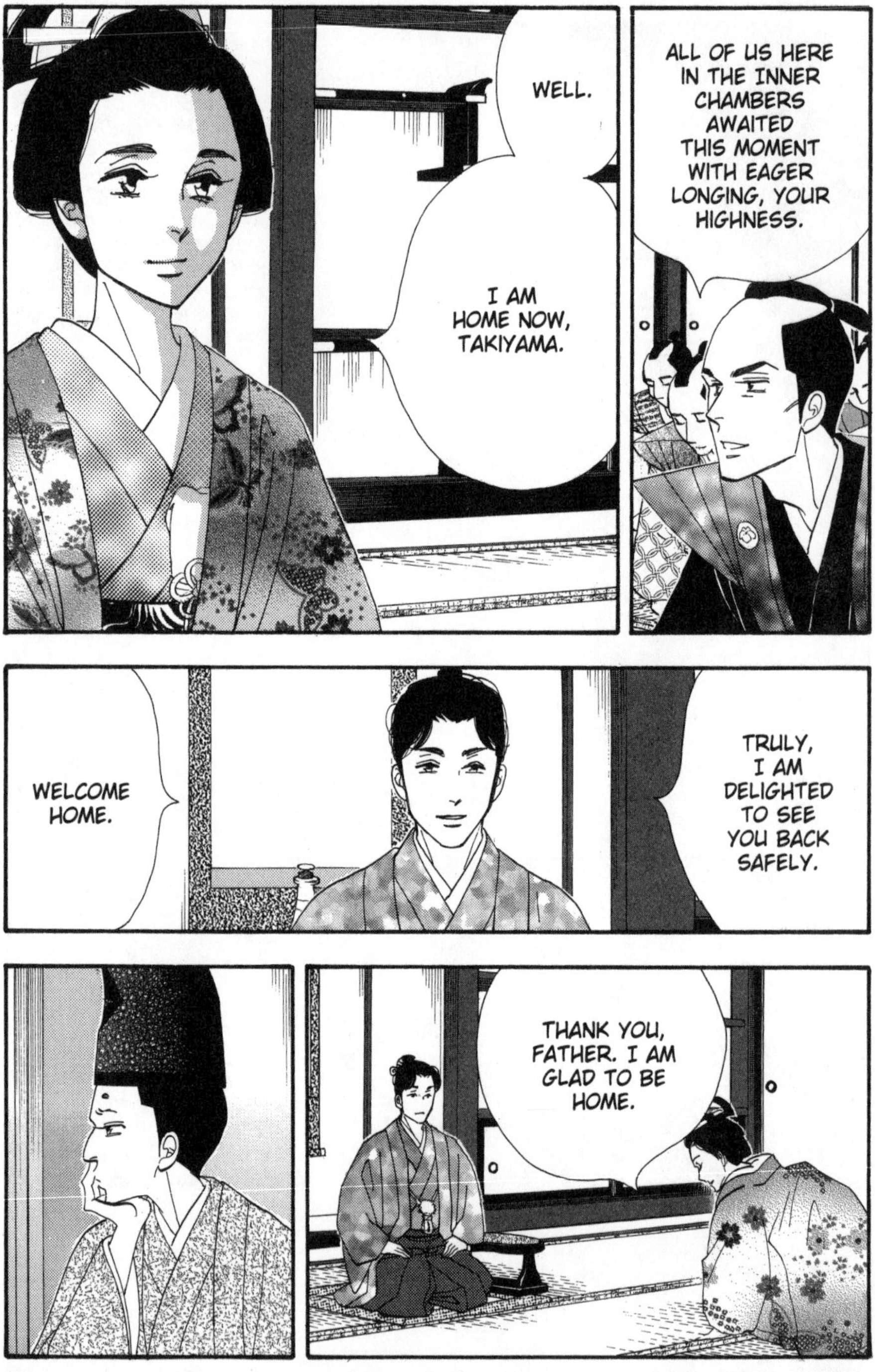
ALL OF US HERE IN THE INNER CHAMBERS AWAITED THIS MOMENT WITH EAGER LONGING, YOUR HIGHNESS.
WELL.
I AM HOME NOW, TAKIYAMA.
TRULY, I AM DELIGHTED TO SEE YOU BACK SAFELY.
WELCOME HOME.
THANK YOU, FATHER. I AM GLAD TO BE HOME.

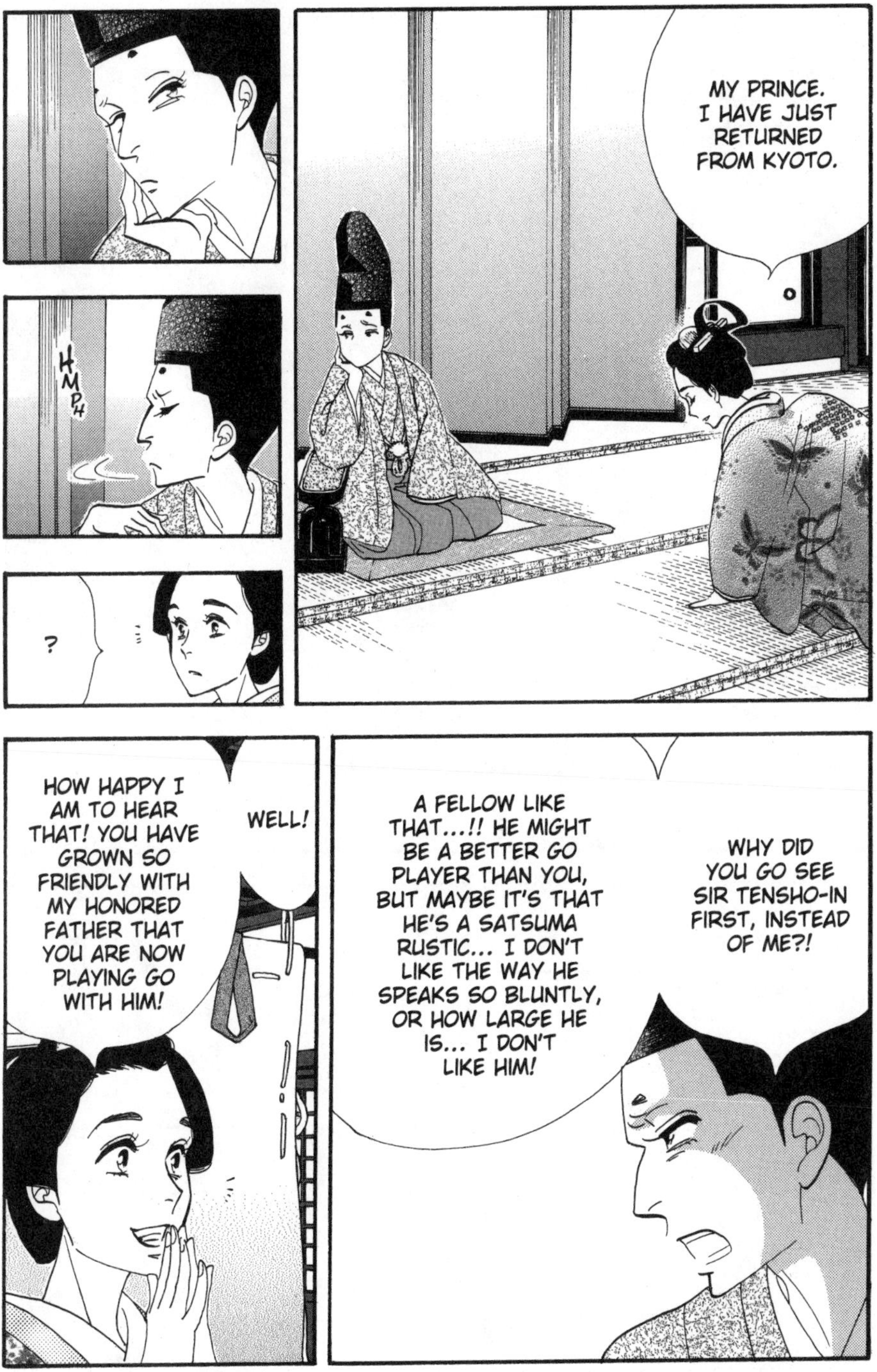
MY PRINCE. I HAVE JUST RETURNED FROM KYOTO.
HMPH
?
WHY DID YOU GO SEE SIR TENSHO-IN FIRST, INSTEAD OF ME?!
A FELLOW LIKE THAT...!! HE MIGHT BE A BETTER GO PLAYER THAN YOU, BUT MAYBE IT'S THAT HE'S A SATSUMA RUSTIC... I DON'T LIKE THE WAY HE SPEAKS SO BLUNTLY, OR HOW LARGE HE IS... I DON'T LIKE HIM!
WELL!
HOW HAPPY I AM TO HEAR THAT! YOU HAVE GROWN SO FRIENDLY WITH MY HONORED FATHER THAT YOU ARE NOW PLAYING GO WITH HIM!

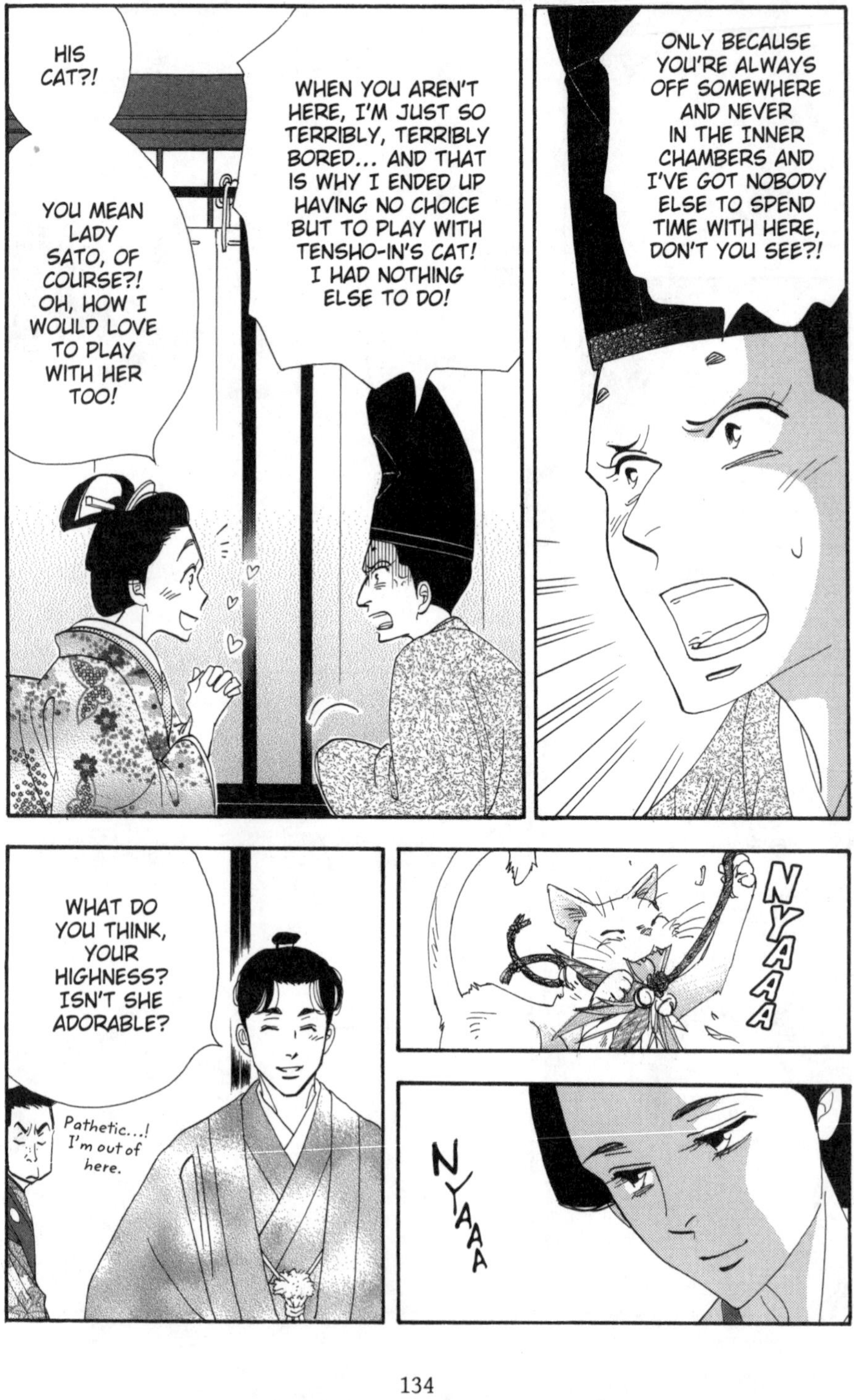
ONLY BECAUSE YOU'RE ALWAYS OFF SOMEWHERE AND NEVER IN THE INNER CHAMBERS AND I'VE GOT NOBODY ELSE TO SPEND TIME WITH HERE, DON'T YOU SEE?!
WHEN YOU AREN'T HERE, I'M JUST SO TERRIBLY, TERRIBLY BORED... AND THAT IS WHY I ENDED UP HAVING NO CHOICE BUT TO PLAY WITH TENSHO-IN'S CAT! I HAD NOTHING ELSE TO DO!
HIS CAT?!
YOU MEAN LADY SATO, OF COURSE?! OH, HOW I WOULD LOVE TO PLAY WITH HER TOO!
NYAAAA
NYAAA
WHAT DO YOU THINK, YOUR HIGHNESS? ISN'T SHE ADORABLE?
Pathetic...! I'm out of here.

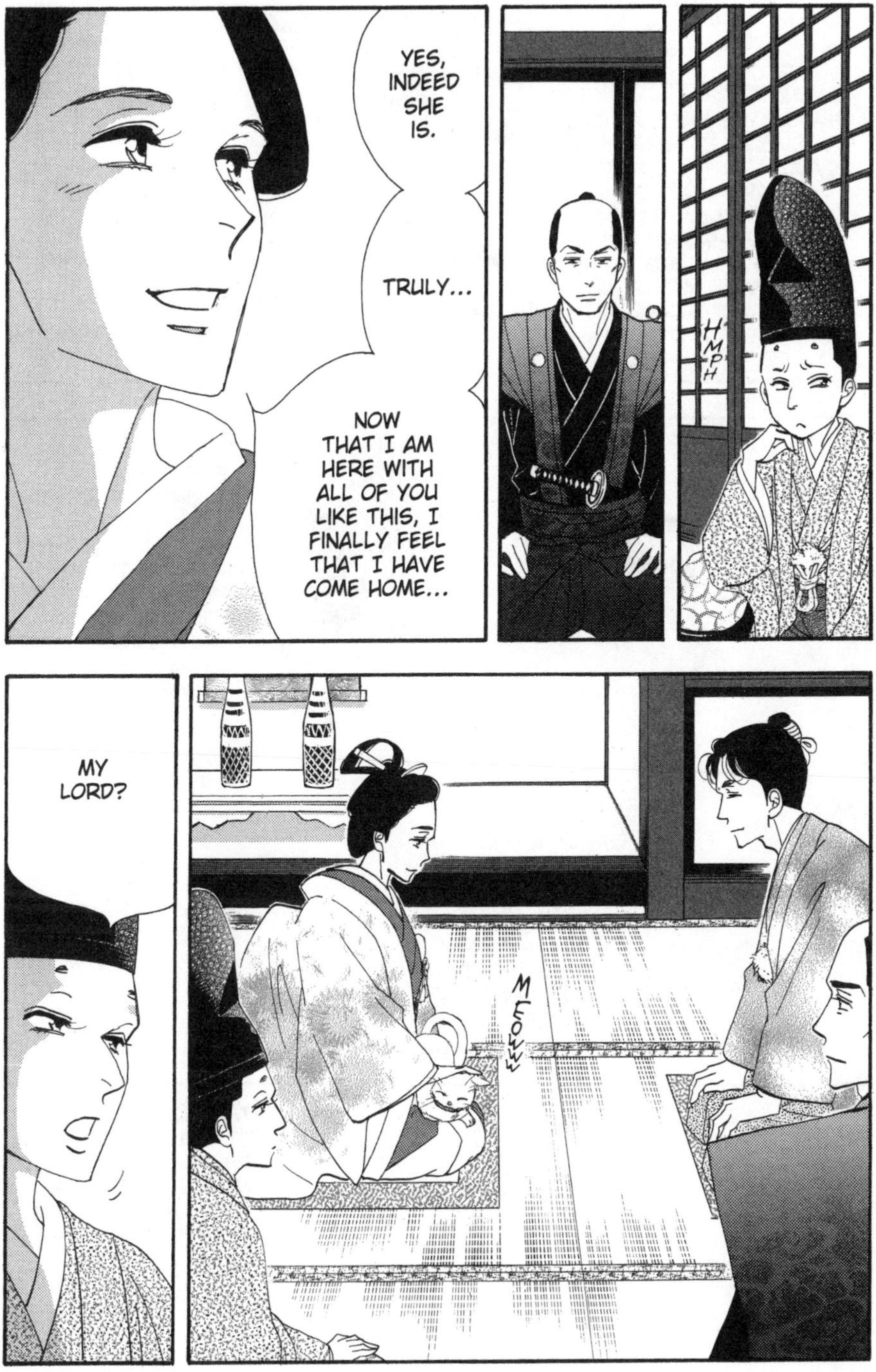
HMPH
YES, INDEED SHE IS.
TRULY...
NOW THAT I AM HERE WITH ALL OF YOU LIKE THIS, I FINALLY FEEL THAT I HAVE COME HOME...
MEOWW
MY LORD?

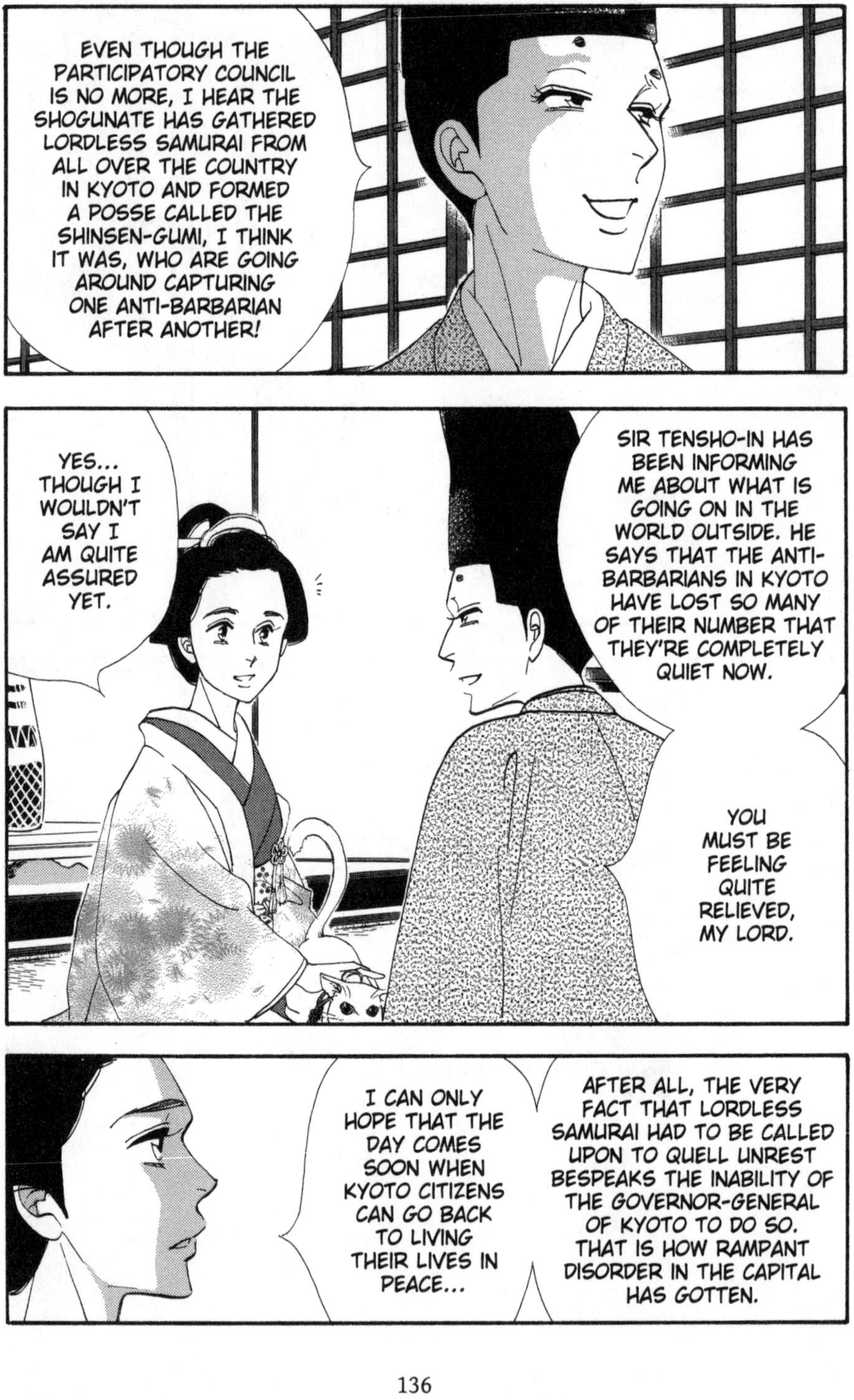
EVEN THOUGH THE PARTICIPATORY COUNCIL IS NO MORE, I HEAR THE SHOGUNATE HAS GATHERED LORDLESS SAMURAI FROM ALL OVER THE COUNTRY IN KYOTO AND FORMED A POSSE CALLED THE SHINSEN-GUMI, I THINK IT WAS, WHO ARE GOING AROUND CAPTURING ONE ANTI-BARBARIAN AFTER ANOTHER!
SIR TENSHO-IN HAS BEEN INFORMING ME ABOUT WHAT IS GOING ON IN THE WORLD OUTSIDE. HE SAYS THAT THE ANTI-BARBARIANS IN KYOTO HAVE LOST SO MANY OF THEIR NUMBER THAT THEY'RE COMPLETELY QUIET NOW.
YOU MUST BE FEELING QUITE RELIEVED, MY LORD.
YES... THOUGH I WOULDN'T SAY I AM QUITE ASSURED YET.
AFTER ALL, THE VERY FACT THAT LORDLESS SAMURAI HAD TO BE CALLED UPON TO QUELL UNREST BESPEAKS THE INABILITY OF THE GOVERNOR-GENERAL OF KYOTO TO DO SO. THAT IS HOW RAMPANT DISORDER IN THE CAPITAL HAS GOTTEN.
I CAN ONLY HOPE THAT THE DAY COMES SOON WHEN KYOTO CITIZENS CAN GO BACK TO LIVING THEIR LIVES IN PEACE...

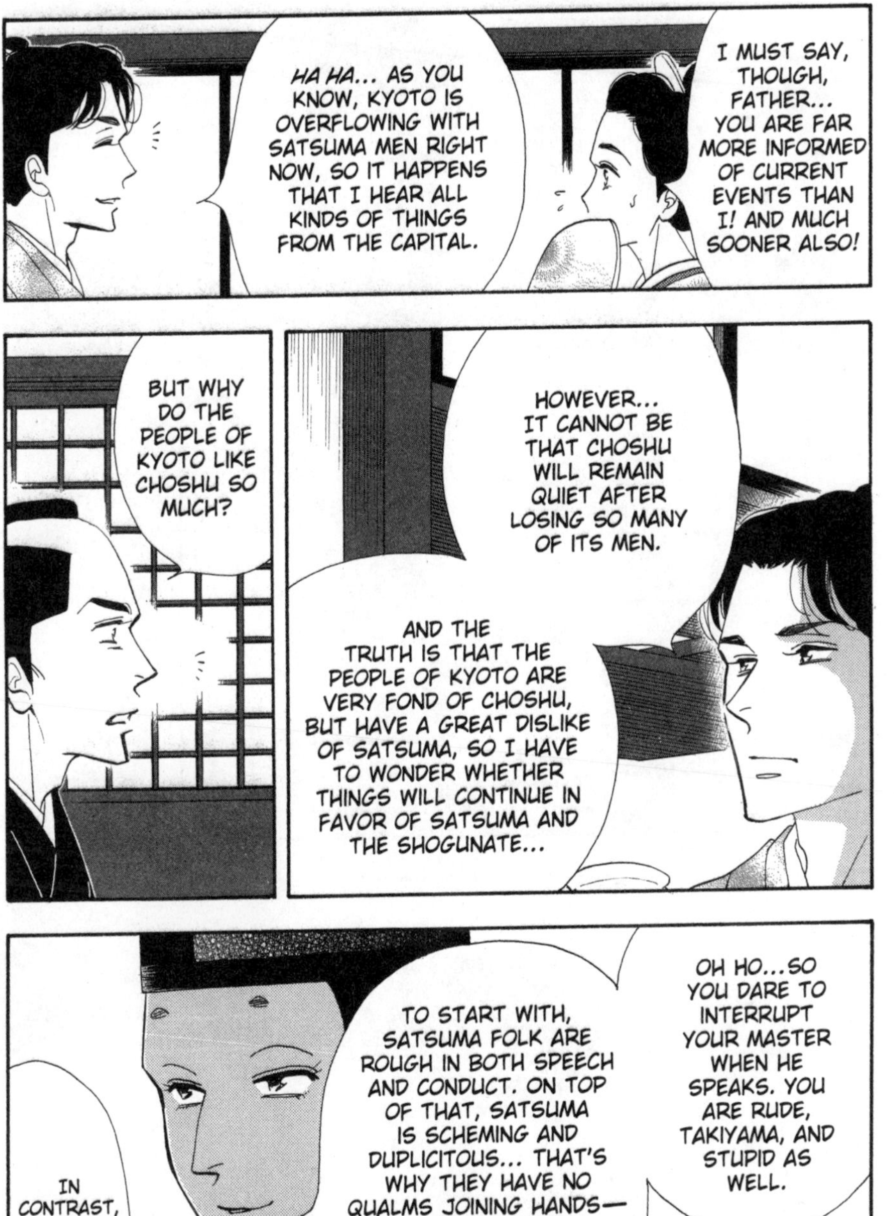
I MUST SAY, THOUGH, FATHER... YOU ARE FAR MORE INFORMED OF CURRENT EVENTS THAN I! AND MUCH SOONER ALSO!
HA HA... AS YOU KNOW, KYOTO IS OVERFLOWING WITH SATSUMA MEN RIGHT NOW, SO IT HAPPENS THAT I HEAR ALL KINDS OF THINGS FROM THE CAPITAL.
HOWEVER... IT CANNOT BE THAT CHOSHU WILL REMAIN QUIET AFTER LOSING SO MANY OF ITS MEN.
AND THE TRUTH IS THAT THE PEOPLE OF KYOTO ARE VERY FOND OF CHOSHU, BUT HAVE A GREAT DISLIKE OF SATSUMA, SO I HAVE TO WONDER WHETHER THINGS WILL CONTINUE IN FAVOR OF SATSUMA AND THE SHOGUNATE...
BUT WHY DO THE PEOPLE OF KYOTO LIKE CHOSHU SO MUCH?
OH HO...SO YOU DARE TO INTERRUPT YOUR MASTER WHEN HE SPEAKS. YOU ARE RUDE, TAKIYAMA, AND STUPID AS WELL.
TO START WITH, SATSUMA FOLK ARE ROUGH IN BOTH SPEECH AND CONDUCT. ON TOP OF THAT, SATSUMA IS SCHEMING AND DUPLICITOUS... THAT'S WHY THEY HAVE NO QUALMS JOINING HANDS—OSTENSIBLY, ANYWAY—WITH THE TOKUGAWA, WHO HAVE BEEN THEIR ENEMY SINCE THE BATTLE OF SEKIGAHARA.
IN CONTRAST, CHOSHU IS STRAIGHT AND TRUE.

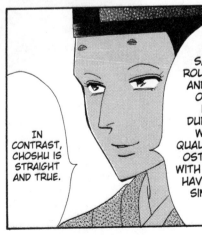

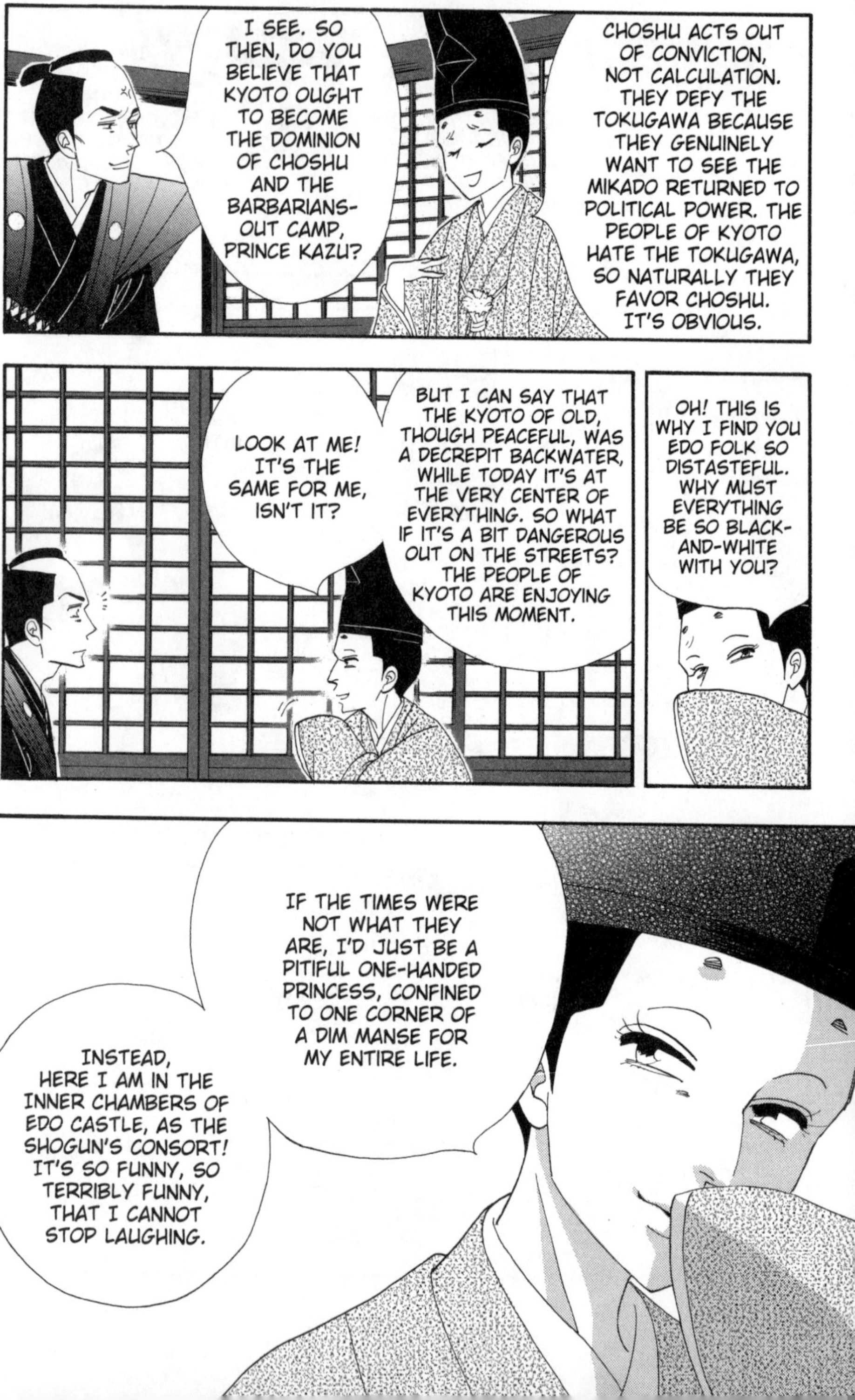
CHOSHU ACTS OUT OF CONVICTION, NOT CALCULATION. THEY DEFY THE TOKUGAWA BECAUSE THEY GENUINELY WANT TO SEE THE MIKADO RETURNED TO POLITICAL POWER. THE PEOPLE OF KYOTO HATE THE TOKUGAWA, SO NATURALLY THEY FAVOR CHOSHU. IT'S OBVIOUS.
I SEE. SO THEN, DO YOU BELIEVE THAT KYOTO OUGHT TO BECOME THE DOMINION OF CHOSHU AND THE BARBARIANS-OUT CAMP, PRINCE KAZU?
OH! THIS IS WHY I FIND YOU EDO FOLK SO DISTASTEFUL. WHY MUST EVERYTHING BE SO BLACK-AND-WHITE WITH YOU?
LOOK AT ME! IT'S THE SAME FOR ME, ISN'T IT?
BUT I CAN SAY THAT THE KYOTO OF OLD, THOUGH PEACEFUL, WAS A DECREPIT BACKWATER, WHILE TODAY IT'S AT THE VERY CENTER OF EVERYTHING. SO WHAT IF IT'S A BIT DANGEROUS OUT ON THE STREETS? THE PEOPLE OF KYOTO ARE ENJOYING THIS MOMENT.
IF THE TIMES WERE NOT WHAT THEY ARE, I'D JUST BE A PITIFUL ONE-HANDED PRINCESS, CONFINED TO ONE CORNER OF A DIM MANSE FOR MY ENTIRE LIFE.
INSTEAD, HERE I AM IN THE INNER CHAMBERS OF EDO CASTLE, AS THE SHOGUN'S CONSORT! IT'S SO FUNNY, SO TERRIBLY FUNNY, THAT I CANNOT STOP LAUGHING.

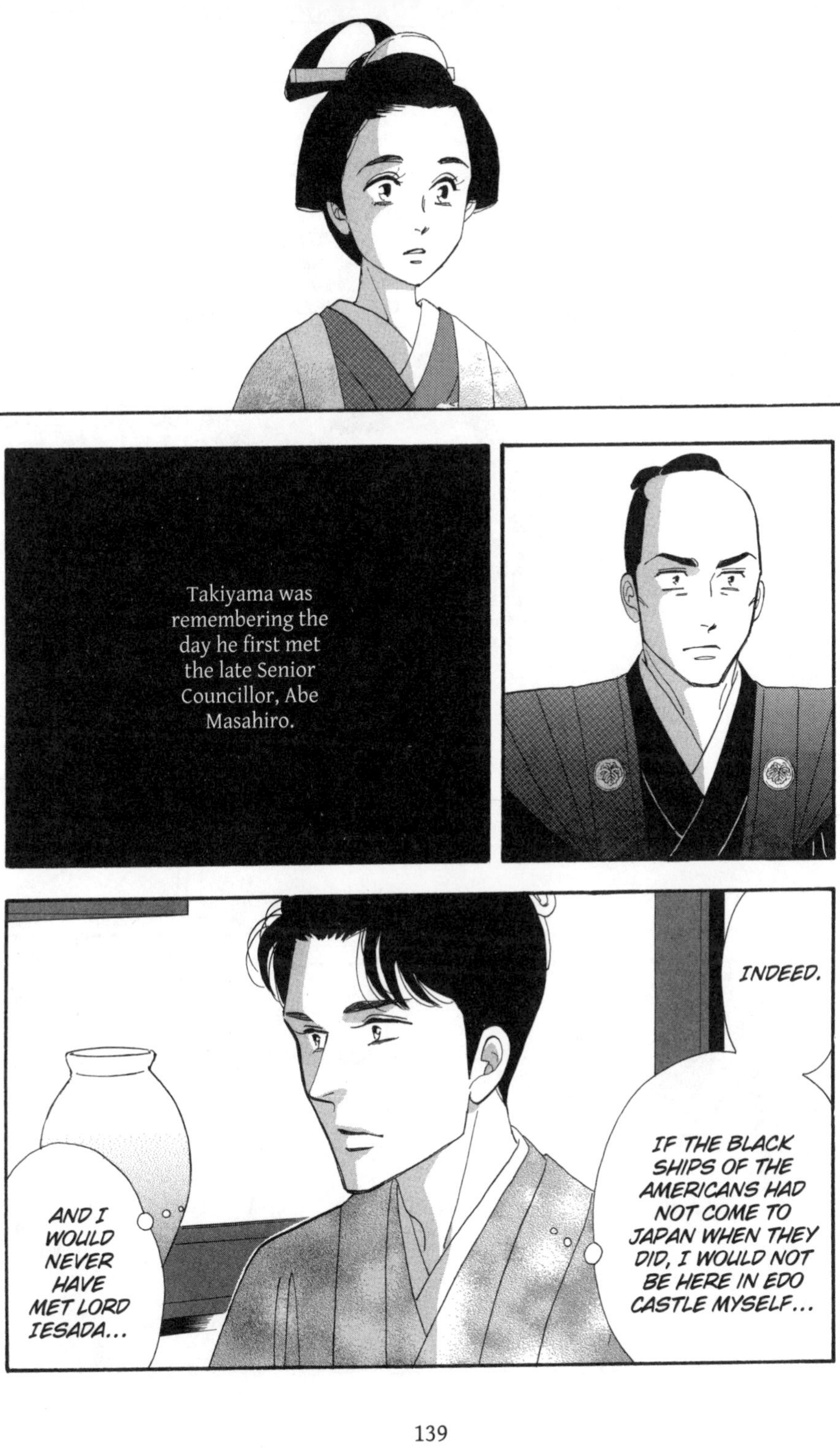
Takiyama was remembering the day he first met the late Senior Councillor, Abe Masahiro.
INDEED.
IF THE BLACK SHIPS OF THE AMERICANS HAD NOT COME TO JAPAN WHEN THEY DID, I WOULD NOT BE HERE IN EDO CASTLE MYSELF...
AND I WOULD NEVER HAVE MET LORD IESADA...

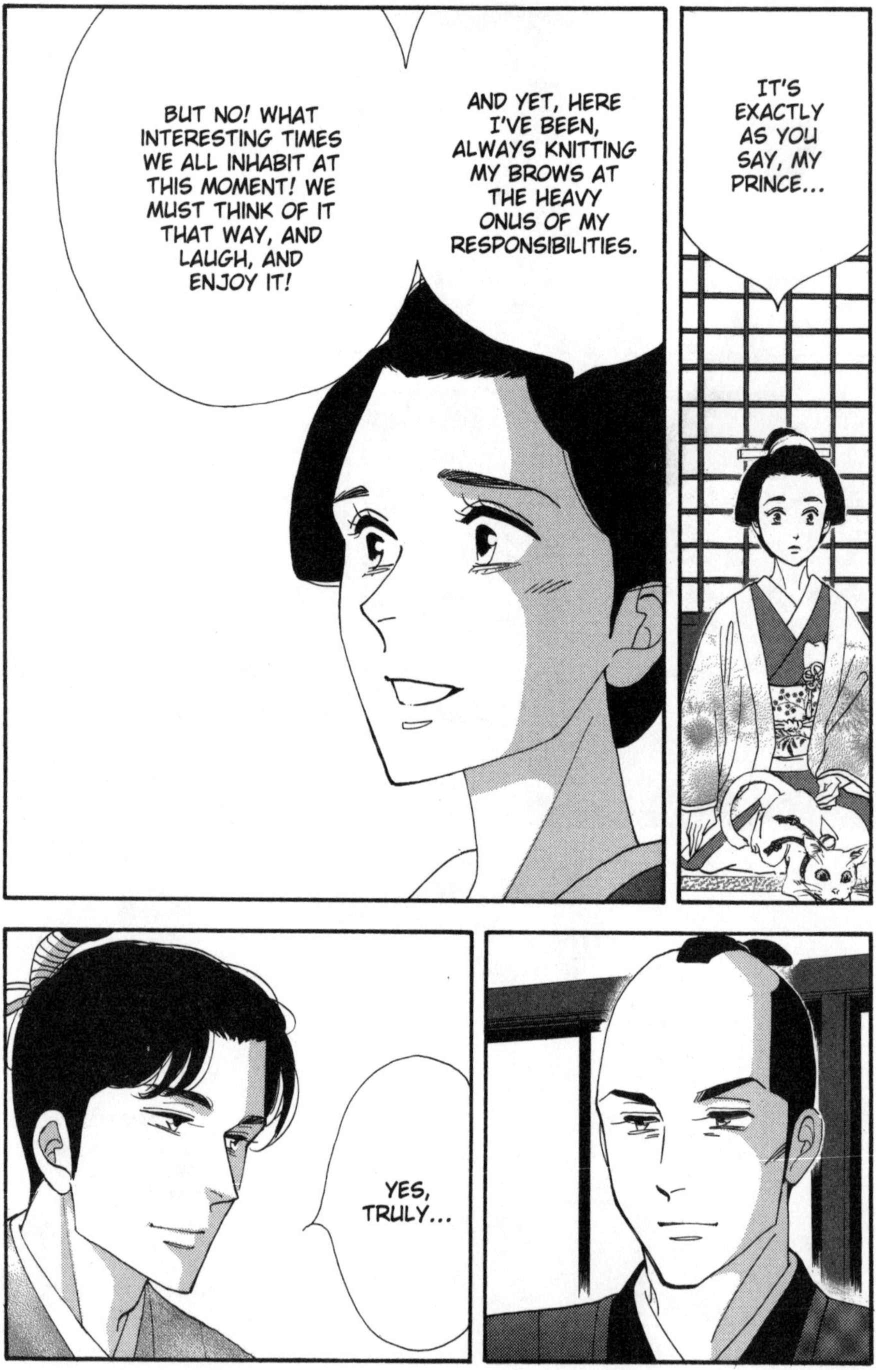
IT'S EXACTLY AS YOU SAY, MY PRINCE...
AND YET, HERE I'VE BEEN, ALWAYS KNITTING MY BROWS AT THE HEAVY ONUS OF MY RESPONSIBILITIES.
BUT NO! WHAT INTERESTING TIMES WE ALL INHABIT AT THIS MOMENT! WE MUST THINK OF IT THAT WAY, AND LAUGH, AND ENJOY IT!
YES, TRULY...

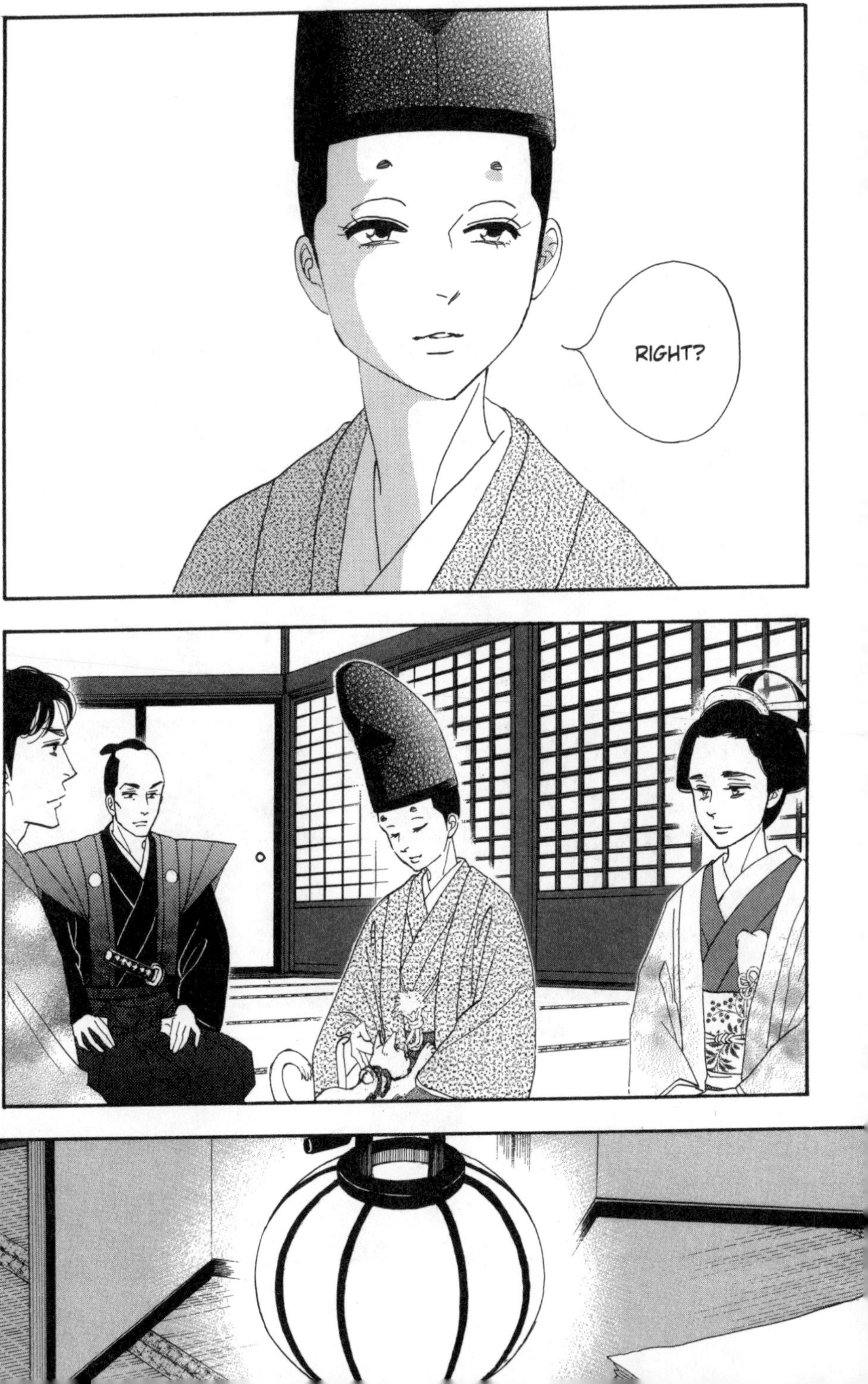
RIGHT?

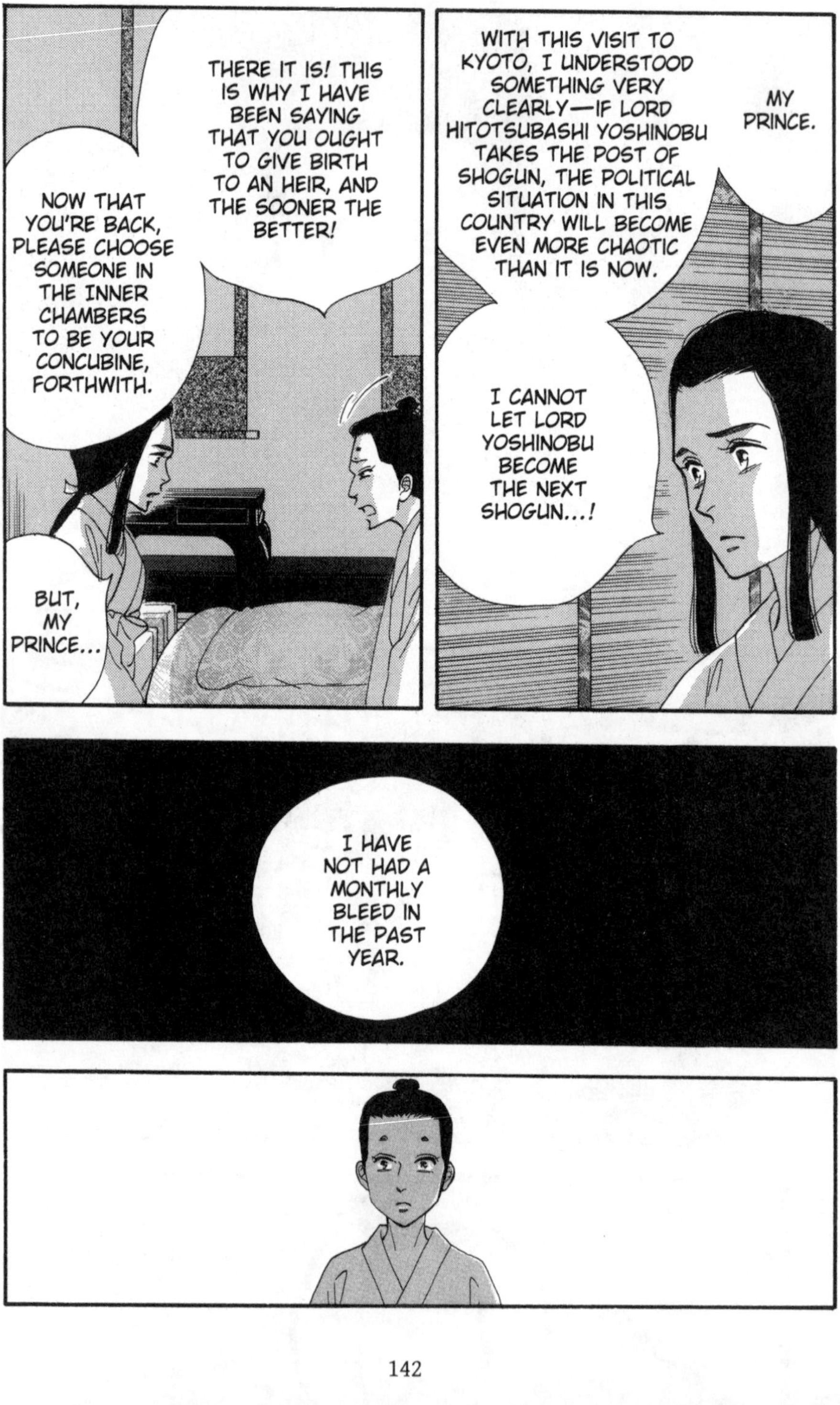
MY PRINCE.
WITH THIS VISIT TO KYOTO, I UNDERSTOOD SOMETHING VERY CLEARLY—IF LORD HITOTSUBASHI YOSHINOBU TAKES THE POST OF SHOGUN, THE POLITICAL SITUATION IN THIS COUNTRY WILL BECOME EVEN MORE CHAOTIC THAN IT IS NOW.
I CANNOT LET LORD YOSHINOBU BECOME THE NEXT SHOGUN...!
THERE IT IS! THIS IS WHY I HAVE BEEN SAYING THAT YOU OUGHT TO GIVE BIRTH TO AN HEIR, AND THE SOONER THE BETTER!
NOW THAT YOU'RE BACK, PLEASE CHOOSE SOMEONE IN THE INNER CHAMBERS TO BE YOUR CONCUBINE, FORTHWITH.
BUT, MY PRINCE...
I HAVE NOT HAD A MONTHLY BLEED IN THE PAST YEAR.

AND SO I AM UNABLE TO BEAR A CHILD AT THIS TIME.

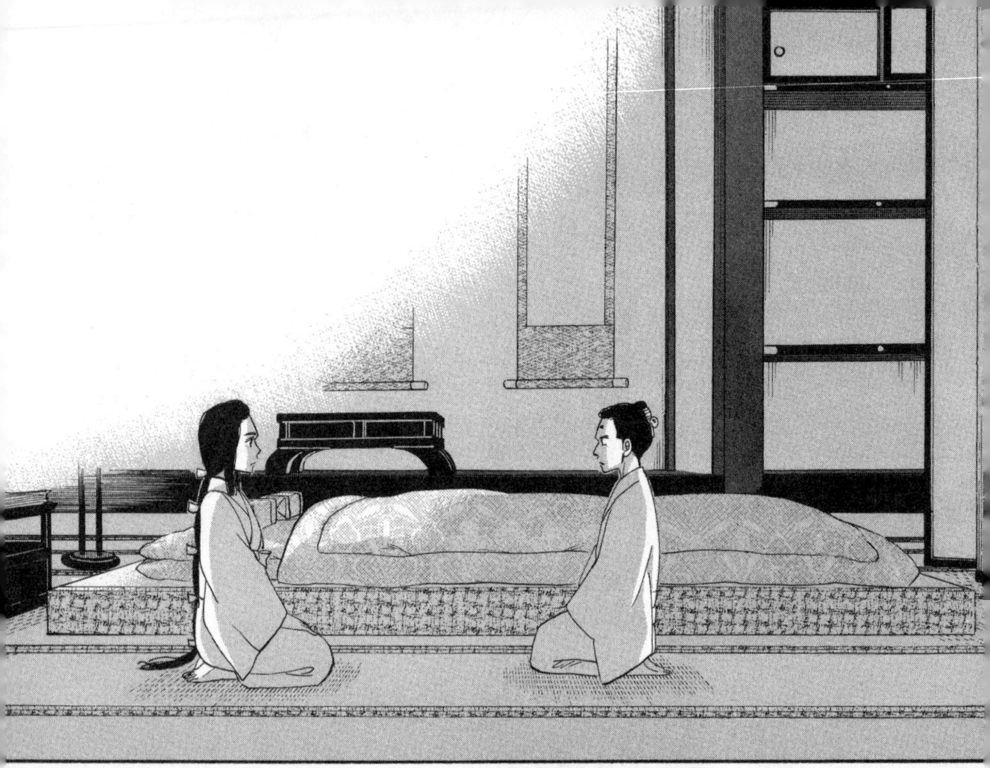

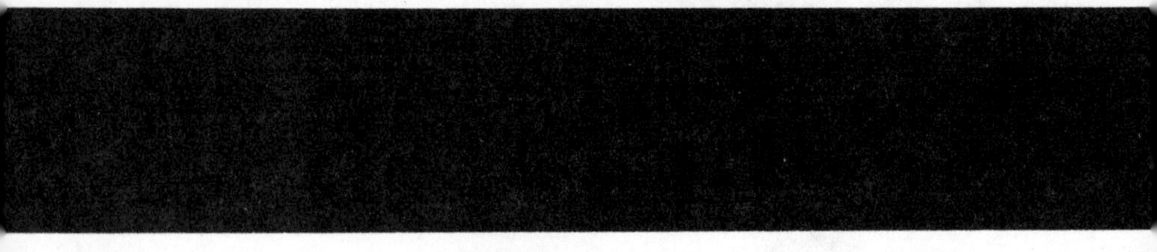

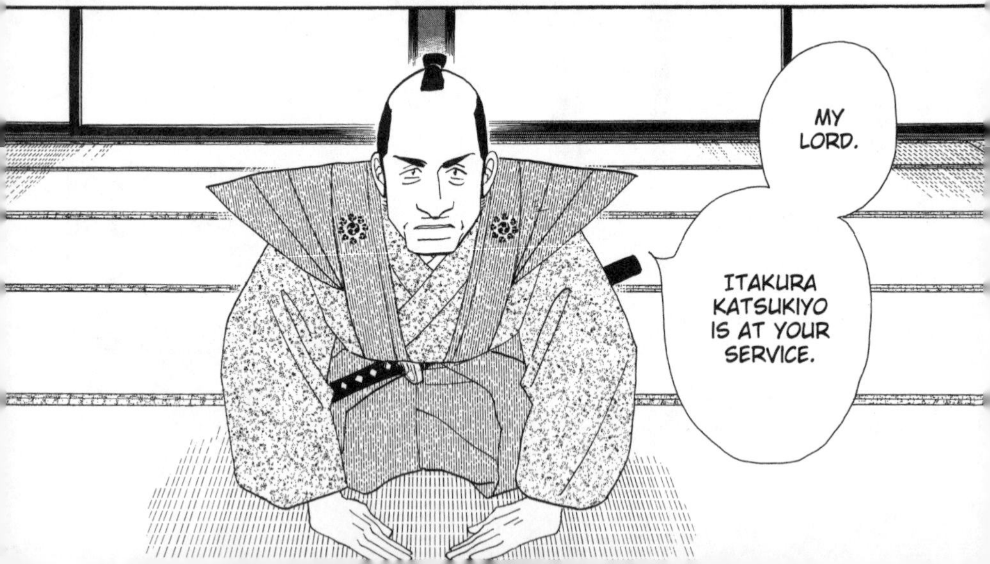
MY LORD.
ITAKURA KATSUKIYO IS AT YOUR SERVICE.

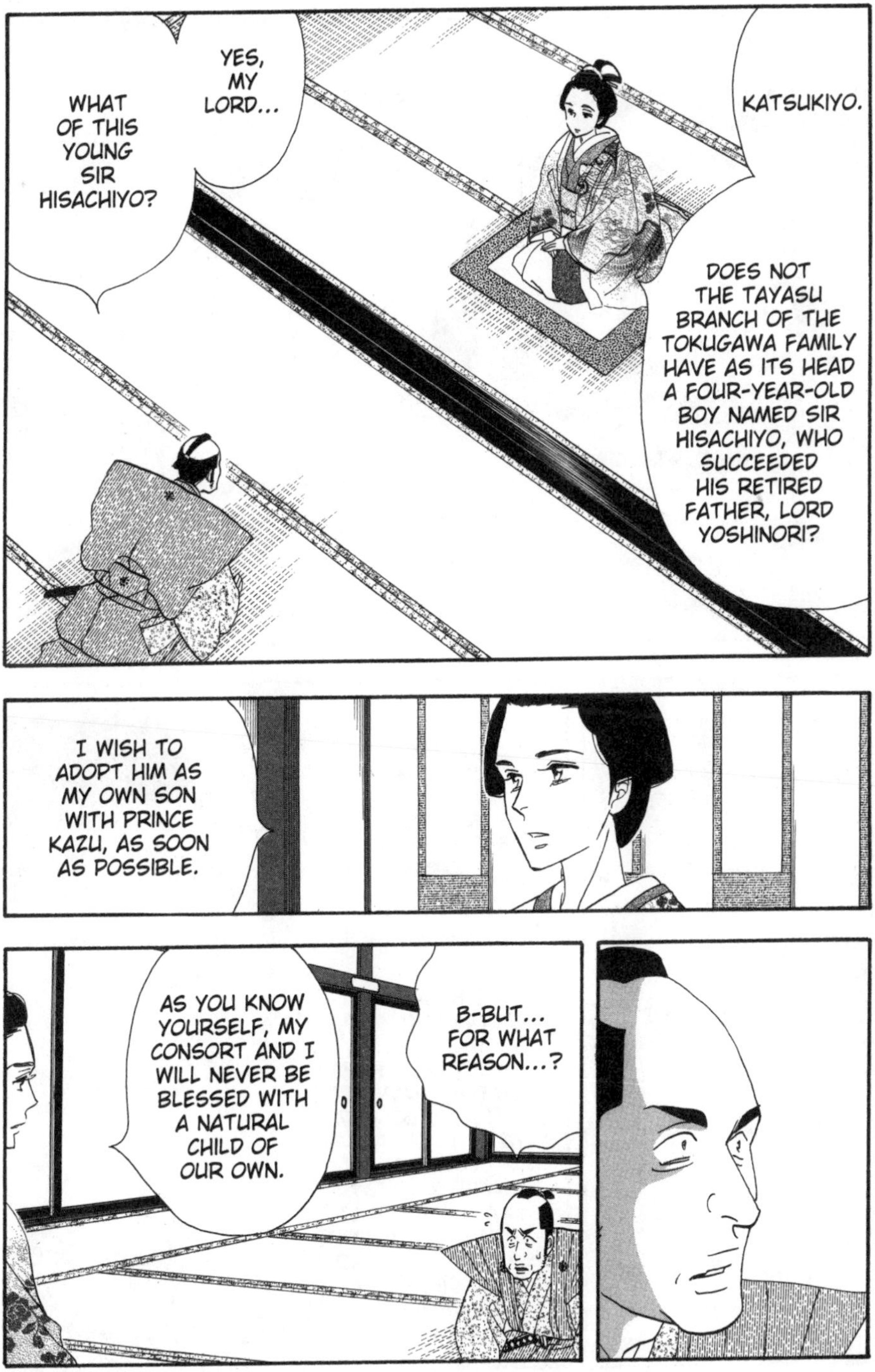
KATSUKIYO.
YES, MY LORD...
DOES NOT THE TAYASU BRANCH OF THE TOKUGAWA FAMILY HAVE AS ITS HEAD A FOUR-YEAR-OLD BOY NAMED SIR HISACHIYO, WHO SUCCEEDED HIS RETIRED FATHER, LORD YOSHINORI?
WHAT OF THIS YOUNG SIR HISACHIYO?
I WISH TO ADOPT HIM AS MY OWN SON WITH PRINCE KAZU, AS SOON AS POSSIBLE.
B-BUT... FOR WHAT REASON...?
AS YOU KNOW YOURSELF, MY CONSORT AND I WILL NEVER BE BLESSED WITH A NATURAL CHILD OF OUR OWN.

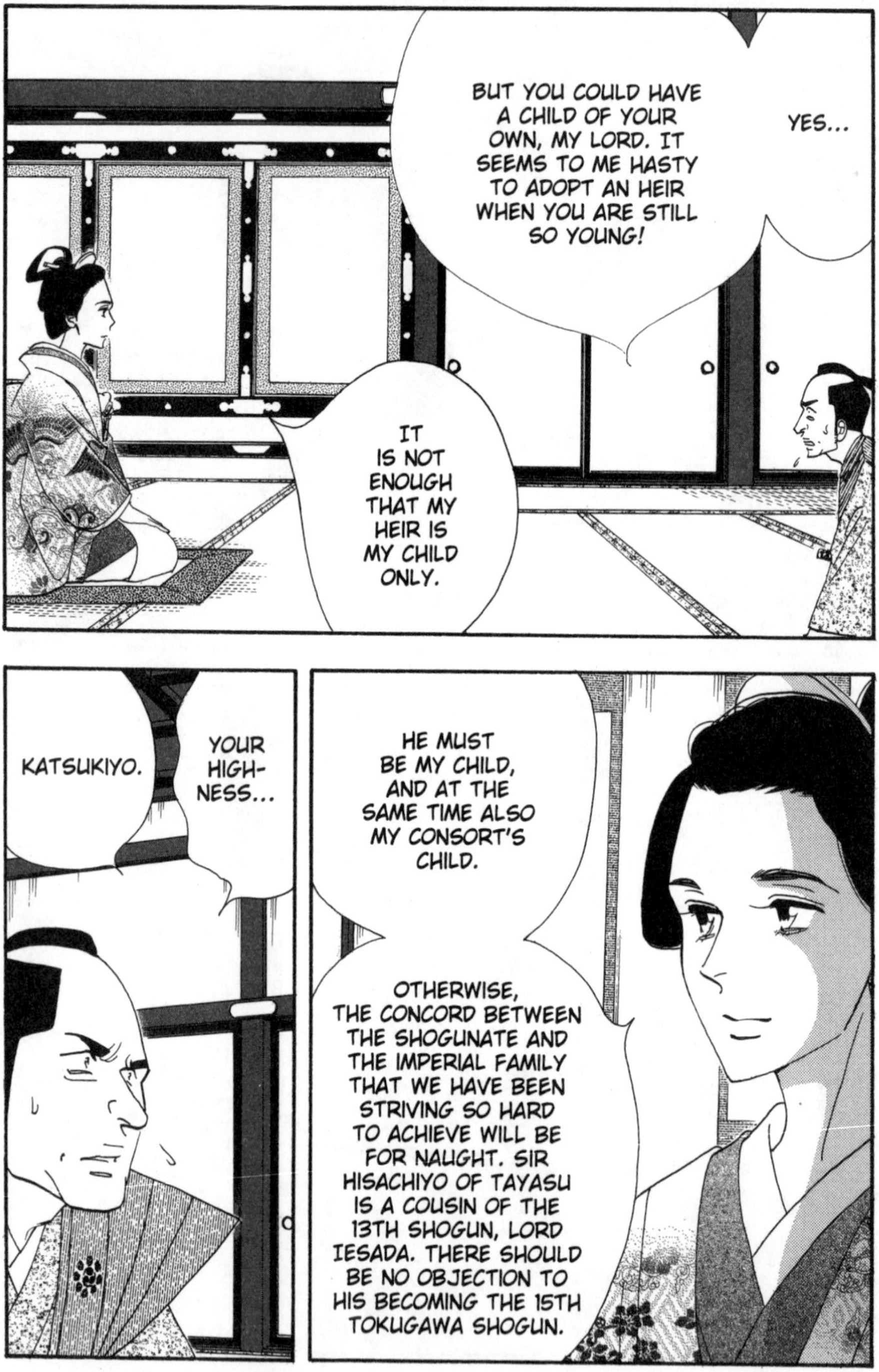
YES...
BUT YOU COULD HAVE A CHILD OF YOUR OWN, MY LORD. IT SEEMS TO ME HASTY TO ADOPT AN HEIR WHEN YOU ARE STILL SO YOUNG!
IT IS NOT ENOUGH THAT MY HEIR IS MY CHILD ONLY.
HE MUST BE MY CHILD, AND AT THE SAME TIME ALSO MY CONSORT'S CHILD.
OTHERWISE, THE CONCORD BETWEEN THE SHOGUNATE AND THE IMPERIAL FAMILY THAT WE HAVE BEEN STRIVING SO HARD TO ACHIEVE WILL BE FOR NAUGHT. SIR HISACHIYO OF TAYASU IS A COUSIN OF THE 13TH SHOGUN, LORD IESADA. THERE SHOULD BE NO OBJECTION TO HIS BECOMING THE 15TH TOKUGAWA SHOGUN.
YOUR HIGHNESS...
KATSUKIYO.

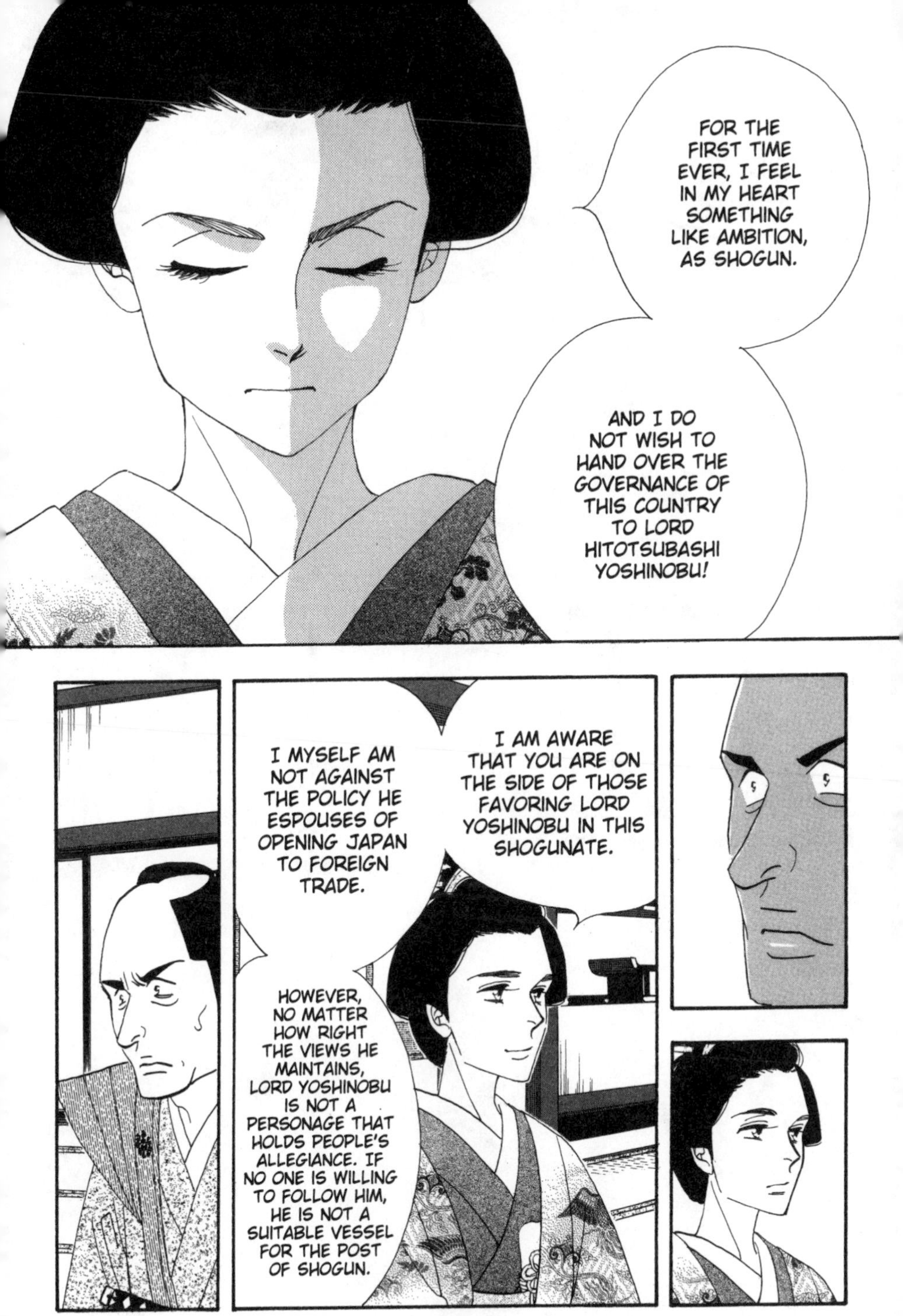
FOR THE FIRST TIME EVER, I FEEL IN MY HEART SOMETHING LIKE AMBITION, AS SHOGUN.
AND I DO NOT WISH TO HAND OVER THE GOVERNANCE OF THIS COUNTRY TO LORD HITOTSUBASHI YOSHINOBU!
I AM AWARE THAT YOU ARE ON THE SIDE OF THOSE FAVORING LORD YOSHINOBU IN THIS SHOGUNATE.
I MYSELF AM NOT AGAINST THE POLICY HE ESPOUSES OF OPENING JAPAN TO FOREIGN TRADE.
HOWEVER, NO MATTER HOW RIGHT THE VIEWS HE MAINTAINS, LORD YOSHINOBU IS NOT A PERSONAGE THAT HOLDS PEOPLE'S ALLEGIANCE. IF NO ONE IS WILLING TO FOLLOW HIM, HE IS NOT A SUITABLE VESSEL FOR THE POST OF SHOGUN.

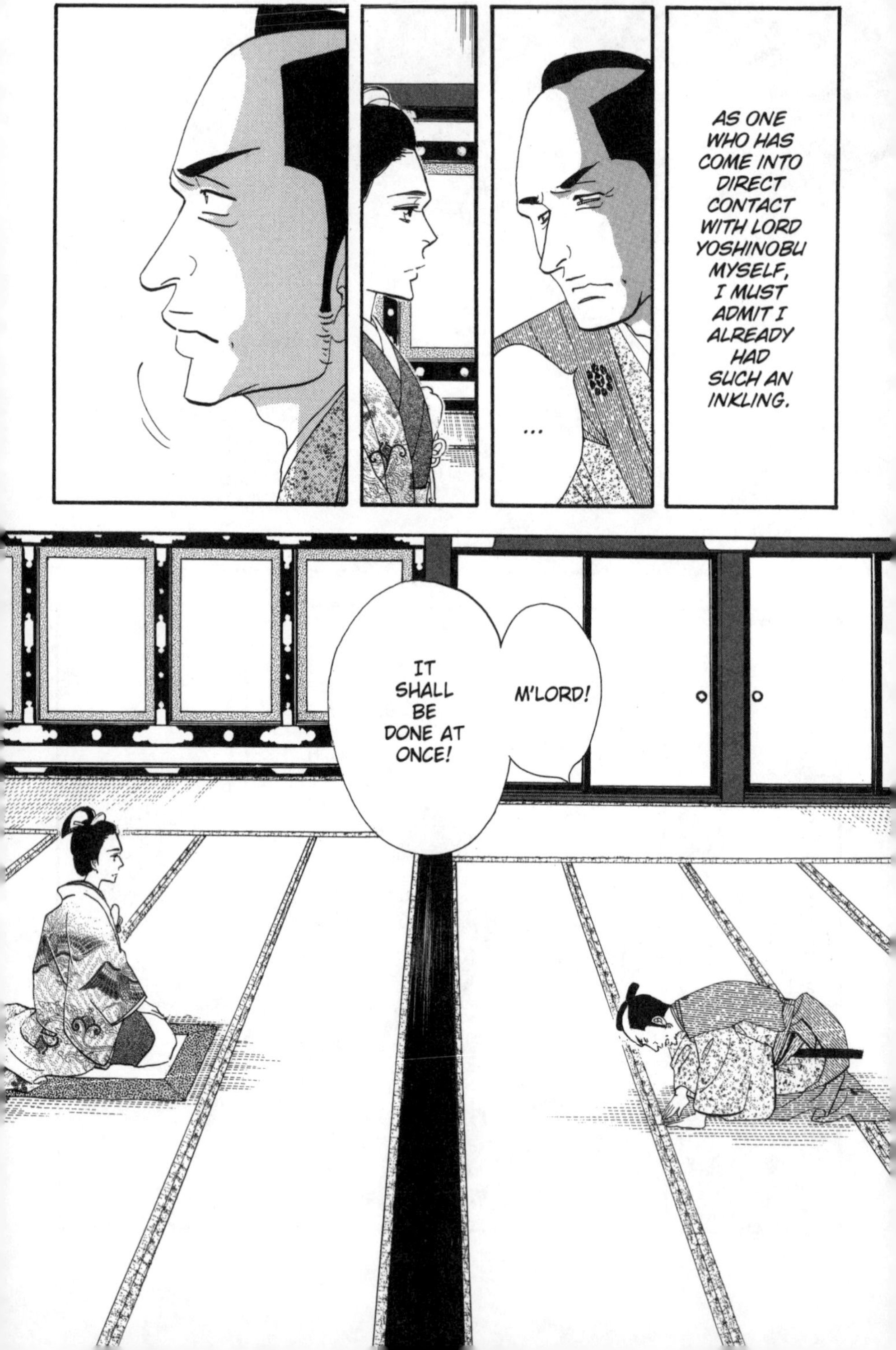
AS ONE WHO HAS COME INTO DIRECT CONTACT WITH LORD YOSHINOBU MYSELF, I MUST ADMIT I ALREADY HAD SUCH AN INKLING.
...
M'LORD!
IT SHALL BE DONE AT ONCE!

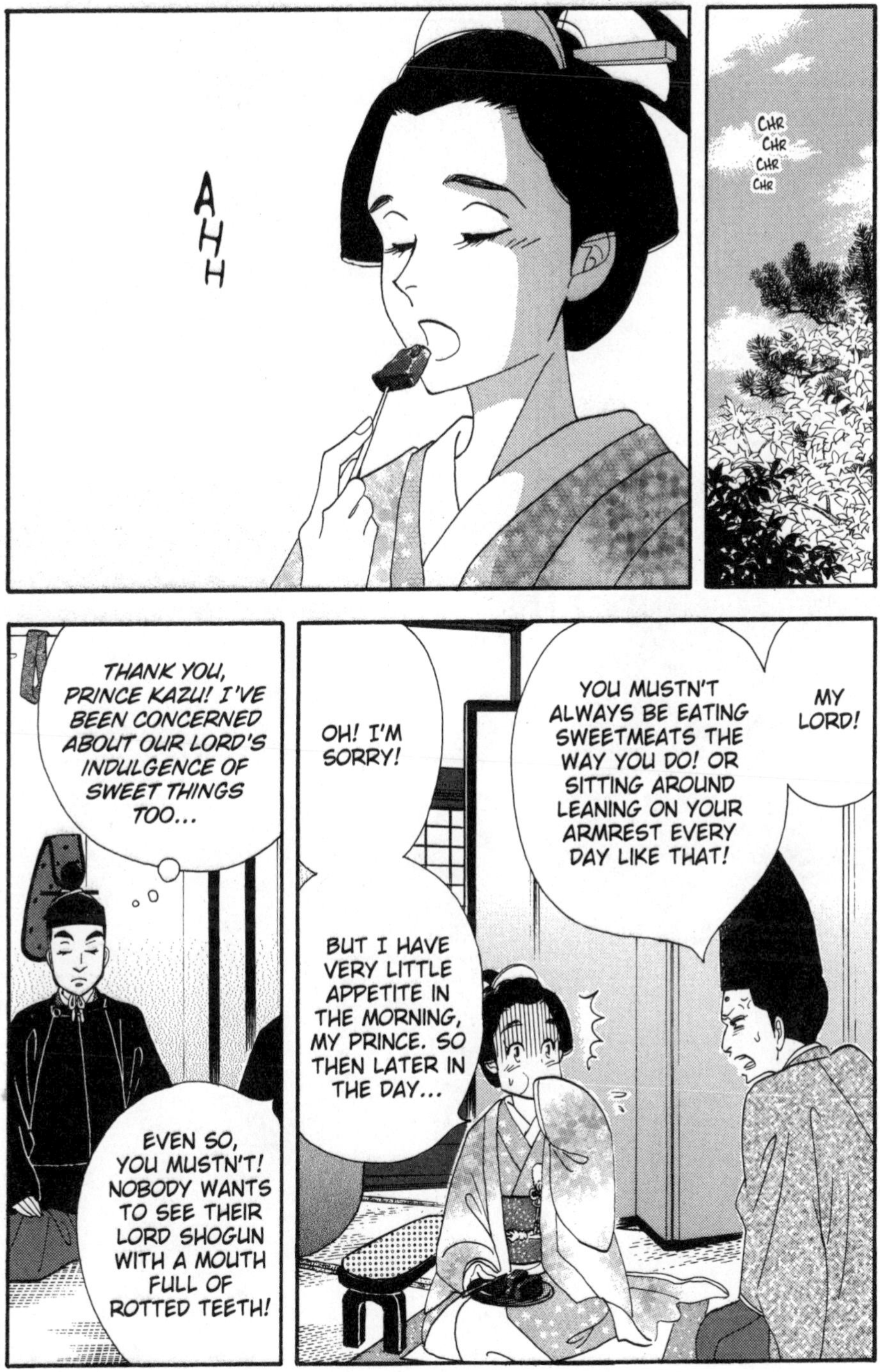
CHR CHR CHR CHR
AHH
MY LORD!
YOU MUSTN'T ALWAYS BE EATING SWEETMEATS THE WAY YOU DO! OR SITTING AROUND LEANING ON YOUR ARMREST EVERY DAY LIKE THAT!
OH! I'M SORRY!
BUT I HAVE VERY LITTLE APPETITE IN THE MORNING, MY PRINCE. SO THEN LATER IN THE DAY...
THANK YOU, PRINCE KAZU! I'VE BEEN CONCERNED ABOUT OUR LORD'S INDULGENCE OF SWEET THINGS TOO...
EVEN SO, YOU MUSTN'T! NOBODY WANTS TO SEE THEIR LORD SHOGUN WITH A MOUTH FULL OF ROTTED TEETH!

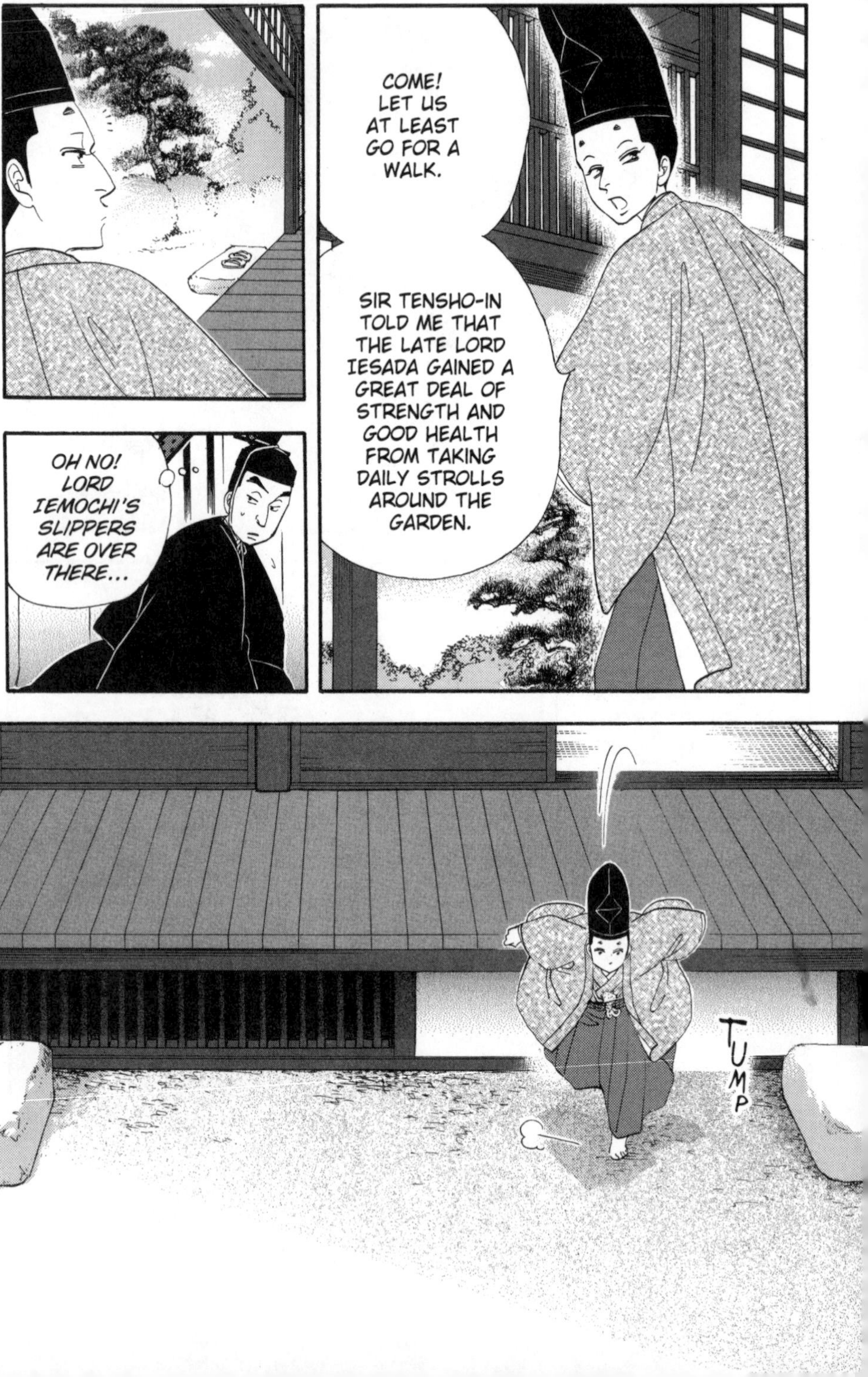
COME! LET US AT LEAST GO FOR A WALK.
SIR TENSHO-IN TOLD ME THAT THE LATE LORD IESADA GAINED A GREAT DEAL OF STRENGTH AND GOOD HEALTH FROM TAKING DAILY STROLLS AROUND THE GARDEN.
OH NO! LORD IEMOCHI'S SLIPPERS ARE OVER THERE...
TUMP

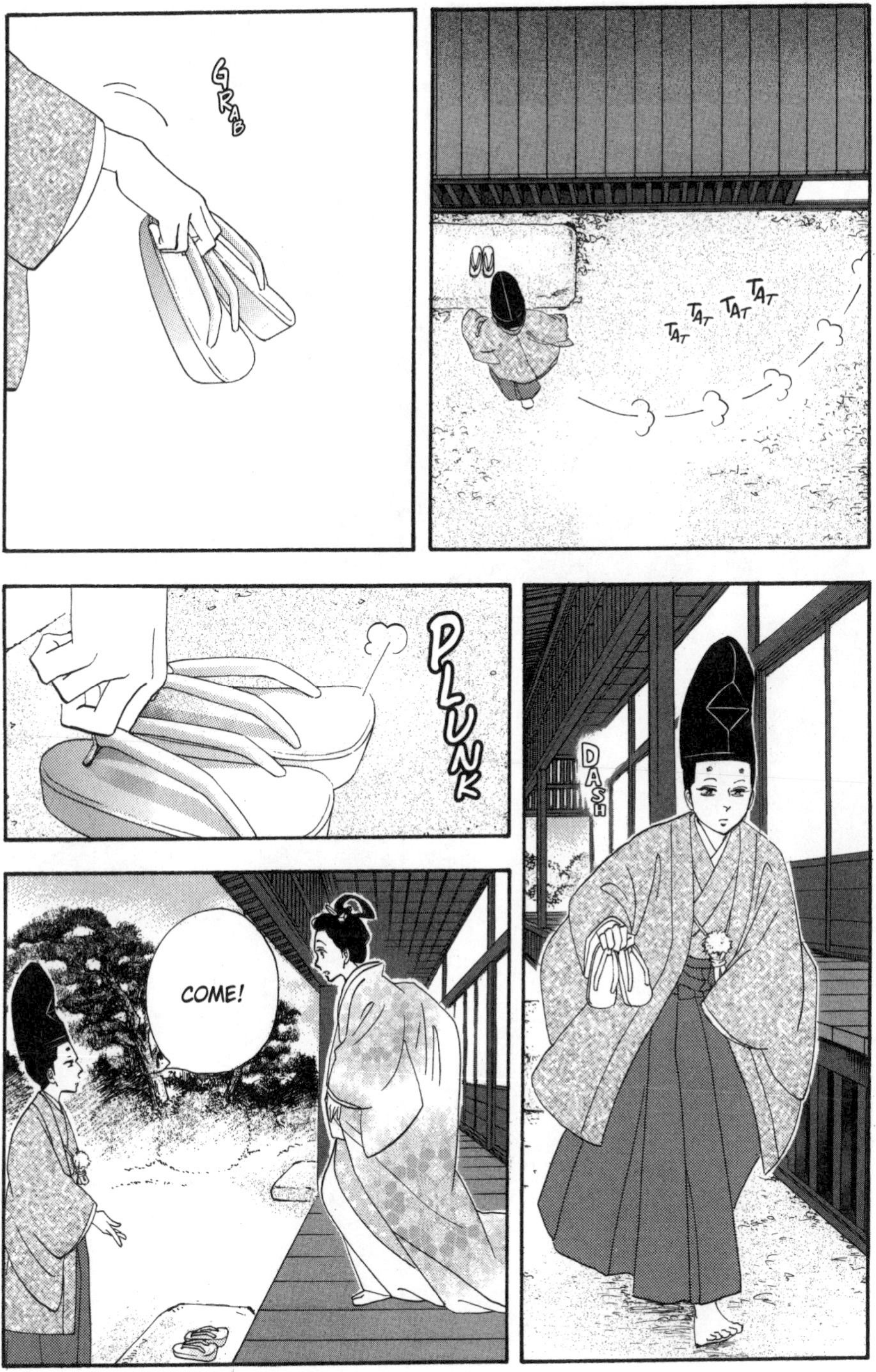
TAT TAT TAT TAT
GRAB
DASH
PLUNK
COME!

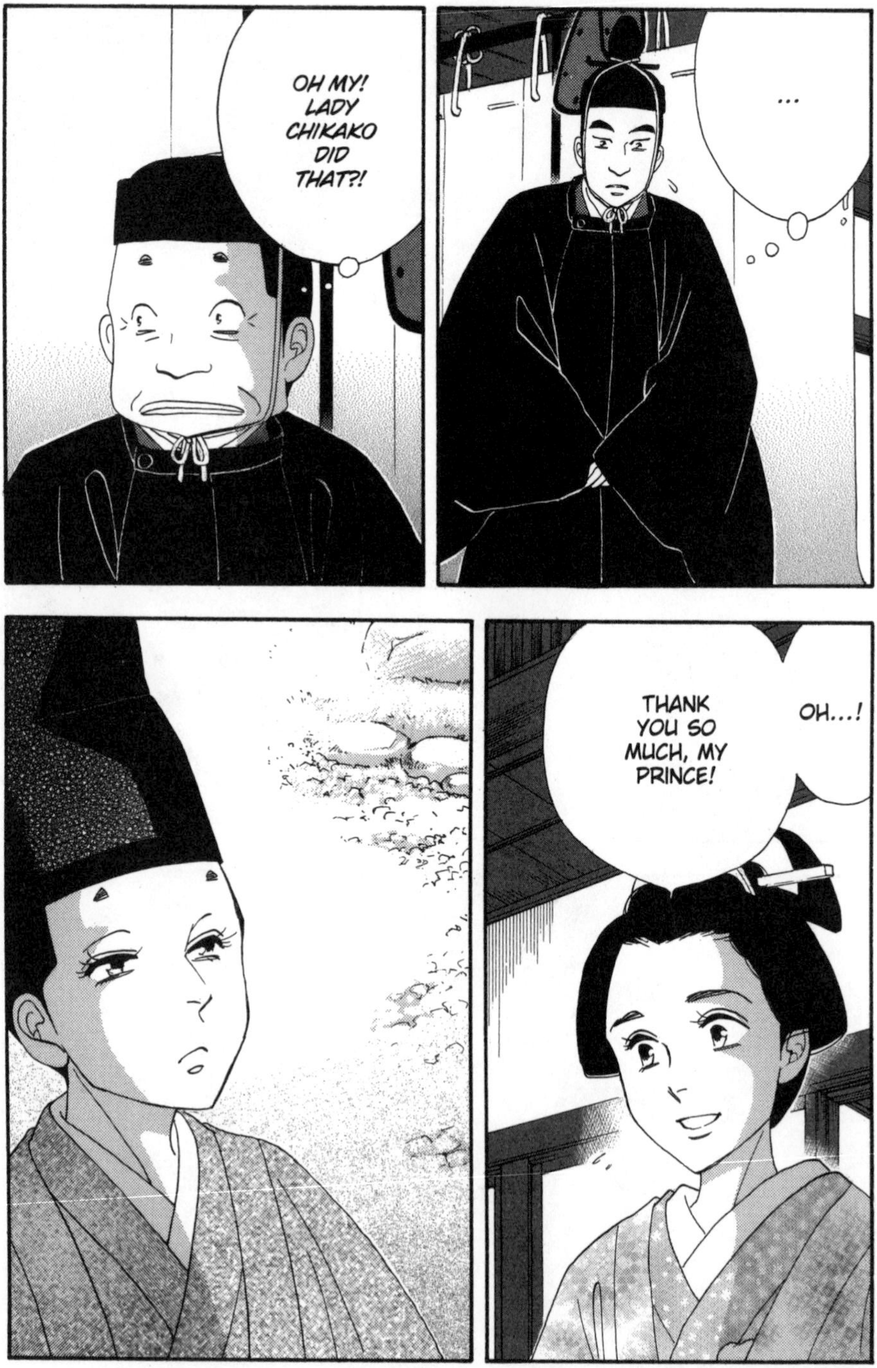
...
OH MY! LADY CHIKAKO DID THAT?!
OH...!
THANK YOU SO MUCH, MY PRINCE!

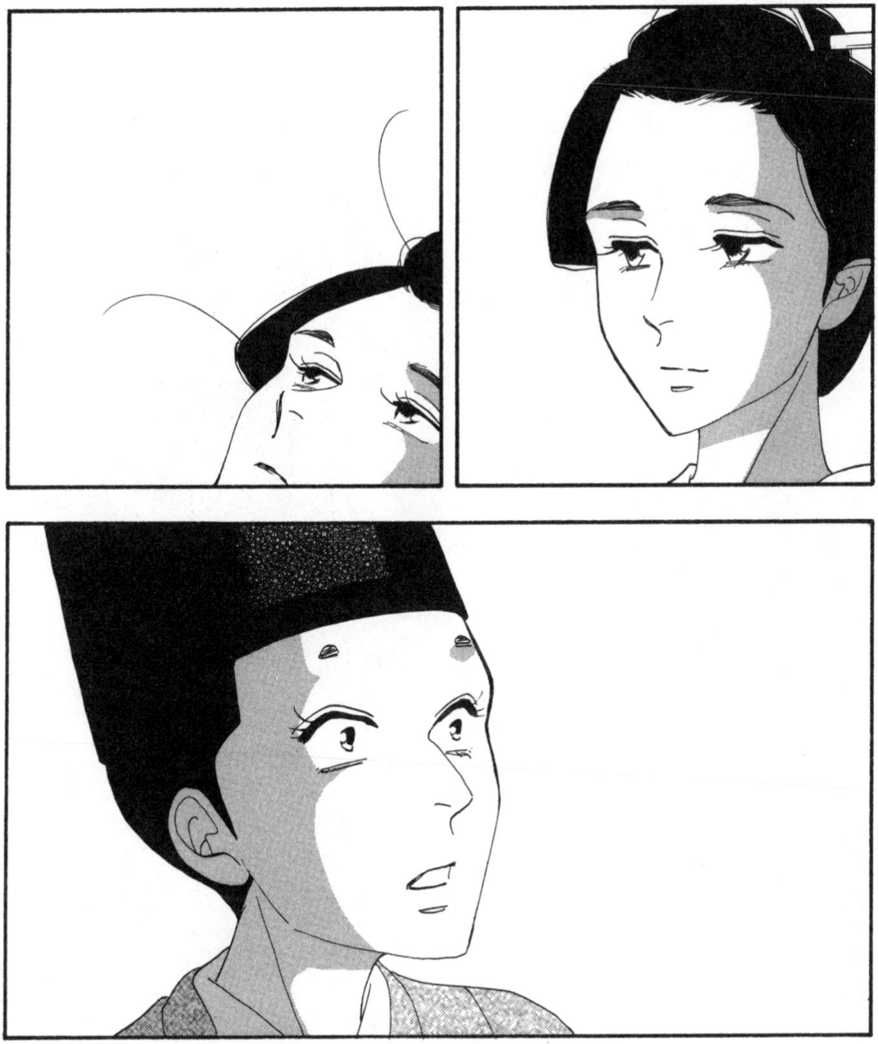
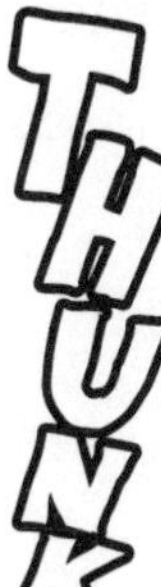
THUNK

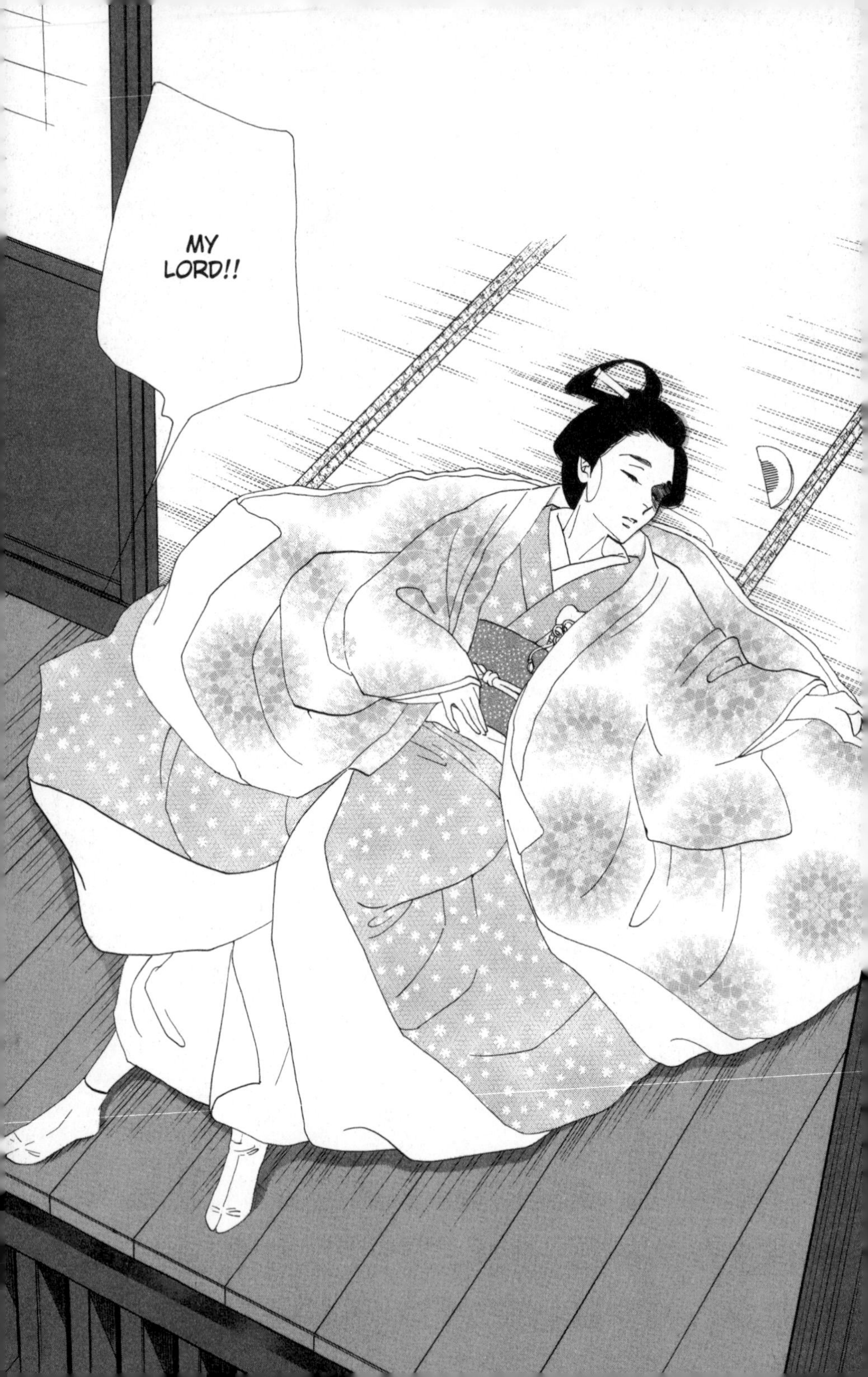
MY LORD!!

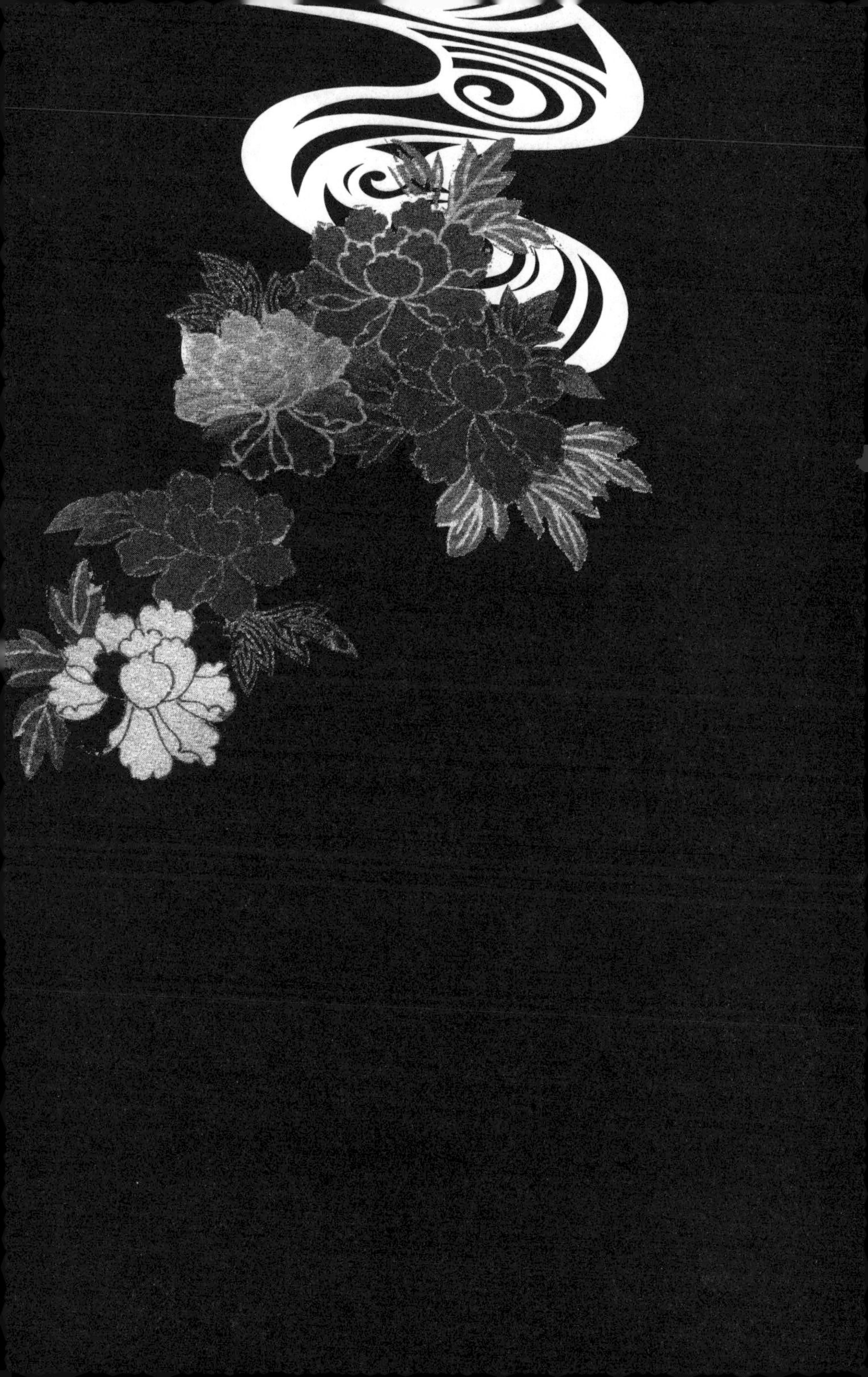

Ōoku

THE INNER CHAMBERS

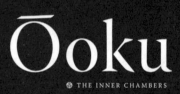

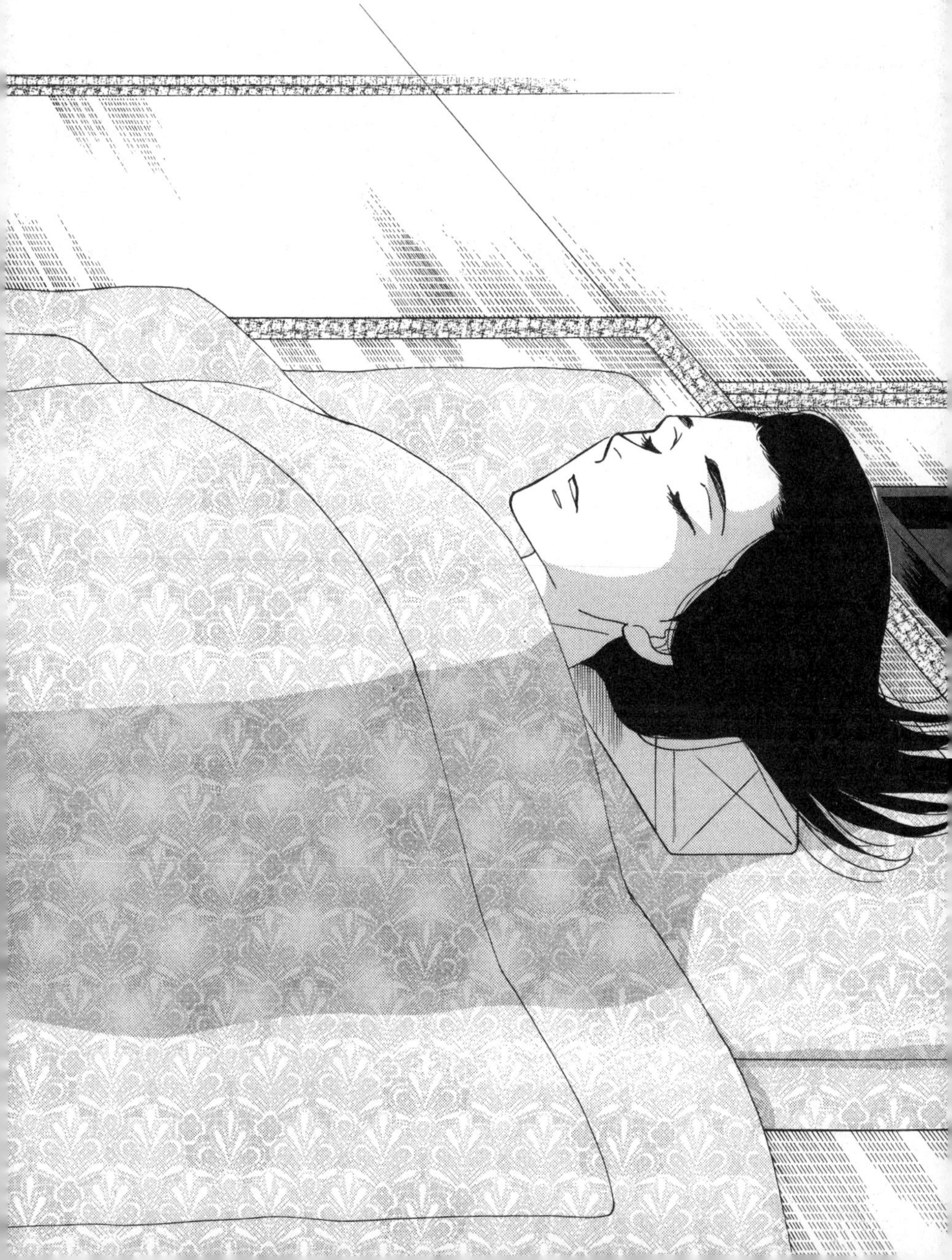

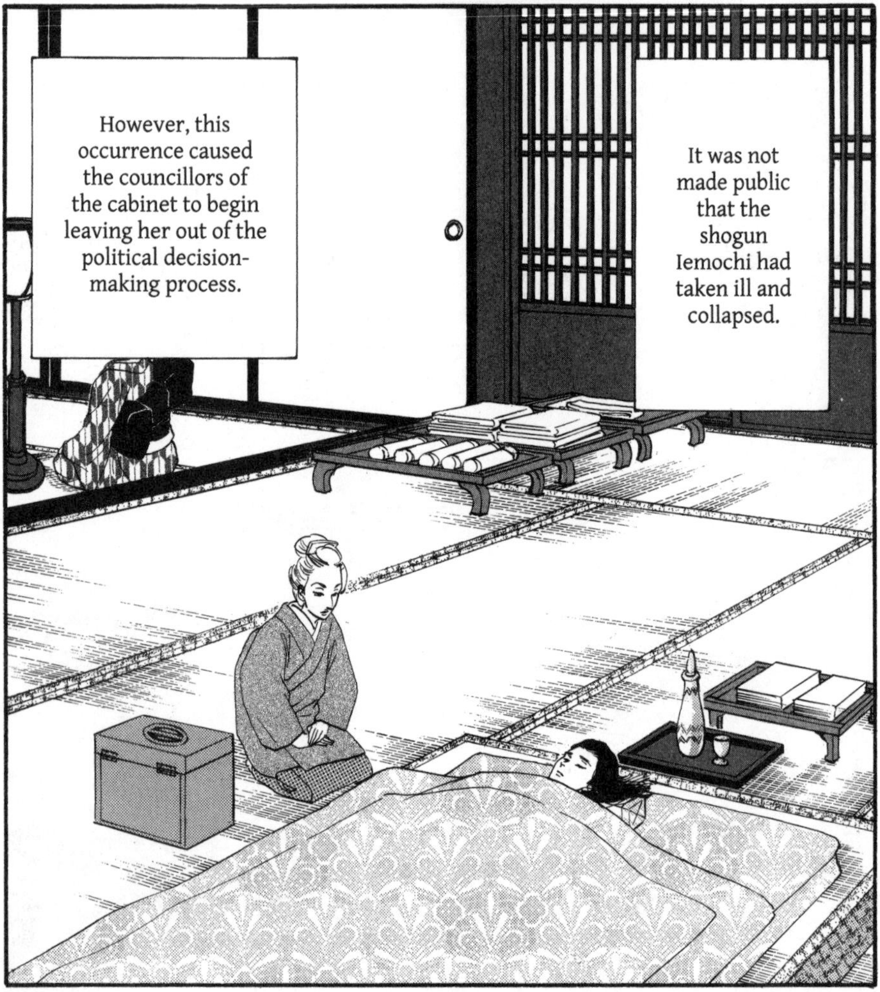
It was not made public that the shogun Iemochi had taken ill and collapsed.
However, this occurrence caused the councillors of the cabinet to begin leaving her out of the political decision-making process.
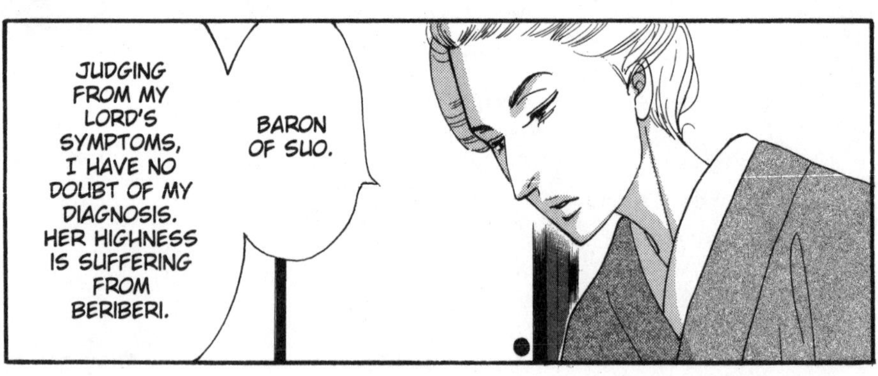
BARON OF SUO.
JUDGING FROM MY LORD'S SYMPTOMS, I HAVE NO DOUBT OF MY DIAGNOSIS. HER HIGHNESS IS SUFFERING FROM BERIBERI.

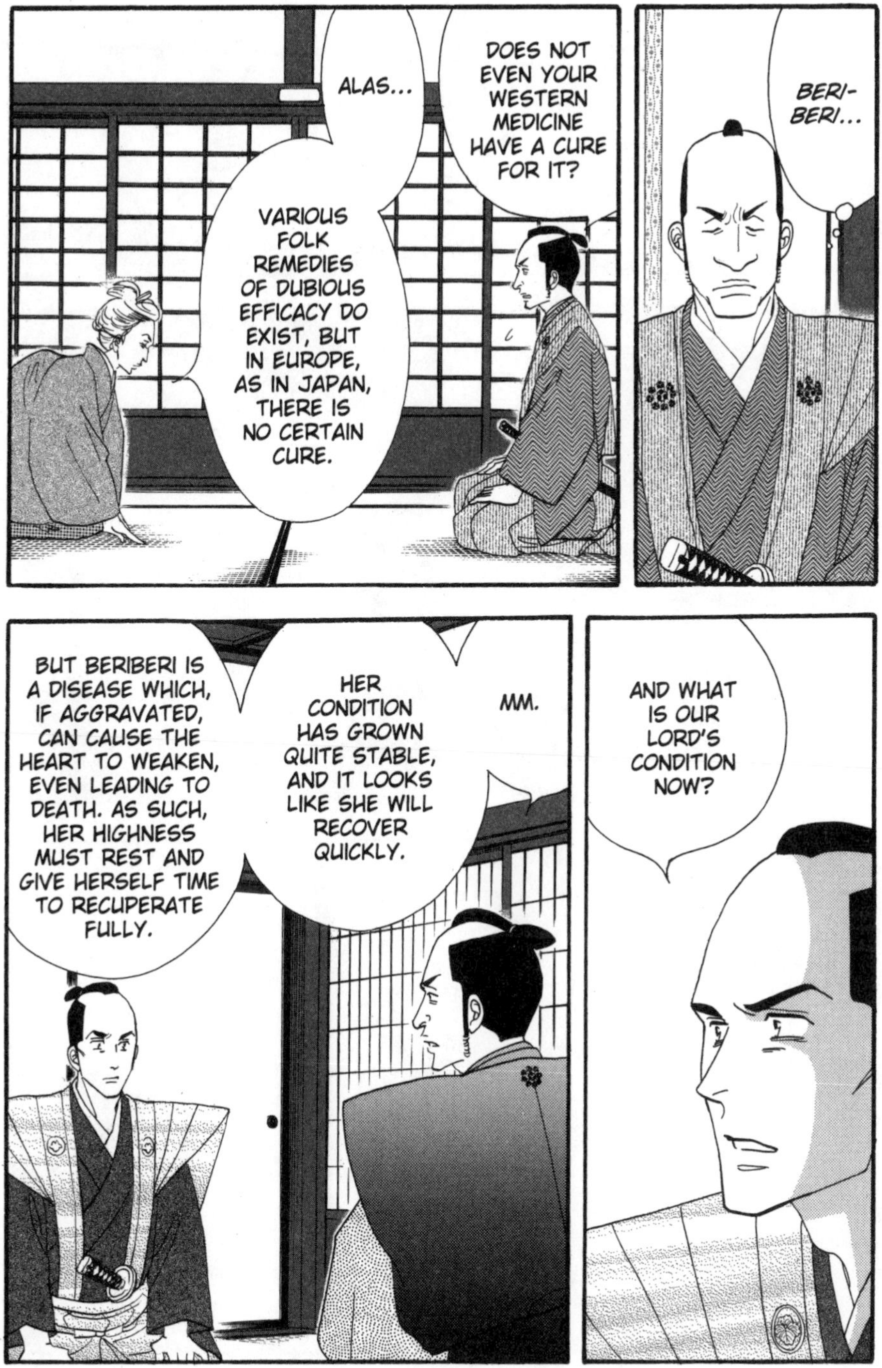
BERI-BERI...
DOES NOT EVEN YOUR WESTERN MEDICINE HAVE A CURE FOR IT?
ALAS...
VARIOUS FOLK REMEDIES OF DUBIOUS EFFICACY DO EXIST, BUT IN EUROPE, AS IN JAPAN, THERE IS NO CERTAIN CURE.
AND WHAT IS OUR LORD'S CONDITION NOW?
HER CONDITION HAS GROWN QUITE STABLE, AND IT LOOKS LIKE SHE WILL RECOVER QUICKLY.
MM.
BUT BERIBERI IS A DISEASE WHICH, IF AGGRAVATED, CAN CAUSE THE HEART TO WEAKEN, EVEN LEADING TO DEATH. AS SUCH, HER HIGHNESS MUST REST AND GIVE HERSELF TIME TO RECUPERATE FULLY.

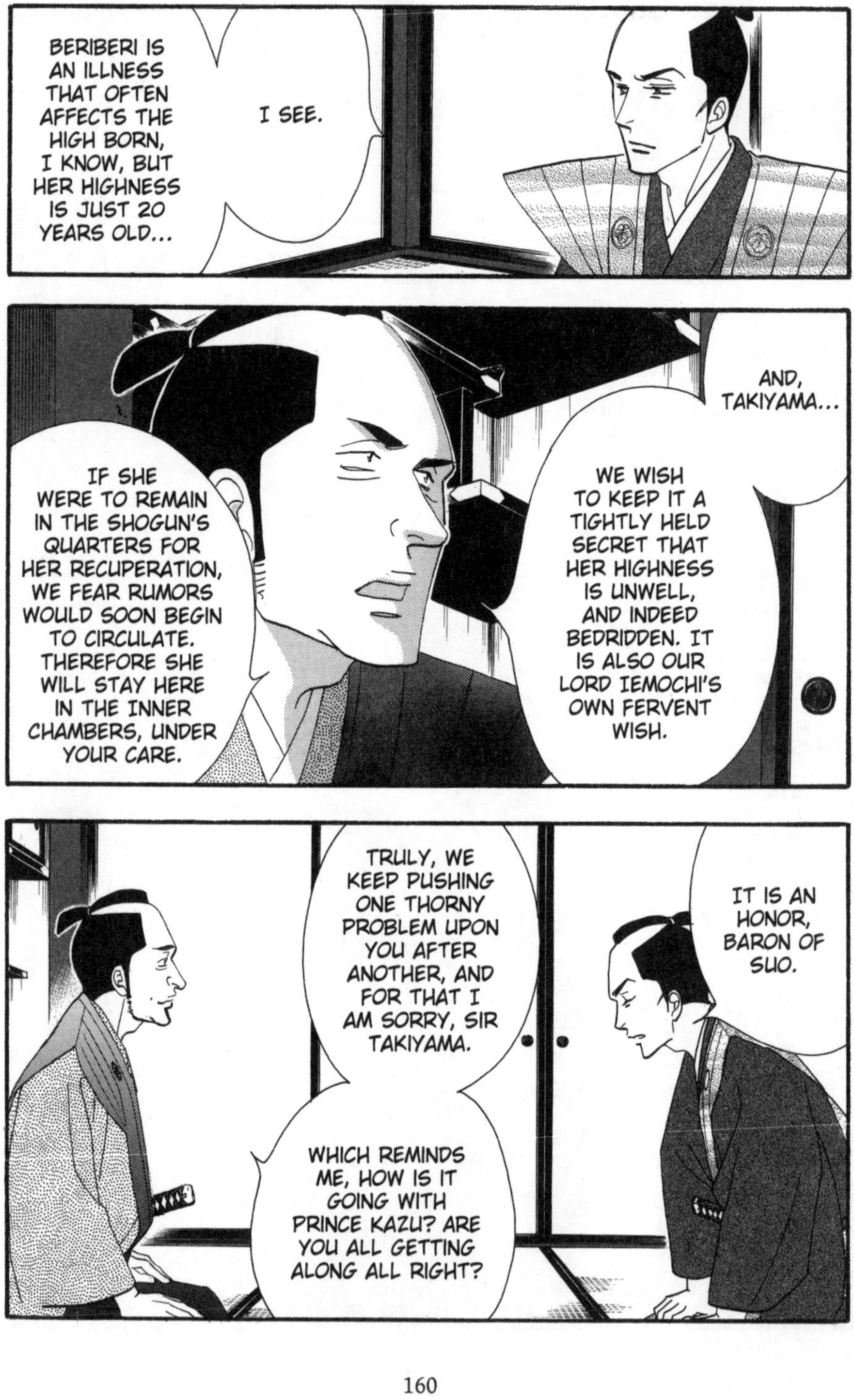
I SEE.
BERIBERI IS AN ILLNESS THAT OFTEN AFFECTS THE HIGH BORN, I KNOW, BUT HER HIGHNESS IS JUST 20 YEARS OLD...
AND, TAKIYAMA...
WE WISH TO KEEP IT A TIGHTLY HELD SECRET THAT HER HIGHNESS IS UNWELL, AND INDEED BEDRIDDEN. IT IS ALSO OUR LORD IEMOCHI'S OWN FERVENT WISH.
IF SHE WERE TO REMAIN IN THE SHOGUN'S QUARTERS FOR HER RECUPERATION, WE FEAR RUMORS WOULD SOON BEGIN TO CIRCULATE. THEREFORE SHE WILL STAY HERE IN THE INNER CHAMBERS, UNDER YOUR CARE.
IT IS AN HONOR, BARON OF SUO.
TRULY, WE KEEP PUSHING ONE THORNY PROBLEM UPON YOU AFTER ANOTHER, AND FOR THAT I AM SORRY, SIR TAKIYAMA.
WHICH REMINDS ME, HOW IS IT GOING WITH PRINCE KAZU? ARE YOU ALL GETTING ALONG ALL RIGHT?

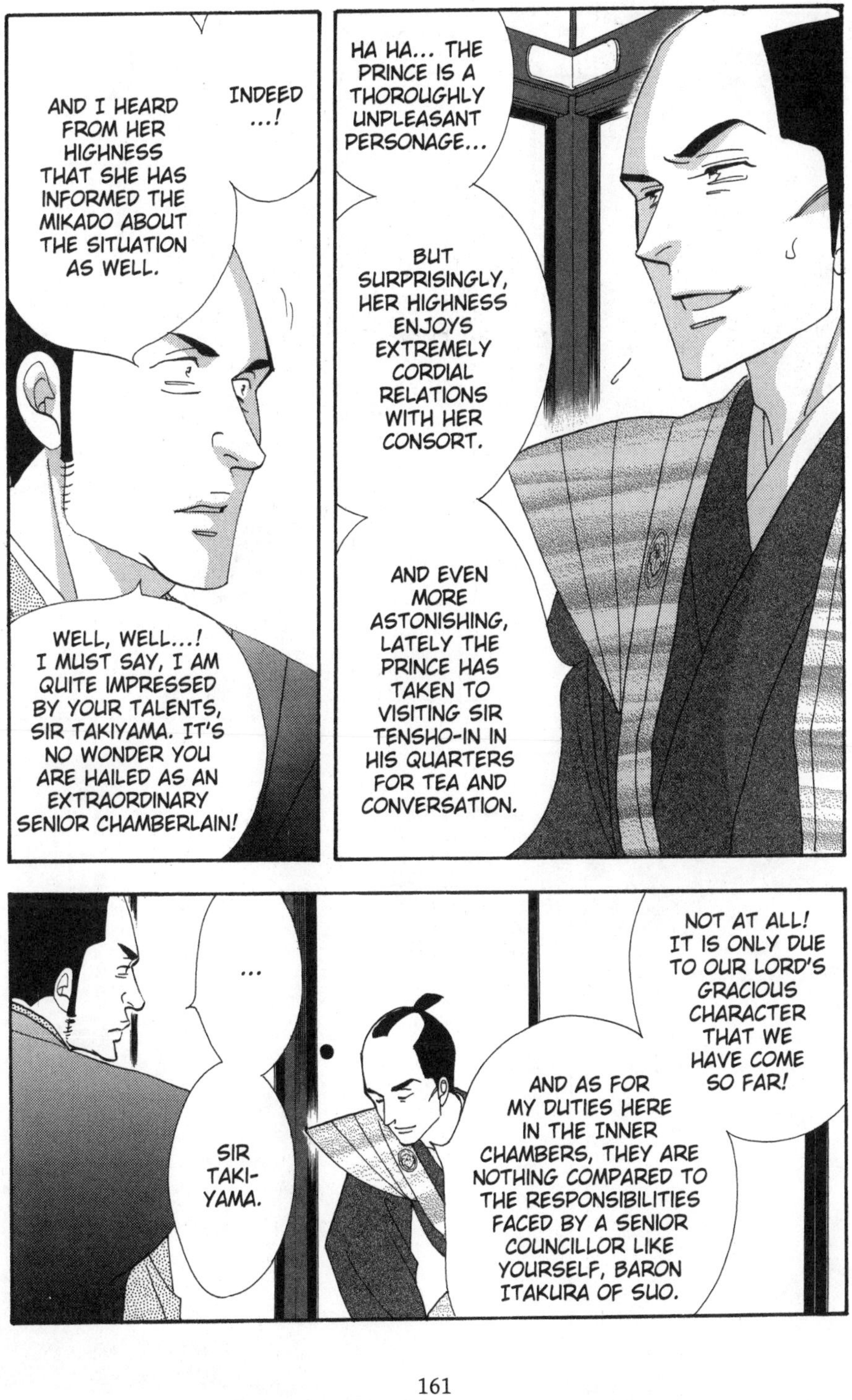
HA HA... THE PRINCE IS A THOROUGHLY UNPLEASANT PERSONAGE...
BUT SURPRISINGLY, HER HIGHNESS ENJOYS EXTREMELY CORDIAL RELATIONS WITH HER CONSORT.
AND EVEN MORE ASTONISHING, LATELY THE PRINCE HAS TAKEN TO VISITING SIR TENSHO-IN IN HIS QUARTERS FOR TEA AND CONVERSATION.
AND I HEARD FROM HER HIGHNESS THAT SHE HAS INFORMED THE MIKADO ABOUT THE SITUATION AS WELL.
INDEED ...!
WELL, WELL...! I MUST SAY, I AM QUITE IMPRESSED BY YOUR TALENTS, SIR TAKIYAMA. IT'S NO WONDER YOU ARE HAILED AS AN EXTRAORDINARY SENIOR CHAMBERLAIN!
NOT AT ALL! IT IS ONLY DUE TO OUR LORD'S GRACIOUS CHARACTER THAT WE HAVE COME SO FAR!
AND AS FOR MY DUTIES HERE IN THE INNER CHAMBERS, THEY ARE NOTHING COMPARED TO THE RESPONSIBILITIES FACED BY A SENIOR COUNCILLOR LIKE YOURSELF, BARON ITAKURA OF SUO.
...
SIR TAKI-YAMA.

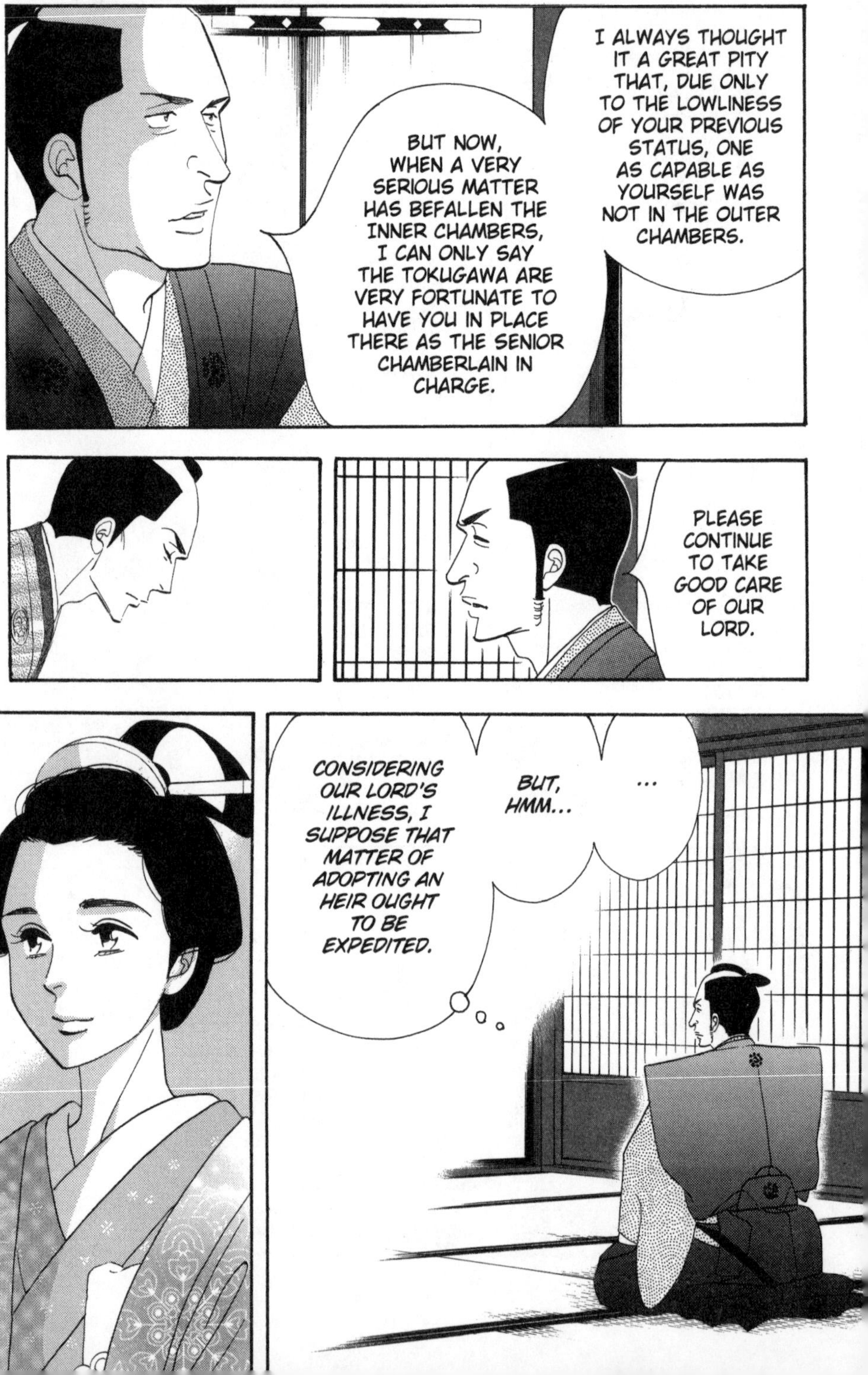
I ALWAYS THOUGHT IT A GREAT PITY THAT, DUE ONLY TO THE LOWLINESS OF YOUR PREVIOUS STATUS, ONE AS CAPABLE AS YOURSELF WAS NOT IN THE OUTER CHAMBERS.
BUT NOW, WHEN A VERY SERIOUS MATTER HAS BEFALLEN THE INNER CHAMBERS, I CAN ONLY SAY THE TOKUGAWA ARE VERY FORTUNATE TO HAVE YOU IN PLACE THERE AS THE SENIOR CHAMBERLAIN IN CHARGE.
PLEASE CONTINUE TO TAKE GOOD CARE OF OUR LORD.
...
BUT, HMM...
CONSIDERING OUR LORD'S ILLNESS, I SUPPOSE THAT MATTER OF ADOPTING AN HEIR OUGHT TO BE EXPEDITED.

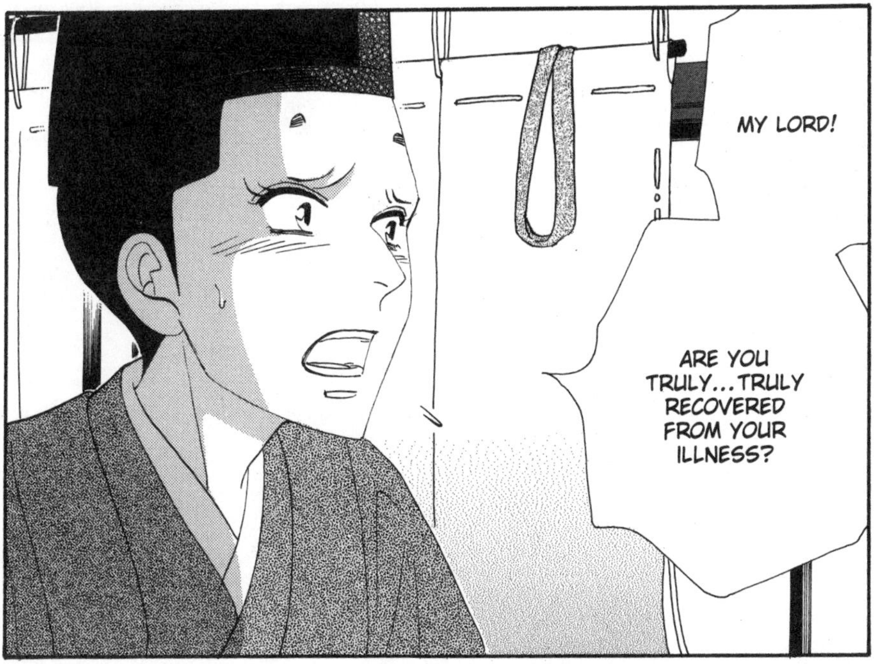
MY LORD!
ARE YOU TRULY...TRULY RECOVERED FROM YOUR ILLNESS?
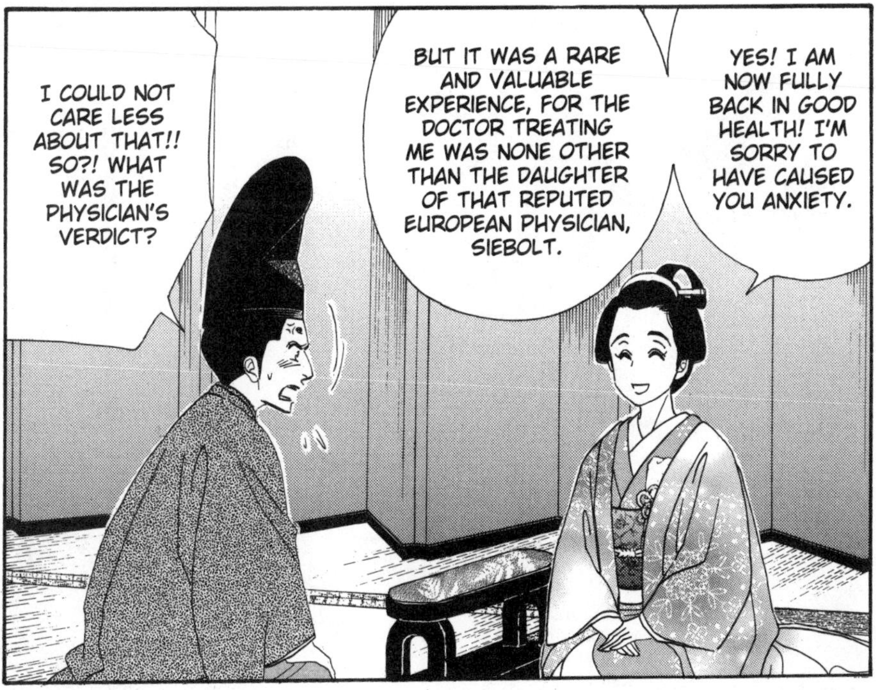
YES! I AM NOW FULLY BACK IN GOOD HEALTH! I'M SORRY TO HAVE CAUSED YOU ANXIETY.
BUT IT WAS A RARE AND VALUABLE EXPERIENCE, FOR THE DOCTOR TREATING ME WAS NONE OTHER THAN THE DAUGHTER OF THAT REPUTED EUROPEAN PHYSICIAN, SIEBOLT.
I COULD NOT CARE LESS ABOUT THAT!! SO?! WHAT WAS THE PHYSICIAN'S VERDICT?

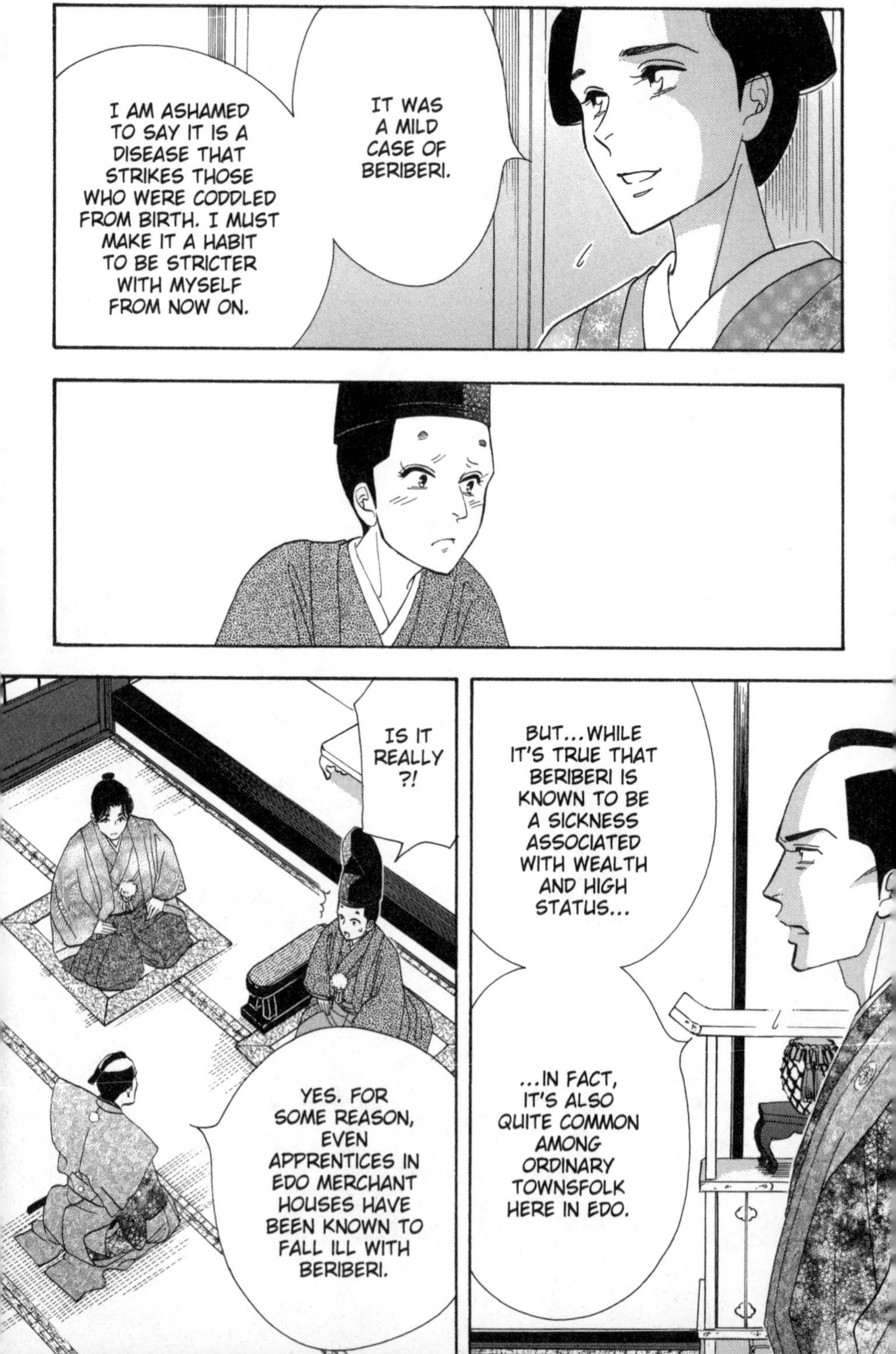
IT WAS A MILD CASE OF BERIBERI.
I AM ASHAMED TO SAY IT IS A DISEASE THAT STRIKES THOSE WHO WERE CODDLED FROM BIRTH. I MUST MAKE IT A HABIT TO BE STRICTER WITH MYSELF FROM NOW ON.
BUT...WHILE IT'S TRUE THAT BERIBERI IS KNOWN TO BE A SICKNESS ASSOCIATED WITH WEALTH AND HIGH STATUS...
...IN FACT, IT'S ALSO QUITE COMMON AMONG ORDINARY TOWNSFOLK HERE IN EDO.
IS IT REALLY ?!
YES. FOR SOME REASON, EVEN APPRENTICES IN EDO MERCHANT HOUSES HAVE BEEN KNOWN TO FALL ILL WITH BERIBERI.

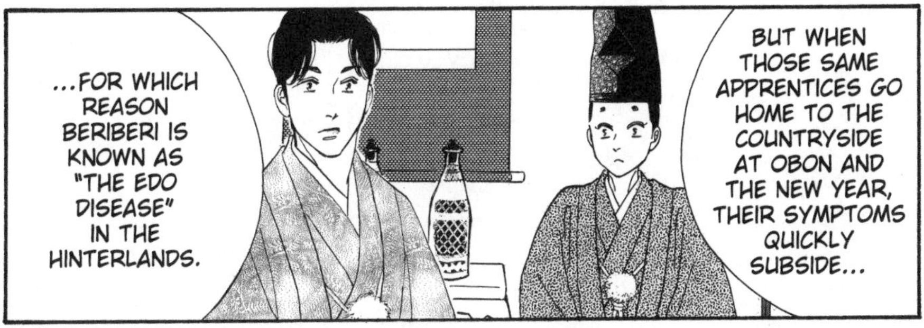
BUT WHEN THOSE SAME APPRENTICES GO HOME TO THE COUNTRYSIDE AT OBON AND THE NEW YEAR, THEIR SYMPTOMS QUICKLY SUBSIDE...
...FOR WHICH REASON BERIBERI IS KNOWN AS "THE EDO DISEASE" IN THE HINTERLANDS.

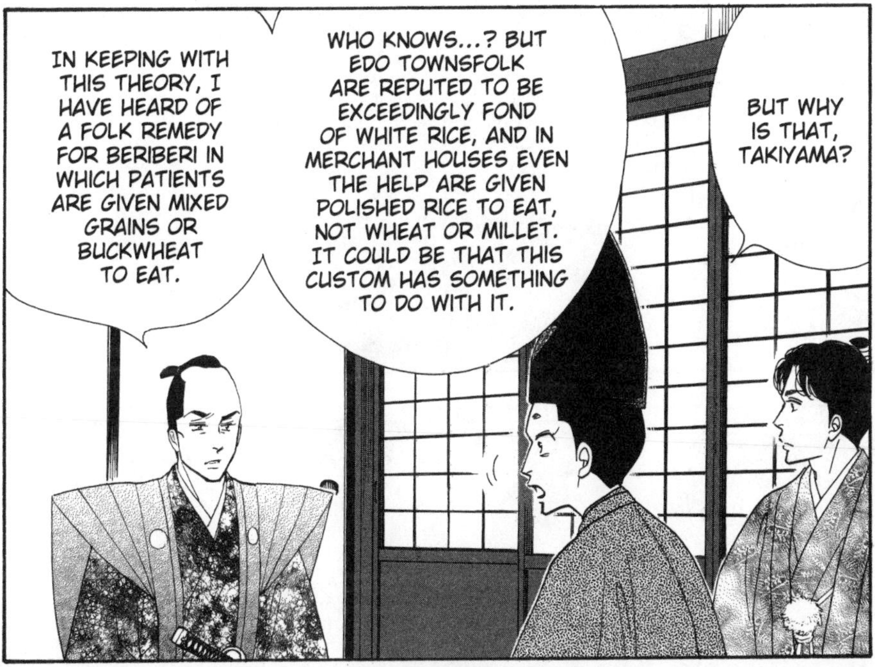
BUT WHY IS THAT, TAKIYAMA?
WHO KNOWS...? BUT EDO TOWNSFOLK ARE REPUTED TO BE EXCEEDINGLY FOND OF WHITE RICE, AND IN MERCHANT HOUSES EVEN THE HELP ARE GIVEN POLISHED RICE TO EAT, NOT WHEAT OR MILLET. IT COULD BE THAT THIS CUSTOM HAS SOMETHING TO DO WITH IT.
IN KEEPING WITH THIS THEORY, I HAVE HEARD OF A FOLK REMEDY FOR BERIBERI IN WHICH PATIENTS ARE GIVEN MIXED GRAINS OR BUCKWHEAT TO EAT.

Beriberi is caused by thiamine deficiency, which damages the peripheral nerves, leading to numbness in the hands and feet, heart failure and other symptoms.

Thiamine, also known as vitamin B1, is found in such foods as pork, eel and brown rice, and as such tended to be lacking in the diet of Japanese people of the time.

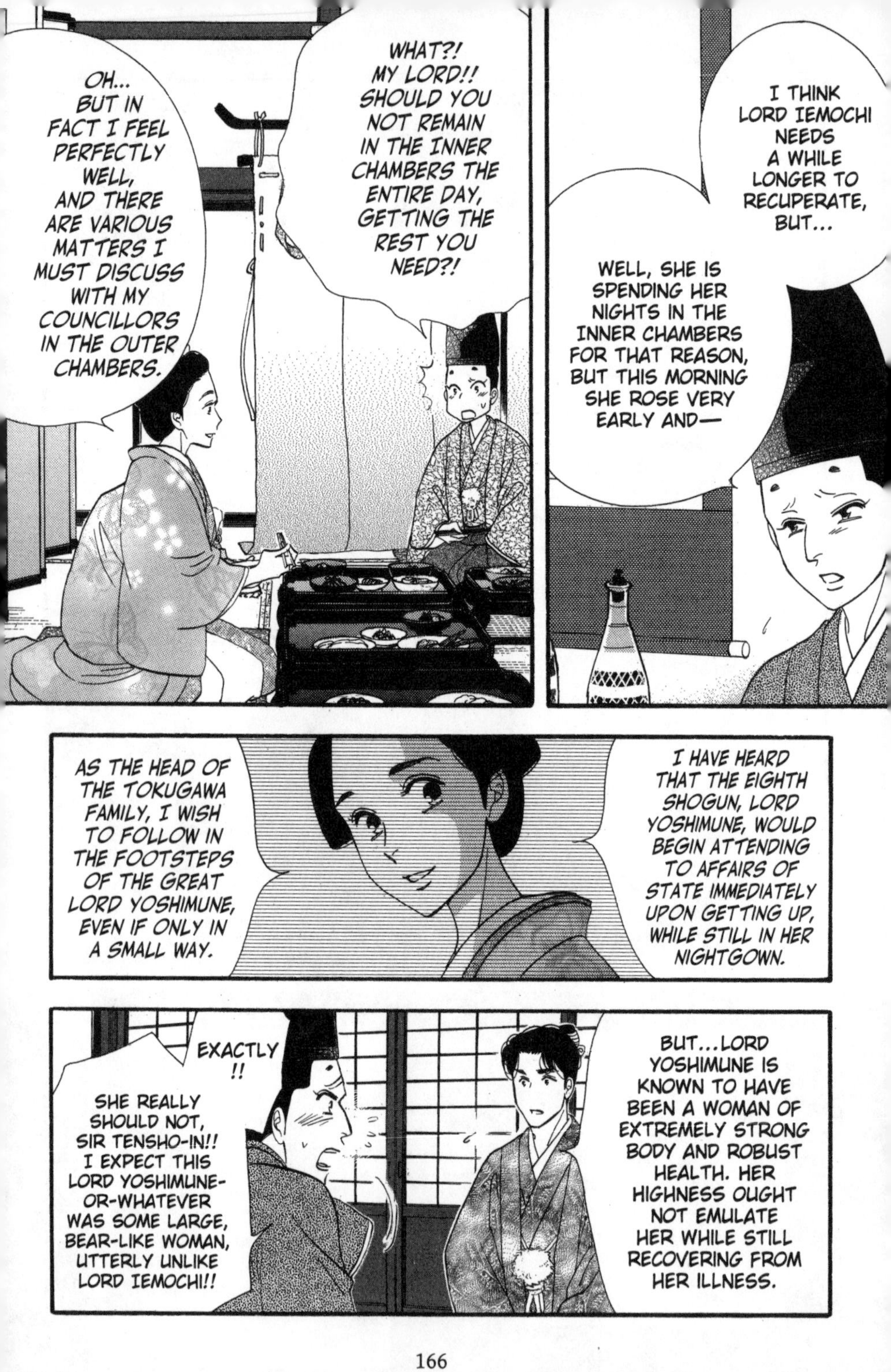
I THINK LORD IEMOCHI NEEDS A WHILE LONGER TO RECUPERATE, BUT...
WELL, SHE IS SPENDING HER NIGHTS IN THE INNER CHAMBERS FOR THAT REASON, BUT THIS MORNING SHE ROSE VERY EARLY AND—
WHAT?! MY LORD!! SHOULD YOU NOT REMAIN IN THE INNER CHAMBERS THE ENTIRE DAY, GETTING THE REST YOU NEED?!
OH... BUT IN FACT I FEEL PERFECTLY WELL, AND THERE ARE VARIOUS MATTERS I MUST DISCUSS WITH MY COUNCILLORS IN THE OUTER CHAMBERS.
I HAVE HEARD THAT THE EIGHTH SHOGUN, LORD YOSHIMUNE, WOULD BEGIN ATTENDING TO AFFAIRS OF STATE IMMEDIATELY UPON GETTING UP, WHILE STILL IN HER NIGHTGOWN.
AS THE HEAD OF THE TOKUGAWA FAMILY, I WISH TO FOLLOW IN THE FOOTSTEPS OF THE GREAT LORD YOSHIMUNE, EVEN IF ONLY IN A SMALL WAY.
BUT...LORD YOSHIMUNE IS KNOWN TO HAVE BEEN A WOMAN OF EXTREMELY STRONG BODY AND ROBUST HEALTH. HER HIGHNESS OUGHT NOT EMULATE HER WHILE STILL RECOVERING FROM HER ILLNESS.
EXACTLY !!
SHE REALLY SHOULD NOT, SIR TENSHO-IN!! I EXPECT THIS LORD YOSHIMUNE-OR-WHATEVER WAS SOME LARGE, BEAR-LIKE WOMAN, UTTERLY UNLIKE LORD IEMOCHI!!

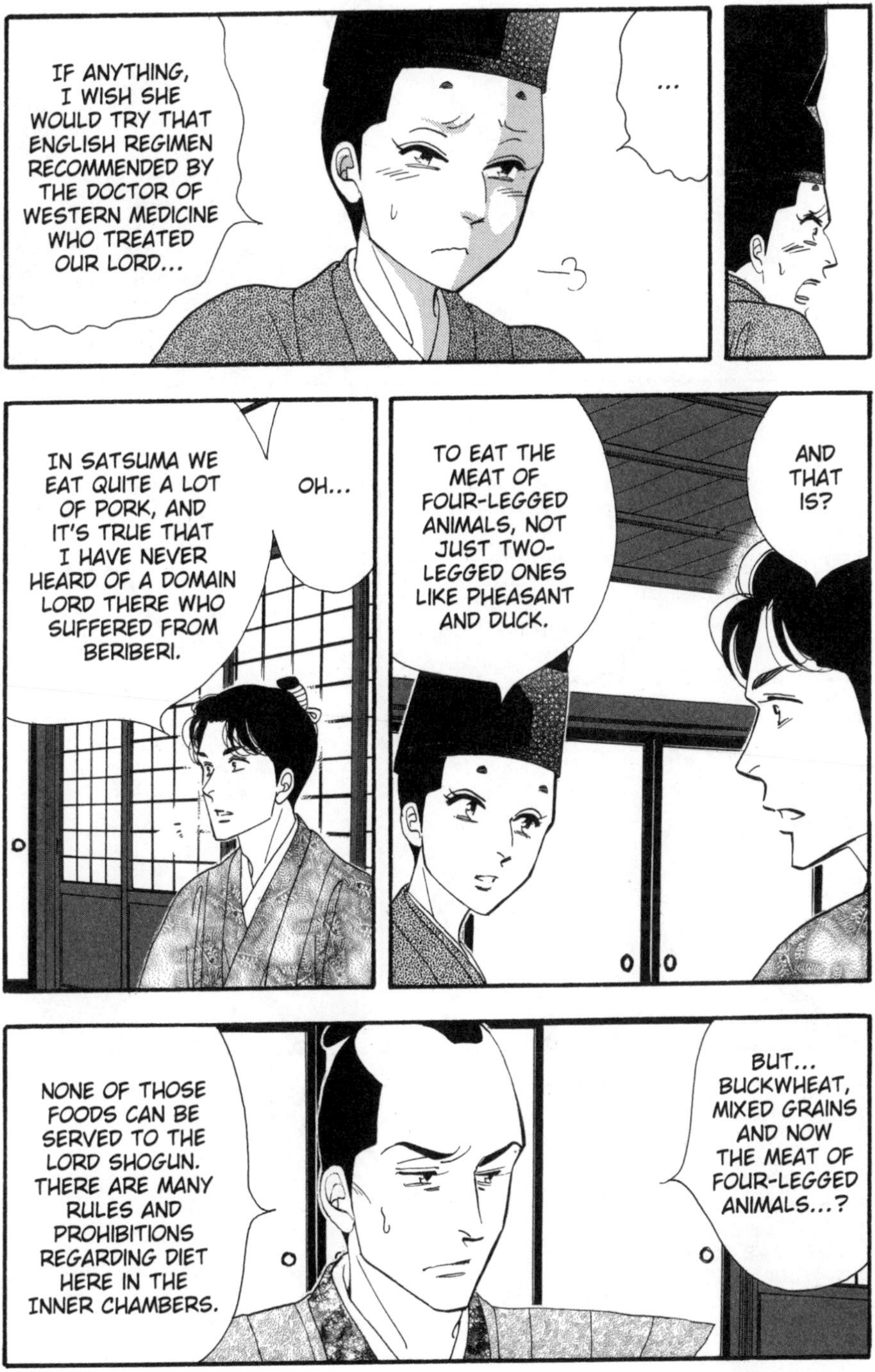
...
IF ANYTHING, I WISH SHE WOULD TRY THAT ENGLISH REGIMEN RECOMMENDED BY THE DOCTOR OF WESTERN MEDICINE WHO TREATED OUR LORD...
AND THAT IS?
TO EAT THE MEAT OF FOUR-LEGGED ANIMALS, NOT JUST TWO-LEGGED ONES LIKE PHEASANT AND DUCK.
OH...
IN SATSUMA WE EAT QUITE A LOT OF PORK, AND IT'S TRUE THAT I HAVE NEVER HEARD OF A DOMAIN LORD THERE WHO SUFFERED FROM BERIBERI.
BUT... BUCKWHEAT, MIXED GRAINS AND NOW THE MEAT OF FOUR-LEGGED ANIMALS...?
NONE OF THOSE FOODS CAN BE SERVED TO THE LORD SHOGUN. THERE ARE MANY RULES AND PROHIBITIONS REGARDING DIET HERE IN THE INNER CHAMBERS.

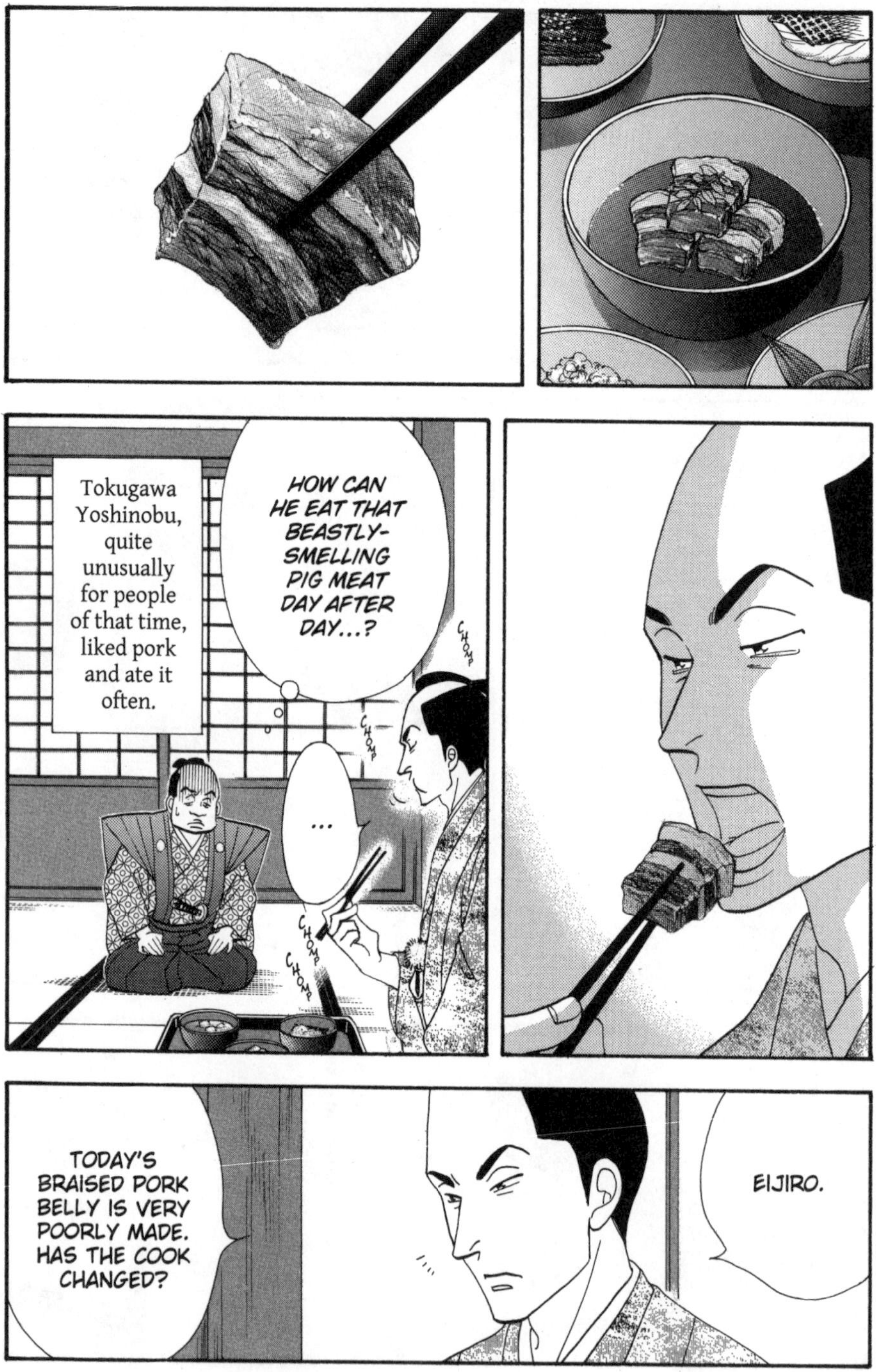
HOW CAN HE EAT THAT BEASTLY-SMELLING PIG MEAT DAY AFTER DAY...?
CHOMP
Tokugawa Yoshinobu, quite unusually for people of that time, liked pork and ate it often.
CHOMP
...
CHOMP
CHOMP
CHOMP
EIJIRO.
TODAY'S BRAISED PORK BELLY IS VERY POORLY MADE. HAS THE COOK CHANGED?

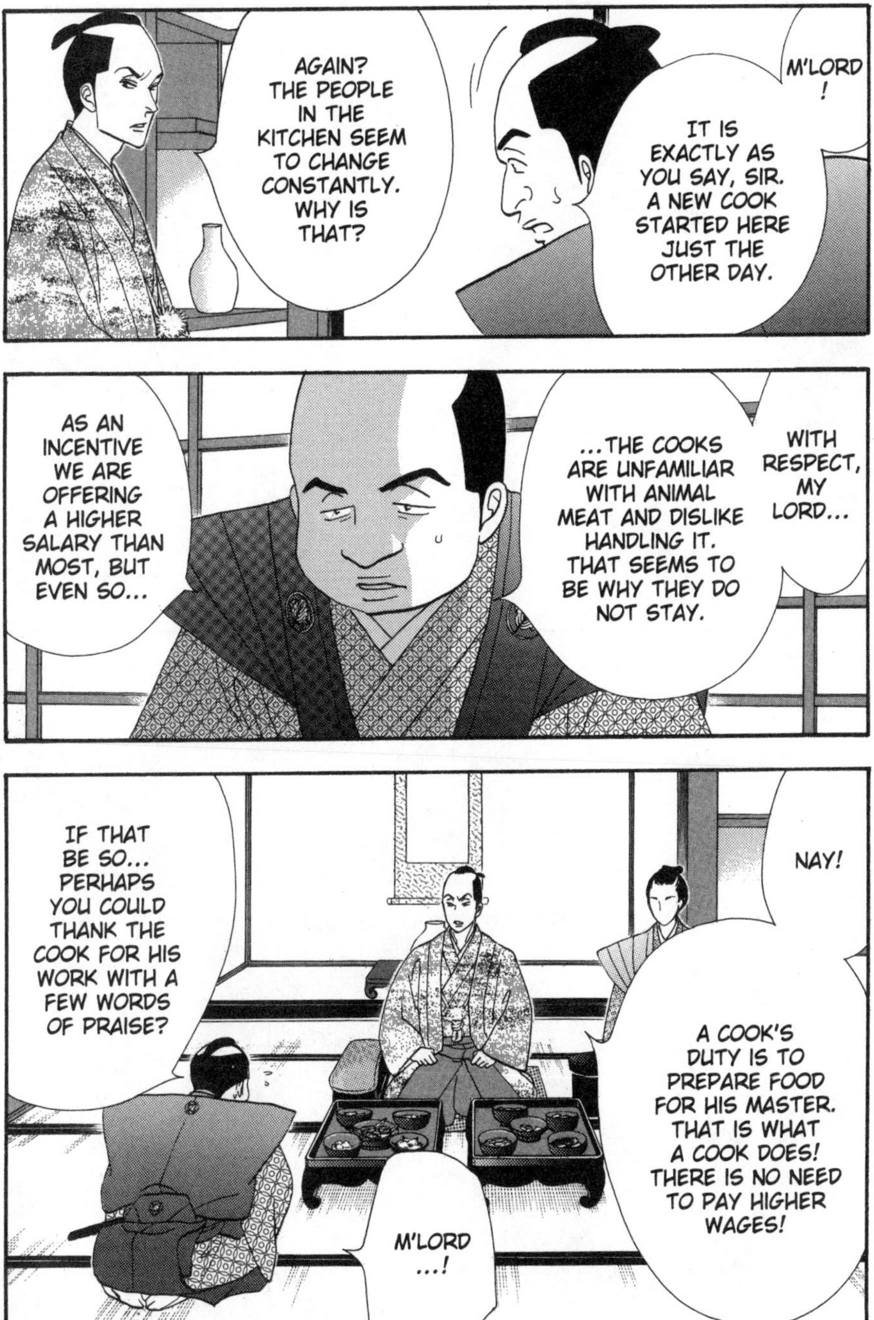
M'LORD!
IT IS EXACTLY AS YOU SAY, SIR. A NEW COOK STARTED HERE JUST THE OTHER DAY.
AGAIN? THE PEOPLE IN THE KITCHEN SEEM TO CHANGE CONSTANTLY. WHY IS THAT?
WITH RESPECT, MY LORD...
...THE COOKS ARE UNFAMILIAR WITH ANIMAL MEAT AND DISLIKE HANDLING IT. THAT SEEMS TO BE WHY THEY DO NOT STAY.
AS AN INCENTIVE WE ARE OFFERING A HIGHER SALARY THAN MOST, BUT EVEN SO...
IF THAT BE SO... PERHAPS YOU COULD THANK THE COOK FOR HIS WORK WITH A FEW WORDS OF PRAISE?
NAY!
A COOK'S DUTY IS TO PREPARE FOOD FOR HIS MASTER. THAT IS WHAT A COOK DOES! THERE IS NO NEED TO PAY HIGHER WAGES!
M'LORD ...!

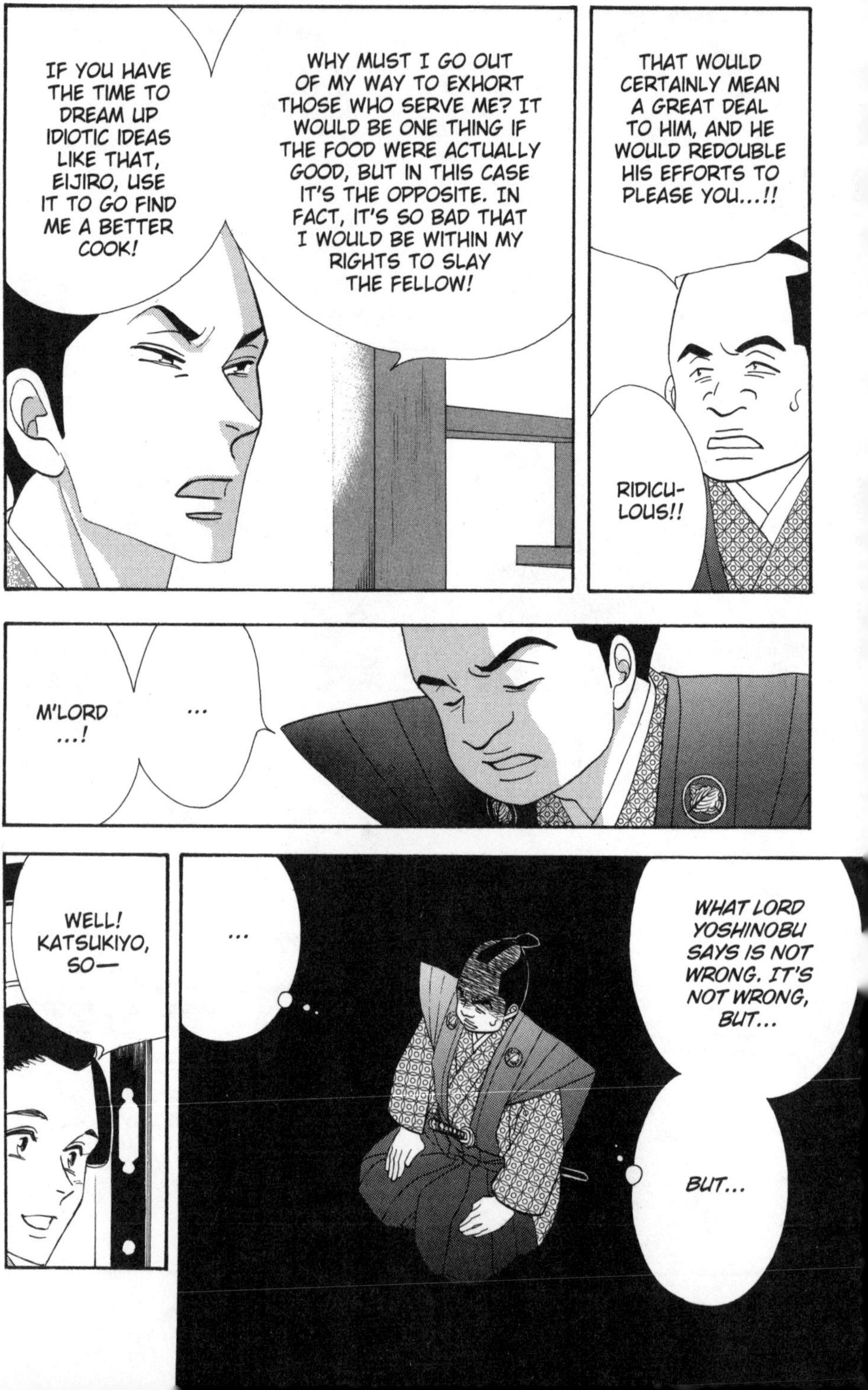
THAT WOULD CERTAINLY MEAN A GREAT DEAL TO HIM, AND HE WOULD REDOUBLE HIS EFFORTS TO PLEASE YOU...!!
RIDICU-LOUS!!
WHY MUST I GO OUT OF MY WAY TO EXHORT THOSE WHO SERVE ME? IT WOULD BE ONE THING IF THE FOOD WERE ACTUALLY GOOD, BUT IN THIS CASE IT'S THE OPPOSITE. IN FACT, IT'S SO BAD THAT I WOULD BE WITHIN MY RIGHTS TO SLAY THE FELLOW!
IF YOU HAVE THE TIME TO DREAM UP IDIOTIC IDEAS LIKE THAT, EIJIRO, USE IT TO GO FIND ME A BETTER COOK!
...
M'LORD ...!
WHAT LORD YOSHINOBU SAYS IS NOT WRONG. IT'S NOT WRONG, BUT...
BUT...
...
WELL! KATSUKIYO, SO—

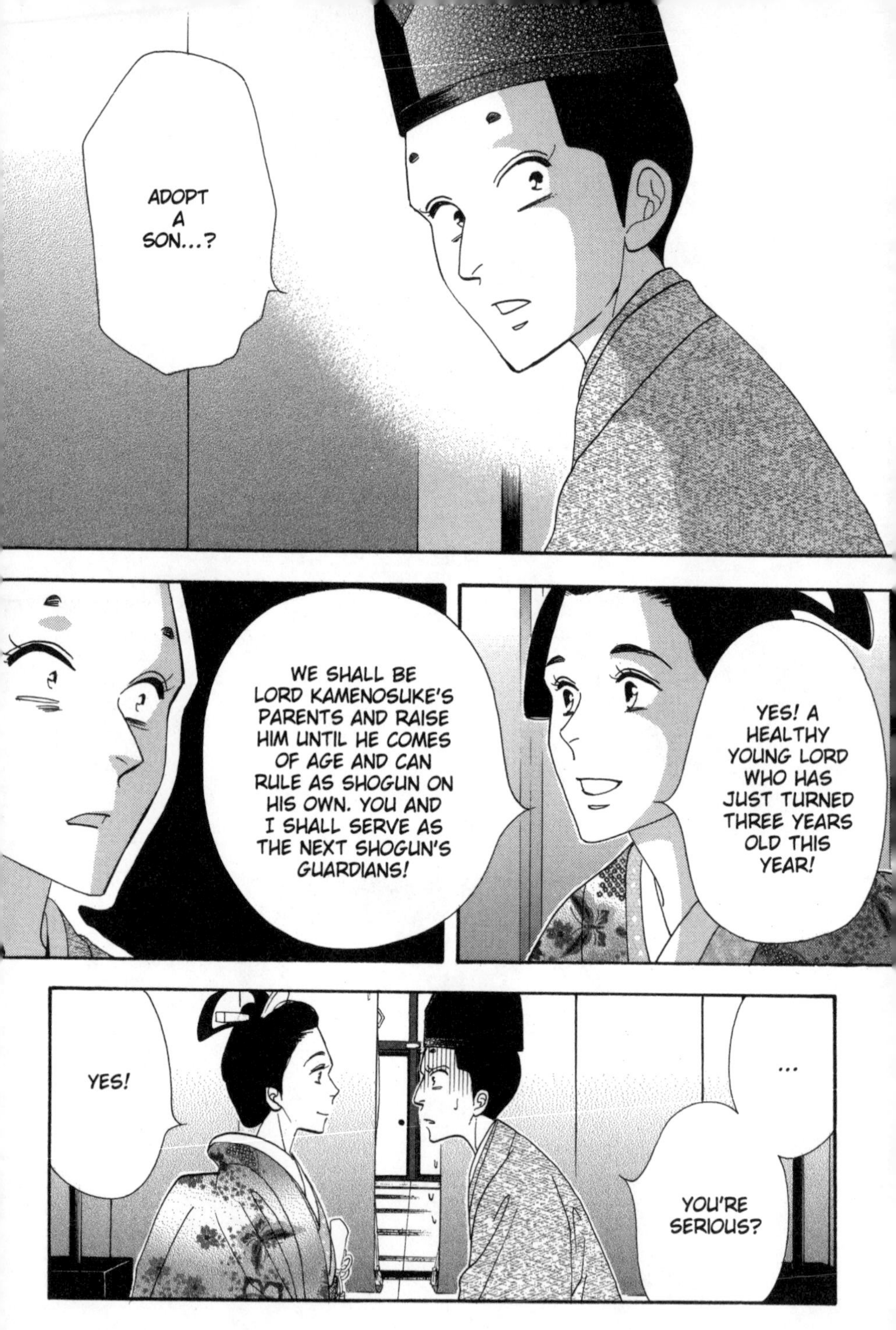
ADOPT A SON...?
YES! A HEALTHY YOUNG LORD WHO HAS JUST TURNED THREE YEARS OLD THIS YEAR!
WE SHALL BE LORD KAMENOSUKE'S PARENTS AND RAISE HIM UNTIL HE COMES OF AGE AND CAN RULE AS SHOGUN ON HIS OWN. YOU AND I SHALL SERVE AS THE NEXT SHOGUN'S GUARDIANS!
...
YOU'RE SERIOUS?
YES!

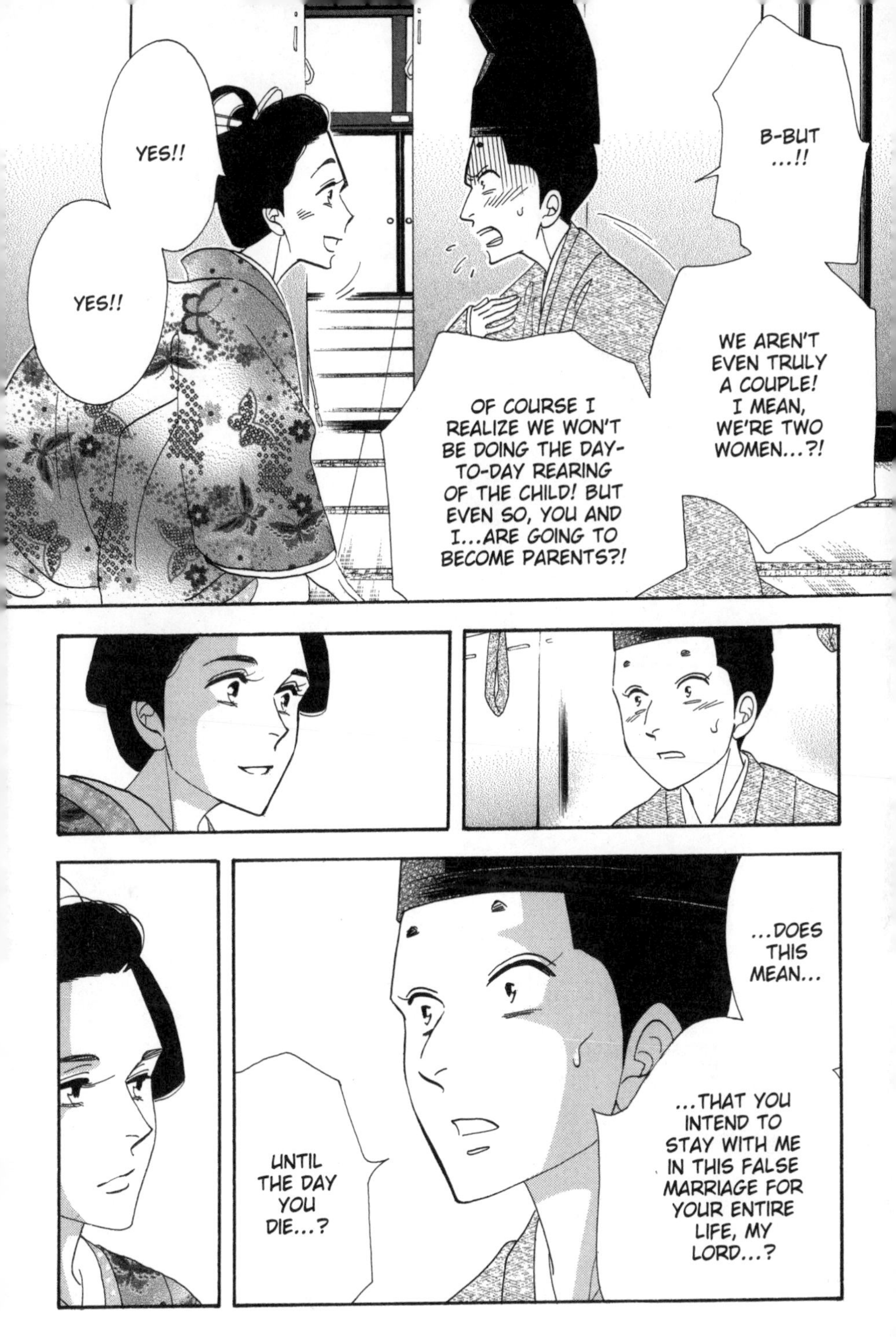
B-BUT ...!!
WE AREN'T EVEN TRULY A COUPLE! I MEAN, WE'RE TWO WOMEN...?!
OF COURSE I REALIZE WE WON'T BE DOING THE DAY-TO-DAY REARING OF THE CHILD! BUT EVEN SO, YOU AND I...ARE GOING TO BECOME PARENTS?!
YES!!
YES!!
...DOES THIS MEAN...
...THAT YOU INTEND TO STAY WITH ME IN THIS FALSE MARRIAGE FOR YOUR ENTIRE LIFE, MY LORD...?
UNTIL THE DAY YOU DIE...?

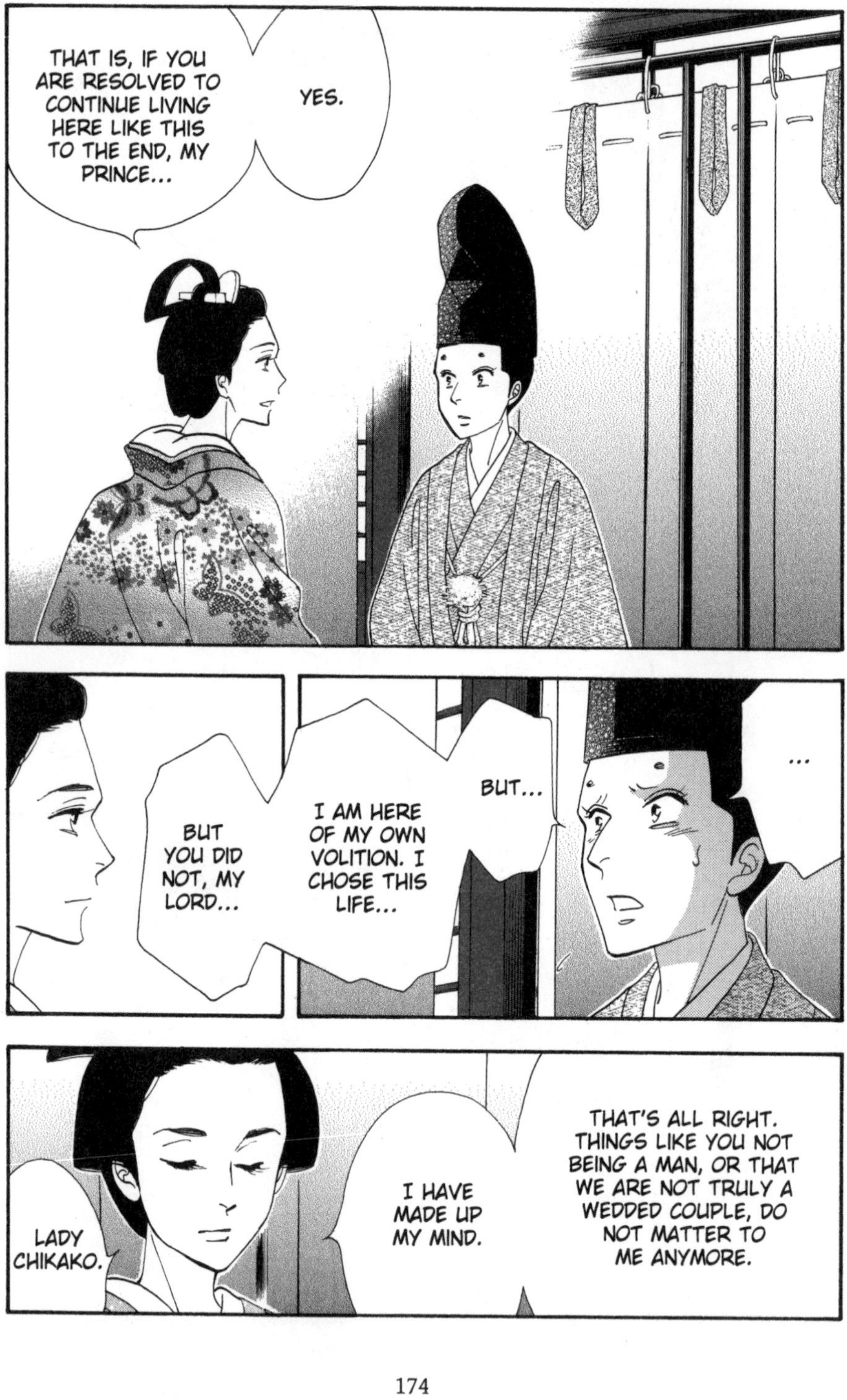
YES.
THAT IS, IF YOU ARE RESOLVED TO CONTINUE LIVING HERE LIKE THIS TO THE END, MY PRINCE...
...
BUT...
I AM HERE OF MY OWN VOLITION. I CHOSE THIS LIFE...
BUT YOU DID NOT, MY LORD...
THAT'S ALL RIGHT. THINGS LIKE YOU NOT BEING A MAN, OR THAT WE ARE NOT TRULY A WEDDED COUPLE, DO NOT MATTER TO ME ANYMORE.
I HAVE MADE UP MY MIND.
LADY CHIKAKO.

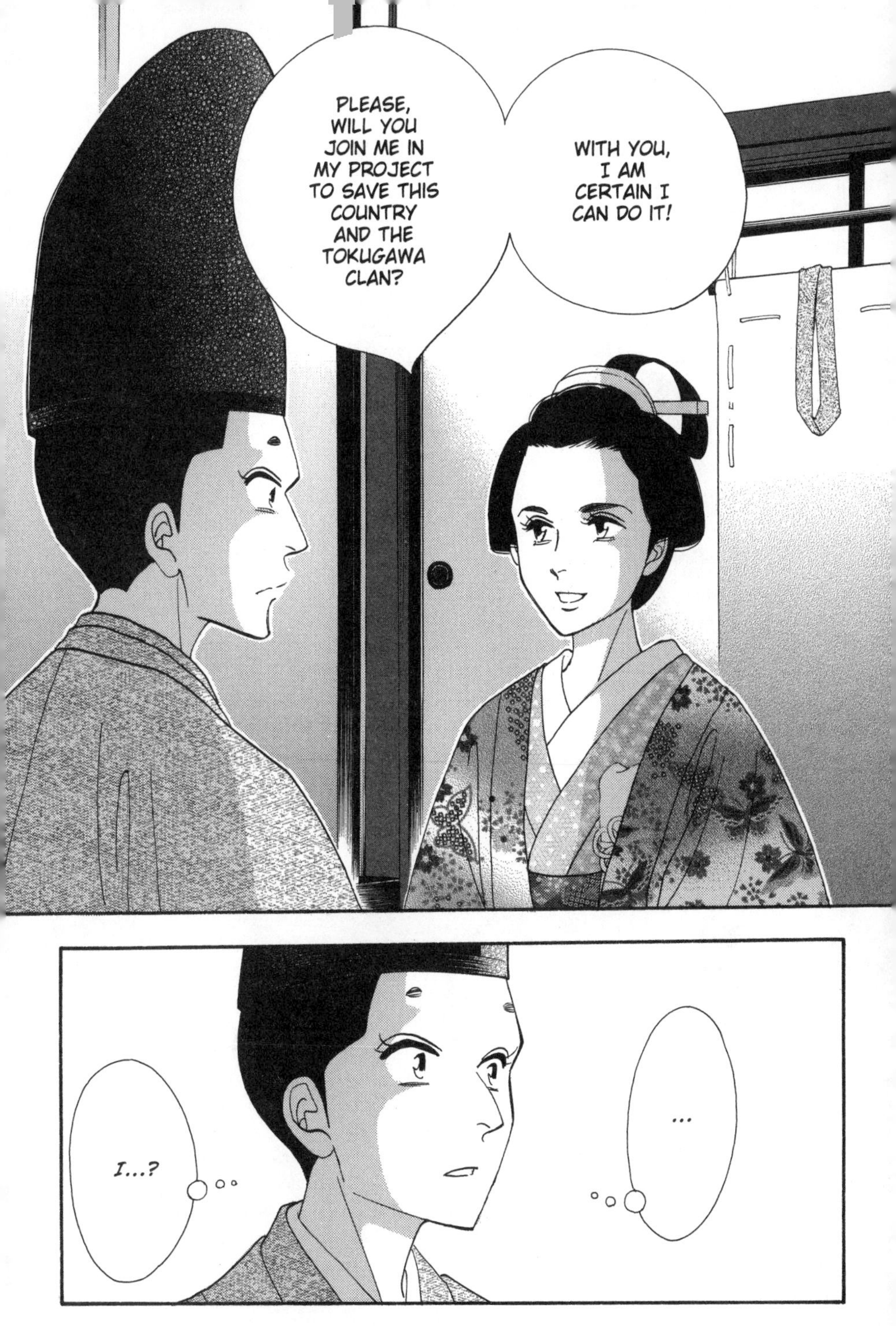
PLEASE, WILL YOU JOIN ME IN MY PROJECT TO SAVE THIS COUNTRY AND THE TOKUGAWA CLAN?
WITH YOU, I AM CERTAIN I CAN DO IT!
...
I...?

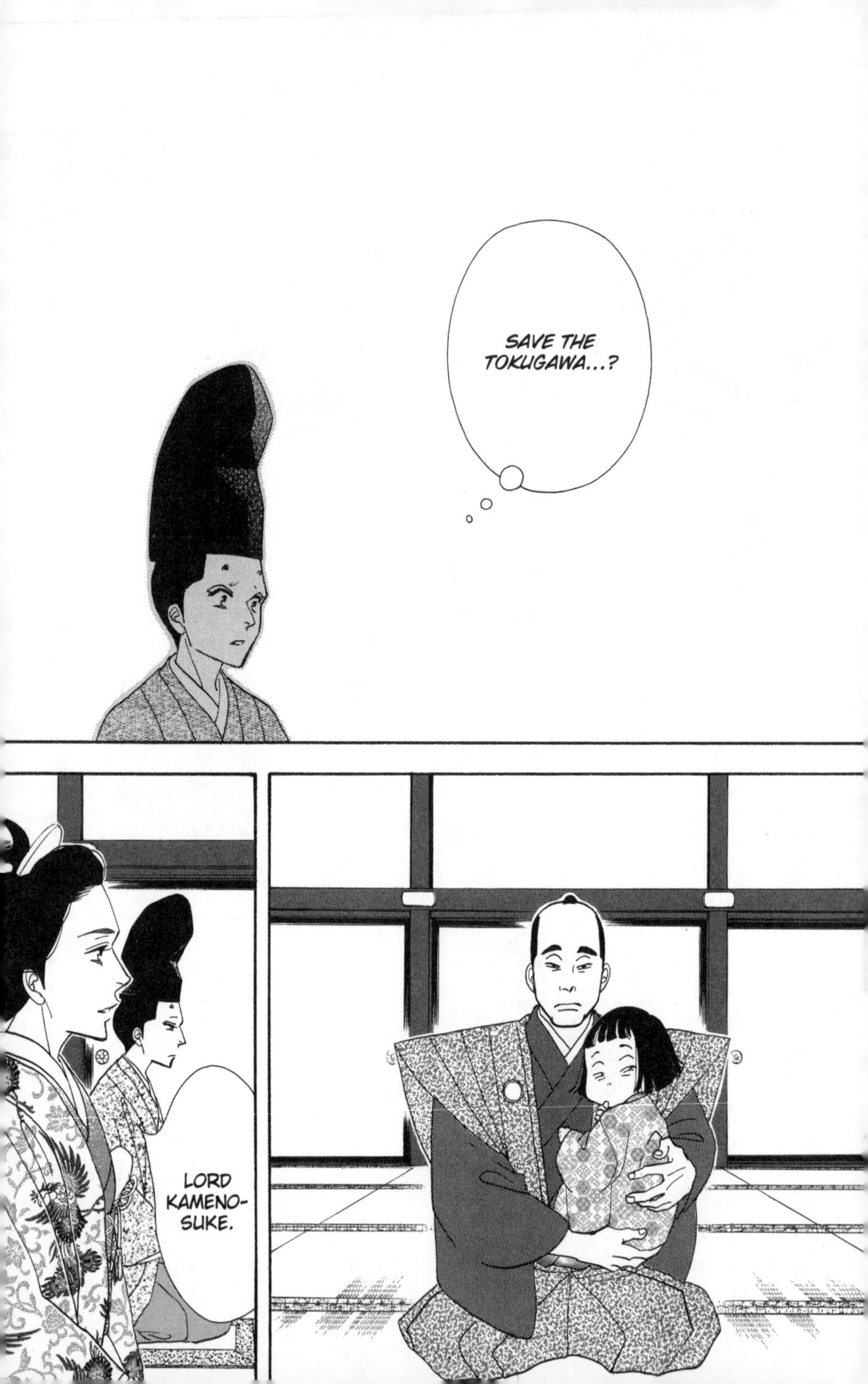
SAVE THE TOKUGAWA...?
LORD KAMENO-SUKE.

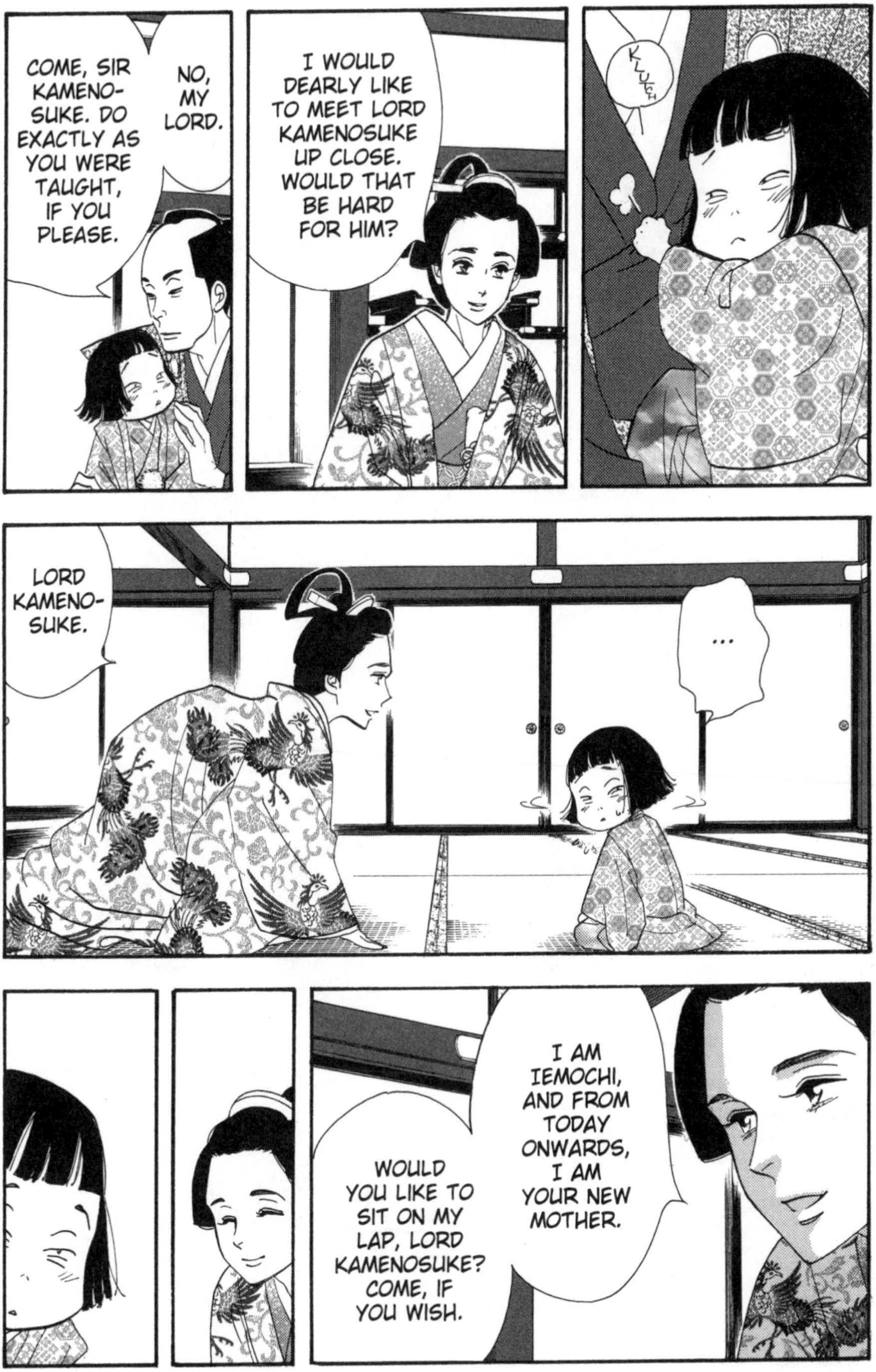
KLUTCH
I WOULD DEARLY LIKE TO MEET LORD KAMENOSUKE UP CLOSE. WOULD THAT BE HARD FOR HIM?
NO, MY LORD.
COME, SIR KAMENO-SUKE. DO EXACTLY AS YOU WERE TAUGHT, IF YOU PLEASE.
LORD KAMENO-SUKE.
...
I AM IEMOCHI, AND FROM TODAY ONWARDS, I AM YOUR NEW MOTHER.
WOULD YOU LIKE TO SIT ON MY LAP, LORD KAMENOSUKE? COME, IF YOU WISH.

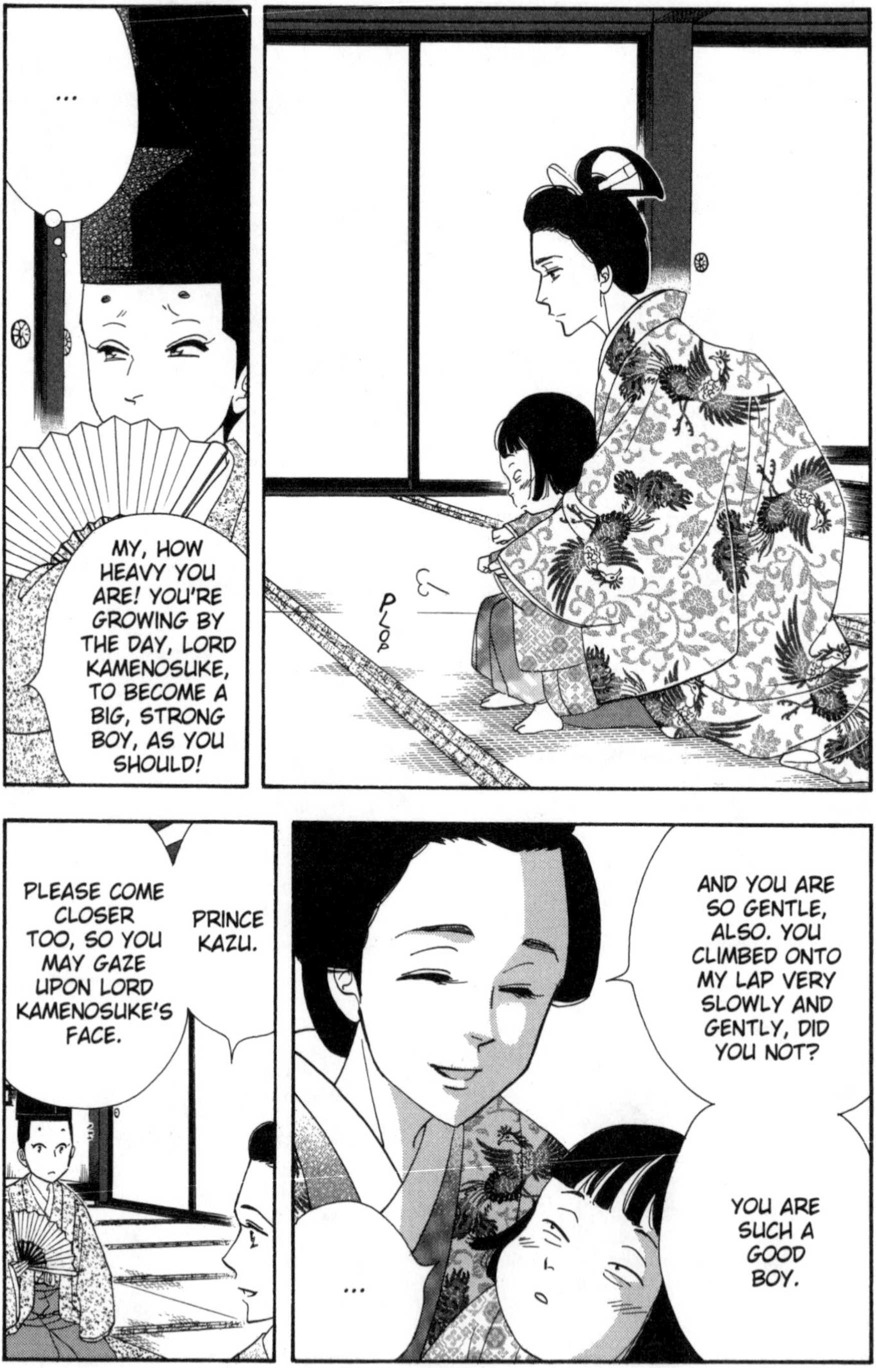
PLOP
...
MY, HOW HEAVY YOU ARE! YOU'RE GROWING BY THE DAY, LORD KAMENOSUKE, TO BECOME A BIG, STRONG BOY, AS YOU SHOULD!
AND YOU ARE SO GENTLE, ALSO. YOU CLIMBED ONTO MY LAP VERY SLOWLY AND GENTLY, DID YOU NOT?
YOU ARE SUCH A GOOD BOY.
...
PRINCE KAZU.
PLEASE COME CLOSER TOO, SO YOU MAY GAZE UPON LORD KAMENOSUKE'S FACE.

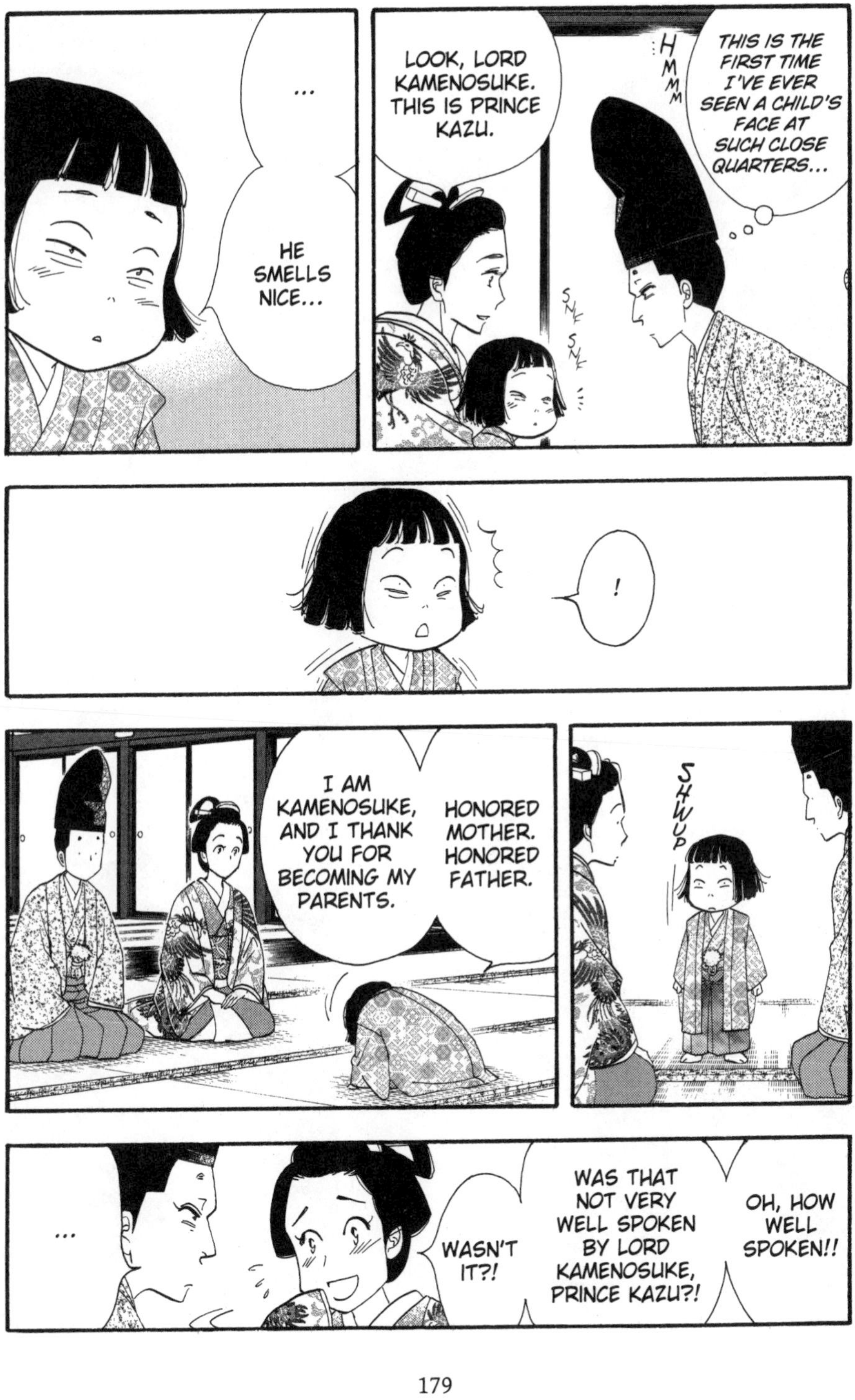
THIS IS THE FIRST TIME I'VE EVER SEEN A CHILD'S FACE AT SUCH CLOSE QUARTERS...
HMMM
LOOK, LORD KAMENOSUKE. THIS IS PRINCE KAZU.
SNF SNF
...
HE SMELLS NICE...
!
SHWUP
I AM KAMENOSUKE, AND I THANK YOU FOR BECOMING MY PARENTS.
HONORED MOTHER. HONORED FATHER.
OH, HOW WELL SPOKEN!!
WAS THAT NOT VERY WELL SPOKEN BY LORD KAMENOSUKE, PRINCE KAZU?!
WASN'T IT?!
...

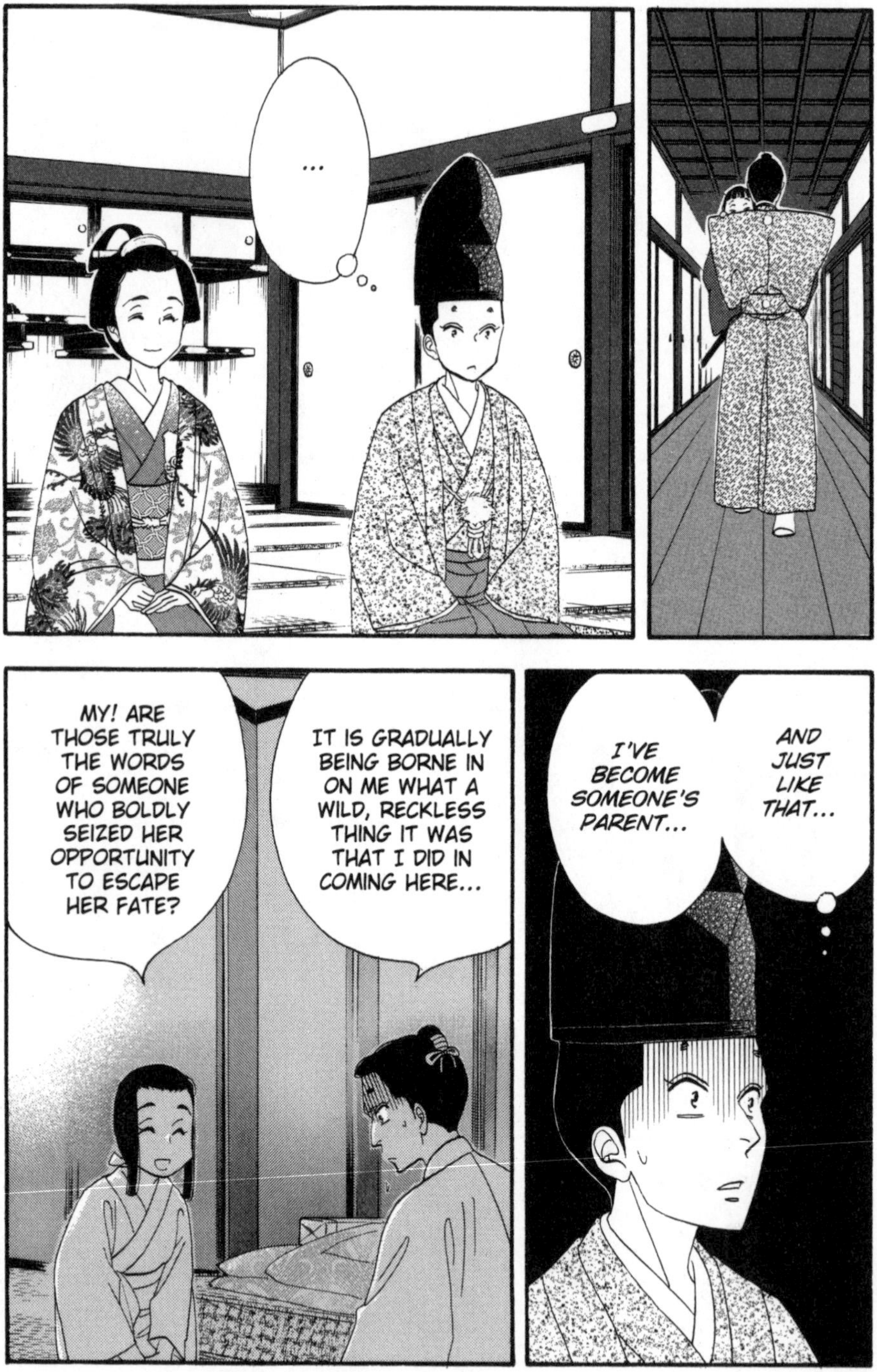
...
AND JUST LIKE THAT...
I'VE BECOME SOMEONE'S PARENT...
IT IS GRADUALLY BEING BORNE IN ON ME WHAT A WILD, RECKLESS THING IT WAS THAT I DID IN COMING HERE...
MY! ARE THOSE TRULY THE WORDS OF SOMEONE WHO BOLDLY SEIZED HER OPPORTUNITY TO ESCAPE HER FATE?

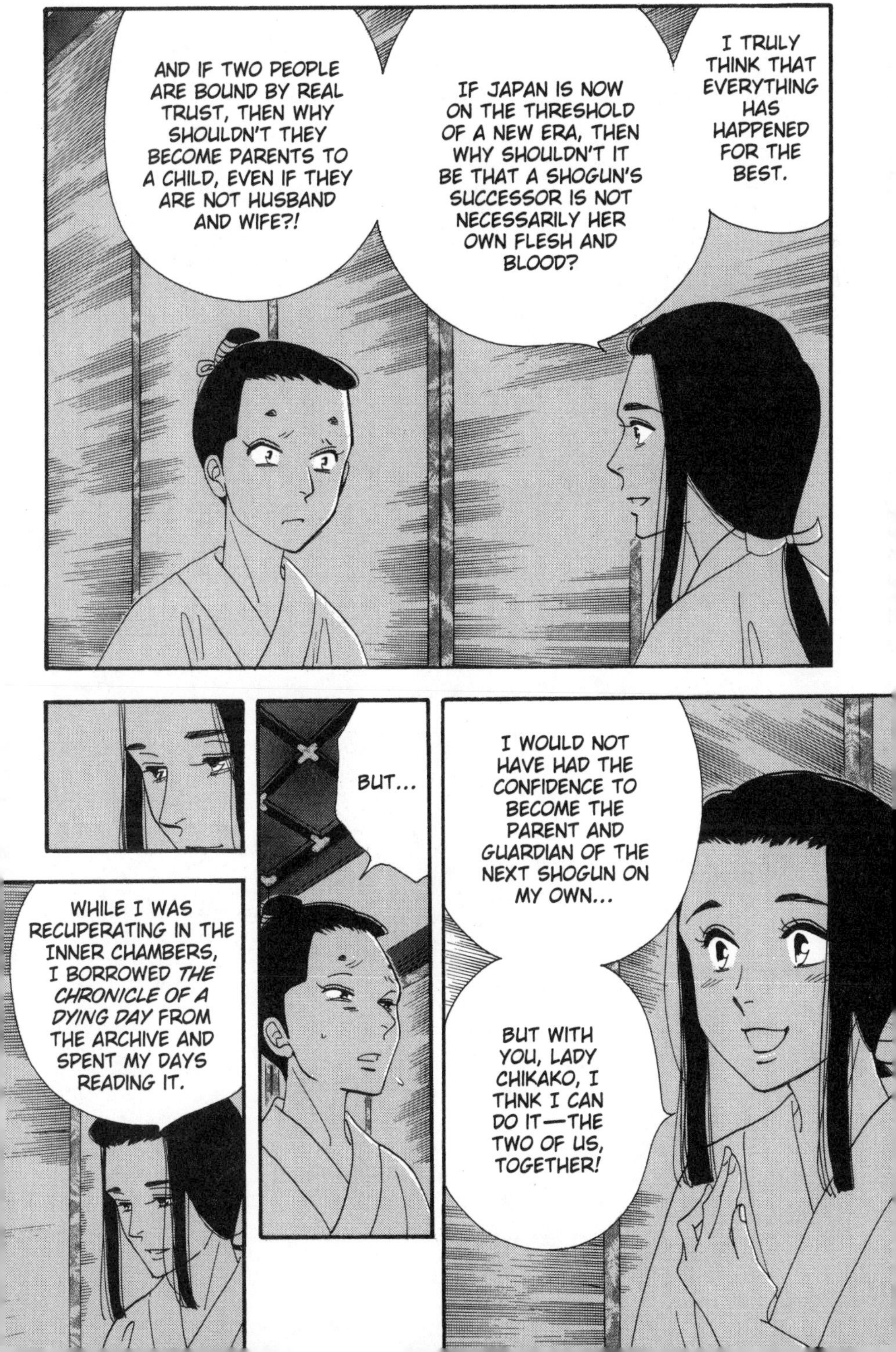
I TRULY THINK THAT EVERYTHING HAS HAPPENED FOR THE BEST.
IF JAPAN IS NOW ON THE THRESHOLD OF A NEW ERA, THEN WHY SHOULDN'T IT BE THAT A SHOGUN'S SUCCESSOR IS NOT NECESSARILY HER OWN FLESH AND BLOOD?
AND IF TWO PEOPLE ARE BOUND BY REAL TRUST, THEN WHY SHOULDN'T THEY BECOME PARENTS TO A CHILD, EVEN IF THEY ARE NOT HUSBAND AND WIFE?!
I WOULD NOT HAVE HAD THE CONFIDENCE TO BECOME THE PARENT AND GUARDIAN OF THE NEXT SHOGUN ON MY OWN...
BUT WITH YOU, LADY CHIKAKO, I THNK I CAN DO IT—THE TWO OF US, TOGETHER!
BUT...
WHILE I WAS RECUPERATING IN THE INNER CHAMBERS, I BORROWED *THE CHRONICLE OF A DYING DAY* FROM THE ARCHIVE AND SPENT MY DAYS READING IT.

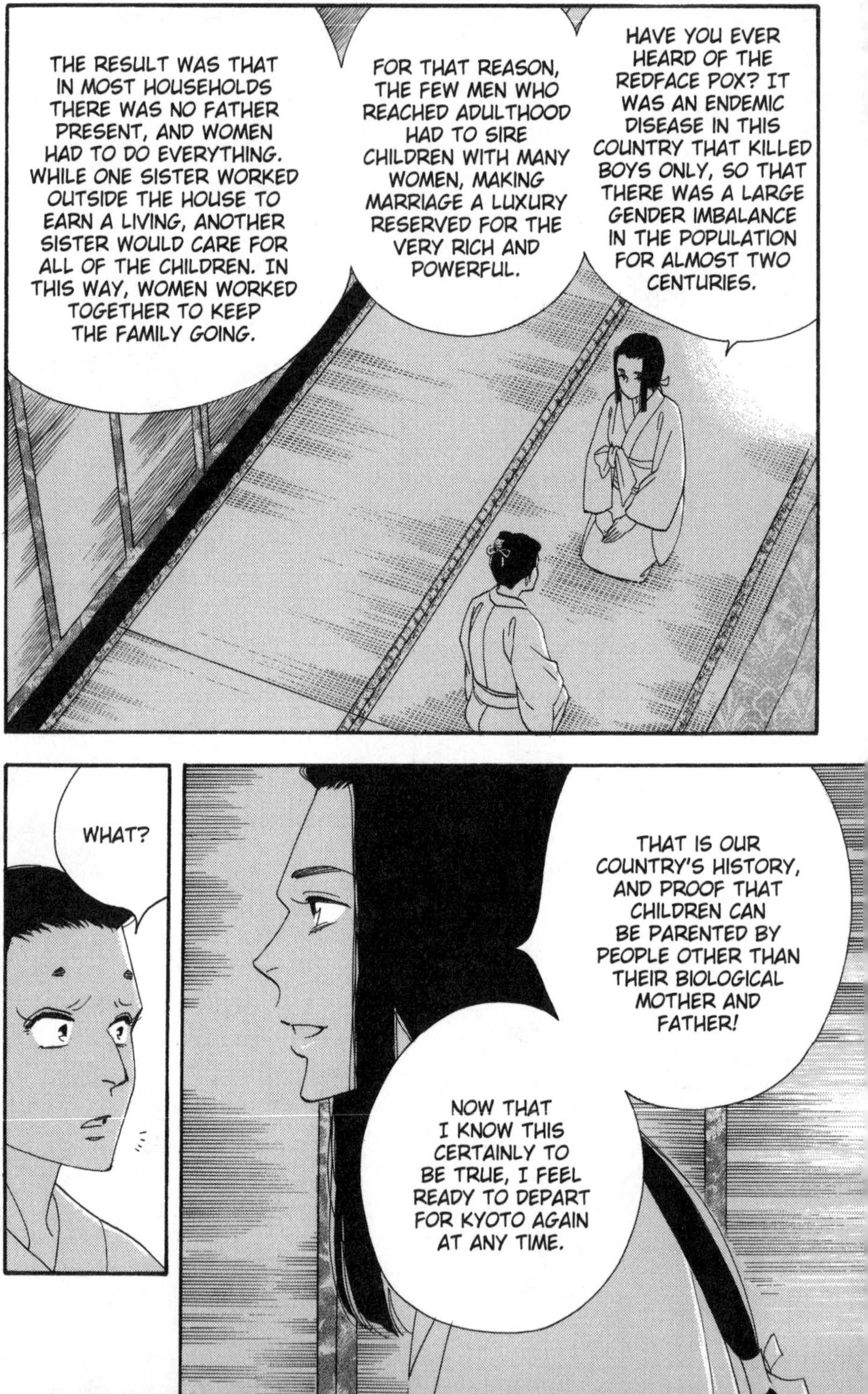
HAVE YOU EVER HEARD OF THE REDFACE POX? IT WAS AN ENDEMIC DISEASE IN THIS COUNTRY THAT KILLED BOYS ONLY, SO THAT THERE WAS A LARGE GENDER IMBALANCE IN THE POPULATION FOR ALMOST TWO CENTURIES.
FOR THAT REASON, THE FEW MEN WHO REACHED ADULTHOOD HAD TO SIRE CHILDREN WITH MANY WOMEN, MAKING MARRIAGE A LUXURY RESERVED FOR THE VERY RICH AND POWERFUL.
THE RESULT WAS THAT IN MOST HOUSEHOLDS THERE WAS NO FATHER PRESENT, AND WOMEN HAD TO DO EVERYTHING. WHILE ONE SISTER WORKED OUTSIDE THE HOUSE TO EARN A LIVING, ANOTHER SISTER WOULD CARE FOR ALL OF THE CHILDREN. IN THIS WAY, WOMEN WORKED TOGETHER TO KEEP THE FAMILY GOING.
THAT IS OUR COUNTRY'S HISTORY, AND PROOF THAT CHILDREN CAN BE PARENTED BY PEOPLE OTHER THAN THEIR BIOLOGICAL MOTHER AND FATHER!
NOW THAT I KNOW THIS CERTAINLY TO BE TRUE, I FEEL READY TO DEPART FOR KYOTO AGAIN AT ANY TIME.
WHAT?

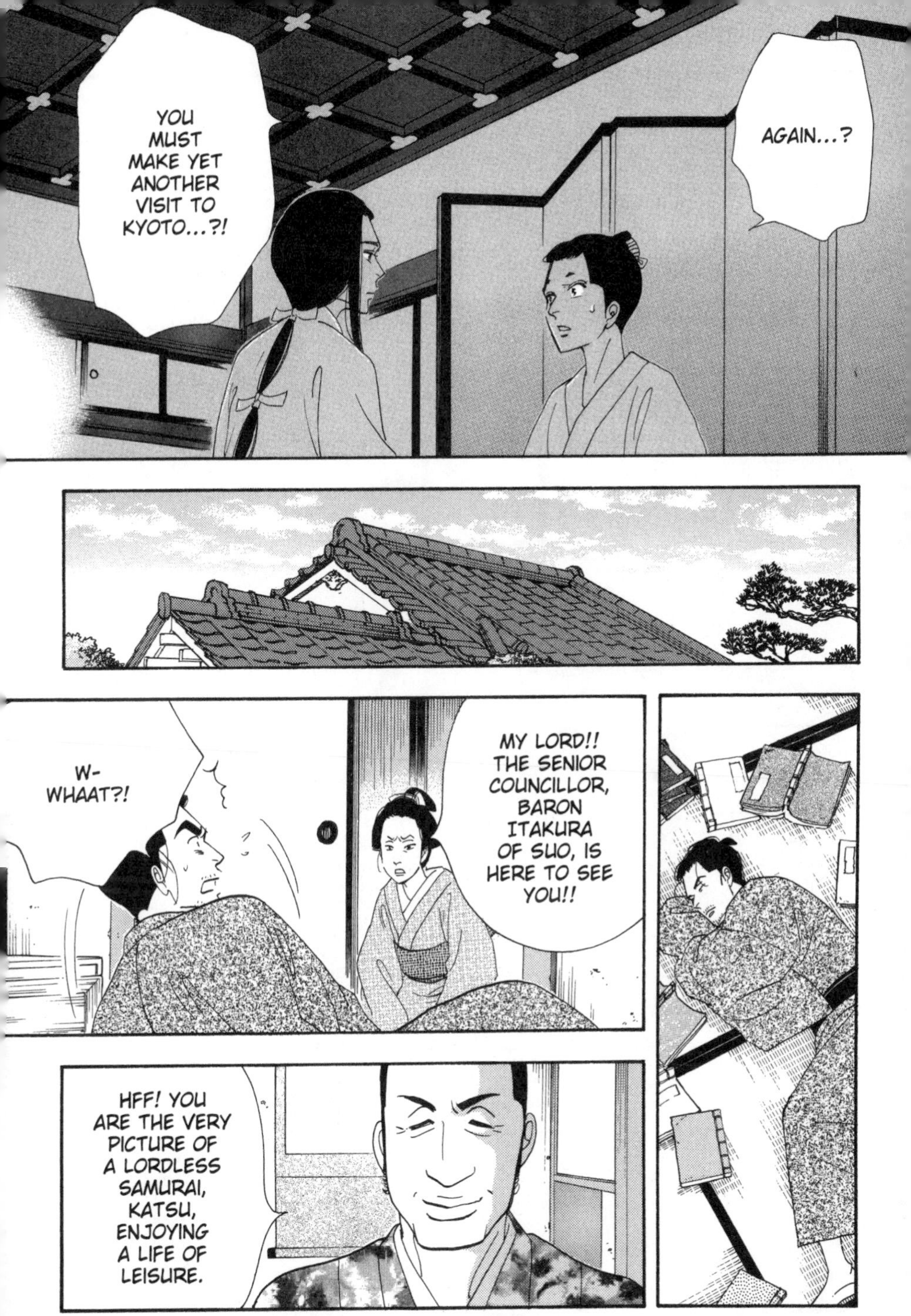
AGAIN...?
YOU MUST MAKE YET ANOTHER VISIT TO KYOTO...?!
MY LORD!! THE SENIOR COUNCILLOR, BARON ITAKURA OF SUO, IS HERE TO SEE YOU!!
W-WHAAT?!
HFF! YOU ARE THE VERY PICTURE OF A LORDLESS SAMURAI, KATSU, ENJOYING A LIFE OF LEISURE.

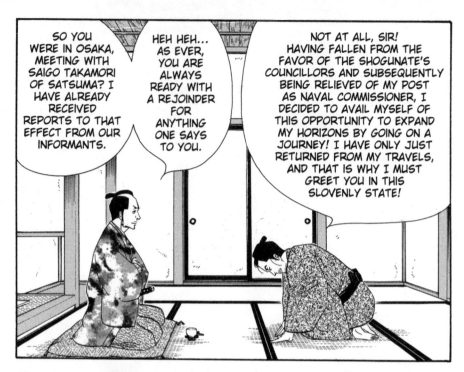

NOT AT ALL, SIR! HAVING FALLEN FROM THE FAVOR OF THE SHOGUNATE'S COUNCILLORS AND SUBSEQUENTLY BEING RELIEVED OF MY POST AS NAVAL COMMISSIONER, I DECIDED TO AVAIL MYSELF OF THIS OPPORTUNITY TO EXPAND MY HORIZONS BY GOING ON A JOURNEY! I HAVE ONLY JUST RETURNED FROM MY TRAVELS, AND THAT IS WHY I MUST GREET YOU IN THIS SLOVENLY STATE!
HEH HEH... AS EVER, YOU ARE ALWAYS READY WITH A REJOINDER FOR ANYTHING ONE SAYS TO YOU.
SO YOU WERE IN OSAKA, MEETING WITH SAIGO TAKAMORI OF SATSUMA? I HAVE ALREADY RECEIVED REPORTS TO THAT EFFECT FROM OUR INFORMANTS.
IT IS BECAUSE OF YOUR FREQUENT MEETINGS WITH SUCH ANTI-BARBARIAN TYPES THAT SOME IN THE GOVERNMENT SEE YOU AS A SECRET AGENT FOR THE ANTI-BARBARIANS.
I FOR ONE FEEL BAD THAT YOU HAVE HAD TO ENDURE INDIGNITIES FOR THAT REASON.
REALLY?! THEN WILL YOU REINSTATE ME TO THE POST OF NAVAL COMMISSIONER, BARON OF SUO?!
SOON ENOUGH, YES.

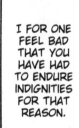

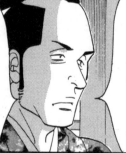

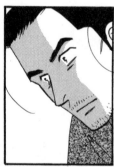

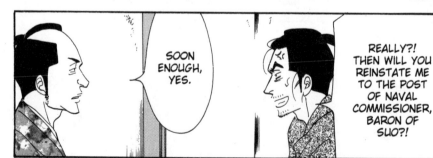

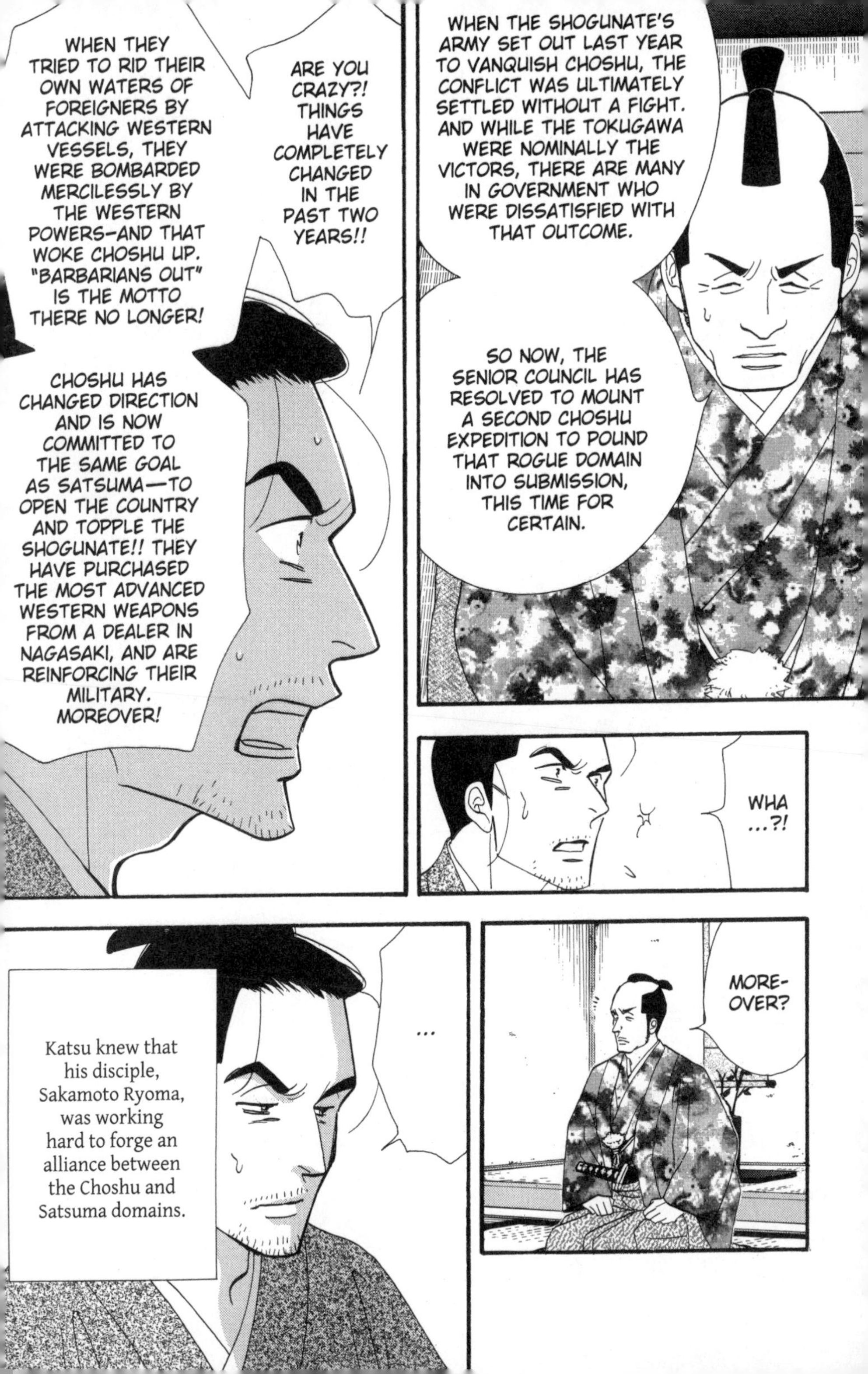
WHEN THE SHOGUNATE'S ARMY SET OUT LAST YEAR TO VANQUISH CHOSHU, THE CONFLICT WAS ULTIMATELY SETTLED WITHOUT A FIGHT. AND WHILE THE TOKUGAWA WERE NOMINALLY THE VICTORS, THERE ARE MANY IN GOVERNMENT WHO WERE DISSATISFIED WITH THAT OUTCOME.
SO NOW, THE SENIOR COUNCIL HAS RESOLVED TO MOUNT A SECOND CHOSHU EXPEDITION TO POUND THAT ROGUE DOMAIN INTO SUBMISSION, THIS TIME FOR CERTAIN.
WHA ...?!
ARE YOU CRAZY?! THINGS HAVE COMPLETELY CHANGED IN THE PAST TWO YEARS!!
WHEN THEY TRIED TO RID THEIR OWN WATERS OF FOREIGNERS BY ATTACKING WESTERN VESSELS, THEY WERE BOMBARDED MERCILESSLY BY THE WESTERN POWERS—AND THAT WOKE CHOSHU UP. "BARBARIANS OUT" IS THE MOTTO THERE NO LONGER!
CHOSHU HAS CHANGED DIRECTION AND IS NOW COMMITTED TO THE SAME GOAL AS SATSUMA—TO OPEN THE COUNTRY AND TOPPLE THE SHOGUNATE!! THEY HAVE PURCHASED THE MOST ADVANCED WESTERN WEAPONS FROM A DEALER IN NAGASAKI, AND ARE REINFORCING THEIR MILITARY. MOREOVER!
MORE-OVER?
...
Katsu knew that his disciple, Sakamoto Ryoma, was working hard to forge an alliance between the Choshu and Satsuma domains.

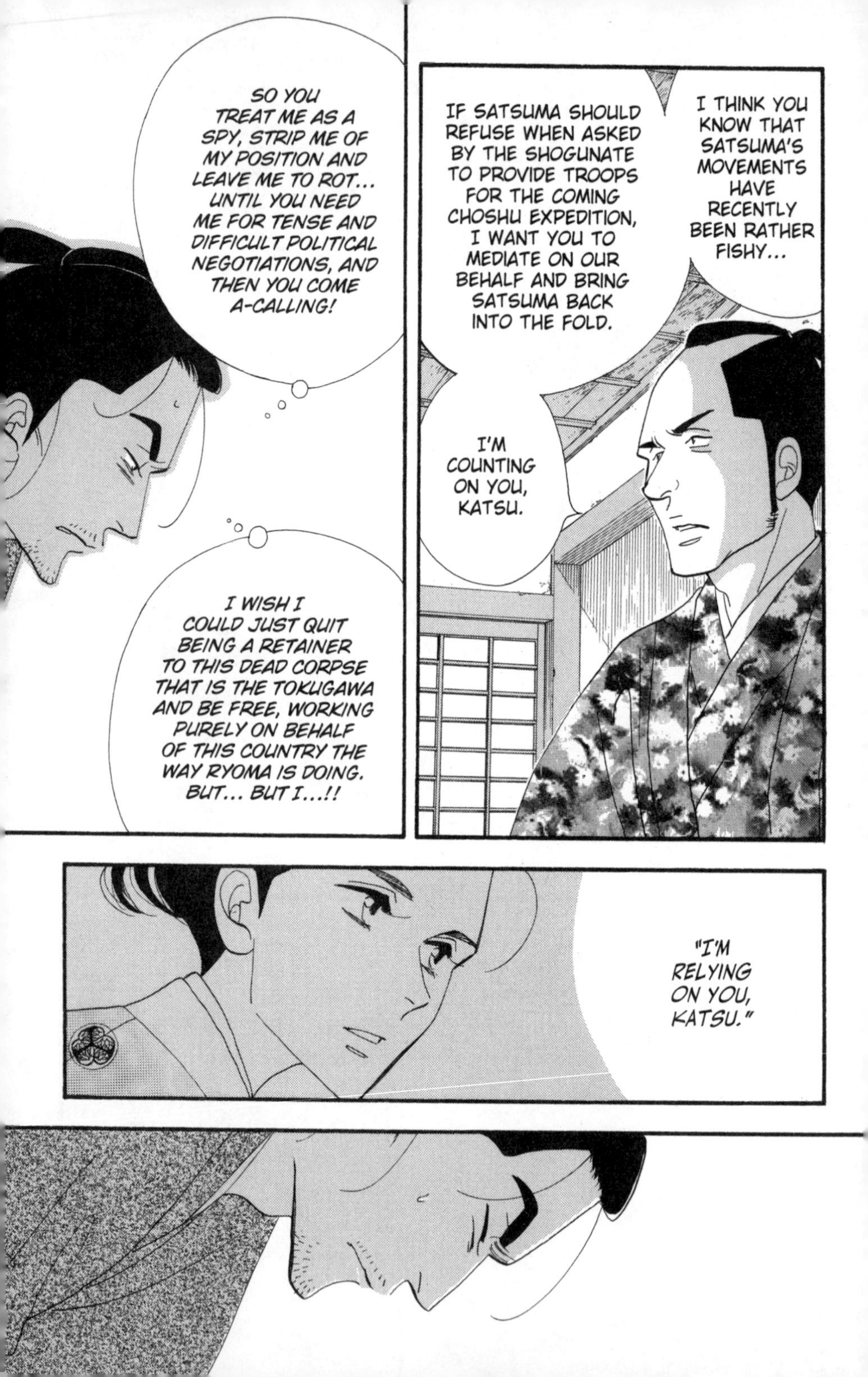
I THINK YOU KNOW THAT SATSUMA'S MOVEMENTS HAVE RECENTLY BEEN RATHER FISHY...
IF SATSUMA SHOULD REFUSE WHEN ASKED BY THE SHOGUNATE TO PROVIDE TROOPS FOR THE COMING CHOSHU EXPEDITION, I WANT YOU TO MEDIATE ON OUR BEHALF AND BRING SATSUMA BACK INTO THE FOLD.
I'M COUNTING ON YOU, KATSU.
SO YOU TREAT ME AS A SPY, STRIP ME OF MY POSITION AND LEAVE ME TO ROT... UNTIL YOU NEED ME FOR TENSE AND DIFFICULT POLITICAL NEGOTIATIONS, AND THEN YOU COME A-CALLING!
I WISH I COULD JUST QUIT BEING A RETAINER TO THIS DEAD CORPSE THAT IS THE TOKUGAWA AND BE FREE, WORKING PURELY ON BEHALF OF THIS COUNTRY THE WAY RYOMA IS DOING. BUT... BUT I...!!
"I'M RELYING ON YOU, KATSU."

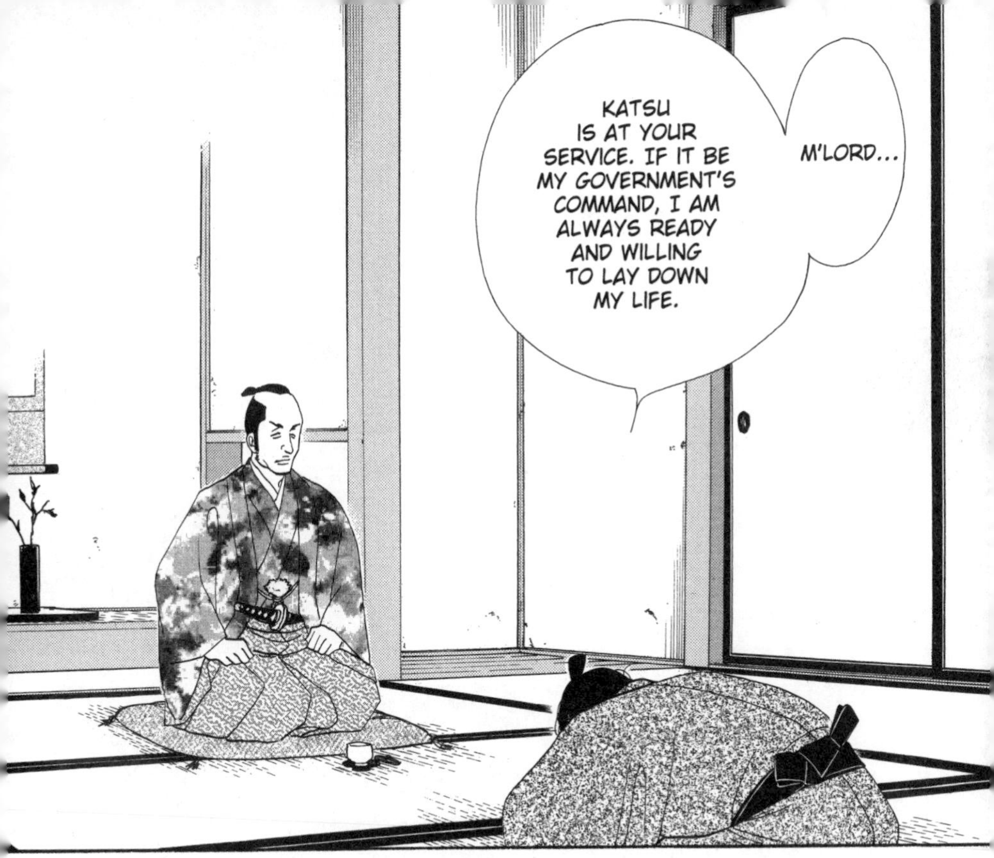
M'LORD...
KATSU IS AT YOUR SERVICE. IF IT BE MY GOVERNMENT'S COMMAND, I AM ALWAYS READY AND WILLING TO LAY DOWN MY LIFE.

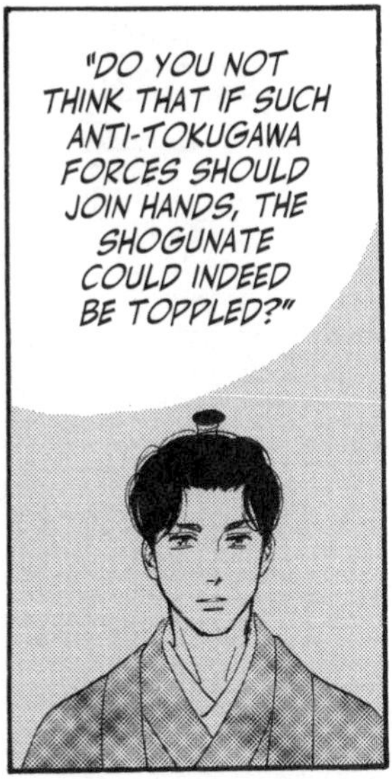
"DO YOU NOT THINK THAT IF SUCH ANTI-TOKUGAWA FORCES SHOULD JOIN HANDS, THE SHOGUNATE COULD INDEED BE TOPPLED?"

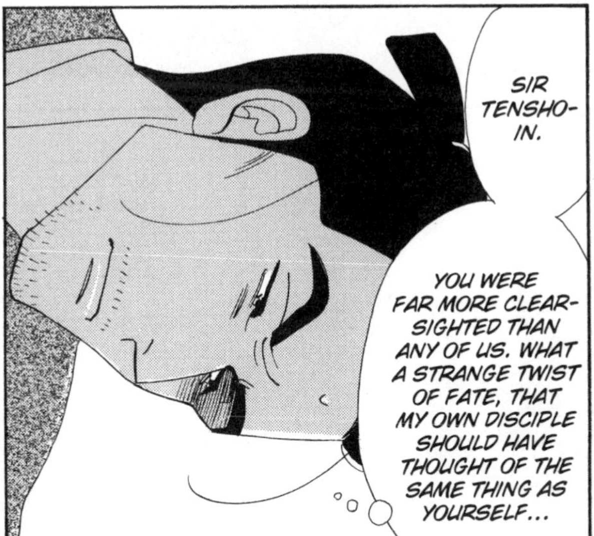
SIR TENSHO-IN.
YOU WERE FAR MORE CLEAR-SIGHTED THAN ANY OF US. WHAT A STRANGE TWIST OF FATE, THAT MY OWN DISCIPLE SHOULD HAVE THOUGHT OF THE SAME THING AS YOURSELF...

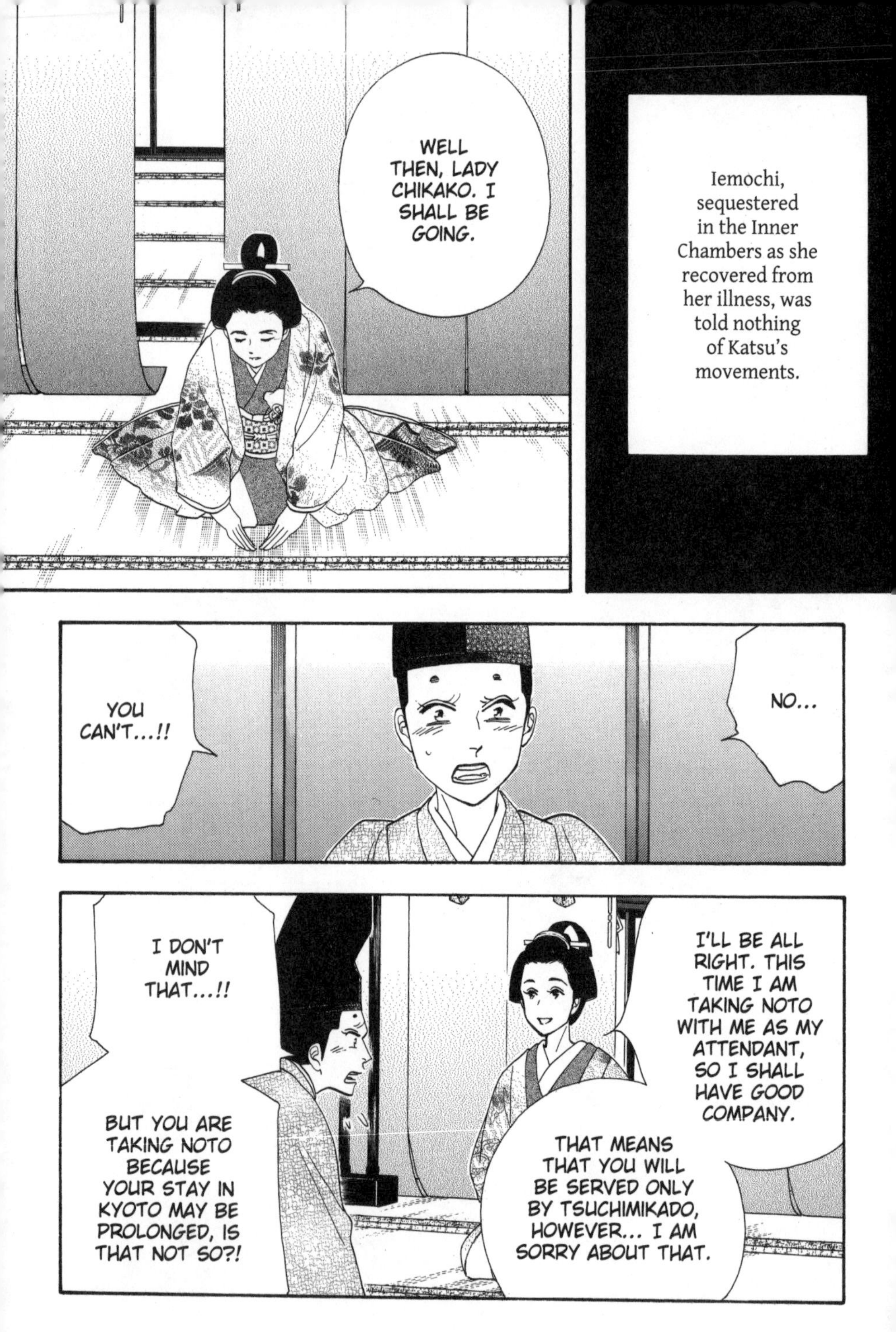

Iemochi, sequestered in the Inner Chambers as she recovered from her illness, was told nothing of Katsu's movements.
WELL THEN, LADY CHIKAKO. I SHALL BE GOING.
NO...
YOU CAN'T...!!
I'LL BE ALL RIGHT. THIS TIME I AM TAKING NOTO WITH ME AS MY ATTENDANT, SO I SHALL HAVE GOOD COMPANY.
THAT MEANS THAT YOU WILL BE SERVED ONLY BY TSUCHIMIKADO, HOWEVER... I AM SORRY ABOUT THAT.
I DON'T MIND THAT...!!
BUT YOU ARE TAKING NOTO BECAUSE YOUR STAY IN KYOTO MAY BE PROLONGED, IS THAT NOT SO?!

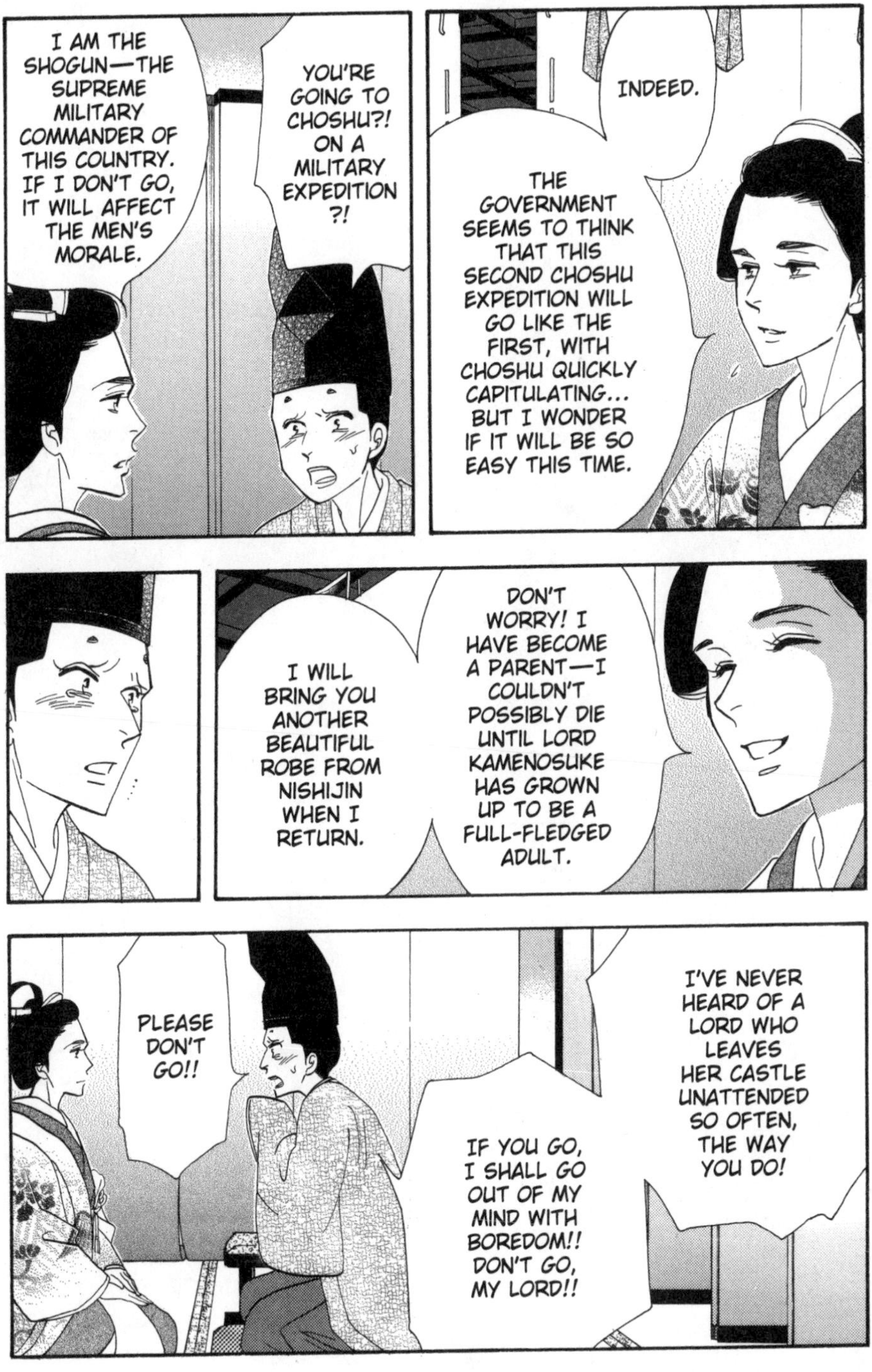
INDEED.
THE GOVERNMENT SEEMS TO THINK THAT THIS SECOND CHOSHU EXPEDITION WILL GO LIKE THE FIRST, WITH CHOSHU QUICKLY CAPITULATING... BUT I WONDER IF IT WILL BE SO EASY THIS TIME.
YOU'RE GOING TO CHOSHU?! ON A MILITARY EXPEDITION ?!
I AM THE SHOGUN—THE SUPREME MILITARY COMMANDER OF THIS COUNTRY. IF I DON'T GO, IT WILL AFFECT THE MEN'S MORALE.
DON'T WORRY! I HAVE BECOME A PARENT—I COULDN'T POSSIBLY DIE UNTIL LORD KAMENOSUKE HAS GROWN UP TO BE A FULL-FLEDGED ADULT.
I WILL BRING YOU ANOTHER BEAUTIFUL ROBE FROM NISHIJIN WHEN I RETURN.
I'VE NEVER HEARD OF A LORD WHO LEAVES HER CASTLE UNATTENDED SO OFTEN, THE WAY YOU DO!
IF YOU GO, I SHALL GO OUT OF MY MIND WITH BOREDOM!! DON'T GO, MY LORD!!
PLEASE DON'T GO!!

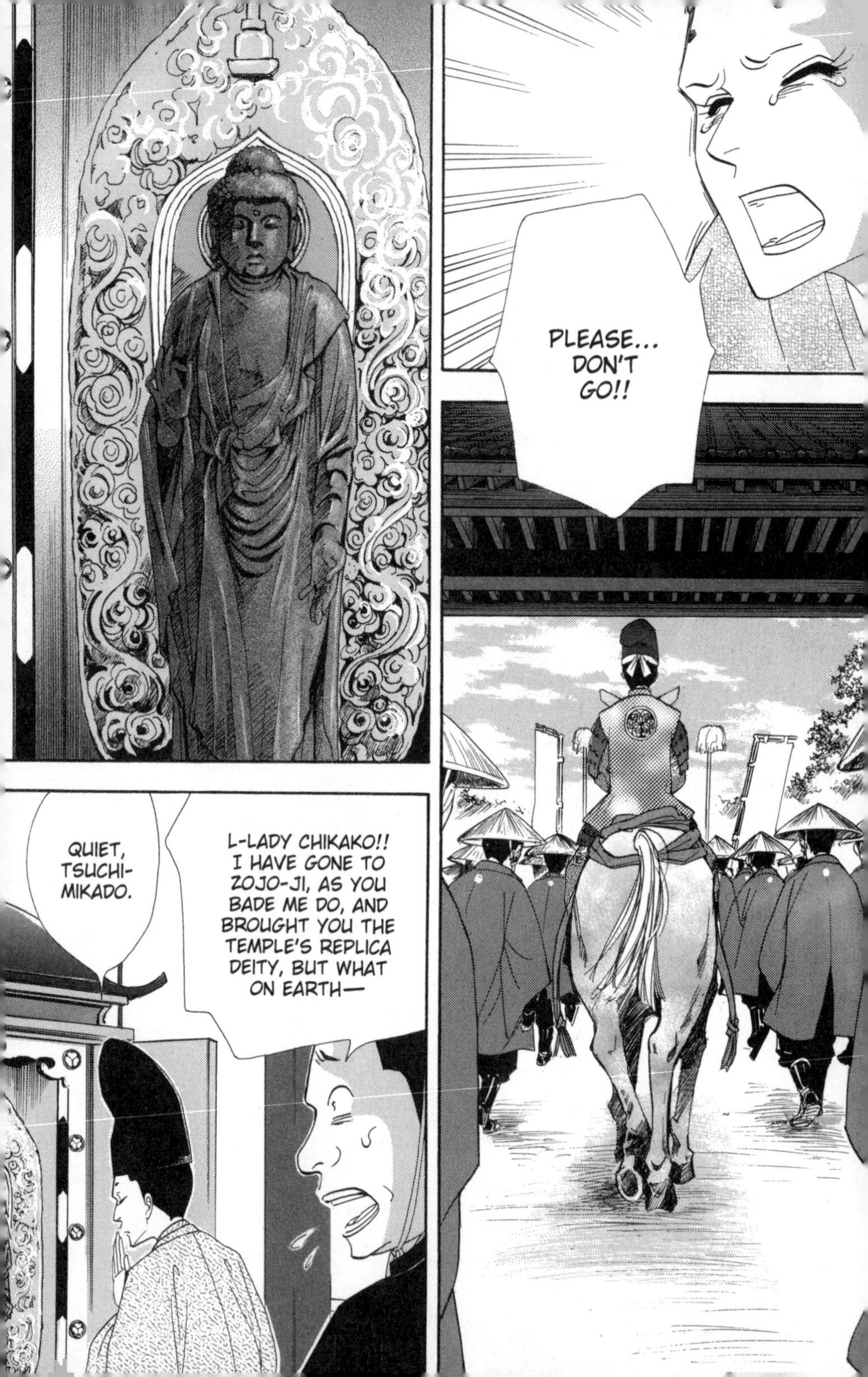
PLEASE... DON'T GO!!
L-LADY CHIKAKO!! I HAVE GONE TO ZOJO-JI, AS YOU BADE ME DO, AND BROUGHT YOU THE TEMPLE'S REPLICA DEITY, BUT WHAT ON EARTH—
QUIET, TSUCHI-MIKADO.

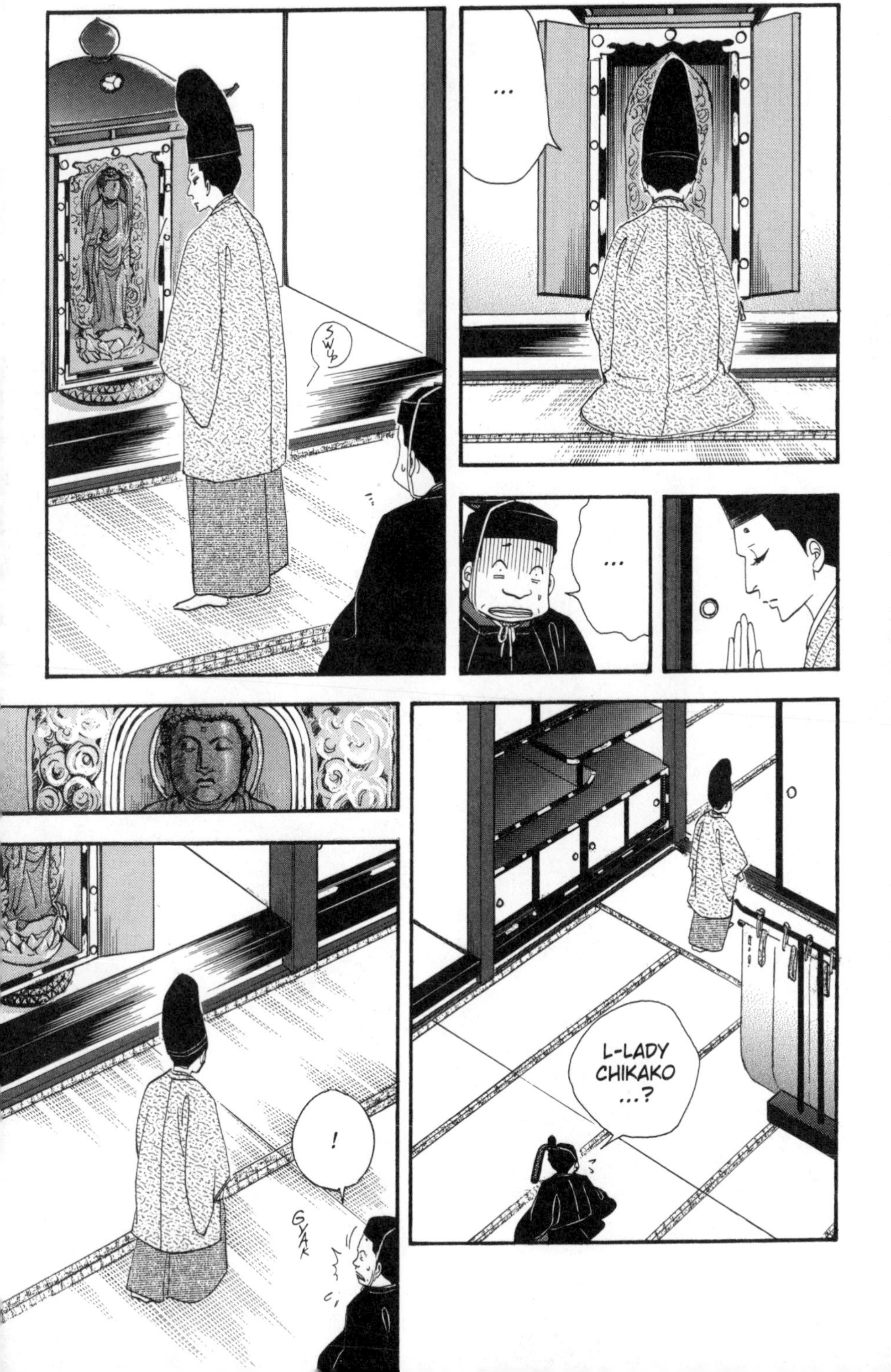
...
...
SWUP
L-LADY CHIKAKO ...?
!
GYAK

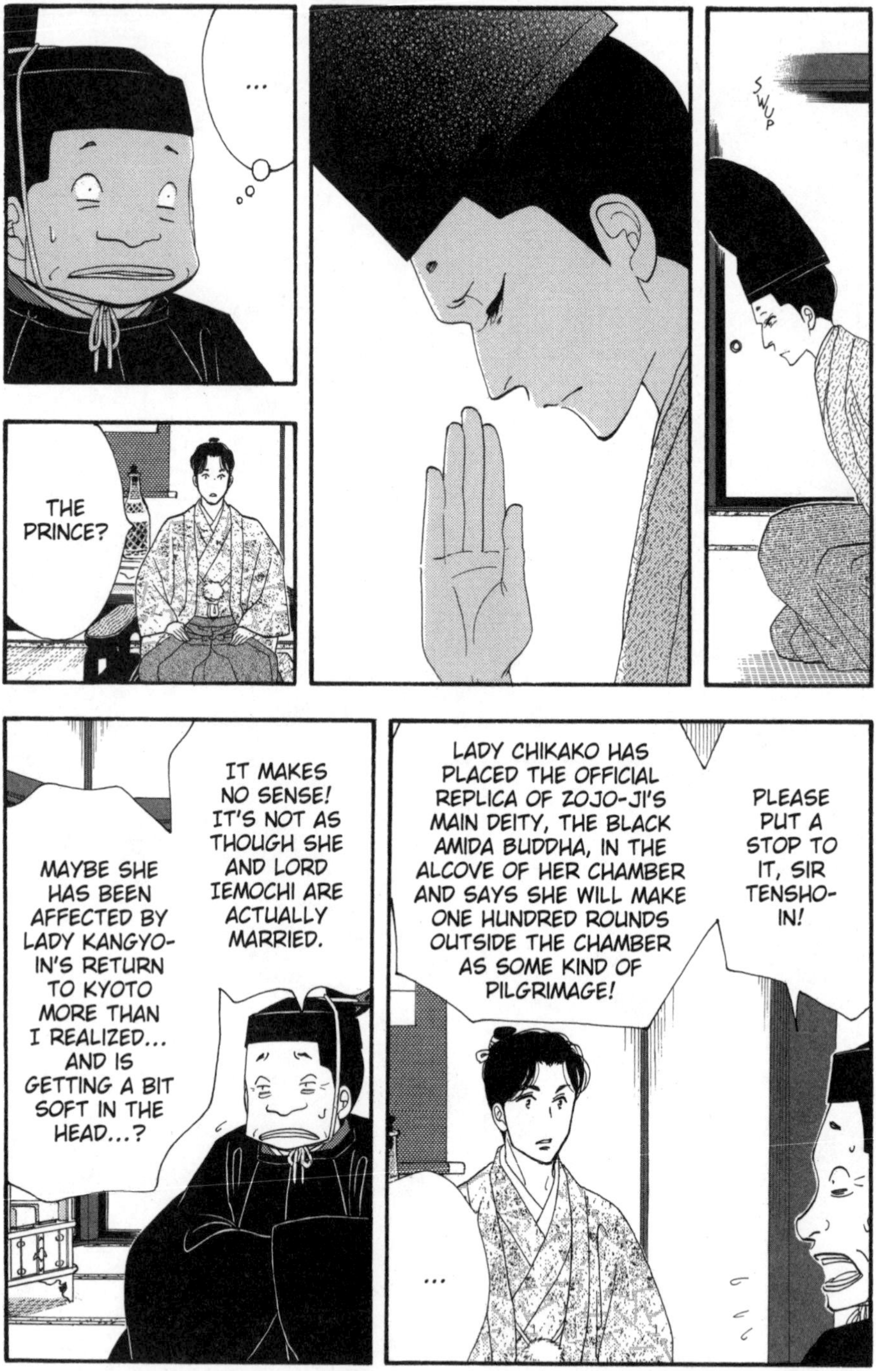
SWUP
...
THE PRINCE?
PLEASE PUT A STOP TO IT, SIR TENSHO-IN!
LADY CHIKAKO HAS PLACED THE OFFICIAL REPLICA OF ZOJO-JI'S MAIN DEITY, THE BLACK AMIDA BUDDHA, IN THE ALCOVE OF HER CHAMBER AND SAYS SHE WILL MAKE ONE HUNDRED ROUNDS OUTSIDE THE CHAMBER AS SOME KIND OF PILGRIMAGE!
...
IT MAKES NO SENSE! IT'S NOT AS THOUGH SHE AND LORD IEMOCHI ARE ACTUALLY MARRIED.
MAYBE SHE HAS BEEN AFFECTED BY LADY KANGYO-IN'S RETURN TO KYOTO MORE THAN I REALIZED... AND IS GETTING A BIT SOFT IN THE HEAD...?

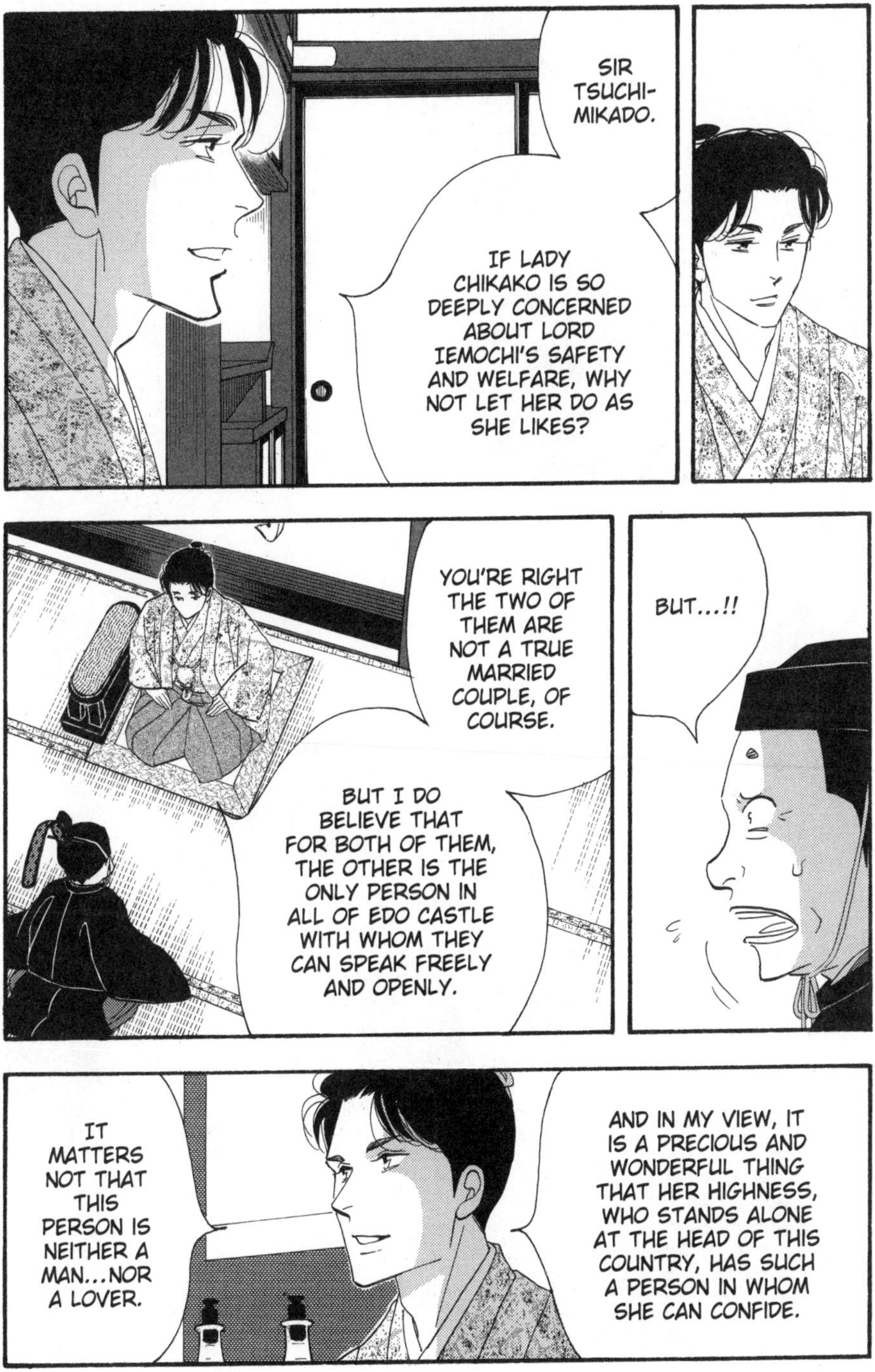
SIR TSUCHI-MIKADO.
IF LADY CHIKAKO IS SO DEEPLY CONCERNED ABOUT LORD IEMOCHI'S SAFETY AND WELFARE, WHY NOT LET HER DO AS SHE LIKES?
BUT...!!
YOU'RE RIGHT THE TWO OF THEM ARE NOT A TRUE MARRIED COUPLE, OF COURSE.
BUT I DO BELIEVE THAT FOR BOTH OF THEM, THE OTHER IS THE ONLY PERSON IN ALL OF EDO CASTLE WITH WHOM THEY CAN SPEAK FREELY AND OPENLY.
AND IN MY VIEW, IT IS A PRECIOUS AND WONDERFUL THING THAT HER HIGHNESS, WHO STANDS ALONE AT THE HEAD OF THIS COUNTRY, HAS SUCH A PERSON IN WHOM SHE CAN CONFIDE.
IT MATTERS NOT THAT THIS PERSON IS NEITHER A MAN...NOR A LOVER.

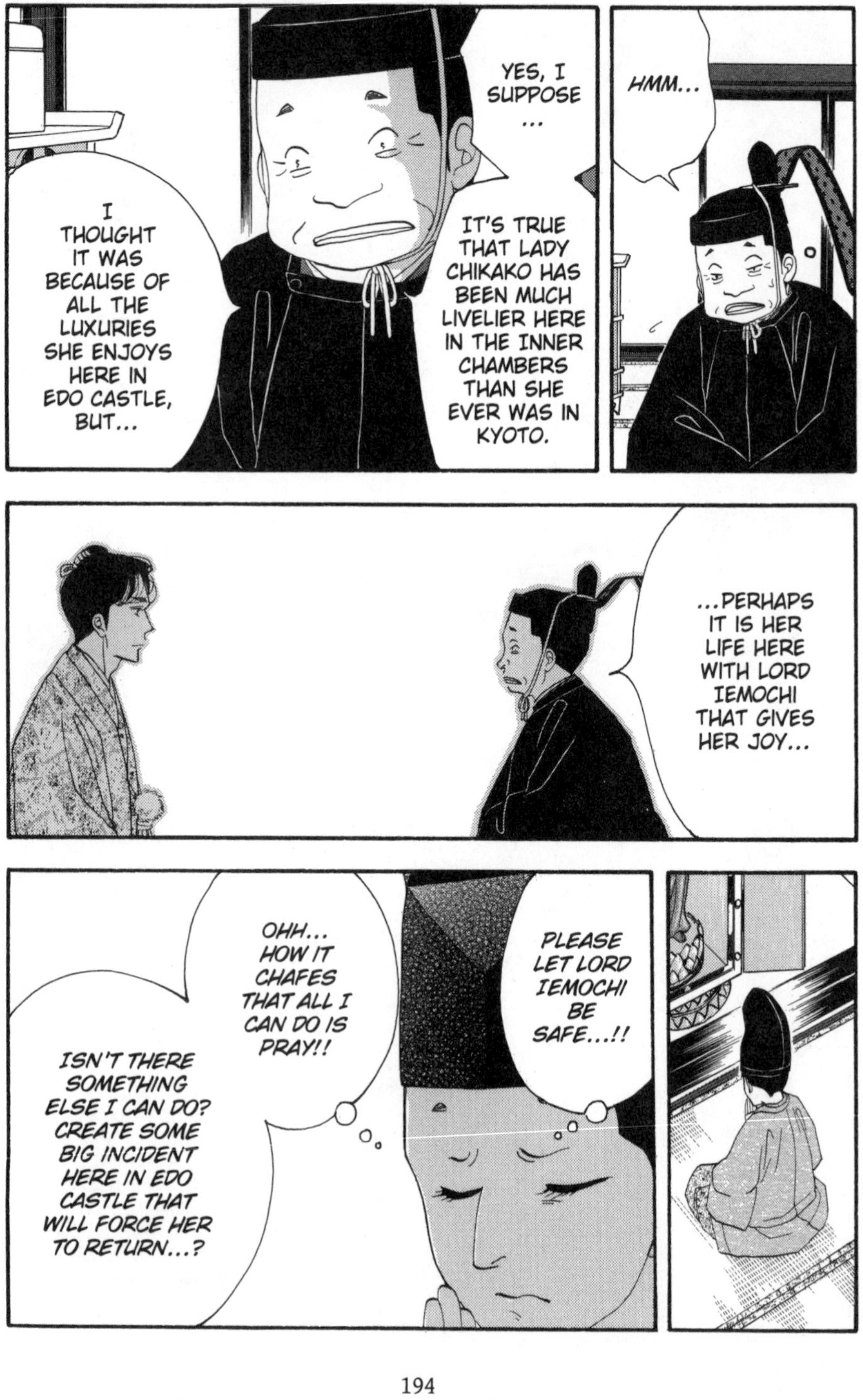
HMM...
YES, I SUPPOSE ...
IT'S TRUE THAT LADY CHIKAKO HAS BEEN MUCH LIVELIER HERE IN THE INNER CHAMBERS THAN SHE EVER WAS IN KYOTO.
I THOUGHT IT WAS BECAUSE OF ALL THE LUXURIES SHE ENJOYS HERE IN EDO CASTLE, BUT...
...PERHAPS IT IS HER LIFE HERE WITH LORD IEMOCHI THAT GIVES HER JOY...
PLEASE LET LORD IEMOCHI BE SAFE...!!
OHH... HOW IT CHAFES THAT ALL I CAN DO IS PRAY!!
ISN'T THERE SOMETHING ELSE I CAN DO? CREATE SOME BIG INCIDENT HERE IN EDO CASTLE THAT WILL FORCE HER TO RETURN...?

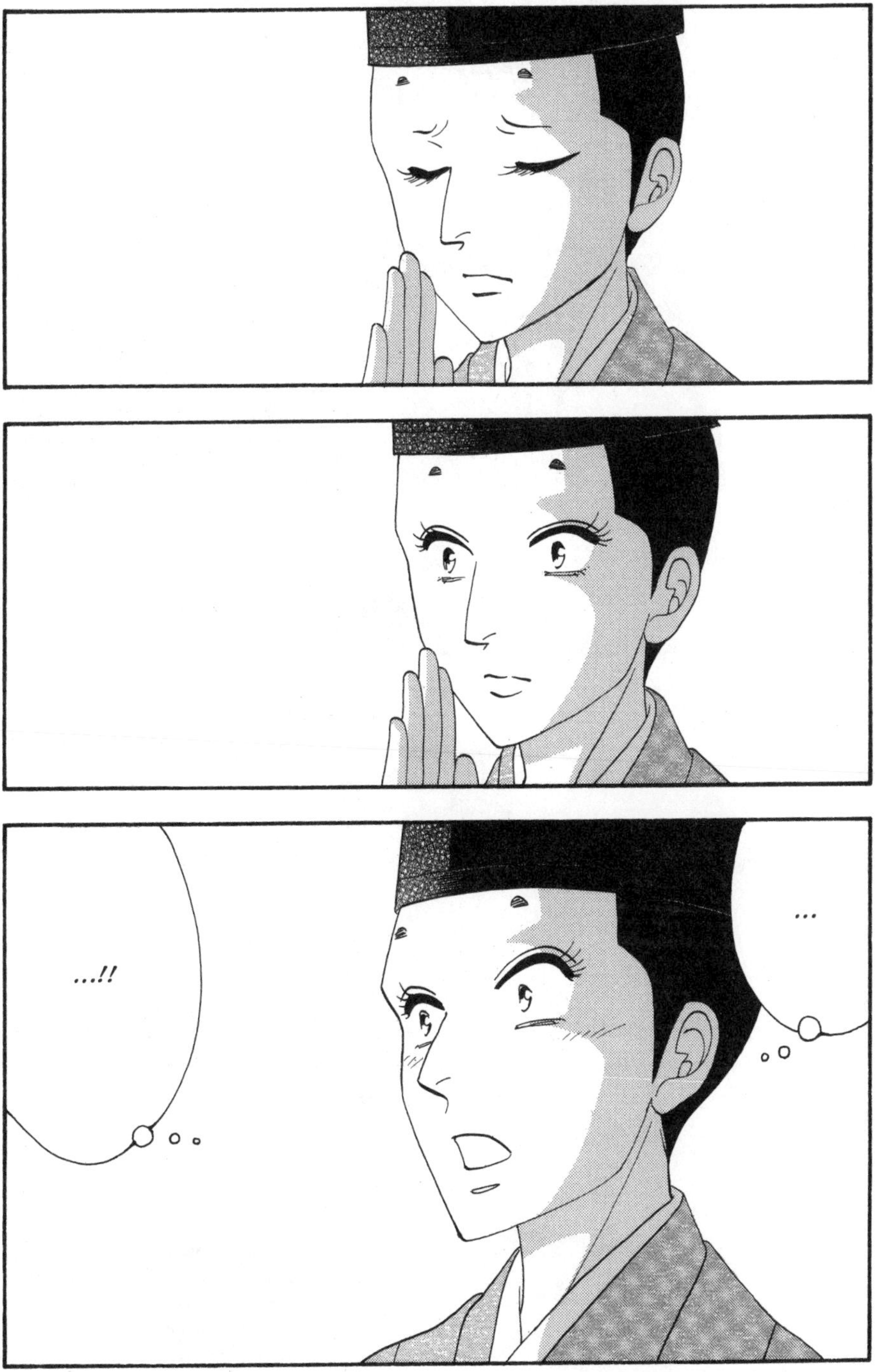
...
...!!

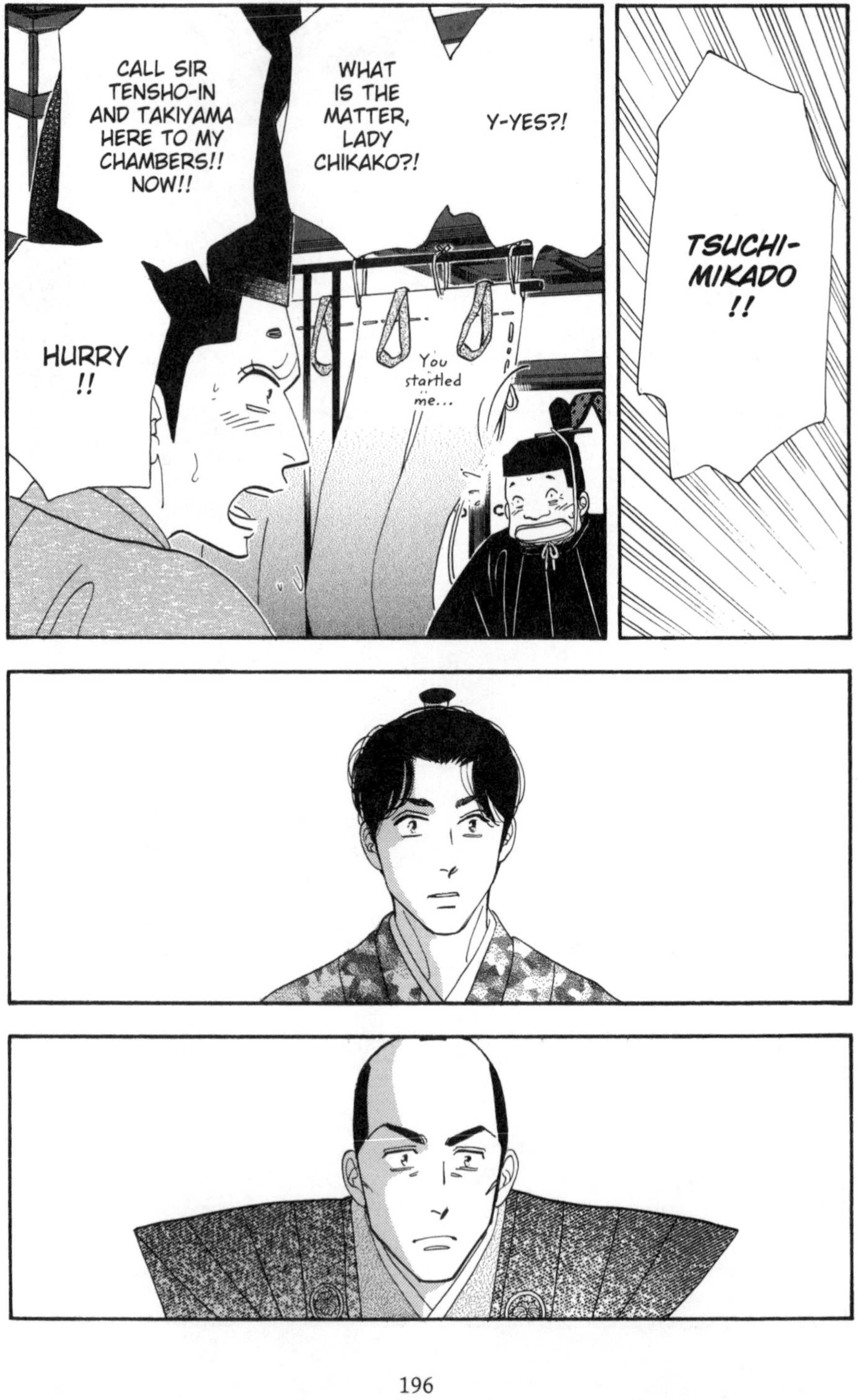
TSUCHI-
MIKADO
!!
Y-YES?!
WHAT
IS THE
MATTER,
LADY
CHIKAKO?!
CALL SIR
TENSHO-IN
AND TAKIYAMA
HERE TO MY
CHAMBERS!!
NOW!!
You
startled
me...
HURRY
!!

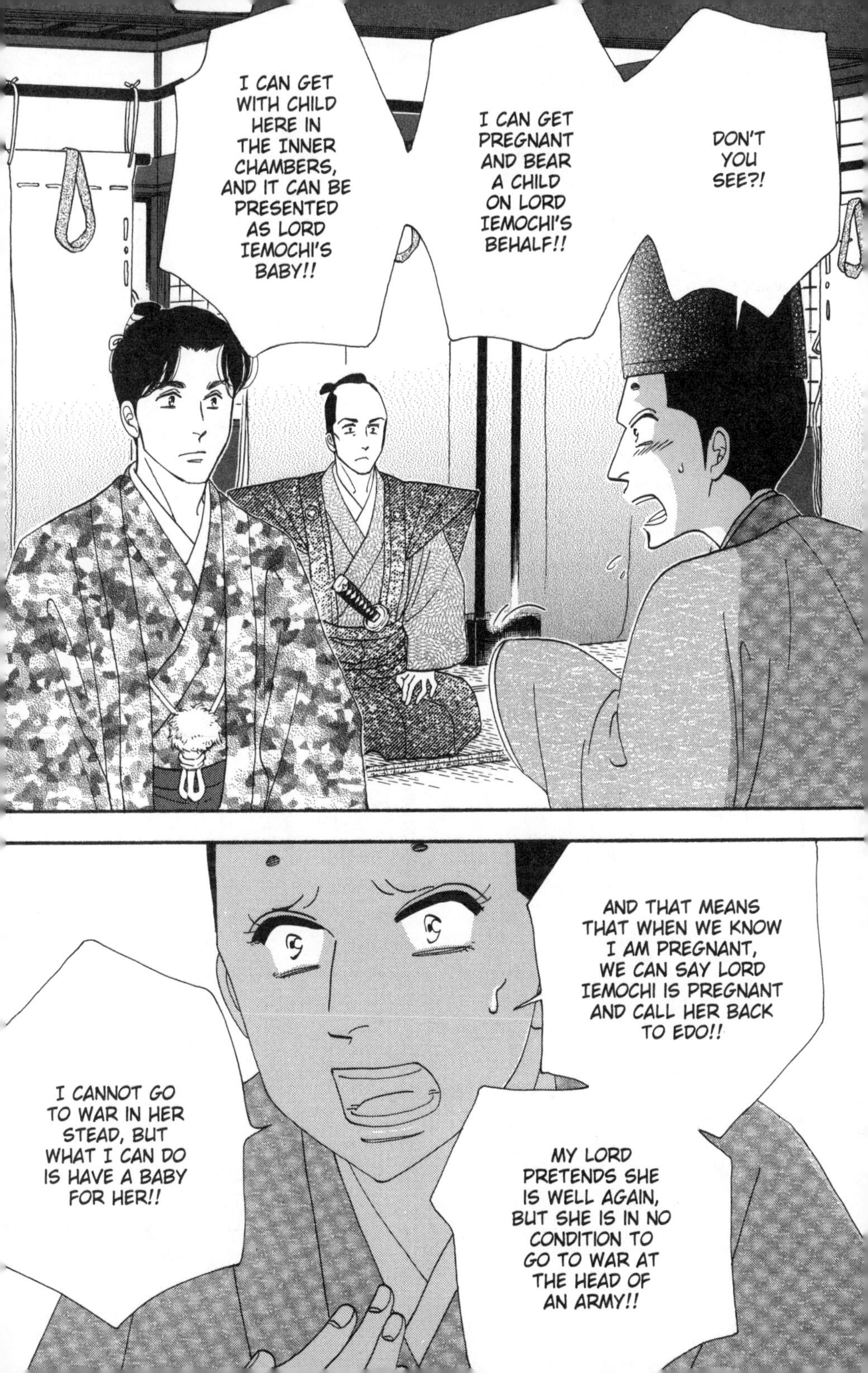
DON'T YOU SEE?!
I CAN GET PREGNANT AND BEAR A CHILD ON LORD IEMOCHI'S BEHALF!!
I CAN GET WITH CHILD HERE IN THE INNER CHAMBERS, AND IT CAN BE PRESENTED AS LORD IEMOCHI'S BABY!!
AND THAT MEANS THAT WHEN WE KNOW I AM PREGNANT, WE CAN SAY LORD IEMOCHI IS PREGNANT AND CALL HER BACK TO EDO!!
MY LORD PRETENDS SHE IS WELL AGAIN, BUT SHE IS IN NO CONDITION TO GO TO WAR AT THE HEAD OF AN ARMY!!
I CANNOT GO TO WAR IN HER STEAD, BUT WHAT I CAN DO IS HAVE A BABY FOR HER!!

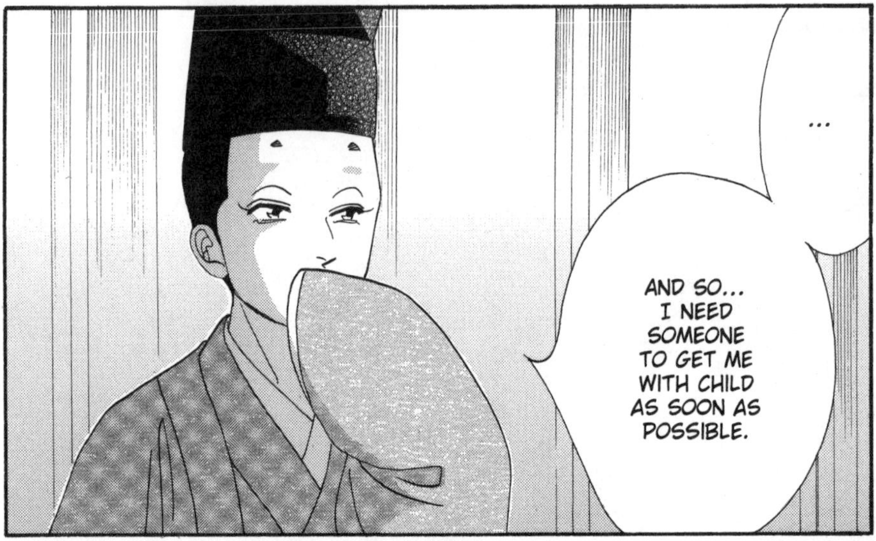
...
AND SO... I NEED SOMEONE TO GET ME WITH CHILD AS SOON AS POSSIBLE.
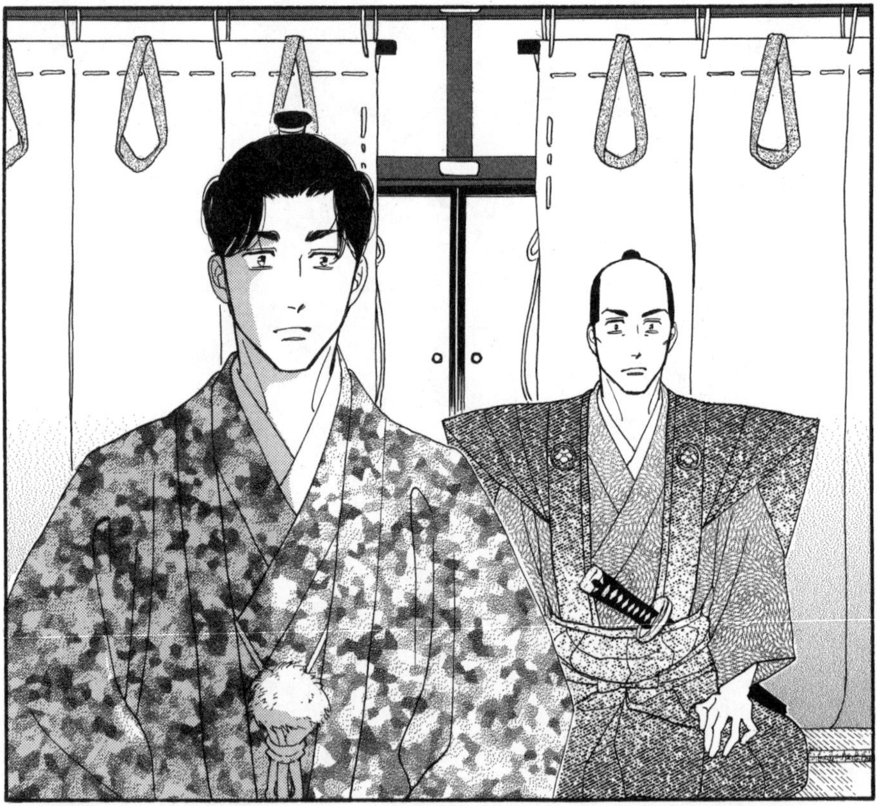

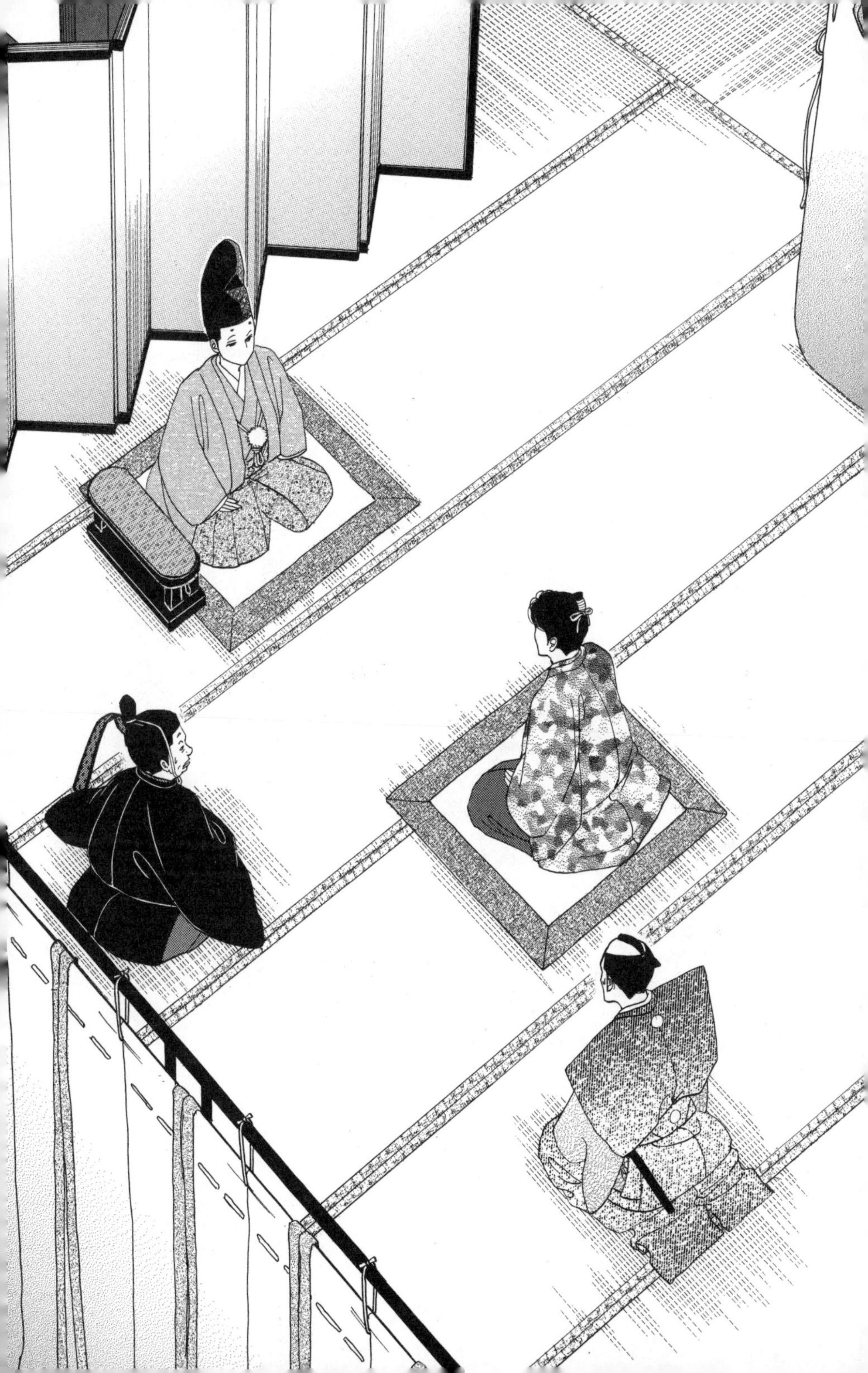

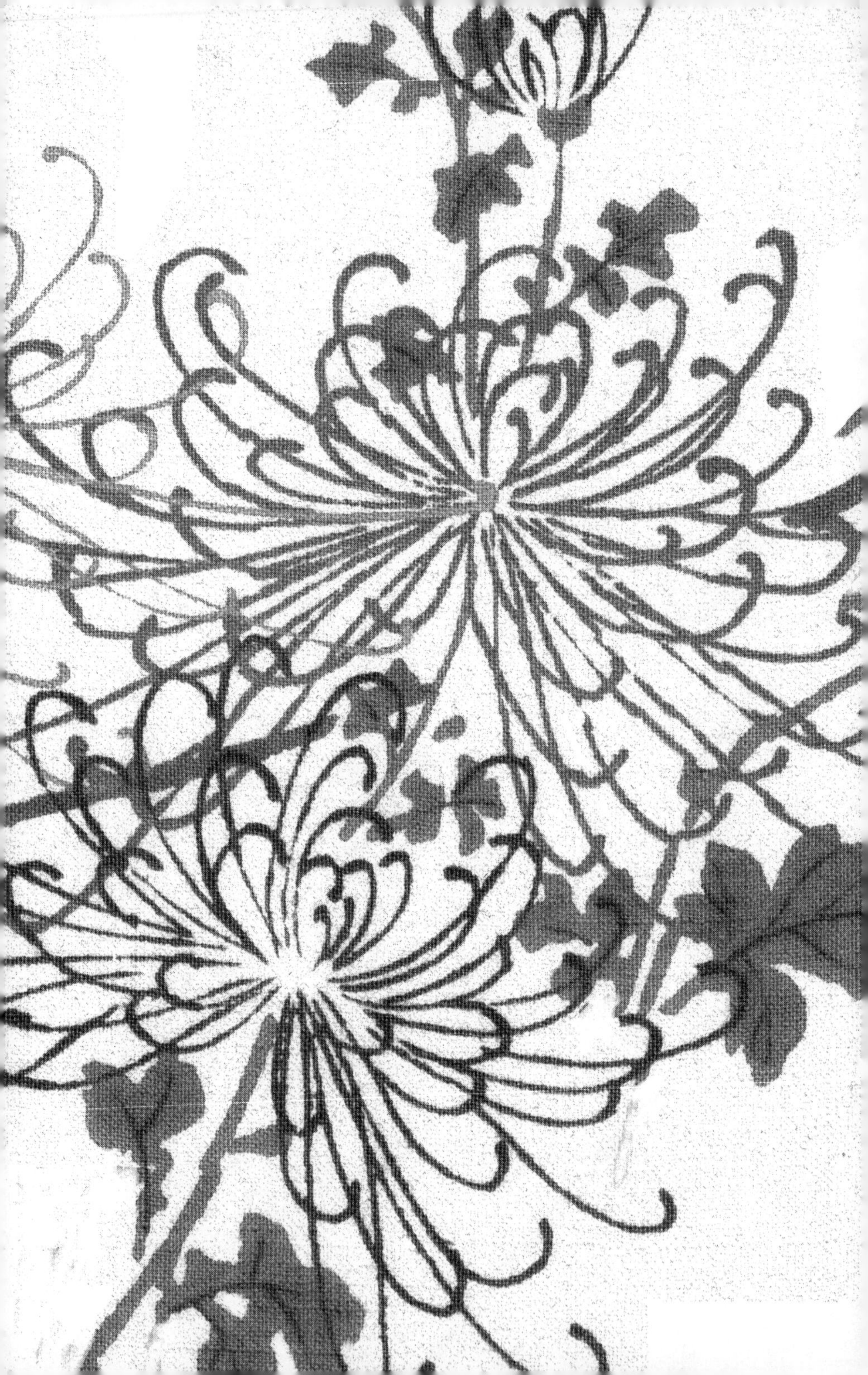

Ōoku

THE INNER CHAMBERS

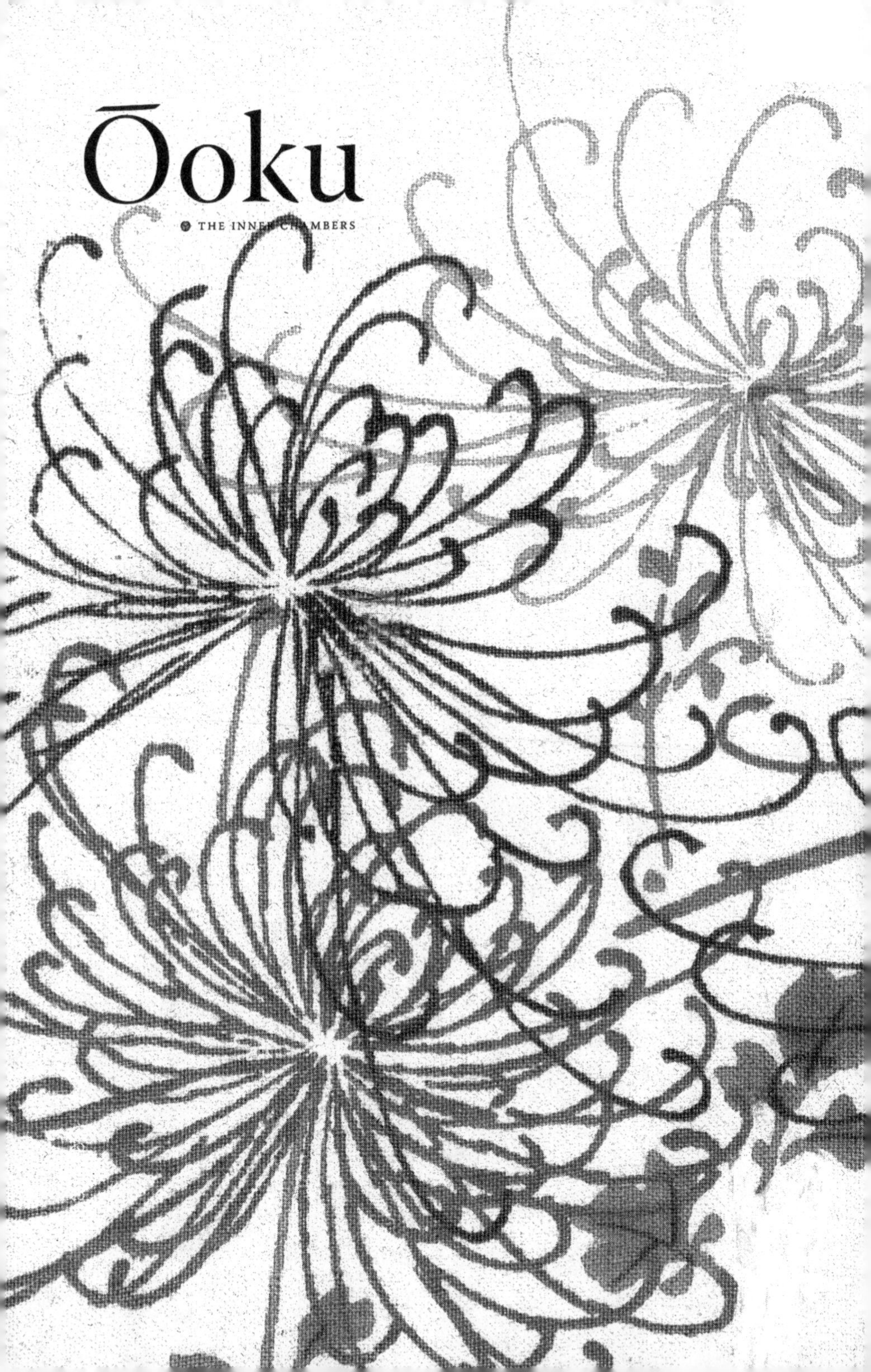

ŌOKU: THE INNER CHAMBERS

VOLUME 17 · END NOTES

by Akemi Wegmüller

Page 34, panel 1 · ARUHEITO

Aruheito is a type of hard candy introduced to Japan by the Portuguese.

Page 81, panel 2 · UCHIKAKE

A highly formal kimono worn by brides or theater performers.

Page 92, panel 3 · SECRET SWAIN

See *Ôoku* volume 1, chapter 1.

Page 103, panel 1 · NISHIJIN DISTRICT

The area of Kyoto where kimono are made.

Ōoku

THE INNER CHAMBERS

Ōoku: The Inner Chambers
Vol. 17

VIZ Signature Edition

Story and Art by Fumi Yoshinaga

Translation & Adaptation/Akemi Wegmüller
Touch-up Art & Lettering/Monaliza De Asis
Design/Yukiko Whitley
Editor/Pancha Diaz

Ōoku by Fumi Yoshinaga © Fumi Yoshinaga 2019
All rights reserved. First published in Japan in 2019 by
HAKUSENSHA, Inc., Tokyo. English language translation
rights arranged with HAKUSENSHA, Inc., Tokyo.

The stories, characters and incidents mentioned in this
publication are entirely fictional.

No portion of this book may be reproduced or transmitted
in any form or by any means without written permission
from the copyright holders.

Printed in Canada

Published by VIZ Media, LLC
P.O. Box 77010
San Francisco, CA 94107

PARENTAL ADVISORY
ŌOKU: THE INNER CHAMBERS is rated M for
Mature and is recommended for ages 18 and up.
Contains violence and sexual situations.

10 9 8 7 6 5 4 3 2 1
First printing, August 2020

VIZ MEDIA
viz.com

VIZ SIGNATUR
vizsignature.com

THIS IS THE LAST PAGE.

Ōoku: The Inner Chambers has been printed in
the original Japanese format in order to preserve
the orientation of the original artwork.